Advance Praise for The VaR Modeling Handbook

This book offers considerable evidence that VaR has grown up as a risk measurement tool. The problems tackled in the papers collected here are both important and subtle, and they cover a surprisingly broad range of issues.

—**Barry Schachter**, Director of Quantitative Resources, Moore Capital Management

This volume edited by Professor Gregoriou is a comprehensive collection of recent advances in risk management. Contributions cover a wide range of topics in this immense area and combine academic rigor with practical relevance and the authors' personal experience from the field. I would highly recommend this book to everyone looking for a comprehensive and up-to-date synthesis of research in risk management.

—**Dr. Bartosz Gebka**, Professor of Finance, Newcastle University Business School

The use of VaR as a risk metric was adopted globally under the 1996 Basel II amendment. Much interest and research in this broad field of risk management followed on its properties as a risk metric and portfolio optimizer. Attention was focused on tail risk and CVaR as extensions to the approach. The latest research on these issues is brilliantly captured in this volume edited by Gregoriou.

—**Professor D. E. Allen**, School of Accounting, Finance and Economics, Edith Cowan University

Value at risk today is one of the most used quantitative risk measures in financial markets. This exquisitely edited volume shows a vast array of applications of this measure—ranging from alternative investments to Solvency II—and also introduces advanced calculation models that go beyond the standard Value at Risk approach and hence highlight how to deal with the caveats of this measure.

—**Dr. Dieter Kaiser**, Director of Hedge Funds, Feri Institutional Advisors GmbH

This timely book contains new research in the vast area of value at risk and will become invaluable for sophisticated and institutional investors and money managers.

—**Fabrice Douglas Rouah**, Vice President and Senior Quantitative Analyst, Enterprise Risk Management, State Street Corporation

THE VaR
MODELING
HANDBOOK

THE VaR MODELING HANDBOOK

GREG N. GREGORIOU

EDITOR

New York   Chicago   San Francisco
Lisbon   London   Madrid   Mexico City
Milan   New Delhi   San Juan   Seoul
Singapore   Sydney   Toronto

This publication is designed to provide accurate and authoritative information in regard to the subject matter covered. It is sold with the understanding that neither the author nor the publisher is engaged in rendering legal, accounting, futures/securities trading, or other professional service. If legal advice or other expert assistance is required, the services of a competent professional person should be sought.

—From a Declaration of Principles jointly adopted by a Committee
of the American Bar Association and a Committee of Publishers

Neither the editors nor the publisher can guarantee the accuracy of individual chapters. All authors are responsible for their own written material

McGraw-Hill books are available at special quantity discounts to use as premiums and sales promotions, or for use in corporate training programs. For more information, please write to the Director of Special Sales, Professional Publishing, McGraw-Hill, Two Penn Plaza, New York, NY 10121–2298. Or contact your local bookstore.

This book is printed on acid-free paper.

CONTENTS

Chapter 6

The Asset–Liability Management Compound Option Model: A Public Debt Management Tool   123

Jorge A. Chan-Lau and André O. Santos

Chapter 7

A Practitioner's Critique of Value-at-Risk Models   147

Robert Dubil

Greg N. Gregoriou is Professor of Finance in the School of Business and Economics at State University of New York (Plattsburgh). He obtained his joint PhD (Finance) from the University of Quebec at Montreal, which pools its resources with Montreal's three other major universities (McGill, Concordia, and HEC). He has published 31 books for John Wiley & Sons, McGraw-Hill, Elsevier-Butterworth-Heinemann, Palgrave-MacMillan, Chapman-Hall/Taylor Francis, and Risk Books. He is coeditor for the peer-reviewed scientific *Journal of Derivatives and Hedge Funds* and an editorial board member for the *Journal of Wealth Management* and the *Journal of Risk Management in Financial Institutions.* He has authored over 50 articles on hedge funds and managed futures in various U.S. and UK peer-reviewed publications, including the *Journal of Portfolio Management, Journal of Futures Markets, European Journal of Operational Research,* and *Annals of Operations Research.*

René Azokli is an economist and formar director of an African Microcredit Bank. Now he is a researcher affiliated with HEC Geneva.

Arjan Berkelaar is principal investment officer of asset allocation and quantitative strategies at the World Bank Treasury. He is responsible for developing multi-asset class investment strategies for the various clients of the World Bank Treasury, including the bank's pension and medical funds. Arjan also advises central banks on reserves management issues and governments in oil-rich developing countries on setting up sovereign wealth funds. He joined the World Bank in July 2000. Before joining the World Bank, he worked at Ortec Consultants, a pension consultancy firm in the Netherlands. Arjan has published several papers in international journals and is a regular speaker at international conferences. Arjan holds a PhD in Finance from the Erasmus University Rotterdam and an MS in Mathematics (summa cum laude) from the Delft University of Technology and is a CFA charter holder

Rossella Bisignani is a postdoctoral student in mathematical methods in economics and finance at the University of Roma, "La Sapienza" (Faculty of Economics), where she obtained her PhD. Her current research interests focus on operational risk management for banks and insurance companies.

Laurent Bodson is PhD candidate in finance and Fonds de la Recherche Scientifique (FNRS) Research fellow at the HEC, Business School of the University of Liège. His areas of expertise include portfolio and risk management, as both a practitioner and researcher. He is also specialized in investment analysis, derivatives, style analysis, stock market price behavior, and integration of higher order moments.

Hans-Peter Burghof has been Professor and Chair of Banking and Financial Services of the University of Hohenheim, Germany since October 2003.

He studied economics at the University of Bonn before he completed his PhD and postdoctoral studies at the Ludwig– Maximilians–University of Munich. Selected articles of Professor Burghof's have appeared in the *Journal of Risk* and the *International Journal of the Economics of Business*.

Tyrone M. Carlin is Professor and Dean of Law at Macquarie University and holds a concurrent posting as Professor of Management at Macquarie Graduate School of Management. His research is concentrated in the areas of corporate governance and corporate financial reporting. He has published more than 100 articles in his fields of interest and is coeditor of the *Journal of Law and Financial Management* and the *Journal of Applied Research in Accounting and Finance*.

Jorge A. Chan-Lau is a senior financial officer at the International Finance Corporation, World Bank Group, where he leads the MATCH project, an International Finance Corporation (IFC) initiative aimed at providing local currency financing in frontier emerging market countries. Prior to joining the IFC, he was a senior economist in the International Monetary Fund, where he conducted work on capital markets and financial stability. He has published scholarly articles and book chapters on asset allocation, credit risk, credit derivatives, financial markets, and institutional investors. Dr. Chan-Lau holds M.Phil. and PhD degrees in Economics and Finance from the Graduate School of Business, Columbia University, and a BS in Civil Engineering (summa cum laude) from the Pontificia Universidad Católica del Perú.

Rosa Cocozza, holds an MA in Banking and Finance and a PhD in Business Administration and is Professor of Financial Risk Management at the Faculty of Economics of the Università di Napoli Federico II. A member of American Risk and Insurance Association (ARIA), of Wolpertinger Club (European Association of University Teachers of Banking and Finance), and of ADEIMF (Associazione dei Docenti di Economia dei Mercati e degli Intermediari Finanziari), she is an editorial board member of the ADEIMF Working Paper Series. Her research focuses on risk management processes and techniques within financial institutions. The author of more than 30 papers on quantitative management modeling for financial intermediaries, she also published two monographs, one on credit pricing and the other on interest rate risk management for life insurers.

Alain Coën is Associate Professor of Finance at the University of Quebec in Montreal (UQAM). He obtained his PhD in Finance from the University of Grenoble and holds an MA in economics with a major in macroeconomics from Laval University and an accreditation to supervise research (HDR) from Dauphine University. He teaches, researches, and consults in the areas of asset pricing and portfolio management. His research interests focus on asset pricing, international finance, business cycles, and financial econometrics. He has published in several international journals and has written a book on financial management.

John Cotter is at the Anderson School of Management, UCLA, and is Director of the Centre for Financial Markets at University College Dublin. John has previously had secondment visits to the London School of Economics and ESSEC Business School. His research is in the areas of volatility modeling and risk management. He has published extensively in journals including the *Journal of Banking and Finance, Journal of International Money and Finance, Journal of Futures Markets*, and *Risk*.

Alfredo D. Egidio dos Reis is Associate Professor at ISEG, Technical University of Lisbon. He presently runs the master's program on Actuarial Science at ISEG and usually teaches courses in the areas of risk theory, probability, and statistics. He holds a PhD in Actuarial Mathematics and Statistics from Heriot-Watt University (Edinburgh), a master's degree in applied mathematics to economics and management and a first degree in business administration, both from ISEG. His main research interests are in the areas of actuarial science and risk theory, particularly ruin theory and credibility.

Kevin Dowd is Professor of Financial Risk Management at Nottingham University Business School, where he works with the Centre for Risk and Insurance Studies. He held previous positions with the University of Sheffield and Sheffield Hallam University. His research interests cover risk management, pensions, insurance, monetary and macroeconomics, financial regulation, and political economy, and he has links with the Cato Institution in Washington, DC, the Institute of Economic Affairs in London, and the Open Republic Institute in Dublin.

Robert Dubil is an Associate Professor and Lecturer of Finance at the University of Utah. He holds a PhD in Finance from University of Connecticut and an MA from Wharton. He was the Director of Risk Analytics in Corporate Risk Management at Merrill Lynch (1999 to 2001), Head of Exotic Derivatives Trading at UBS (1996 to 1999) and Chase (1994 to 1995), an options trader at Merrill Lynch (1992 to 1994), a quant at Nomura (1990 to 1992) and JPMorgan (1989 to 1990). He has written articles on banking regulation, venture capital, risk management, and personal finance. His book is titled *An Arbitrage Guide to Financial Markets* (Wiley, 2004).

João L. C. Duque completed his PhD at the Manchester Business School, UK and subsequently joined ISEG, Technical University of Lisbon, where he is presently Professor of Finance. He teaches financial derivatives, portfolio management, and financial management. Until 1998, he was the head of the Research Department at the Portuguese securities markets regulator Comissão do Mercado de Valores Mobiliários (CMVM). His research interests are financial markets, financial derivatives, and portfolio management. He recently published on subjects such as initial public offerings and financial regulation.

Nigel Finch is a Lecturer in Management at the Macquarie Graduate School of Management, specializing in the areas of managerial accounting and financial management. His research interests are in the areas of accounting and management decision making, finance and investment management, and financial services management. Prior to joining Macquarie Graduate School of Management, Nigel worked as a financial controller for both public and private companies operating in the manufacturing, entertainment, media, and financial services industries. Subsequently, he worked as an investment manager specializing in Australian growth stocks for institutional investment funds.

Guy Ford is Associate Professor of Management at Macquarie Graduate School of Management, where he teaches in the areas of financial management, corporate acquisitions, corporate reconstructions, and financial institution management. Formerly of the Treasury Risk Management Division of the Commonwealth Bank of Australia, he has published in refereed research papers in a range of Australian and international journals and is the coauthor of two books, *Financial Markets and Institutions in Australia* (Pearson Education Australia, 2003) and *Readings in Financial Institutions Management* (Prentice-Hall Australia, 1999). He is a founding co-editor of the *Journal of Law and Financial Management*.

Emmanuel Fragnière, Certified Internal Auditor (CIA), is a professor of service management at the Haute Ecole de Gestion of Geneva, Switzerland. He is also a lecturer at the Management School of the University of Bath, UK. He specializes in energy, environmental, and financial risk and has published several papers in academic journals such as *Annals of Operations Research, Environmental Modeling,* and *Assessment, Interfaces, and Management Science.*

Ricardo Garcia is senior risk and solvency analyst at the Portuguese Insurance and Pension Funds Supervisory Authority. He is presently a member of the Internal Models Expert Working Group of the Committee of European Insurance and Occupational Pensions Supervisors (CEIOPS). He holds a master's degree in Actuarial Science and a first degree on Management, both from ISEG, Technical University of Lisbon.

Raquel M. Gaspar has been Assistant Professor at ISEG, Technical University of Lisbon, since February 2006. She has a PhD in Finance from the Stockholm School of Economics with postgraduate studies in risk management and derivatives from IDEFE, Nova Forum, and IMC and a master's degree in Applied Mathematics to Economics and Management from ISEG; she did undergraduate studies in economics at New University of Lisbon. Her research interests are in mathematical finance and particularly in credit risk, energy markets, portfolio optimization, and term structure models.

Georges Hübner (PhD, INSEAD) is the Deloitte Professor of Financial Management and is cochair of the Finance Department at HEC,

Management School of the University of Liège. He is an Associate Professor of Finance at Maastricht University and Academic Expert at the Luxembourg School of Finance, University of Luxembourg. He is also the founder and CEO of Gambit Financial Solutions, a financial software spin-off company of the University of Liège. Georges Hübner has taught at the executive and postgraduate levels in several countries in Europe, North America, Africa, and Asia. He regularly provides executive training seminars for the preparation of the Global Association of Risk Professionals (GARP) and CAIA (Chartered Alternative Investment Analyst) certifications. His research articles have been published in leading scientific journals including *Journal of Banking and Finance, Journal of Empirical Finance, Review of Finance, Financial Management,* and *Journal of Portfolio Management.* Georges Hübner was the recipient of the prestigious 2002 Iddo Sarnat Award for the best paper published in the *Journal of Banking and Finance* in 2001.

Adam Kobor is a principal investment officer at the quantitative strategies, risk, and analytics department of the World Bank Treasury. He is responsible for strategic asset allocation and risk budgeting recommendations for several internal and external clients of the World Bank Group. He is also advising central banks, UN agencies, and public pension plans on investment policy, asset allocation, and risk-management-related topics. In addition, Mr. Kobor developed several quantitative financial models used either in the strategic asset allocation process or in the active portfolio management. Prior to joining the World Bank Group in 2001, he worked for the National Bank of Hungary as a risk analyst. His main responsibilities covered the preparation and periodic revision of the investment policy and the development of several risk analytics for the foreign exchange reserves portfolio. Adam Kobor holds a PhD in Business Administration from the Budapest University of Economic Sciences and Public Administration (currently, Corvinus University), and he is a CFA charter holder. He is author and coauthor of several publications, and he speaks at conferences.

Roy Kouwenberg is Assistant Professor at Mahidol University, College of Management, in Bangkok. He received a PhD degree in Finance from

Erasmus University Rotterdam in 2001 and is a CFA charterholder. Previously, Roy worked as a postdoctoral fellow at the University of British Columbia and as a quantitative analyst at the equity department of AEGON Asset Management. His research interests are in the areas of portfolio choice, asset pricing, and empirical finance. His work has been published in various journals, including the *Review of Economics and Statistics*, the *Journal of Banking and Finance*, the *Journal of International Money and Finance* and the *Journal of Economic Dynamics and Control*.

Giovanni Masala is a researcher in mathematical methods for economy and finance at the Faculty of Economics in the University of Cagliari (Italy). He got his Ph D. in differential geometry in the University of Mulhouse (France). His current research interests include mathematical risk modeling for financial and actuarial applications.

Francesco Menoncin is Associate Professor at Brescia University. He teaches courses in Market Risks and Derivatives, and Financial Hedging. His research interests are mainly focused on: financial risks, actuarial risks, optimal portfolio, and pension funds. On these sujbects, he has published in: *Insurance, Mathematics and Economics, Annals of Operations Research, European Journal of Finance, Revue Economique, Managerial Finance, and International Economics*.

Albert Mentink is currently operational manager at the Asset and Liability Management department of AEGON Netherlands. He received his PhD degree in Finance from the Erasmus University Rotterdam in 2005. His work has been published in chapters in books (Wiley & Sons and Elsevier) and journal articles (*Journal of Banking and Finance* and the *Journal of Derivatives*). His research interests are in the fields of interest rate, credit and liquidity risk of corporate bonds.

Marco Micocci is Full Professor of Financial Mathematics and Actuarial Science at the University of Cagliari. From 1996 to 2001 he was Researcher of Financial and Actuarial mathematics at the University of Rome "La Sapienza". He has a degree in Economics, a degree in Banking,

Financial and Insurance Science and a degree in Actuarial Statistics. His fields of research are financial and actuarial management of pension funds, mathematical finance, and credit risk. He is author of over 60 publications (papers, articles, books) and is a consultant actuary.

Jan Müller is a Ph. D. student at the Chair of Banking and Financial Services of the University of Hohenheim, Germany. He has studied economics at the University of Hohenheim.

Akimou Ossé works as a quantitative analyst and risk manager at Banque SYZ & CO, a private bank based in Geneva. He is also a Lecturer at the Haute Ecole de Gestion of Geneva, Switzerland and holds a PhD in Mathematics from Université de Neuchâtel in Switzerland.

Juliane Proelss, is a research assistant at the chair of Empirical Capital Market Research at the WHU, Otto Beisheim School of Management in Vallendar, Germany. Her research focuses on strategy optimization for alternative investments. Juliane also works as an academic assistant in the field of executive education in alternative investments and finance at the EBS Finanzakademie. She completed the postgraduate programs Kontaktstudium Finanzökonomie, and Intensivstudium Estate Planning and passed the exams for the Certified Financial Planner and the Certified Foundation and Estate Planner at the Financial Planning Standards Board. Prior to this, she studied at the Catholic University of Eichstaett-Ingolstadt, where she graduated in 2005 with a diploma in business administration, and at the Lincoln University, New Zealand, where she graduated with a postgraduate diploma in commerce. Her major subjects where financial markets and econometrics. During her studies, she worked as a student assistant at the chair for statistics and operations research and as a student trainee for FondsConsult and Siemens Management Consulting.

André O. Santos is a senior economist in the International Monetary Fund, where he conducts work on capital markets and financial stability. In particular, he has worked extensively on corporate and sovereign default risk and derivatives markets in emerging market countries including credit derivatives. Dr. Santos holds an M.Phil. and a PhD in International Economics from the Graduate Institute of International

Studies, University of Geneva, Switzerland, and a BS in Economics from the University of Brasília, Brazil.

Mark Schouten holds two MS degrees in Econometrics (specializing in operations research) and Economics (specializing in finance of aging) from Tilburg University. Currently he works at AEGON Netherlands Asset and Liability Management department as junior analyst. His research interests cover hedging financial risks and asset allocation in the presence of liabilities.

Denis Schweizer is a PhD student and research assistant at the chair of Empirical Capital Market Research at the WHU, Otto Beisheim School of Management in Vallendar, Germany. His research focus is on asset allocation and pricing of alternative investments. At the same time he works as an academic assistant in the design and structuring of executive educational programs in alternative investments and finance at the EBS Finanzakademie. Denis Schweizer also lectures in those programs. He completed the postgraduate programs Kontaktstudium Finanzökonomie, Intensivstudium Capital Markets and Portfolio Management and passed the exams for the Certified Financial Planner at the Financial Planning Standards Board. In 2005 he graduated from Johann-Wolfgang Goethe University in Frankfurt with a diploma in business administration and worked for the chair of international banking and finance, the chair of corporate finance, and the chair of investments, portfolio-management, and pension finance. During his studies, he worked for the UBS Investment Bank and for the SEB AG as a student trainee.

Robin Sonnenberg holds an MS in Econometrics (with a specialization in quantitative finance) from Erasmus University Rotterdam. He wrote his master's thesis during an internship at the Asset and Liability Management department of AEGON Netherlands. Currently he works at the Securities department of Kempen and Co Merchant Bank as member of the Institutional Equity Sales Team.

Ana T. Vicente has worked as a member of a supervisory team integrated on the Department of Financial Supervision of Insurance Companies at the Portuguese Insurance Supervisory Authority since March 2003. She has a master's degree in Actuarial Science from ISEG, Technical University of Lisbon. Her first degree is also from ISEG, in the field of Management. Her main research interest is in the area of risk analysis, namely, insurance underwriting and market risks.

PART ONE

Alternative Investments and Optimization

CHAPTER 1

Asset Allocation for Hedge Fund Strategies: How to Better Manage Tail Risk

Arjan Berkelaar, Adam Kobor, and Roy Kouwenberg

ABSTRACT

Most approaches to risk budgeting are based on tracking error and value at risk (VaR). In addition, the return streams from any investment process are usually assumed to be serially uncorrelated and normally distributed. This assumption, however, does not necessarily hold in reality. In this chapter, we consider two relatively new risk measures that are better suited to deal with nonnormal and serially correlated return streams and that are superior to tracking error (or volatility) and value at risk. We show how these measures can be used in determining an optimal risk allocation, allowing investors to better manage the tail and drawdown risks in their portfolios. By better managing these risks, investors can achieve superior risk-adjusted returns.

INTRODUCTION

Many institutional investors are searching for sources of diversification and return-enhancing strategies in order to improve the performance of their portfolios. An area where many of them hope to achieve superior risk-adjusted returns is hedge funds.[1] Shifting asset allocations toward hedge funds is not a guarantee of success, however. Unlike equity and bond markets that compensate investors with a positive risk premium over the long term, returns from selecting hedge fund managers are conditional on skill. To be successful in picking hedge funds, a strong risk management process and a disciplined investment approach are required.

Most approaches to risk and asset allocation, both in practice and in the academic literature, are based on standard deviation and value at risk. In addition, the return streams are usually assumed to be normally distributed. This assumption is quite convenient, allowing investors to use the well-known mean-variance workhorse to derive optimal allocations. We refer interested readers to Berkelaar et al. (2006) for a risk budgeting framework when investment returns are normally distributed. In the case of hedge funds, however, the normal distribution fails to adequately describe the return distribution. Basing risk allocations on mean-variance optimization may result in a considerable misallocation of risk that could result in suboptimal portfolios and lower investment returns.

In this chapter, we consider conditional value at risk (CVaR)—a relatively new risk measure that is better suited to deal with nonnormal return streams. The advantage of this risk measure is that it is easy to use and allows for numerical tractability. In this chapter, we derive optimal portfolios for mean-CVaR investors and compare results with those of a mean-variance investor. Others have also studied the impact of skewness and fat tails on optimal portfolios. Krokhmal et al. (2003) consider a portfolio of individual hedge funds and study the performance of various risk constraints, including CVaR and conditional drawdown at risk (CDaR), with in-sample and out-of-sample tests. Amin and Kat (2003) study the optimal allocation among stocks, bonds, and hedge funds in a mean-variance-skewness optimization framework. Kouwenberg (2003) studies the added value of investment in individual hedge funds for investors with passive stock and bond portfolios, taking into account the nonnormality of the return distribution.

---

[1] In the last decade the growth in the hedge fund industry has been phenomenal. In 1990 the assets under management (AUM) in the hedge fund industry were on the order of US$39 billion with about 530 hedge funds in operation. At the end of 2007, the AUM had increased to US$1.5 trillion with almost 10,000 hedge funds in operation.

We use the Hedge Fund Research, Inc. (HFRI) indexes for several hedge fund strategies to determine optimal allocations.[2] The period for the historical time series is January 1990 to December 2007. We show that investors who manage tail risk by basing their portfolios on mean-CVaR optimization should be able to produce superior returns on their hedge fund portfolio. Using historical returns for several hedge fund strategies, the incremental return could be as much as 100 to 200 basis points (bps). We also present results based on a forward-looking simulation model for hedge fund returns with more modest assumptions about expected returns. In this case, the incremental return is about 40 to 60 bps.

This chapter is organized as follows. The second section of this chapter discusses the CVaR measure. We also show to what extent risk could be underestimated by assuming that returns are serially uncorrelated and normally distributed. This chapter's third section discusses a framework that can be applied to develop forward-looking return scenarios for a wide range of hedge fund strategies. In our simulation approach, we separate the systematic market (or beta) exposures prevalent in hedge fund returns from an alpha component that can be attributed to skill. Our factor model is kept simple, and we only decompose the hedge fund returns into an equity beta and fixed-income beta. The sensitivities of hedge fund returns to equity and fixed-income returns are time varying. We use a Kalman filtering approach to capture the time-varying nature of the beta factors. To simulate realistic return scenarios for equities and bonds, we use regime switching models. By capturing both normal and stressful periods, regime switching models can describe the empirically observed skewness and kurtosis in stock and bond returns. By linking the return on hedge funds to the returns on public asset classes, they will also exhibit skewed and fat-tailed distributions. In the fourth section of this chapter, we compare the optimal asset allocations based on mean-variance optimization with the optimal asset allocations based on mean-CVaR optimization. First, we study the results based on the historical return distribution, and then we present optimal allocations derived using our forward-looking simulation framework. The final section summarizes our conclusions.

---

[2] We refer to www.hedgefundresearch.com for more details on the construction of the HFRI hedge fund indexes.

DOWNSIDE RISK AND RISK ALLOCATION

We assume that the investor wants to maximize the expected return across different hedge fund strategies subject to a constraint on the maximum allowable risk. This portfolio optimization problem can be formulated mathematically as

$$\max_{w} \mu' w$$
$$\text{such that } R(w) \leq R_{\max} \qquad (1.1)$$
$$\iota' w = 1, w \geq 0$$

where w is the vector of portfolio weights, $\mu' w$ equals the expected return of the portfolio, $R(w)$ indicates the risk measure used to measure portfolio risk, and $R_{\max}$ is the overall risk budget. We assume that the portfolio weights are nonnegative and sum to 100 percent.

Most approaches to risk budgeting are based on volatility and value at risk (VaR) and rely on the assumption that returns are serially uncorrelated and normally distributed. While these two assumptions are convenient and allow for simple formulas for the optimal allocation of risk, they may not be realistic for hedge fund returns.

We consider several hedge fund indexes from HFRI. Table 1.1 shows the skewness, kurtosis, and serial correlation for various hedge fund strategies based on monthly historical returns from January 1990 to December 2007. As the numbers in Table 1.1 show, the assumption that hedge fund returns are normally distributed and serially uncorrelated is violated in many cases. This has been observed by several others in the literature. Typically, however, these violations are dealt with through ad hoc adjustments, e.g., to the returns or by inflating historical volatilities to make the resulting return streams closer to that of a normal distributed and independent and identically distributed (i.i.d.) variable.

In the presence of positive serial correlation, volatilities tend be underestimated and Sharpe ratios overestimated. When returns are serially correlated, we can no longer annualize monthly volatilities by multiplying with the $\sqrt{12}$. An extensive discussion and some analytical results on the effect of serial correlation on Sharpe ratios can be found in Lo (2002).

T A B L E   1.1

Deviation from normality and serial correlation in hedge fund returns*

	Normality				Serial Correlation			
	Skewness	Kurtosis	JB	p-value	1st order SC	p-value	2nd order SC	p-value
Convertible Arbitrage	−1.40	6.51	172	0.0%	0.54	0.0%	0.26	0.0%
Distressed	−0.66	8.43	265	0.0%	0.50	0.0%	0.18	0.8%
Equity Long/Short	0.09	4.45	18	0.0%	0.14	3.7%	0.09	20.7%
Equity Market Neutral	0.07	3.78	5	6.9%	−0.01	86.8%	0.04	55.8%
Event-Driven	−1.27	7.57	233	0.0%	0.30	0.0%	0.08	22.3%
FI Arbitrage	−1.78	14.06	1,147	0.0%	0.39	0.0%	0.15	3.1%
Global Macro	0.36	3.72	9	1.1%	0.16	2.1%	−0.01	88.8%
Managed Futures	0.38	3.61	8	1.7%	0.06	35.5%	−0.14	4.2%
Merger Arbitrage	−2.67	15.42	1,554	0.0%	0.18	0.6%	0.04	53.7%
Relative Value	−0.91	13.37	943	0.0%	0.27	0.0%	0.19	0.4%
Short Selling	0.11	5.12	39	0.0%	0.09	19.2%	−0.06	38.8%

* Statistics based on log-excess returns over 1-month London Interbank Offered Rate (LIBOR) return.

In this chapter we are concerned with investment processes that may generate return streams that have outliers (indicated, for example, by skewness and tails that are fatter than for a normal distribution). In these situations, volatility is no longer a meaningful indicator of risk, and using it to determine an optimal hedge fund portfolio may result in a misallocation of risk. Value at risk is often advocated in the investment industry as a risk measure that is superior to volatility as it captures potential downside risk. Value at risk has several weaknesses, however, that make it a poor risk measure for the purpose of risk budgeting.

These weaknesses are widely documented in the literature [see, e.g., Artzner et al. (1999)]. Probably, the most severe drawback is that VaR, in general, is not a coherent risk measure in a sense defined by Artzner et al. (1999). Value at risk does not, in general, satisfy the property of subadditivity defined by Artzner et al. (1999). This means that diversification may, in fact, increase risk. This is a serious shortcoming when we try to allocate risk.[3] Basak and Shapiro (2001) show that the optimal portfolio that maximizes expected utility over wealth subject to a constraint on VaR results in adverse investment behavior, and may, e.g., increase extreme losses in the tail. Finally, VaR is, in general, a nonconvex and nonsmooth function. This can lead to multiple optima, which creates problems for portfolio optimization.

In this chapter we use CVaR. Basak and Shapiro (2001) also consider an investor that maximizes expected utility over wealth subject to a constraint on CVaR.[4] They show that the optimal portfolio is much better behaved compared to an investor that constrains the VaR of the portfolio. Conditional VaR is a conditional tail expectation. In general, CVaR is the weighted average of VaR and losses exceeding VaR. As a result, CVaR always exceeds VaR and is useful in quantifying risks beyond VaR, taking into account both the likelihood and the magnitude of possible losses. Conditional VaR should be considered superior to VaR for quantifying downside risks. Unlike VaR, it is easily verified that CVaR is a coherent risk measure and consistent with risk-aversion (second-order stochastic dominance). In addition, CVaR is a smooth and convex function, making it better suited for the purpose of portfolio optimization. Finally, Rockafeller and Uryasev (2000; 2002) have shown that mean-CVaR optimization can be formulated as a linear programming problem that can be solved easily even in the case of nonnormal return distributions. (The linear programming formulation is provided in Appendix A.)

We are interested in determining the optimal risk allocation from portfolio optimization problem (1) with $R\ (W)\ CVaR = -E(r'\ w\ |\ r'\ w \le VaR_\alpha)$. In the special case when returns are normally distributed with mean μ and volatility σ, the $\alpha\%$ CVaR over an investment horizon T can be calculated as

$$\text{CVaR}_\alpha = -\mu T + \frac{\phi(\xi)}{1-\alpha}\sigma\sqrt{T} = \text{VaR}_\alpha + \frac{\phi(\xi)-(1-\alpha)\xi}{1-\alpha}\sigma\sqrt{T}$$

---

[3] In the special case when returns are normally (or more generally, elliptically) distributed, it can be shown, that VaR is a coherent risk measure (i.e., it also satisfies the subadditive criterion). This result is not very helpful, however, as we are interested in allocating risk when returns are not normally distributed and display serial correlation.

[4] Conditional value at risk is also known as *expected shortfall* or *tail VaR*.

where $\xi = N^{-1}(\alpha)$ and where $N(\cdot)$ denotes the cumulative normal distribution function and $\phi(\cdot)$ denotes the normal density function. For example, the 95 percent CVaR for one year for a portfolio with annual mean and volatility μ and σ, is given by $-\mu + 2.06\,\sigma$ (in contrast, the 95 percent VaR equals $-\mu + 1.64\,\sigma$).

For a time series of returns of length N, the $\alpha\%$ CVaR can be calculated as

$$\text{CVaR}_\alpha = \text{VaR}_\alpha + \frac{1}{(1-\alpha)N}\sum_{k=1}^{N}\max[-\text{VaR}_\alpha - R_k, 0]$$

The confidence level α effectively determines how much weight the investor puts on tail risk. When $\alpha \to 0$, the $\alpha\%$ CVaR will be equal to the average return. When $\alpha \to 1$, the $\alpha\%$ CVaR will be equal to the worst-case return.

As mentioned above, a portfolio optimization with CVaR constraints can be reformulated as a linear programming problem. The linear programming formulation allows an investor to maximize the expected portfolio return subject to CVaR constraints while simultaneously calculating the VaR of the optimal portfolio. Linear programming problems can be solved easily with most commercially available optimization packages. Table 1.2 shows the monthly 99 percent VaR and CVaR for several hedge fund strategies for historical monthly returns from January 1990 to December 2007.

To get a better sense of how much tail risk could be underestimated by using a normal distribution for hedge fund returns, we calculated the ratio of the 99 percent CVaR based on the historical distribution to the 99 percent CVaR based on a normal distribution with a mean and volatility equal to the historical mean and volatility. Figure 1.1 shows this ratio on the vertical axis versus the Jarque-Bera statistic (on a logarithmic scale) on the horizontal axis. Clearly, the more returns deviate from a normal distribution, the more risk is being underestimated by a normal distribution.

A nice property of mean-CVaR optimization models is that when returns are normally distributed and serially uncorrelated, the optimal risk allocations are identical to those derived from mean-variance optimization. In other words, mean-variance analysis is a special case of the mean-CVaR optimization.

T A B L E   1.2

Comparative VaR figures for various hedge fund strategies*

	Normal Distribution		Empirical Distribution	
	99% VaR	99% CVaR	99% VaR	99% CVaR
Convertible Arbitrage	2.11%	2.48%	3.06%	4.19%
Distressed	3.24%	3.82%	3.95%	6.42%
Equity Long/Short	4.86%	5.69%	4.78%	6.35%
Equity Market Neutral	1.63%	1.92%	1.74%	2.10%
Event-Driven	3.60%	4.23%	5.07%	7.70%
FI Arbitrage	2.49%	2.89%	2.95%	6.45%
Global Macro	4.53%	5.31%	4.22%	5.44%
Managed Futures	6.20%	7.16%	5.85%	7.01%
Merger Arbitrage	2.37%	2.78%	4.85%	6.69%
Relative Value	1.84%	2.19%	1.57%	4.07%
Short Selling	13.32%	15.25%	14.74%	19.05%

* Statistics based on excess returns over 1-month LIBOR return. The *positive* figures represent potential *loss* relative to LIBOR.

F I G U R E   1.1

Impact of nonnormality on tail risk

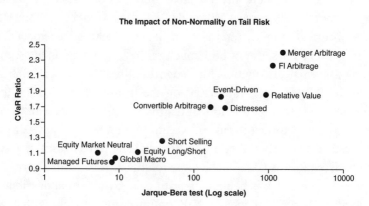

Some investors may shun the use of risk measures such as CVaR for fear that it will require a huge investment in new technology to upgrade their current risk systems that rely heavily on VaR. We believe that CVaR will eventually take over the popularity of VaR in the investment industry. While many banks and institutional investors have heavily invested in VaR technology in the last several years, upgrading existing VaR-based risk systems to CVaR is relatively cheap. The CVaR for a portfolio can be calculated as the average of several VaR numbers for the portfolio at different confidence levels. If risk systems can spit out VaR numbers for a portfolio at different confidence levels, it is relatively easy to calculate (or approximate) the CVaR of the portfolio.

MODELING HEDGE FUND RETURN DISTRIBUTIONS

The Simulation Framework

When constructing an optimal portfolio across a wide range of hedge fund strategies, several approaches can be taken. The simplest approach is to run an optimization based on historical returns. By now, we indeed have a reasonably long history of hedge fund returns, and we will present historical optimization results in the section Optimal Hedge Fund Allocations. The historical approach is naïve however. Historical returns are not necessarily representative going forward. As the hedge fund industry grows and matures, it is reasonable to expect lower alphas in the future due to, e.g., increased competition. In addition, historical hedge fund data potentially suffers from several biases, such as survivorship bias or backfill bias. *Survivorship bias* means that hedge funds that run out of business may disappear from the database. *Backfill bias*, on the other hand, refers to the fact that hedge funds can voluntarily report their performance to databases and typically report historical performance after having had a good run.

We need a more rigorous approach to determine optimal hedge fund portfolios. Our main considerations are the following: While hedge funds follow active strategies, their performance cannot be entirely attributed to skill (i.e., alpha, or uncorrelated excess returns). Several studies have shown that a significant portion of the returns on various hedge fund strategies can be explained by the returns on stocks and bonds. For each hedge fund strategy, we build a simple factor model with both a beta component linked to the performance of public asset classes and an alpha component that is independent from the beta factors.

The sensitivity of hedge fund returns relative to the returns on public asset classes is not constant over time. Style drifts and changing bets, among others, explain why it would be unrealistic to assume constant betas exposures. We apply a Kalman filter methodology to capture this time-varying behavior. We model the return of hedge fund strategy h in period t as follows: $r_{\mathrm{h.t}} = +\alpha_{h.t}\,\beta_{h.t}^{EQ}\,r_t^{EQ} + \beta_{h.t}^{FI}\,r_t^{FI} + \varepsilon_t$, where $\alpha_{h.t}$ is the time-varying alpha component of strategy h and the other two components represent the systematic beta components. This means that the performance in every period can be attributed partially to the performance of equity and fixed-income markets as well as to the skill and success of the fund manager.

To properly quantify tail risk, we need to model the returns on fixed income and equities in a realistic fashion. We use regime switching models to estimate and simulate the return processes of these two asset classes. Regime switching models do a reasonable job at fitting the empirically observed skewness and kurtosis in asset returns. By linking hedge fund returns to the returns on public asset classes, they will also inherit the regime switching property, and thus, potentially exhibit asymmetric and leptokurtic distributions.

While we rely on historical time series to fit the return distribution, we set the expected returns for the public asset classes, as well as the expected alphas for the hedge fund strategies, independently from the historical returns.

Several studies have been performed to explain hedge fund returns. Schneeweis et al. (2001) review several fund-specific microlevel factors, and they estimate different linear multifactor models for the performance of various hedge fund strategies. As they point out, the estimated alpha is very sensitive to the model specification, i.e., the number of factors used. While the classic linear regression model is a tractable approach, time-invariant factor loadings may be misleading. Mamaysky et al. (2007; 2008) apply linear factor models with time-varying betas to assess the performance of different mutual funds. In order to estimate time-varying betas properly, they apply Kalman filter models. Swinkels and Van Der Sluis (2006) present a return-based-style analysis to estimate the factor exposure of mutual funds. Since the investment style, and thus the factor exposures may vary over time, they argue that a rolling regression model would be inappropriate as it cannot properly account for time-varying betas, and the selected window size is ad hoc. Instead, they propose estimating time-varying factor sensitivities using Kalman filter techniques.

As we discussed earlier, hedge fund returns are typically serially correlated, reflecting smoothing and stale pricing. Before using hedge fund return data for fitting time-varying factor models, we "unsmooth" the return data time series in order to correct for these effects. We follow Geltner's (1991) approach and use only one lag to unsmooth hedge fund returns:

$$r_{u,t} = \frac{r_t^* - \rho r_{t-1}^*}{1-\rho}$$

where $r_{\mu,t}$ is the unsmoothed, estimated return, based on the observed return series r_t^* and ρ denotes the first-order serial correlation coefficient.

Time-Varying Factors

As discussed earlier, it is unrealistic to assume constant factor sensitivities for hedge fund returns. In addition, the alpha component will likely fluctuate over time as well depending on available opportunities in the market. Typically, time-varying betas are modeled as a driftless random walk. We deem this inappropriate as it would allow the beta's to drift away significantly over time, resulting in unrealistic factor exposures. Instead, a mean-reverting process seems more intuitive. We propose the following process for the alpha and beta factors:

$$\begin{bmatrix} \alpha_{h,t} \\ \beta_{h,t}^{EQ} \\ \beta_{h,t}^{FI} \end{bmatrix} = \begin{bmatrix} c_{1,h} \\ c_{2,h} \\ c_{3,h} \end{bmatrix} + \begin{bmatrix} \phi_{1,h} & 0 & 0 \\ 0 & \phi_{2,h} & 0 \\ 0 & 0 & \phi_{3,h} \end{bmatrix} \begin{bmatrix} \alpha_{h,t-1} \\ \beta_{h,t-1}^{EQ} \\ \beta_{h,t-1}^{FI} \end{bmatrix} + \begin{bmatrix} \eta_{1,h,t} \\ \eta_{2,h,t} \\ \eta_{3,h,t} \end{bmatrix}$$

We assume that the $\eta_{t,h,t}$ error terms are independent from each other.

The structure of this model is fairly intuitive, but the estimation is not straightforward. While we can use ordinary least squares to estimate linear regressions with static coefficients, this is not the case if the regression coefficients are changing over time. Such models can be estimated, however, using the Kalman filter. In our estimation, we follow the approach described by Kim and Nelson (1999). Figures 1.2 and 1.3 illustrate the beta and alpha processes for two selected hedge fund strategies, fixed-income arbitrage, and long/short equity funds.

Table 1.3 shows the estimation results for the factor models for each of the hedge fund strategies that we will use in the optimization.

F I G U R E   1.2

Time-varying betas and alpha of the fixed-income arbitrage strategy

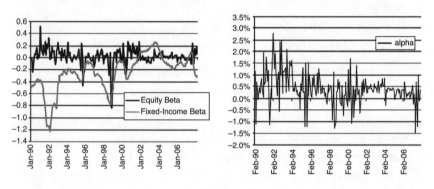

F I G U R E   1.3

Time-varying betas and alpha of the long/short equity strategy

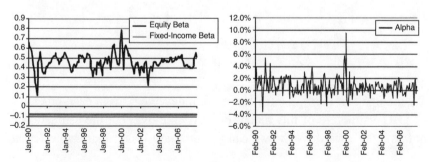

T A B L E   1.3

Estimated parameters for the time-varying factor model

		Alpha	Beta EQ	Beta FI
FI Arbitrage	c	0.0037	0.0151	−0.0282
	ϕ	0.1024	0.2712	0.8839
	LT-mean	0.0041	0.0207	−0.2429
Convertible Arbitrage	c	0.0020	0.0578	0.0423
	ϕ	0.5004	−0.2046	−0.3329
	LT-mean	0.0040	0.0480	0.0317
Distressed	c	0.0035	0.2021	0.0045
	ϕ	0.5302	−0.2389	0.7753
	LT-mean	0.0074	0.1631	0.0200
Equity Market Neutral	c	0.0029	0.0342	0.1889
	ϕ	−0.1060	0.3048	−0.6230
	LT-mean	0.0026	0.0492	0.1164
Equity Long/Short	c	0.0063	0.2062	−0.1175
	ϕ	0.1177	0.5492	−0.4190
	LT-mean	0.0071	0.4574	−0.0828
Relative Value	c	0.0025	0.0951	0.0141
	ϕ	0.5298	−0.0279	0.3252
	LT-mean	0.0053	0.0925	0.0209
Event-Driven	c	0.0030	0.3196	−0.0045
	ϕ	0.5649	−0.0781	−0.0490
	LT-mean	0.0069	0.2964	−0.0043
Merger Arbitrage	c	0.0020	0.0913	0.0166
	ϕ	0.5670	0.2702	−0.2804
	LT-mean	0.0046	0.1251	0.0130
Global Macro	c	0.0049	0.1510	0.2161
	ϕ	0.1463	0.3232	0.6078
	LT-mean	0.0057	0.2231	0.5510

Capturing Fat Tails: Regime Switching Model

As we showed in the second section of this chapter, returns on various hedge fund strategies are skewed and fat tailed. Applying a normal distribution and ignoring these features may result in an underestimation of the downside risk an investor is exposed to. In order to produce more reliable estimates of downside risk, we need a simple model that fits the return distribution and captures the fat tails and skewness.

We use regime switching models to describe the return distribution of the two factors, i.e., equities and fixed income. Regime switching models produce a better fit of the historical return distribution than a normal distribution. We keep the model specification simple. We assume the presence of K regimes and assume that equity and bond returns r_t are normally distributed with expected values μ_i and covariance matrices Ω_i, conditional on regime i. The return distribution is given by

$$f(r_{it} \mid s_t = i) = \frac{1}{(2\pi)^{m/2} \det(\Omega_i)^{1/2}} \exp\left\{ -\frac{1}{2}(y_t - \mu_i)'\Omega_i^{-1}(y_t - \mu_i) \right\}$$

where s_t denotes the regime or state in period t. The regimes are assumed to evolve as a Markov chain: the probability of regime $s_t = j$ ($j = 1, \ldots, N$) only depends on the previous observation: $P\{s_t = j \mid s_{t-1} = i,\ s_{t-2} = k,\ldots\} = P\{s_t = j \mid S_{t-1} = i\} = P_{ij}$. Regime switching models can be estimated using the so-called expectation maximization algorithm, as described by Kim and Nelson (1999) and Hamilton (1990; 1994).

We estimate a 2-regime model for equities and bonds based on the past 20 years of history. The estimated parameters are summarized in Table 1.4.

T A B L E   1.4

Regime switching parameters

	Regime 1	Regime 2
Equity Return*	−13.38%	17.80%
Fixed-Income Return*	10.42%	6.40%
Equity Volatility*	22.47%	11.36%
Fixed-Income Volatility*	3.32%	4.12%
Correlation	−0.51	0.38

* Annualized Statistics: based on excess returns over 1-month LIBOR.

As the statistics suggest, we can clearly distinguish between a regime when equities perform poorly with high volatility (annualized return and volatility of -13.4 and 22.5 percent, respectively) and a regime where equities perform extremely well with a lower volatility (annualized return and volatility of 17.8 and 11.4 percent, respectively). In the first regime, fixed income acts as diversifier: the correlation between the two asset classes is negative. This phenomenon is known as *flight to quality*. The state probabilities of these two regimes are 20 and 80 percent, respectively. The normal regime (regime 2) is more persistent with a transition probability of 80 percent, whereas the stressful regime (regime 1) shows a lower persistence with a transition probability of 20 percent. Note that it is unusual to find the same values for the state and transition probabilities.

Figure 1.4 shows the cumulative performance of equities and the estimated state probability for the stressful regime (regime 1). The crash of 1987, the long-term capital management (LTCM) crisis, and the collapse of the tech bubble are all attributed to the stressful regime.

In our simulation approach, we use forward-looking expected return assumptions for bond and equity returns for each of the two regimes. These forward-looking expected return assumptions are summarized in Table 1.5.

F I G U R E   1.4

Cumulative equity performance and state probability

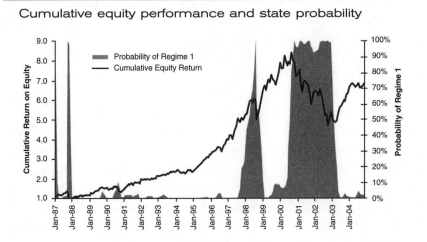

T A B L E   1.5

Forward-looking expected excess returns

	Regime 1	Regime 2
Equities	−10%	7.5%
Fixed Income	5%	0%

Simulation Approach

We now describe the steps to generate return scenarios for each of the various hedge fund strategies:

1. First, we simulate r_t^{EQ} and r_t^{Fl} in a 2-state regime switching framework, where the conditional means are forward-looking as discussed above.

2. In the second step, we simulate $(\alpha_{h,t}, \beta_{h,t}^{EQ}, \beta_{h,t}^{Fl})$ using AR(1) processes as described in a previous section, where the long-term mean of $\alpha_{h,t}$ is set on a forward-looking basis.

3. In the third step, based on the simulated paths of the previous two steps, we construct hedge fund returns and add simulated error terms.

To set the long-term average alpha for each hedge fund on a forward-looking basis we simply modify the intercept $c_{1,h}$. In general, the long-term mean of a first-order vector autoregressive process $y_t = V + Ay_{t-1} + \mu_t$ is given by the following formula: $Y = (1-A)^{-1} \cdot v$. To modify the long-term expected value Y^*, we can simply modify the intercept of the VAR(1) process as follows: $v^* = (1-A)Y^*$. We assume that the time-varying alphas for each of the hedge fund strategies mean-revert to an expected alpha that is different from their long-term historical average. We have chosen the forward-looking (expected) alpha in such a way as to produce comparable Sharpe ratios for each of the hedge fund strategies. This assumption is simply for illustrative purposes. The expected alphas for each hedge fund strategy as well as the long-term historical average are summarized in Table 1.6. Note that our expected alphas are below the long-term historical average for each strategy.

T A B L E   1.6

Forward-looking expected alphas

Strategy	Expected Annualized Alpha	Average Annualized Alpha 1990–2007
FI Arbitrage	3.60%	5.22%
Convertible Arbitrage	2.10%	4.52%
Distressed	3.30%	9.30%
Equity Market Neutral	1.98%	3.08%
Equity Long/Short	4.80%	8.80%
Relative Value	2.10%	6.48%
Event Driven	3.00%	8.54%
Merger Arbitrage	2.10%	5.97%
Global Macro	4.20%	6.78%

Results for the Simulation

In this section we show the moments of the distribution of the simulated returns for each of the hedge fund strategies. To generate realistic return distributions, we need to select a time horizon long enough to simulate the impact of the different regimes. We selected 120 months for the simulation, i.e., 10 years. To get a sense for the impact of sampling error, we repeat the simulation 100 times. Table 1.7 shows the skewness and kurtosis for equities and fixed income on a historical basis and for the simulated returns.

Our regime switching model for equity and fixed-income returns does a good job a mimicking the historically observed skewness and kurtosis.

Table 1.8 shows the expected (annualized) excess return over 1-month LIBOR for each hedge fund strategy as well as the average, minimum, and maximum Sharpe ratio and 99 percent Conditional VaR. The Sharpe ratios for each of the hedge fund strategies are comparable. Note also that the conditional VaR exhibits a wide range—particularly for those strategies that have fatter tails such as fixed-income arbitrage, distressed, equity long/short, event driven, and merger arbitrage.

T A B L E   1.7

Skewness and kurtosis for equity and fixed-income returns

	Historical Returns		Simulated Returns			
	Skewness	**Kurtosis**	**Skewness**		**Kurtosis**	
			Average	[Min, Max]	Average	[Min, Max]
Equities	−0.60	4.1	−0.26	[−1.3, 0.95]	4.4	[2.5, 7.9]
Fixed Income	−0.34	3.4	−0.04	[−0.66, 0.52]	3.0	[2.4, 5.1]

T A B L E   1.8

Expected returns, Sharpe ratios, and CVaRs for simulated returns

	Expected Annualized Return	Sharpe Ratio			99% CVaR		
		Average	Minimum	Maximum	Average	Minimum	Maximum
FI Arbitrage	3.18%	0.65	0.48	0.87	−4.45%	−10.40%	−1.73%
Convertible Arbitrage	2.11%	0.65	0.52	0.78	−2.31%	−3.41%	−1.20%
Distressed	4.29%	0.76	0.62	0.96	−4.34%	−10.51%	−2.47%
Equity Market Neutral	2.43%	0.73	0.59	0.97	−2.48%	−4.93%	−1.48%
Equity Long/Short	6.06%	0.69	0.49	0.95	−7.74%	−14.00%	−3.46%
Relative Value	2.28%	0.71	0.57	0.93	−2.64%	−6.51%	−1.49%
Event-Driven	3.83%	0.66	0.46	0.89	−5.55%	−11.67%	−1.82%
Merger Arbitrage	2.71%	0.82	0.51	1.22	−3.38%	−10.50%	−1.19%
Global Macro	5.52%	0.69	0.55	0.80	−5.82%	−11.21%	−3.60%

Table 1.9 shows the skewness and kurtosis for the simulated hedge fund returns. For some of the hedge fund strategies the range over our 100 repeated simulation paths is quite wide. This should result in a wide range for the optimal portfolio weights to those strategies.

Our simulation approach produces fat-tailed return distributions. Several of the hedge fund strategies exhibit significant kurtosis, e.g., fixed-income arbitrage, event driven, and merger arbitrage. These strategies also

T A B L E   1.9

Skewness and kurtosis for simulated returns

	Skewness			Kurtosis		
	Average	Minimum	Maximum	Average	Minimum	Maximum
FI Arbitrage	−0.10	−1.87	3.07	5.3	2.4	25.3
Convertible Arbitrage	−0.03	−0.65	0.74	3.1	2.2	5.4
Distressed	−0.09	−1.94	0.72	3.5	2.2	13.5
Equity Market Neutral	0.05	−0.95	1.25	3.7	2.4	7.9
Equity Long/Short	−0.20	−1.33	1.31	4.2	2.2	8.4
Relative Value	−0.09	−1.85	0.78	4.1	2.4	13.9
Event-Driven	−0.15	−2.67	2.17	5.9	2.6	19.2
Merger Arbitrage	−0.10	−3.76	3.31	7.6	3.5	28.6
Global Macro	−0.01	−0.59	0.64	3.3	2.3	5.7

exhibit significant kurtosis in the historical return data, but the historical return distribution is more extreme. There is room for improvement, however, as the simulation approach does not capture the skewness in hedge fund returns very well. Our model for hedge fund returns is very simplistic as we only allow for two factors (equity returns and fixed-income returns). Many other factors have been found to be statistically significant in the literature. Extending the number of factors in our simulation approach is a topic for future research. Another possible extension is to allow for regime switches in the alpha component of the various hedge fund returns.

OPTIMAL HEDGE FUND ALLOCATIONS

In this section we contrast the risk allocation derived from mean-variance optimization to the risk allocation derived from mean-CVaR using the empirical distribution and simulated returns from the regime switching and time-varying factor models discussed in the third section of this chapter. In the following section, we study optimal risk allocations based on the historical distribution. We also discuss optimal risk allocations based on our forward-looking simulation framework. The optimizations were carried out in MATLAB[5] using MOSEK,[6] a commercial optimization package for solving a variety of optimization models.

Historical Optimization Results

In this section we compare the optimal allocation of a mean-variance investor with that of an investor that wants to manage tail risk through mean-CVaR optimization. Table 1.10 shows the optimal allocations for different 99 percent CVaR risk budgets (300, 400, and 500 bps on a monthly basis) using the historical return distribution for various hedge fund strategies from January 1990 to December 2007. We compare these optimal allocations with mean-variance optimal portfolios for the same risk budget.

T A B L E   1.10

Optimal CVaR versus mean-variance-based risk allocation*

	Sharpe Ratio	Skew	Kurt	99% CVaR Allocation (%)		99% CVaR Allocation (%)		99% CVaR Allocation (%)	
				M-V	M-CVaR	M-V	M-CVaR	M-V	M-CVaR
FI Arbitrage	0.77	−1.78	14.06	0%	17%	0%	0%	0%	0%
Conv. Arbitrage	1.19	−1.40	6.51	2%	0%	0%	0%	0%	0%
Distressed	1.51	−0.66	8.43	7%	0%	21%	0%	47%	0%
Equity M/N	1.32	0.07	3.78	32%	25%	3%	21%	0%	0%
Equity L/S	1.24	0.09	4.45	0%	25%	9%	36%	24%	40%
Rel. Val.	1.80	−0.91	13.37	48%	0%	55%	0%	14%	0%
Event-Dr.	1.33	−1.27	7.57	0%	0%	0%	0%	0%	0%
Merger Arb.	1.21	−2.67	15.42	5%	0%	0%	0%	0%	0%
Glob. Macro	1.24	0.36	3.72	6%	32%	11%	43%	16%	60%
99% CVaR (Monthly)				300	300	400	400	500	500
Volatility				278	463	400	603	542	733
Ann. Mean				604	749	788	902	943	1031

*Based on empirical return distribution.

[5] See www.mathworks.com for more details.
[6] See www.mosek.com for more details.

Several differences stand out from the results in Table 1.10. First, it is important to note that the mean-CVaR-based allocations produce superior expected returns for a given risk budget. For a 99 percent monthly CVaR risk budget of 300 bps, the difference in annualized expected returns is on the order of 150 bps, which is substantial. Even for a risk budget of 500 bps, the annualized expected return differential is about 90 bps. Second, it should be noted that for the same CVaR risk budget, the volatility of the mean-variance-based allocations is lower than that of the mean-CVaR-based risk allocation. Volatility simply measures the dispersion in returns and is not a good measure of tail risk. By better managing the tail risk, the mean-CVaR investor can run a portfolio with a higher volatility even though the monthly 99 percent CVaR risk budget is identical to that of the mean-variance-based risk allocation.

If we compare individual allocations by strategy, some important differences stand out as well. The mean-variance-based risk allocations spend a large portion of the risk budget on relative value arbitrage. Relative value arbitrage has the highest Sharpe ratio. The mean-variance-based risk allocation picks out this strategy as it seemingly provides superior risk-adjusted returns. Relative value arbitrage also exhibits negative skewness and extremely fat tails. These features are ignored in a mean-variance setting. The mean-CVaR-based risk allocations, however, spend none of the risk budget on relative value arbitrage as its negative skewness and extreme kurtosis make it a very unattractive strategy for an investor who wants to manage the tail risk of her portfolio. In general, the mean-CVaR-based risk allocation tends to prefer strategies that have low or positive skewness and low kurtosis. Merger arbitrage or relative value arbitrage never show up in the optimal risk allocation for a mean-CVaR investor. The reason is that these strategies exhibit negative skewness and excessive kurtosis. On the other hand, the mean-CVaR-based risk allocations spend a considerable portion of the risk budget on equity long/short, equity market neutral, or global macro strategies. These strategies have positive skewness (an attractive feature for investors) and relatively low kurtosis.

The differences between mean-variance-based allocations and mean-CVaR-based allocations are most pronounced for conservative and moderate investors. For more aggressive investors who have a relatively large risk budget, the optimal allocations for a mean-variance investor and a mean-CVaR investor become more similar. Aggressive investors that focus less on tail risk will start to behave increasingly like mean-variance investors. This is also borne out by the efficient frontier plotted in Figure 1.5.

Figure 1.6 shows the underlying optimal portfolios corresponding to the efficient frontiers presented in Figure 1.5. In Figure 1.6, Panel A shows the allocations based on the mean-variance framework, whereas Panel B shows the mean-CVaR optimal allocations. Note that putting less emphasis on tail-risk can also be achieved by reducing the confidence level α for the CVaR budget.

F I G U R E   1.5

Mean-CVaR optimal portfolios versus mean-variance portfolios

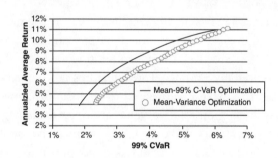

F I G U R E   1.6

Mean-CVaR optimal portfolios versus mean-variance portfolios

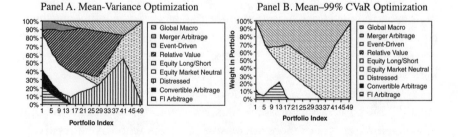

Forward-Looking Optimization Results

In this section we present the optimization results based on the simulation framework described in this chapter's third section. Performing mean-CVaR optimization based on historical returns is relatively straightforward: we take the historical time series of hedge fund returns, and apply the optimization methodology discussed in this chapter's second section. On a forward-looking basis, the principle is the same: we generate hypothetical time series for hedge fund returns based on our forward-looking and modeling assumptions, and complete the optimization accordingly. To generate realistic return distributions for equities, fixed income, and thus ultimately for the selected hedge funds, we have to select a time horizon long enough to bring the regime switching alive, in other words, to expose the simulated returns to both regimes.

We selected 120 periods for the simulation, i.e., 10 years. However, when we rerun the simulation with new random numbers, the optimal portfolios may be different. This is because the optimization process, especially the downside-risk-driven optimizations are sensitive to the extreme values that we generate. This problem is also known as *sampling error*; for further details on this issue see, e.g., Schrerer (2002). Thus, we present our optimization results based on 120-month simulated time series, repeated 100 times. The output thus not only reflects optimal portfolios but also highlights on the uncertainty in the output of the model. In Tables 1.11a and 1.11b we compare the mean-variance and the mean-CVaR-based optimization results, subject to a 200 and 300-bps 99 percent CVaR risk budget. In these tables we show both the optimal portfolio weights and the minimum and maximum weights based on the 100 simulation runs over a period of 120 months.

As in the case of the historical returns, the mean-CVaR investor tends to allocate less to strategies that exhibit fat tails. However, the differences are less dramatic compared to the optimization results using historical returns as the regime switching model does not fully capture the skewness and fat tails in hedge fund returns. The mean-CVaR optimal portfolios produce slightly better expected returns for a given CVaR risk budget, 56 and 40 bps, respectively. Compared to the mean-variance optimal portfolios, the mean-CVaR optimal portfolios allocate less to fixed-income arbitrage and merger arbitrage—strategies that exhibit relatively

T A B L E   1.11A

Optimal CVaR risk allocation versus mean-variance-based risk allocation. Based on a regime switching model, with a 99 percent CVaR budget of 200 bps

	Simulated			Mean-Variance Allocation		CVaR Allocation	
	Sharpe Ratio	Skewness	Kurtosis	Average	[Min, Max]	Average	[Min, Max]
FI Arbitrage	0.65	−0.10	5.3	23.3%	[5.5%, 43%]	13.7%	[0%, 59%]
Conv. Arb.	0.65	−0.03	3.1	5.9%	[0%, 32%]	4.5%	[0%, 51%]
Distressed	0.76	−0.09	3.5	18.2%	[0%, 37%]	18.9%	[0%, 55%]
Equity M/N	0.73	0.05	3.7	12.9%	[0%, 41%]	5.7%	[0%, 45%]
Equity L/S	0.69	−0.20	4.2	12.0%	[0%, 37%]	17.6%	[0%, 52%]
Rel. Val.	0.71	−0.09	4.1	3.3%	[0%, 22%]	2.1%	[0%, 30%]
Event-Dr.	0.66	−0.15	5.9	1.7%	[0%, 18%]	4.2%	[0%, 38%]
Merger Arb.	0.82	−0.10	7.6	7.2%	[0%, 39%]	5.7%	[0%, 45%]
Glob. Macro	0.69	−0.01	3.3	15.5%	[2.6%, 33%]	27.6%	[0%, 53%]
Target 99% CVaR (monthly)				200 bps			
Expected Annualized Return				3.9%	[2.5%, 5.0%]	4.4%	[3.2%, 5.4%]
Annualized Standard Deviation				2.9%	[1.7%, 4.5%]	4.1%	[2.9%, 5.3%]

T A B L E   1.11B

Optimal CVaR risk allocation versus mean-variance-based risk allocation. Based on a regime switching model, with a 99 percent CVaR risk budget of 300 bps

	Simulated			Mean-Variance Allocation		CVaR Allocation	
	Sharpe Ratio	Skewness	Kurtosis	Average	[Min, Max]	Average	[Min, Max]
FI Arbitrage	0.65	−0.10	5.3	17.4%	[0%, 41%]	7.0%	[0%, 40%]
Conv. Arb.	0.65	−0.03	3.1	1.4%	[0%, 26%]	0.6%	[0%, 19%]
Distressed	0.76	−0.09	3.5	21.2%	[0%, 40%]	15.4%	[0%, 66%]
Equity M/N	0.73	0.05	3.7	4.4%	[0%, 34%]	2.1%	[0%, 38%]
Equity L/S	0.69	−0.20	4.2	25.5%	[0%, 68%]	29.8%	[0%, 87%]
Rel. Val.	0.71	−0.09	4.1	0.5%	[0%, 16%]	1.0%	[0%, 29%]
Event-Dr.	0.66	−0.15	5.9	0.9%	[0%, 20%]	2.3%	[0%, 40%]
Merger Arb.	0.82	−0.10	7.6	1.7%	[0%, 32%]	1.4%	[0%, 33%]
Glob. Macro	0.69	−0.01	3.3	27.0%	[7%, 50%]	40.4%	[0%, 74%]
Target 99% CVaR (monthly)				300 bps			
Expected Annualized Return				4.7%	[3.3%, 5.9%]	5.1%	[3.9%, 5.9%]
Annualized Standard Deviation				4.3%	[2.4%, 6.2%]	5.5%	[4%, 6.6%]

F I G U R E   1.7

Histograms of optimal portfolio weights for mean-variance versus mean-CVaR investors

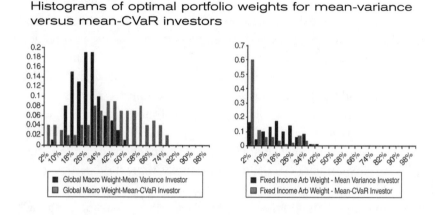

high kurtosis—and more to long/short equity and global macro (see Tables 1.11a and 1.11b).

Another important difference is the range of optimal weights. The weights for the mean-CVaR optimal portfolios display a wider range for most of the strategies (see also Figure 1.7). The reason is that downside risk measures, such as the 99 percent CVaR, are more sensitive to outliers than the standard deviation. In real life, however, investors are more concerned with rare but major downside losses rather than everyday fluctuations, so this is a desirable feature of the mean-CVaR optimization framework. Our framework should potentially help investors select portfolios that result in less negative surprises in those bad days.

CONCLUSION

In this chapter we discussed how investors can build a better asset allocation and risk budgeting approach when faced with investment strategies with returns that are not normally distributed. We discussed CVaR, a relatively new risk measure, as a promising candidate for this purpose. This risk measure has desirable theoretical properties (i.e., it satisfies the axioms for a coherent risk measure) while still being easy to use. Another advantage is that it can easily be incorporated into standard optimization methods. Mean-CVaR optimization can be formulated as a linear programming problem. Such optimization models can be solved with most standard commercial optimization packages.

To illustrate the differences between mean-CVaR and standard mean-variance optimization, we used several hedge fund indexes. These hedge fund indexes exhibit skewness and fat tails. We showed that the optimal allocation across hedge fund strategies when taking into account these fat-tailed and skewed return streams is quite different from that suggested by standard mean-variance models. By better managing tail risk, investors should be able to achieve superior risk-adjusted returns.

In this chapter, we presented a simulation framework for hedge fund returns. We took into account that (1) hedge fund returns can partially be explained by the performance of equities and fixed income, but the sensitivities vary over time; (2) asset returns exhibit different properties in different regimes, and this characteristic explains some of the skewness and kurtosis in their distribution; and (3) a mean CVaR optimization approach can protect investors against rare but severe losses, however, the portfolio weights in the optimal portfolio display a wider range due to sampling error as downside risk measures are more sensitive to outliers. Our approach not only helps investors arrive at a better portfolio, but also allows for a better understanding of the drivers and attributes of hedge returns. The case study in this chapter is kept simple and is for illustrative purposes. The factor model, for instance, can and should be extended to more factors beyond just the returns on bonds and equities.

In the optimization approach, additional risk constraints, such as drawdown constraints should be incorporated to deal with the serial correlation that is observed for many hedge fund strategies. In this chapter we optimized repeatedly using a single path for hedge fund returns (120 simulated monthly returns). The optimization model should be extended to incorporate multiple paths for the different hedge fund strategies simultaneously. Alternatively, the mean-CVaR approach could be extended to a multi-stage stochastic programming framework. These types of optimization models can be solved with fast decomposition methods, such as the method developed by Berkelaar et al. (2005).

APPENDIX A: MEAN-CVAR OPTIMIZATION

In this appendix we present the equivalent linear programming problems for the mean-CVaR optimization [we refer to Rockafeller and Uryasev

(2000; 2002) for a complete derivation]. First, we consider the mean-CVaR optimization problem, given by

$$\max_{w} \mu' w$$

$$\text{such that} - E(r'w \mid r'w \leq \text{VaR}_{\alpha}) \leq \text{CVaR}_{\max} \qquad \text{(A1.1)}$$

$$\iota'w = 1, \; w \geq 0$$

For discrete return observations r_t (where r_t denotes the N-vector of returns at time t), the $\alpha\%$-CVaR for a portfolio with weights w, can be calculated as

$$\text{VaR}_{\alpha} + \frac{1}{(1-\alpha)T} \sum_{t=1}^{T} \max[-\text{VaR}_{\alpha} - r_t'w, 0]$$

Introducing auxiliary variables, it is straightforward to show that Equation (A1.1) can be reformulated as

$$\max_{w, \xi, z} \mu' w$$

$$\xi + \frac{1}{(1-\alpha)T} \iota' z_t \leq \text{CVaR}_{\max}$$

$$-\xi - r_t'w \leq z_t, \; z_t \geq 0 \; t = 1, \ldots, T$$

$$\iota'w = 1, w \geq 0$$

Note that we optimize over the portfolio weights w and the auxiliary variables z and x. For the optimal portfolio, the variable x will be equal to the $\alpha\%$ VaR.

REFERENCES

Amin, G.S. and H.M. Kat (2003) Stocks, Bonds, and Hedge Funds. *Journal of Portfolio Management*, Vol. 29, No 4, pp. 111–122.

Artzner, P., F. Delbaen, J.M. Eber, and D. Heath (1999) Coherent Measures of Risk. *Mathematical Finance*, Vol. 9, No. 3, pp. 203–228.

Basak, S. and A. Shapiro (2001) Value-at-Risk Based Risk Management: Optimal Policies and Asset Prices. *Review of Financial Studies*, Vol. 14, No. 2, pp. 371–405.

Berkelaar, A., J. Gromicho, R. Kouwenberg, and S. Zhang (2005) A Primal-Dual Decomposition Algorithm for Multistage Stochastic Convex Programming. *Mathematical Programming*, Vol. 104, No. 1, pp. 153–177.

Berkelaar, A., A. Kobor, and M. Tsumagari (2006) The Sense and Nonsense of Risk Budgeting. *Financial Analyst Journal*, Vol. 62, No. 5, pp. 63–75.

Geltner, D.M. (1991) Smoothing in Appraisal-Based Returns. *Journal of Real Estate Finance and Economics*, Vol. 4, No. 3, pp. 327–345.

Hamilton, J.D. (1990) Analysis of Time Series Subject to Changes in Regime. *Journal of Econometrics*, Vol. 45, No. 1–2, pp. 39–70.

Hamilton, J.D. (1994) *Time Series Analysis*. Princeton, NJ: Princeton University Press.

Kim, C. and C.R. Nelson. (1999) *State-Space Models with Regime Switching—Classical and Gibbs-Sampling Approaches and Applications*. Cambridge, MA: MIT Press.

Kouwenberg, R. (2003) Do Hedge Funds Add Value to a Passive Portfolio? Correcting for Non-Normal Returns and Disappearing Funds. *Journal of Asset Management*, Vol. 3, No. 4, pp. 361–382.

Krokhmal, P., S. Uryasev, and G. Zrazhesky. (2003) Numerical Comparison of CVaR and CDaR Approaches: Application to Hedge Funds. In W.T. Ziemba (ed.), *The Stochastic Programming Approach to Asset Liability and Wealth Management*. Malden, MA: Blackwell Publishers.

Lo, A. (2002) The Statistics of Sharpe Ratios. *Financial Analyst Journal*, Vol. 58, No. 4, pp. 36–52.

Mamaysky, H., M. Spiegel, and H. Zhang. (2007) Improved Forecasting of Mutual Fund Alphas and Betas. *Review of Finance*, Vol. 11, No. 3, pp. 1–42.

Mamaysky, H., M. Spiegel, and H. Zhang. (2008) Estimating the Dynamics of Mutual Fund Alpha and Betas. *Review of Financial Studies*, Vol. 21, No. 1, pp. 233–264.

Rockafellar, R.T. and S. Uryasev. (2000) Optimization of Conditional Value at Risk. *Journal of Risk*, Vol. 2, No. 3, pp. 21–42.

Rockafellar, R.T. and S. Uryasev. (2002) Conditional Value at Risk for General Loss Distributions. *Journal of Banking and Finance*, Vol. 26, No. 7, pp. 1443–1471.

Schrerer, B. (2002) *Portfolio Construction and Risk Budgeting.* London: Risk Books.

Schneeweis, T., H. Kazemi, and G. Martin. (2001) Understanding Hedge Fund Performance: Research Results and Rules of Thumb for the Institutional Investor. Working paper, Lehman Brothers, New York.

Swinkels, L., and P.J. Van Der Sluis. (2006) Return-Based Style Analysis with Time-Varying Exposures. *The European Journal of Finance*, Vol. 12, No. 6–7, pp. 529–552.

CHAPTER 2

Estimating Value at Risk of Institutional Portfolios with Alternative Asset Classes[1]

Roy Kouwenberg, Albert Mentink, Mark Schouten, and Robin Sonnenberg

ABSTRACT

This chapter presents a vector autoregressive (VaR) model, used to generate future return scenarios for a broad set of traditional and alternative asset classes. Our VaR model has the desirable property that it can deal with historical time series that differ in length. This is especially relevant for alternative asset classes, which typically have a short history. Furthermore, we model the distribution of asset returns using a skewed Student's t distribution, which captures the skewness and fat tails of the historical time series of many asset classes. We generate scenarios of future asset returns to calculate (conditional) value-at-risk values for European institutional investors with five different strategic allocations ranging from very conservative to very aggressive. Furthermore, we calculate the required economic capital for investment risk under the Solvency II regulations using two

---

[1] The views expressed in this chapter are those of the authors and do not necessarily reflect those of our employer and our colleagues. We thank Dick van Dijk for his helpful suggestions.

specifications of the VaR model. Our results show that using a VaR model with normally distributed asset returns underestimates the downside risk of investing in alternative asset classes.

INTRODUCTION

Institutional investors have access to a broad set of investment opportunities nowadays. Whereas in the past the strategic allocation mainly consisted of bonds and stocks, institutional investors now can choose between several alternative asset classes, such as private equity, hedge funds, and low-rated corporate bonds. Many of the alternative asset classes are relatively new, which imply short historical time series. This complicates the generation of future scenarios of alternative asset returns, since the estimations will be based on a limited number of observations. Furthermore, the returns of (especially alternative) asset classes do not follow the standard assumption of a normal distribution: see, e.g., Harris and Küçüközmen (2001) for stock indexes in the United States and United Kingdom; Theodossiou (1998) for stock indexes in the United States, Canada, and Japan; Jondeau and Rockinger (2005) for stock indexes in emerging Asian countries; and Kouwenberg and Ziemba (2007) for hedge fund data. Misspecification of the distribution of asset returns may lead to misleading results in portfolio choice and risk management, especially when tail behavior is modeled incorrectly.

We overcome these problems by introducing a vector autoregressive (VaR) model that optimally uses the longer historical data for traditional asset classes to estimate the return generating process for alternative asset classes with short historical time series, following the approach introduced by Stambaugh (1997). We extend the framework of Stambaugh (1997) to cope with multiple time series that differ in length and nonnormal error distributions. Because the returns of many asset classes suffer from skewness and fat tails, we apply a skewed Student's t error distribution (Fernández and Steel, 1998) for the VaR model. Depending on the maximum likelihood estimate of the skewed Student's t distribution parameters the asset classes can be modeled as a skewed normal distribution or a skewed Student's t distribution. This extends the standard framework, which only includes normally distributed asset returns.

We use the VaR model to generate future return scenarios for the asset classes. Based on these scenarios we estimate the (conditional) value at risk for five model portfolios for European institutional investors. We calculate the value-at-risk estimates using scenarios from the VaR model based on the standard assumption of normally distributed asset returns and using scenarios from the VaR model with a skewed Student's t error distribution. Then we compare whether the two VaR model specifications generate large differences in the (conditional) value-at-risk results. Large differences between the two methods imply that the simplifying assumption of normally distributed asset returns gives misleading results in terms of the risk characteristics of the strategic portfolios.

We also analyze the results from the perspective of the Solvency II framework that requires institutional investors to hold a percentage of their assets as economic required capital (ERC) in order to cope with extreme shocks in the investment portfolio value. Our results show that for a very conservative, average, and very aggressive strategic asset allocation an institutional investor must hold 4.0, 9.3, and 12.9 percent, respectively, as ERC using the normal VaR model compared to 4.5, 10.0, and 13.2 percent based on our skewed Student's t model. These differences may seem small but have a large impact in terms of monetary amounts considering the large portfolios held by typical institutional investors.

This chapter extends the current literature in a number of ways. Firstly, Stambaugh (1997) only analyzes two groups of time series of different length. Since we want to use many alternative asset classes with different lengths, we extend the Stambaugh (1997) framework such that we can divide the historical data into four groups based on the length of the time series.

Secondly, VaR models traditionally focus on traditional asset classes such as stocks and bonds. An exception is the study by Hoevenaars et al. (2007), who consider the asset-classed stocks, government bonds, real estate, commodities, and hedge funds. This chapter considers a larger set of alternative asset classes, including real estate, hedge funds, private equity, corporate bonds, high-yield bonds, emerging market bonds, leveraged loans, asset-backed securities, and inflation-linked bonds. Thirdly, Hoevenaars et al. (2007) consider a VaR model with normally distributed asset returns instead of the more general skewed Student's t distribution in this chapter. Further, we investigate whether the nonnormal return distribution of asset classes, especially the alternative ones, contributes to larger value-at-risk estimates and economic capital requirements for well-diversified institutional portfolios.

The structure of this chapter is as follows. The second section of this chapter describes the data, consisting of the historical time series of asset returns and state variables and our model portfolios for institutional investors. This chapter's third section presents the VaR model, the scenario generator for future asset returns, and the method for calculating (conditional) value at risk. In the fourth section, an overview of the (conditional) value-at-risk and economic capital results for our institutional portfolios is given, and a short study of the fraud case at Société Générale in 2008 is presented.

DATA

This section provides an overview of the historical time series we use for asset classes and state variables, including descriptive statistics. We further present and discuss our five model portfolios for European institutional investors.

Asset Classes

Table 2.1 shows the data sources for our empirical analysis. For all asset classes we use monthly total returns hedged to euro.[2] We divide the asset classes into four groups, depending on the historical time-series length.

State Variables

We also include a number of state variables in our model, to help explain the variation of the asset returns. The four state variables fall into group 1

---

[2] We hedge the total returns to euro since we focus on European institutional investors.

T A B L E   2.1

Overview of the index and length of the historical time series
per asset class

Group	Asset Class	Index	Period
1	Global equity	MSCI World Index	May 1977–Jun. 2007
1	European government bonds	A. German benchmark bond yield 10 year*	May 1977–Aug. 1996
		B. ML European Union government bond index	Sep. 1996–Jun 2007
1	Commodities	GSCI total return index	May 1977–Jun. 2007
2	Global real estate	S&P/Citigroup BMI global real estate index	Jan. 1990–Jun. 2007
2	Hedge funds	HFR FoF index†	Jan. 1990–Jun. 2007
3	Emerging market bonds	JPM EMBI index	Jan. 1994–Jun. 2007
3	Private equity	LPX50 global listed private equity‡	Jan. 1994–Jun. 2007
4	European corporate bonds	Lehman Brothers euro aggregate corporate bond index	Jan. 1999–Jun. 2007
4	European high yield bonds	Lehman high yield pan European	Jan. 1999–Jun. 2007
4	European asset-backed securities	Lehman euro-aggregate ABS index	Jan. 1999–Jun. 2007
4	European inflation-linked bonds	A. Barclays France government inflation-linked all maturities	Jan. 1999–Oct. 2001
		B. Barclays euro government EMU HICP-linked all maturities	Nov. 2001–Jun. 2007
4	European leveraged loans	CSFB western European leveraged loan index§	Jan. 1999–Jun. 2007

* For this period index B is not available. Instead, we approximate constant maturity government bond returns using the German 10-year bond yield series following Campbell et al. (1997).

† For more information, see http://www.hedgefundresearch.com.

‡ For more information, see http://www.lpx.ch/index.php?id=30.

§ For more information, see http://www.styleadvisor.com/support/download/hyidxlevloan_desc.pdf.

due to their long historical time-series length. Table 2.2 shows more information about the indexes used for the state variables.

T A B L E   2.2

Overview index and length historical time series
per state variable

State Variable	Index	Period
Risk-free rate	A. German 1-month interest rate	May 1977–Nov. 1998
	B. EURIBOR 1-month interest rate	Dec. 1998–Jun. 2007
Term spread	A. German benchmark bond yield 10-year German 1-month interest rate	May 1977–Nov. 1998
	B. European government bond yield 10 year – EURIBOR 1-month interest rate	Dec. 1998–Jun. 2007
Credit spread	U.S. credit spread Baa–Aaa (Moody's)*	May 1977–Jun. 2007
Dividend yield	Dividend yield MSCI world index	May 1977–Jun. 2007

* We use U.S. credit spread data, because euro-zone credit spread data with a sufficiently long history is not available. Moody's determines this credit spread for long-term bonds with remaining maturities as close as possible to 30 years. For more information: http://research.stlouisfed.org/fred2/series/AAA?cid=119.

Model Portfolios European Institutional Investors

In order to evaluate the asset return scenarios generated with our VaR model, we will calculate the value at risk and economic capital required for five fictitious model portfolios for European institutional investors. The weights of these model portfolios are based on general trends in European institutional investment portfolios. Firstly, we use as a source the findings from a survey by Russell Investment Group in 2007 on investments in alternative asset classes among institutional investors. For European institutional investors the report finds an average weight of 4.6 percent invested in private equity, 7.4 percent in hedge funds, and 8.9 percent in real estate in 2007. Furthermore, our second source is the Dutch Central Bank: Rooij et al. (2005) find relatively stable average weights among Dutch pension funds from 2000 onward, consisting of 45 percent in fixed income, 45 percent in equity, and 10 percent in "other" classes (such as real estate and other alternatives). Based on this information, we have constructed five model portfolios for European institutional investors shown in Table 2.3, ranging from "very conservative" to "very aggressive."

T A B L E   2.3

Five asset mix strategies for European institutional investors
with weight asset class in percentages

Weight Asset Class(%)	Strategy				
	Very Conservative	Conservative	Average	Aggressive	Very Aggressive
Government bonds*	55	35	20	15	10
Corporate bonds	20	20	20	20	10
Global equity	20	35	40	40	45
Commodities	2	2	2	2	4
Real estate	3	5	8	10	12
Private Equity	0	1	4	5	7
Hedge funds	0	2	6	8	12

* We indicate government bonds with AAA Standard & Poor's rating.

DESCRIPTIVE STATISTICS

Table 2.4 depicts the descriptive statistics of all asset classes. Besides the annualized mean return and volatility, Table 2.4 also shows the skewness and kurtosis. *Skewness* is defined as the third moment about the mean divided by the standard deviation to the power three. It provides a measure of the asymmetry of a distribution function. *Kurtosis* is defined as the fourth moment about the mean divided by the standard deviation to the power four. It gives an estimate of the amount of variation in the distribution function caused by infrequent extreme events. A normally distributed time series has zero skewness and a kurtosis of three (excess kurtosis zero).

Table 2.4 shows that the return distribution of many asset classes exhibits negative skewness. This indicates that most asset classes have a longer tail at the left side of the probability distribution than on the right side. In other words, the probability of negative returns is larger than a normal distribution identifies. Furthermore, we see that many asset classes exhibit kurtosis in excess of three, indicating that the probability of extreme returns is higher than for a normal distribution.

T A B L E   2.4

Descriptive statistics for asset class returns

Asset class	Mean	Volatility	Skewness	Kurtosis
Global equity	0.1358	0.1388	−0.5561	4.4683
Government bonds	0.0765	0.0430	−0.2196	4.3197
Commodities	0.1121	0.1757	0.2202	4.2819
Real estate	0.1032	0.1559	−0.2246	3.9526
Hedge funds	0.1026	0.0543	−0.2878	7.2101
Emerging market bonds	0.0591	0.0258	−0.1710	3.0069
Private equity	0.1687	0.2011	0.2801	7.5414
Corporate bonds	0.0441	0.0279	−0.1326	2.4115
High yield	0.0666	0.1027	−0.6474	5.8609
Asset-backed securities	0.0417	0.0319	−0.4082	2.9335
Inflation-linked bonds	0.0526	0.0449	−0.2747	3.7244
Leveraged loans	0.0602	0.0060	−0.6791	6.8216

Note: Statistics based on monthly data; mean and volatility are annualized.

We test whether our time series are stationary, i.e., the mean and variance of the time series do not depend on time, using the Dickey–Fuller test. We find that the risk-free return, the credit spread, and the dividend yield are nonstationary, and therefore we difference[3] these series to obtain stationary time series. Retesting with the differenced time series gives that all time series are now stationary at a significance level of 5 percent.

METHODOLOGY

This section describes the VaR model for the time series of the asset classes and the scenario generation method for simulating future return. Furthermore, we describe the value-at-risk and conditional value-at-risk measures that we use to evaluate the risk of the five model portfolios for European institutional investors.

---

[3] We transform the time series into a differenced time series $x_{\text{difference},t}=x_t-x_{t-1}$, where indicates the observation number in the historical time series.

Vector Autoregressive Model

In order to model the return generating process for the asset classes we use a set of autoregressive equations. A standard autoregressive equation of order p is defined as

$$y_t = c + \beta_1 y_{t-1} + \dots \beta_p y_{t-p} + \varepsilon_t \qquad (2.1)$$

where y_t is an observation of a time-series variable, $\beta_1, \dots, \beta_p$ are the p autoregressive coefficients, and ε_t is a normally distributed error term with mean 0 and variance σ_ε^2. We use ordinary least squares to estimate the autoregressive coefficients. In a VaR model y_t not only depends on its own history but also on the history of other $n-1$ time series. This gives a VaR model of order p:

$$Y_t = \Phi_0 + \Phi_1 Y_{t-1} + \dots + \Phi_p Y_{t-p} + \varepsilon_t \qquad (2.2)$$

where $Y_t = (Y_{1t}, \dots, y_{nt})$ is a $(n \times 1)$ vector of time-series variables, Φ_0 is a $(n \times 1)$ vector of constants, $\Phi_1 \dots \Phi_p$ are $(n \times n)$ autoregressive coefficient matrices, and ε_t is a $(n \times 1)$ Gaussian white noise vector process. The VaR model can also be estimated with ordinary least squares, as well as other, more elaborate methods such as seemingly unrelated regression (SUR). We refer to Lütkepohl (2005), amongst others, for more detailed information on VaR models.

A drawback of this standard VaR model is that all time series must have an equal number of observations. In our case especially, this leads to discarding much data, since for the alternative asset classes we have only a small number of observations. We overcome this problem by extending the methodology proposed by Stambaugh (1997). Stambaugh (1997) introduces a model for time series that differ in length (similar to VaR) and improves the estimation of the properties of the shorter time series by using all observations available for the longer time series. For more details, we refer to Stambaugh (1997).

Stambaugh (1997) analyses only time series that can be divided into two groups based on the number of observations. Since we have four distinct groups in our historical data series, we extend the Stambaugh (1997) methodology from two to four groups. Firstly, we divide the time series in four groups (L_t, $S_{1,t}$, $S_{2,t}$, and $S_{3,t}$), sorted from the series with the largest number of observations to the smallest number of observations. The number of time series in each group L_t, $S_{1,t}$, $S_{2,t}$, and $S_{3,t}$ is denoted by n_L, n_{S_1}, n_{S_2}, and n_{S_3}, respectively. In vector notation

$$Y_t = \begin{bmatrix} L_t \\ S_{1,t} \\ S_{2,t} \\ S_{3,t} \end{bmatrix} \tag{2.3}$$

The econometric equation for the longest time series is VaR, as follows:

$$L_t = c_0 + \Phi_1 L_{t-1} + \varepsilon_t \tag{2.4}$$

Note, that the shorter time series $S_{1,t}$, $S_{2,t}$, and $S_{3,t}$ do not influence the estimation of Equation (2.4), and hence we can use the maximum number of observations. The estimation equations for the three shorter time series exploit contemporaneous information about the longer series, as follows:

$$S_{1,t} = c_1 + \Theta_1 L_t + \Theta_2 L_{t-1} + \Theta_3 S_{1,t-1} + \eta_t \tag{2.5}$$

$$S_{2,t} = c_2 + \Delta_1 L_t + \Delta_2 L_{t-1} + \Delta_3 S_{1,t} + \Delta_4 S_{1,t-1} + \Delta_5 S_{2,t-1} + \upsilon_t \tag{2.6}$$

$$\begin{aligned} S_{3,t} = c_3 + \Psi_1 L_t + \Psi_2 L_{t-1} + \Psi_3 S_{1,t} + \Psi_4 S_{1,t-1} \\ + \Psi_5 S_{2,t} + \Psi_6 S_{2,t-1} + \Psi_7 S_{3,t-1} + v_t \end{aligned} \tag{2.7}$$

where Σ_η is the covariance matrix of the error term η, Σ_υ is the covariance matrix of the error term υ, and Σ_v is the covariance matrix of the error term v. Note, that the longer time series are used to model the process of the short time series, both contemporaneously and in lagged form, but not the other way around. This implies that $S_{2,t}$ and $S_{3,t}$ do not influence the estimation for $S_{1,t}$ and that $S_{3,t}$ does not influence the estimation for $S_{2,t}$. By substituting Equation (2.4) into (2.5), Equation (2.5) into (2.6), and Equation (2.6) into (2.7), we rewrite the equations to

$$Y_t = \Omega_0 + \Omega_1 Y_{t-1} + \omega_t \tag{2.8}$$

where Ω_0 is defined as

$$\Omega_0 = \begin{bmatrix} c_0 \\ c_1 + \Theta_1 c_0 \\ c_2 + \Delta_1 c_0 + \Delta_3 (c_1 + \Theta_1 c_0) \\ c_3 + \Psi_1 c_0 + \Psi_3 (c_1 + \Theta_1 c_0) + \Psi_5 (c_2 + \Delta_1 c_0 + \Delta_3 (c_1 + \Theta_1 c_0)) \end{bmatrix} \tag{2.9}$$

The four columns of $\Omega_1 = [\Omega_1 (:, 1)\ \Omega_1(:, 2)\ \Omega_1(:, 3)\ \Omega_1(:, 4)]$ are defined as follows:

$$\Omega_1(:,1) = \begin{bmatrix} \Phi_1 \\ \Theta_1 \Phi_1 + \Phi_2 \\ \Delta_1 \Phi_1 + \Delta_2 + \Delta_3 (\Theta_1 \Phi_1 + \Theta_2) \\ \Psi_1 \Phi_1 + \Psi_2 + \Psi_3 (\Theta_1 \Phi_1 + \Theta_2) + \Psi_5 \\ (\Delta_1 \Phi_1 + \Delta_2 + \Delta_3 (\Theta_1 \Phi_1 + \Theta_2)) \end{bmatrix} \tag{2.10}$$

$$\Omega_1(:,2) = \begin{bmatrix} 0 \\ \Theta_3 \\ \Delta_3 \Theta_3 + \Delta_4 \\ \Psi_3 \Delta_3 + \Psi_4 + \Psi_5 (\Delta_3 \Theta_3 + \Delta_4) \end{bmatrix} \tag{2.11}$$

where 0 is an $n_L \times n_{S_1}$ null matrix.

$$\Omega_1(:,3) = \begin{bmatrix} 0 \\ 0 \\ \Delta_5 \\ \Psi_5 \Delta_5 + \Psi_5 \end{bmatrix} \tag{2.12}$$

where the first entry of the vector is a $n_L \times n_{S_2}$ null matrix and the second entry of the vector is a $n_{S_1} \times n_{S_2}$ null matrix.

$$\Omega_1(:,4) = \begin{bmatrix} 0 \\ 0 \\ 0 \\ \Psi_7 \end{bmatrix} \tag{2.13}$$

where the first entry of the vector is a $n_L \times n_{S_3}$ null matrix, the second entry of the vector is a $n_{S_1} \times n_{S_3}$ null matrix, and the third entry of the vector is a $n_{S_2} \times n_{S_3}$ null matrix.

Concluding, the covariance matrix $\Sigma_\omega = [\Sigma_\omega(:, 1)\ \Sigma_\omega(:, 2)\ \Sigma_\omega(:, 3)\ \Sigma_\omega(:, 4)]$ of ω in Equation (2.8) is defined as

$$\Sigma_\omega(:,1) = \begin{bmatrix} \Sigma_\varepsilon \\ \Theta_1\Sigma_\varepsilon \\ (\Delta_1+\Delta_3\Theta_1)\Sigma_\varepsilon \\ (\Psi_1+\Psi_3\Theta_1+\Psi_5(\Delta_1+\Delta_3\Theta_1))\Sigma_\varepsilon \end{bmatrix} \tag{2.14}$$

$$\Sigma_\omega(:,2) = \begin{bmatrix} \Sigma_\varepsilon\Theta_1^T \\ \Sigma_\eta+\Theta_1\Sigma_\varepsilon\Theta_1^T \\ (\Delta_1+\Delta_3\Theta_1)\Sigma_\varepsilon\Theta_1^T+\Delta_3\Sigma_\eta \\ (\Psi_1+\Psi_3\Theta_1+\Psi_5(\Delta_1+\Delta_3\Theta_1))\Sigma_\varepsilon\Theta_1^T+(\Psi_3+\Psi_5\Delta_3)\Sigma_\eta \end{bmatrix} \tag{2.15}$$

$$\Sigma_\omega(:,3) = \begin{bmatrix} \Sigma_\varepsilon(\Delta_1+\Delta_3\Theta_1)^T \\ \Theta_1\Sigma_\varepsilon(\Delta_1+\Delta_3\Theta_1)^T+\Sigma_\eta\Delta_3^T \\ \Sigma_\upsilon+(\Delta_1+\Delta_3\Theta_1)\Sigma_\varepsilon(\Delta_1+\Delta_3\Theta_1)^T+\Delta_3\Sigma_\eta\Delta_3^T \\ (\Psi_1+\Psi_3\Theta_1+\Psi_5(\Delta_1+\Delta_3\Theta_1))\Sigma_\varepsilon(\Delta_1+\Delta_3\Theta_1)^T+ \\ (\Psi_3+\Psi_5\Delta_3)\Sigma_\eta\Delta_3^T+\Psi_5\Sigma_\upsilon \end{bmatrix} \tag{2.16}$$

$$\Sigma_\omega(:,4) = \begin{bmatrix} \Sigma_\varepsilon(\Psi_1+\Psi_3\Theta_1+\Psi_5(\Delta_1+\Delta_3\Theta_1))^T \\ \Theta_1\Sigma_\varepsilon(\Psi_1+\Psi_3\Theta_1+\Psi_5(\Delta_1+\Delta_3\Theta_1))^T+\Sigma_\eta(\Psi_3+\Psi_5\Delta_3)^T \\ (\Delta_1+\Delta_3\Theta_1)\Sigma_\varepsilon(\Psi_1+\Psi_3\Theta_1+\Psi_5(\Delta_1+\Delta_3\Theta_1))^T \\ \Delta_3\Sigma_\eta(\Psi_3+\Psi_5\Delta_3)^T+\Sigma_\upsilon\Psi_5^T \\ \Sigma_V+(\Psi_1+\Psi_3\Theta_1+\Psi_5(\Delta_1+\Delta_3\Theta_1))\Sigma_\varepsilon \\ (\Psi_1+\Psi_3\Theta_1+\Psi_5(\Delta_1+\Delta_3\Theta_1))^T+... \\ ...(\Psi_3+\Psi_5\Delta_3)\Sigma_\eta(\Psi_3+\Psi_5\Delta_3)^T+\Psi_5\Sigma_\upsilon\Psi_5^T \end{bmatrix} \tag{2.17}$$

ASSET RETURN DISTRIBUTION

Normal Distribution

We first estimate a standard VaR model with normally distributed error terms, implying normal asset return distributions with zero skewness and no excess kurtosis. We call this model the *normal* VaR *model*. However, as this may not be a realistic assumption, especially for the alternative asset classes, we now propose alternative error distributions for the VaR model.

Skewed Student's t Distribution

In our second model, called the *skewed Student's t* VaR *model*, we allow the error terms to follow either a normal or Student's t distribution depending on the characteristics of the time series. An advantage of the Student's t distribution compared to the normal distribution are the fatter tails, which can be used for historical time series with a large number of extreme observations far from the mean. The degree to which the Student's t distribution has fat tails depends on the number of degrees of freedom v. For relatively small values of v (close to 2) the distribution has very fat tails. For larger values of v the Student's t distribution approaches the normal distribution (in the limit, as $v \to \infty$).

In order to improve our model further, we create a skewed version of the normal and Student's t distribution with the method of Fernández and Steel (1998), who transform a symmetric probability distribution function $f(\cdot)$ with the positive scalar γ in the following way:

$$p(x\,|\,\gamma) = \frac{2}{\gamma + \dfrac{1}{\gamma}}\left(f\!\left(\frac{x}{\gamma}\right)\!I_{[0,\infty)}(x) + f(x\gamma)I_{(-\infty,0)}(x)\right) \qquad (2.18)$$

where I is the indicator function. For $\gamma = 1$ the distribution remains unchanged, as $p(x\,|\,\gamma = 1) = f(\cdot)$. However, for $0 < \gamma < 1$ the distribution becomes negatively skewed, and for $\gamma > 1$ the distribution becomes positively skewed. Note that, for example, Kouwenberg and Ziemba (2007) use this method to model skewed hedge fund returns.

By introducing two different probability distribution functions and skewness parameter, we have in total four options for the distribution of the error term in the VaR model. We choose one of the four options by maximizing the likelihood for a skewed Student's t error distribution and applying likelihood ratio tests for skewness and nonfat tails. For more details, see Fernández and Steel (1998) and Kouwenberg and Ziemba (2007). Note, that the normal distribution is a special case of the skewed Student's t distribution, thereby making our skewed Student's t VaR model more flexible and general, compared to the standard normal VaR model.

GENERATING FUTURE ASSET RETURN SCENARIOS

After estimating the coefficients of the VaR model, we use the calibrated model to generate future asset return scenarios for the asset classes. To do so, we draw random deviates from the error distributions, which are specified by the estimated skewness parameter and degrees of freedom following from the maximum likelihood procedure. Then we generate m scenarios for the coming h periods in the following way (Hoevenaars et al., 2003):

$$y_{m,t+h} = \left[\sum_{i=0}^{h-1} \Omega_1^i \right] \Omega_0 + \Omega_1^h y_t + \sum_{i=0}^{h-1} \Omega_1^i L_\omega^T x_{m,t+h-i} \qquad (2.19)$$

where $\mathbf{y}$ is an $(n \times 1)$ vector of n asset returns for period $t + h$ in scenario m, L_ω is the Choleski decomposition of the unconditional covariance matrix Σ_ω such that $L_\omega^T L_\omega = \Sigma_\omega$, and $\mathbf{x}$ is an $(n \times 1)$ vector of random drawings from the corresponding error distribution.

VALUE AT RISK AND CONDITIONAL VALUE AT RISK

To assess the risk of our five model portfolios we use two measures, namely, value at risk (VaR) and conditional value at risk (CVaR). Value at risk with confidence level α for the period of n months ahead indicates that the probability for a variable y to have loss equal to or larger than VaR_α equals $(1 - \alpha)$. Conditional value at risk, also known as *tail* VaR, gives the expected loss value, given that a loss larger than VaR_α occurs: $CVaR_\alpha = E(y \mid y \leq VaR_\alpha)$. Conditional value at risk provides a better measure of the tail risk of an asset return distribution than unconditional

VaR. For example, two simulated time series can have equal VaR_α but a large difference in CVaR_α. This indicates that the simulated time series with the largest CVaR_α has a relatively fat tail at the left side of the probability distribution function compared to the time series with a relatively small CVaR_α.

We calculate our conditional and unconditional VaR values by generating 10, 000 scenarios for our asset classes, for a period of 12 months ahead. A relatively short horizon of one year is chosen to provide an estimation of the investment risk for an institutional investor in the Solvency II framework. This framework demands that institutional investors must hold a buffer to ensure solvency over a one-year horizon. This buffer, which is referred to as *economic required capital* (ERC), must be such that in 99.5 percent of the cases the investor can cover losses due to adverse investment returns. Since we base our VaR estimates also on a confidence level of 99.5 percent, we can estimate the ERC using our two different models.

RESULTS

Estimation Results Normal and Skewed Student's t VaR Model

A brief description of the most salient characteristics of the normal and skewed Student's *t* VaR model estimation results is given in this section. The estimation results are not presented in tables to save space, but available upon request from the corresponding author.

Normal VaR Model

The estimated VaR model shows that the returns of global equity and commodities cannot be predicted well, as none of the lagged explanatory variables is significant at a level of 5 percent. The returns of real estate, hedge funds, and emerging market bonds are explained well by the returns on the "traditional" asset classes of global equity, government bonds, and commodities. Third, it is remarkable to see the wide range of significant predictors for the return on asset-backed securities, namely, government bonds, real estate, hedge funds, emerging market bonds, and corporate bonds. Fourth, we see an intuitively appealing set of predictor variables for inflation-linked bonds, namely, government bonds, the risk-free rate, commodities, and real estate. The first two variables influence the return on inflation-linked bonds via the nominal interest rate, whereas the influence of the latter two can possibly be explained by changes in inflation.[4] We also find that private equity is a significant predictor variable for a large set of asset classes, namely, private equity itself, corporate bonds, and high-yield and asset-backed securities.

Finally, the R^2 is generally lower (smaller than 0.10) for the traditional asset classes compared to the "alternative" asset classes. Especially the R^2 of 0.63 for private equity, 0.69 for inflation-linked bonds, 0.88 for corporate bonds, and 0.88 for asset-backed securities are relatively high. The reason is that the shorter time series are modeled as a function of the contemporaneous returns on all asset classes with longer series, while the longest time series (including the traditional asset classes) are only predicted with lagged series.

Skewed Student's t VaR Model

Our skewed Student's VaR model only fits a symmetric normal error distribution for real estate, emerging market bonds, and corporate bonds. For all other asset classes the hypothesis of normally distributed returns is rejected. This shows that the normal VaR model does not give a proper representation of the historical time series in terms of the statistical distribution.

Another important observation is the relatively small difference in significant predictor variables (at 5 percent significance level) for the normal and skewed Student's t VaR models. The normal VaR model and the skewed Student's t VaR model have a total of 45 and 39, respectively, significant predictor variables, of which 31 coincide. The largest difference in significant variables occurs for the risk-free rate series. In the normal VaR model the significant variables are the risk-free rate itself, government bonds, the term spread, and the dividend yield, while in the skewed Student's t VaR model only government bonds are significant.

---

[4] See, for example, Hoesli et al. (1997) for a discussion of inflation hedging qualities for UK real estate in the short run and Hoevenaars et al. (2007) for a discussion of U.S. real estate and commodities inflation hedging qualities at different horizons.

Value at Risk and CVaR for Institutional Investment Portfolios

This section evaluates and compares the VaR and CVaR results for our 10,000 scenarios for a period of 12 months ahead. We give the results for each of the 12 asset classes individually and the five model portfolios for institutional investors, with two different confidence levels, namely, 95.0 and 99.5 percent.

Normal VaR Model

Table 2.5 shows the VaR and CVaR results in percentage losses, using scenarios from the normal VaR model. This table shows nicely that the five model portfolios increase in risk in both VaR and CVaR terms. When we

T A B L E   2.5

One-year horizon VaR and CVaR results based on the normal VaR model

Portfolio	95.0% VaR	99.5% VaR	95.0% CVaR	99.5% CVaR
Global equity	−9.3	−21.0	−14.7	−23.9
Government bonds	−1.6	−6.2	−3.7	−7.6
Commodities	−16.5	−30.8	−22.9	−34.3
Real estate	−12.8	−25.2	−18.6	−28.9
Hedge funds	0.2	−5.2	−2.3	−7.2
Emerging market bonds	1.1	−1.6	−0.1	−2.6
Private equity	−17.7	−35.8	−25.8	−39.8
Corporate bonds	−0.9	−5.1	−2.9	−6.4
High yield	−13.4	−21.9	−17.2	−24.5
Asset-backed securities	−1.7	−6.3	−3.8	−7.7
Inflation-linked bonds	−4.4	−11.0	−7.6	−13.2
Leveraged loans	5.0	4.4	4.7	4.2
Very conservative	0.5	−4.0	−1.4	−5.4
Conservative	−1.1	−6.8	−3.7	−8.8
Average	−2.4	−9.3	−5.7	−11.8
Aggressive	−2.9	−10.1	−6.3	−12.7
Very aggressive	−4.3	−12.9	−8.2	−15.5

Note: All numbers in the table are percentages, representing losses on the portfolio.

focus on the Solvency II VaR level of 99.5 percent, this implies that in a very aggressive portfolio an institutional investor must be able to cope with a downward shock in the portfolio value of 12.9 percent. Note, that this loss is relatively small, because we calculate the loss over a period of 12 months and the portfolio is diversified over seven asset classes. In order to have a large yearly loss, we must have multiple months with very low returns, which is quite unlikely. Furthermore, we see that the CVaR results do not dramatically differ from the VaR results. This is due to the fact that we use normally distributed asset returns, which do not give rise to many extreme observations. Lastly, we see some surprising VaR and CVaR results for leveraged loans. This is because in our relatively short historical time series the annualized volatility is only equal to 0.6 percent whereas the annualized mean return is 6.0 percent.

Skewed Student's t VaR Model

Table 2.6 shows the VaR and CVaR results using the skewed Student's *t* VaR. The results show a similar ordering of asset classes in terms of risk compared to the normal VaR model with, for example, high yield as very risky investment and leveraged loans as a safe investment. The 99.5 percent VaR results, which correspond with Solvency II regulations, show that an investor in global equity must hold 21.9 percent of its investment as ERC. Moreover, investing in our model portfolios results in a required economic capital (as percentage of the value of the investment portfolio) of 10.0 percent for our average portfolio and 13.2 percent for our very aggressive portfolio. Over the complete range of portfolios, we see more extreme VaR results based on the skewed Student's *t* VaR model than based on the normal VaR model. This indicates that using a normal VaR model underestimates tail risk. This observation becomes even clearer when we inspect the CVaR results, demonstrating that our skewed Student's *t* VaR model gives rise to fatter tails. For example, for the average, aggressive, and very aggressive model portfolios the 99.5 percent CVaR results are 0.9 percent higher when using the skewed Student's *t* VaR model in comparison with the normal VaR model. The differences are most pronounced for risky investments such as private equity, where the difference between the normal and skewed Student's *t* VaR model is equal to 7.4 percent in terms of 99.5 percent CVaR.

T A B L E   2.6

One-year horizon VaR and CVaR results of the skewed
Student's t VaR model

Portfolio	95.0% VaR	99.5% VaR	95.0% CVaR	99.5% CVaR
Global equity	−10.6	−21.9	−15.9	−25.8
Government bonds	−1.7	−7.0	−4.0	−8.3
Commodities	−17.0	−31.0	−22.9	−33.7
Real estate	−13.6	−26.4	−19.3	−30.4
Hedge funds	−2.0	−9.2	−5.2	−11.3
Emerging market bonds	1.1	−1.9	−0.3	−2.9
Private equity	−16.7	−37.2	−26.1	−47.2
Corporate bonds	−1.0	−5.6	−3.0	−6.8
High yield	−9.3	−26.3	−16.4	−37.8
Asset-backed securities	−1.4	−6.6	−3.7	−9.0
Inflation-linked bonds	−3.3	−11.3	−7.2	−16.7
Leveraged loans	4.5	3.3	3.9	2.0
Very conservative	0.2	−4.5	−1.9	−6.0
Conservative	−1.5	−7.5	−4.4	−9.7
Average	−3.0	−10.0	−6.4	−12.7
Aggressive	−3.5	−10.7	−7.0	−13.6
Very aggressive	−4.7	−13.2	−8.9	−16.4

All numbers in the table are percentages, representing losses on the portfolio.

These results demonstrate that using a normal VaR model underestimates (tail) risk, which may lead to an overestimation of the attrac-
tiveness of investing in risky alternative asset classes. Furthermore, this
underestimation problem becomes most clear when using CVaR as a
risk measure. Although the differences may appear small, they still can
have a huge impact on institutional investors that typically hold a large
investment portfolio. For example, the required economic capital for
our "average" investment portfolio is 0.7 percent higher using the
skewed Student's *t* compared to the normal VaR model. For a portfolio
of € 1 billion, this amounts to a difference of € 70 million in required
economic capital.

Practical Application: Société Générale

As a practical application we now evaluate the probability of the losses incurred by the rogue derivatives trader at Société Générale (SG), using our two VaR models. Jerôme Kerviel, a derivatives trader at SG, speculated with huge sums of money using futures contracts on stock indexes. Kerviel realized a loss of € 4.9 billion on futures positions with a total underlying value of € 50 billion.[5] In order to realize this loss, the underlying index must decrease approximately 10 percent in value. We calculate the likelihood of such an event using our normal and skewed Student's t VaR model, assuming an investment horizon of one month, which corresponds to the strong stock market decline in the month January 2008 when the fraud was discovered.[6] According to our normal VaR model the probability of a monthly loss in global equity in excess of 10 percent is only 0.27 percent, which implies a frequency of once in every 31 years. The skewed Student's t VaR model assesses a larger probability of 0.89 percent for this event, corresponding to a frequency of once in every nine years. These results demonstrate that the normal VaR model underestimates the tail risk severely compared to the skewed Student's t VaR model.

CONCLUSION

This chapter introduces an approach for calibrating a VaR model with the purpose to generate future return scenarios for a broad set of traditional and alternative asset classes, such as real estate, hedge funds, private equity, corporate bonds, high yield, asset-backed securities, and inflation-linked bonds. Our approach optimally uses the longer historical data from traditional asset classes such as stock and bonds to estimate future return scenarios for alternative asset classes that have relatively short historical time series available, building upon and extending the method proposed by Stambaugh (1997). As the return distributions of many asset classes suffer from skewness and fat tails, we apply a skewed Student's t distribution

---

[5] For more information, see http://www.sueddeutsche.de/finanzen/artikel/17/154616/.
[6] Therefore, we assume that Kerviel traded in MSCI index futures.

(Fernández and Steel, 1998) to obtain the VaR estimates and generate future return scenarios.

We compare risk measured and/or estimated with two versions of the econometric model for asset returns, namely, (1) a normal VaR model with the traditional assumption of normally distributed error terms and (2) a skewed Student's t VaR model with the more general assumption of a skewed Student's t error distribution. Note, that the latter model is a generalization of the former because the skewed Student's t distribution includes the normal distribution as a special case.

We use our set of future return scenarios to assess the VaR and CVaR for European institutional investors with five different asset allocation strategies ranging from very conservative to very aggressive. The VaR estimates for a confidence level of 99.5 percent also provide the basis for the required economic capital under new Solvency II regulations. These rules try to ensure that the institutional investor holds sufficient capital to be able to cope with extreme negative shocks to the investment portfolio value. We find that the institutional investor must hold 4.0, 9.3, and 12.9 percent of the portfolio value as ERC for a very conservative, average, and very aggressive investment portfolio, respectively, based on the normal VaR model, compared to 4.5, 10.0, and 13.2 percent based on our skewed Student's t model. Our results clearly show that the normal VaR model underestimates the downside risk of investing in alternative asset classes such as private equity and high-yield bonds, which may give misleading risk estimates for these asset classes, as well as biased results at the portfolio level. The differences may appear small in percentage terms, but they have a large impact in terms of potential losses and economic capital required, considering the large investment portfolios held by typical institutional investors.

REFERENCES

Campbell, J.Y., A.W. Lo, and A.C. MacKinlay (1997) *The Econometrics of Financial Markets*. Princeton, NJ: Princeton University Press.

Fernández, C. and M. Steel (1998) On Bayesian Modeling of Fat Tails and Skewness. *Journal of the American Statistical Association*, Vol. 93, No. 441, pp. 359–371.

Harris, D.F. and C.C. Küçüközmen (2001) The Empirical Distribution of UK and US Stock Return. *Journal of Business Finance & Accounting,* Vol. 28, No. 5–6, pp. 715–740.

Hoesli, M., B.D. MacGregor, G. Matysiak, and N. Nanthakumaran (1997) The Short-Term Inflation-Hedging Characteristics of U.K. Real Estate. *Journal of Real Estate Finance and Economics,* Vol. 15, No. 1, pp. 27–57.

Hoevenaars, R.P.M.M., R.D.J. Molenaar, and T.B.J. Steenkamp (2003) Simulation for the Long Run. In B. Scherer (ed.), *Asset Liability Management Tools.* London: Risk Books.

Hoevenaars, R.P.M.M., R.D.J. Molenaar, P. Schotman, and T.B.J. Steenkamp (2007) Strategic Asset Allocation with Liabilities: Beyond Stocks and Bonds. Working paper, Tilburg University, Tilburg, Netherlands.

Jondeau, E. and M. Rockinger (2005) Conditional Asset Allocation under Non-Normality: How Costly Is the Mean-Variance Criterion? Working paper, Lausanne University, Lausanne, Switzerland.

Kouwenberg, R. and W.T. Ziemba (2007) Incentives and Risk Taking in Hedge Funds. *Journal of Banking & Finance,* Vol. 31, No. 11, pp. 3291–3310.

Lütkepohl, H. (2006) *New Introduction to Multiple Time Series Analysis.* Berling, Germany: Springer-Verlag

Rooij, M.C.J. van., A.H. Siegmann, and P.J.G. Vlaar (2005) Beleidsopties voor Pensioenfondsen. *Economic Statistical Notes,* Vol. 25, No. 3, pp. 124–127.

Russell Investment Group (2007) Russell Investments Survey on Alternative Investing. Survey, Tacoma, WA.

Stambaugh, R. (1997) Analysing Investments Whose Histories Differ in Length. *Journal of Financial Economics,* Vol. 45, No. 3; pp. 285–331.

Theodossiou, P. (1998) Financial Data and the Skewed Generalized T Distribution. *Management Science,* Vol. 44, No. 12; pp. 1650–1661.

CHAPTER 3

A Comparison between Optimal Allocations Based on the Modified VaR and Those Based on a Utility-Based Risk Measure

Laurent Bodson, Alain Cöen, and Georges Hübner

ABSTRACT

Many empirical analyses have demonstrated that some financial asset returns like those of hedge funds depart from the normal distribution. From this observation, several new risk measures have been created to take into consideration the skewness and the kurtosis of the return distributions. We propose in this chapter to present the impact of higher moments on the optimal portfolio allocation comparing two 4-moment risk measures, namely, a utility-based risk measure with the preference-free modified value at risk (MVaR).

INTRODUCTION

Since the explanatory studies of Samuelson (1970) showing that several financial asset classes exhibit large deviations from the normal distribution, the financial literature has investigated measures integrating higher order moments. In asset-allocation problems, the well-known mean-variance framework of Markowitz (1952) has revealed its difficulties to treat assets that are nonnormally distributed. Generally, the metrics based on higher moments outperform the traditional mean-variance-based measures and tend to explain a larger part of the financial asset behaviors.

There is evidence in the literature that extreme risks affect the optimal allocation of a traditional portfolio in the presence of hedge funds. Galeano and Favre (2001), Favre and Galeano (2002), and Capocci et al. (2007) emphasize that risk metrics based on higher moments of the return distribution significantly affect efficient frontiers and, in particular, the diversification properties of heavily nonnormal asset classes such as hedge fund portfolios.

However, the approximation of risk using a higher order moment risk estimate has met some pitfalls. For instance, we observe that asset returns have time-varying moments. This difficulty has been managed for the variance using stochastic volatility models as generalized autoregressive conditional heteroscedasticity (GARCH), but concerning the higher moments (the skewness and the kurtosis), few articles have proposed solutions to model this variability.

In this chapter, we propose to compare the risk measure stability of two portfolios of equities created on two different higher order moments risk measures: one portfolio optimized using the modified value at risk (MVaR) and the other one optimized using a utility-based risk measure (UBR).

The chapter is organized as follows. The first section depicts the optimization models used in the study. In the second section, we present the empirical method used. In the third section, we report the ex-ante and ex-post distributions of optimal risk measures and the results of the correspondence of risk measures. The last section provides conclusive remarks and suggestions for future research.

OPTIMIZATION MODELS

We assume the traditional constraints made on the weights, i.e., the weights of the assets composing the portfolio sum up to one and all the weights are positive or null (no short selling). The optimization program uses a traditional risk–return framework, where the risk metric is defined according to a particular measure, and in general, the investor averse to risk seeks a portfolio that minimizes risk for a target level of expected return with a budget constraint (long only asset allocation and the sum of portfolio weights adds up to one).

Modified Value at Risk

Value at risk can be defined as the potential loss from an adverse market move within a specified confidence level (typically, 95 or 99 percent) over a specified trading horizon (e.g., one day, one week, or one month).

To compensate for the drawbacks of the Gaussian VaR, an alternative is the Cornish–Fisher "semiparametric" approach (1937), which allows the extreme risks associated with nonnormal return distribution to be taken into account (Favre and Galeano, 2002). The optimal allocation of the portfolio is the allocation maximizing the $\text{MVaR}_{p\alpha}$ of the portfolio p at the confidence level α under the budget and return constraints.[1] $\underset{w_i}{\text{Max}}\ \text{MVaR}_{p\alpha}$ subject to

$$\sum_{i=1}^{n} w_i = 1,\ w_i \geq 0\ (\text{for}\ i=1,...,n)\ \text{and}\ \sum_{i=1}^{n} w_i . \overline{R}_i = \overline{R}_p \tag{3.1}$$

where w_i is the optimal weight of the asset i in the portfolio p, $\overline{R}_i$ is the average return of the asset i, and $\overline{R}_p$ is the required average return of the portfolio, and where

$$\text{MVaR}_{p\alpha} = M_p - \left(\begin{array}{c} z_\alpha - \dfrac{1}{6}(z_\alpha^2 - 1)S_p^* + \dfrac{1}{24}(z_\alpha^3 - 3z_\alpha)K_p^* \\[2mm] -\dfrac{1}{36}(2z_\alpha^3 - 5z_\alpha)S_p^{*2} \end{array} \right) V_p^{0.5} \tag{3.2}$$

where M_p is the portfolio average return, V_p is the portfolio variance, S_p^* is the portfolio standardized skewness (i.e., the third centered moment divided by the third power of the standard deviation), K_p^* is the portfolio standardized excess kurtosis (i.e., the fourth centered moment divided by the fourth power of the standard deviation, this quotient minus 3), and z_α is the quantile of the

---

[1] The program maximizes the MVaR because it is defined as a measure of return, and thus the MVaR is inversely related to the risk level of the investment.

normal distribution (X) such as $P(X > z_\alpha) = \alpha$. If we consider a portfolio of n components, w_i is the optimal allocation in asset i (for $i = 1, \ldots, n$) maximizing the $\text{MVaR}_{p\alpha}$ of the portfolio.

The Cornish–Fisher expansion is simply an adjustment of the quantile of the normal distribution [equation between the brackets in Equation (3.2)]. Naturally, if the portfolio returns are characterized by a normal distribution $(S_p^* = K_p^* = 0)$, Equation (3.2) is reduced to the following traditional Gaussian VaR formula: $\text{MVaR}_{p\alpha} = M_p - (z_\alpha)V^{0.5}{}_p$.

We know from (Favre and Galeano, 2002) that the $\text{MVaR}_{p\alpha}$ does not provide reliable results for highly skewed portfolios. Thus, we suggest an alternative: the use of a UBR.

Utility-Based Risk Measure

Bell's (1988; 2000) utility function, also called the *linex utility function* (because it is in the same time linear and exponential), is commonly written as $U(W) = W - be^{-cW}$, where b (the "risk aversion" coefficient) and c (the "risk perception" coefficient) are positive investor-specific coefficients. This utility function allows the investor to rank the expected wealth levels (W), that result from alternative investment opportunities. Investors with high cs put more emphasis on the possibility of bad outcomes while parameter b controls for their degree of risk aversion (Bell, 1988).

It is widely acknowledged that the investment choice of the investor is based on expected utility. Let W_0 be the initial wealth of the investor I and be the global amount invested in the risky asset with a return equal to m. The total amount invested in the risk-free asset $W_0 - I$ gives a return of r.

If the risk free asset gives a return of r(constant) and the risky asset a return of m (with a defined statistical distribution), and if we consider that the investor invests all her wealth in the risk-free or the risky asset, her final wealth in one period (cf frequency of the returns) is given by

$$W = (W_0 - I)(1+r) + I(1+m) = W_0(1+r) + I(m-r) \qquad (3.3)$$

Define the risk premium as $x = m - r$. The utility function becomes

$$U(W(x)) = U(W_0(1+r) + Ix) = W_0(1+r) + Ix - be^{-c(W_0(1+r)+Ix)} \qquad (3.4)$$

and the expected utility is[2]

$$
\begin{aligned}
E[U(W(x))] &= W_0(1+r) + IE[x] - bE[e^{-c(W_0(1+r)+Ix)}] \\
&= W_0(1+r) + I\bar{x} - be^{-cW_0(1+r)}E[e^{-clx}]
\end{aligned}
\tag{3.5}
$$

where $\bar{x}$ is the expected value of the risk premium.

Knowing that

$$
E[e^{-clx}] = e^{-cl\bar{x}}E[e^{-clx+cl\bar{x}}] = e^{-cl\bar{x}}E[e^{-cl(x-\bar{x})}]
\tag{3.6}
$$

we have, therefore,

$$
E[U(W(x))] = W_0(1+r) + I\bar{x} - be^{-c(W_0(1+r)+I\bar{x})}E[e^{-cl(x-\bar{x})}]
\tag{3.7}
$$

Some authors argue that the expected utility function may be more appropriately approximated by a function of higher moments (Arditti, 1967; Samuelson, 1970). Bell's utility function is designed to integrate the first four moments of any distribution using the Taylor development around the mean risk premium return. This Taylor series expansion yields a good polynomial approximation of c in terms of the second, third, and fourth moments of the risk premium return distribution (or, equivalently, of the risky asset return distribution). Effectively, if we approximate the Bell's function realizing the fourth-order Taylor series expansion of the expression $E[e^{-cl(x-\bar{x})}]$ around $\bar{x}$ (the expected risk premium value), this leads to the following expression:

$$
\begin{aligned}
E[e^{-cl(x-\bar{x})}] = E\Bigg[1 - cl(x-\bar{x}) + \frac{1}{2}c^2I^2(x-\bar{x})^2 \\
- \frac{1}{6}c^3I^3(x-\bar{x})^3 + \frac{1}{24}c^4I^4(x-\bar{x})^4 \Bigg]
\end{aligned}
\tag{3.8}
$$

$$
\begin{aligned}
E[e^{-cl(x-\bar{x})}] = 1 + \frac{1}{2}c^2I^2E[(x-\bar{x})^2] - \frac{1}{6}c^3I^3E[(x-\bar{x})^3] \\
+ \frac{1}{24}c^4I^4E[(x-\bar{x})^4]
\end{aligned}
\tag{3.9}
$$

---

[2] The parameters b and c are assumed to be constant over a short period of time.

where $E[(x - \bar{x})^2]$ is the variance of the risky asset returns, denoted V_x (i.e., the second centered moment), $E[(x - \bar{x})^3]$ is the (nonstandardized) skewness of the risky asset returns, denoted S_x (i.e., the third centered moment); and $E[(x - \bar{x})^4]$ is the (nonstandardized) kurtosis of the risky asset returns, denoted K_x (i.e., the fourth centered moment).

Using Equations (3.7) and (3.9), we obtain the following expression of the expected utility of the investor:

$$E[U(W)] = W_0(1+r) + I\bar{x} - be^{-cW_0(1+r)}e^{-cI\bar{x}}\left(1 + \frac{1}{2}c^2I^2V_x\right.$$
$$\left. - \frac{1}{6}c^3I^3S_x + \frac{1}{24}c^4I^4K_x\right)$$

(3.10)

The variance, skewness, and kurtosis of the risk premium (respectively V_x, S_x, and K_x) are identical to the variance, the skewness, and the kurtosis of the risky asset return distribution (respectively, V_m, S_m, and K_m) because the riskless asset has a constant return r.

As a result, we may infer a utility-based risk measure (UBR) of the risky investment or, more generally, the portfolio p (UBR$_{pC}$) for any decision maker (i.e., with a specific parameter C) satisfying the assumptions of the Bell's utility function:

$$\text{UBR}_{pC} = \frac{1}{2}V_p - \frac{C}{6}S_p + \frac{C^2}{24}K_p$$

(3.11)

where V_p is the portfolio variance, S_p is the portfolio skewness (i.e., the third centered moment), K_p is the portfolio kurtosis (i.e., the fourth centered moment), and C is the "global" risk perception parameter depending on the risk profile and the wealth-related investment of the investor. This last parameter varies, according to our empirical analysis, from 5 to 50.

This is the only definition of risk (or a monotonic transformation thereof) compatible with an increasing, risk averse utility function, with risk consistency and that is independent of return derived from the Bell's utility function.

The optimization of our particular UBR consists simply in the following optimization system: $\underset{wi}{Min}$ UBR$_{pC}$, subject to

$$\sum_{i=1}^{n} w_i = 1, \, w_i \geq 0 \text{ (for } i = 1, ..., n) \text{ and } \sum_{i=1}^{n} w_i.\bar{R}_i = \bar{R}_p$$

(3.12)

where w_i is the optimal weight of the asset i in the portfolio p, $\bar{R}_i$ is the average return of the asset i, and $\bar{R}_p$ is the required average return of the portfolio, and

$$\text{UBR}_{pC} = \frac{1}{2}V_p - \frac{C}{6}S_p + \frac{C^2}{24}K_p \qquad (3.13)$$

EMPIRICAL METHOD

We have chosen to focus our comparison on the equity asset class. We have selected a large set of 889 potential (U.S.) equity components from Datastream with an historical record of 121 months (more precisely, the monthly returns from January 1998 to February 2008).

We propose to compare the stability of the two risk measures between two dates (after 36 months and after 121 months). We test the stability of the risk measures, beginning with an optimization of the portfolio allocation at 36 months (we optimize with the values of the first 36 months) and comparing the risk measures at this date with their corresponding values at the end of the dataset (i.e., computed over the last 85 months).

We assume an α of 1 percent for the MVaR metric, which is the traditional value for the threshold of the VaR used by practitioners.

The parameter c for the UBR measure is equal to 10 because this is the value that equalizes the risk part of the MVaR and the UBR for the historical returns of the S&P 500 taken has a median portfolio record of accomplishment.

For each simulation, we randomly select 10 different equities[3] from our database of 889 equities. We construct two types of optimal portfolios: a first portfolio whose MVaR is maximized and a second portfolio whose UBR is minimized. For both optimizations, we apply the constraints developed in Equations (3.1) and (3.12) and these optimizations are executed over the 36 first historical monthly data. The required return of the portfolio created must be equal to the average of the mean monthly return (over the 36 months) of the selected equities series. We let the allocations of these two optimal portfolios remain unchanged until the end of the series (i.e., 121 months) and we compute the values of the MVaR and of

---

[3] The results are identical for 5, 20, 30, and 40 different equities (randomly chosen) in the analyzed portfolio.

the UBR for each portfolio over the remaining 85 months (121 minus 36) of fixed optimal allocation. We repeat this procedure 1, 000 times. We have then 1, 000 draws/selections of 10 equities in our database.

EMPIRICAL RESULTS

Ex-Ante and Ex-Post Distribution of Optimal Risk Measures

We report the empirical density and cumulative distribution functions in each pair of portfolios [i.e., when we compute the MVaR for the MVaR optimized portfolio (Figure 3.1), the UBR for the MVaR optimized portfolio (Figure 3.2), the MVaR for the UBR optimized portfolio (Figure 3.3), and the UBR for the UBR optimized portfolio (Figure 3.4)]. The empirical cumulative distribution function (ecdf) permits to avoid the assumption of a specific distribution for the underlying process. In addition, the ecdf is useful for examining the difference between the distribution of the risk measure at

F I G U R E   3.1

Histograms of the MVaR at 36 months (black) and after 121 months (white) of the portfolio optimized (at 36 months) with the MVaR measure

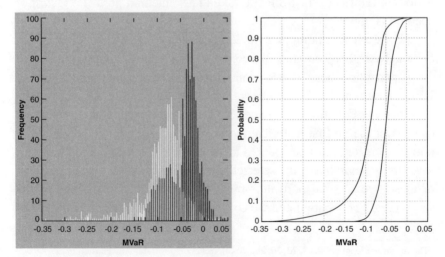

F I G U R E 3.2

Histograms of the utility-based risk at 36 months (black)
and after 121 months (white) of the portfolio optimized
(at 36 months) with the MVaR measure

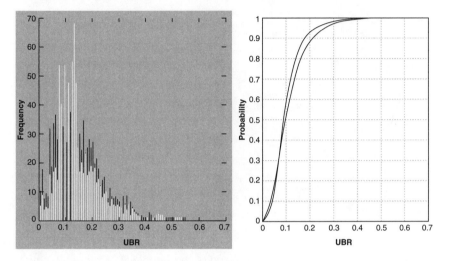

F I G U R E 3.3

Histograms of the MVaR at 36 months (black) and after
121 months (white) of the portfolio optimized (at 36 months)
with the UBR

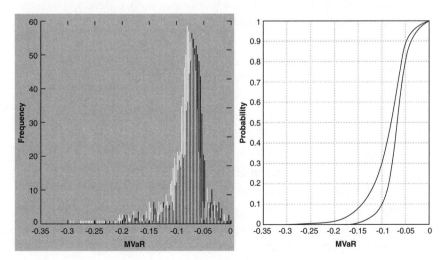

F I G U R E   3.4

Histograms of the utility-based risk at 36 months (black)
and after 121 months (white) of the portfolio optimized
(at 36 months) with the UBR

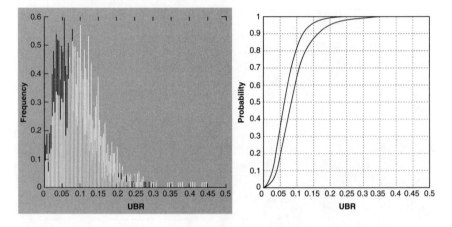

the beginning (36 months) and at the end of the sample (121 months), which
represent the ex-ante and ex-post risk measures, respectively, as the portfolio formation period takes place after the first 36 months.

We observe that the UBR distribution is much more stable through
time than the MVaR measure distribution. Figure 3.1 shows that the distributions (at the beginning and at the end) are completely different in the case
of MVaR optimization. An interesting result is the stability of the UBR
measure even for the MVaR optimization. According to the Figures 3.3
and 3.4, the UBR optimization leads to a more stable estimation of risk
through time.

In Table 3.1, we compute the (centered) moments, quantiles, and
J-B statistics of each risk measure distribution. We compute the MVaR
for the MVaR optimized portfolio (MVaR OptMVaR), the UBR for the
MVaR optimized portfolio (UBR OptMVaR), the MVaR for the UBR
optimized portfolio (MVaR OptUBR), and the UBR for the UBR optimized portfolio (UBR OptUBR)). Note that the skewness is standardized and the kurtosis is the standardized excess kurtosis. The first,
second, and third quantiles and the Jarque-Bera statistics are computed
and are reported in Table 3.1.

T A B L E   3.1

Moments (centered), quantiles, and Jarque-Bera statistic of the distribution in each case at 36 months and after 121 months

	Mean	Var	Skew	Kurt	Q0.25	Q0.5	Q0.75	J-B test
After 36 Months								
MVaR OptMVaR	−0.0504	0.0004	−0.2415	1.1369	−0.0626	−0.0493	−0.0379	62.7606*
UBR OptMVaR	0.1125	0.0057	1.4775	3.4572	0.0583	0.0971	0.1462	857.0237*
MVaR OptUBR	−0.0727	0.0007	−0.4644	1.0068	−0.0868	−0.0709	−0.0562	77.4067*
UBR OptUBR	0.0670	0.0015	1.1768	2.5815	0.0397	0.0612	0.0876	505.3906*
From 36 to 121 Months								
MVaR OptMVaR	−0.0960	0.0019	−1.7288	4.5409	−0.1100	−0.0872	−0.0702	1350.0734*
UBR OptMVaR	0.1040	0.0040	1.9860	6.9725	0.0632	0.0896	0.1295	2669.4889*
MVaR OptUBR	−0.0902	0.0019	−1.8004	4.5760	−0.1043	−0.0802	−0.0647	1405.3220*
UBR OptUBR	0.0915	0.0031	1.8141	5.6661	0.0550	0.0826	0.1125	1876.3627*
Difference								
MVaR OptMVaR	−0.0456				−0.0474	−0.0379	−0.0323	
UBR OptMVaR	−0.0085				0.0049	−0.0075	−0.0167	
MVaR OptUBR	−0.0175				−0.0175	−0.0093	−0.0085	
UBR OptUBR	0.0245				0.0153	0.0214	0.0249	

* At 1 percent.

The results confirm the insights obtained from the above graphs. The Jarque-Bera statistics reject the hypothesis of normality for all portfolios. The third part of the table reports the difference between relevant statistics computed on the ex-ante and ex-post distributions. Surprisingly, the least stable results are obtained for the MVaR ex-post measure based on MVaR optimization (first line of results). Meanwhile, the mean and quartiles of the utility-based measure remain very stable when optimization is performed based on MVaR (second line of results).

Correspondence of Risk Measures for Each Portfolio

The preceding results only compare the distribution at the beginning and at the end of the simulations without linking one specific initial value to its final value. In order to test the direct variation of a risk measure through time, we compute the difference between the risk measure calculated at the beginning (at the optimization of the portfolio) and its final value (after the 121 months). We obtain the following histograms for the variations of the risk measures.

The histograms in Figures 3.6 to 3.8 are much more concentrated around zero meaning that the UBR, contrarily to the MVaR measure, has a better predictive capacity through its constancy.

Table 3.2 includes descriptive statistics as the (centered) moments (the skewness and the excess kurtosis are standardized as already mentioned), the quantiles, and the Jarque-Bera statistic of each histogram. This table shows notably that the UBR measure of the MVaR optimized portfolio has an average value closer to zero but it has a larger variance.

There again, Table 3.2 confirms the visual inspection of the preceding figures. Overall, the optimization specification that yields the most consistent ex-ante and ex-post measures is the UBR approach, as evidenced by the value of the mean return and the K-S test, that takes the

F I G U R E   3.5

Histogram of the difference between the MVaR value at 36 months and its value after 121 months if the portfolio is optimized (at 36 months) using the MVaR measure

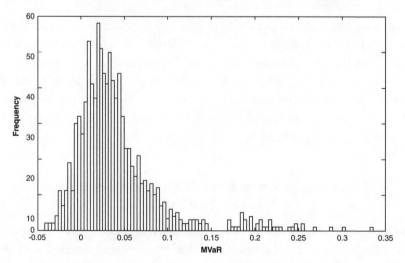

F I G U R E   3.6

Histogram of the difference between the utility-based risk at 36 months and its value after 121 months if the portfolio is optimized (at 36 months) using the MVaR measure

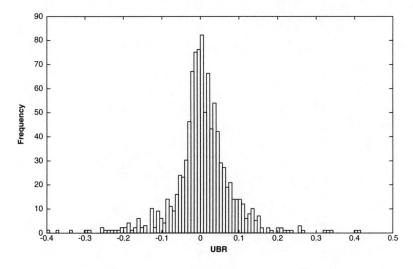

F I G U R E   3.7

Histogram of the difference between the MVaR at 36 months and its value after 121 months if the portfolio is optimized (at 36 months) using the UBR

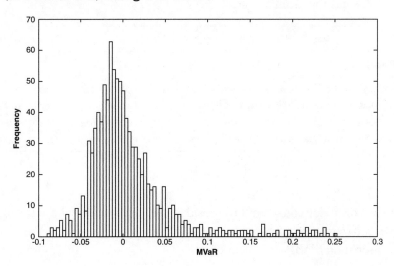

F I G U R E   3.8

Histogram of the difference between the utility-based risk at 36 months and its value after 121 months if the portfolio is optimized (at 36 months) using the UBR

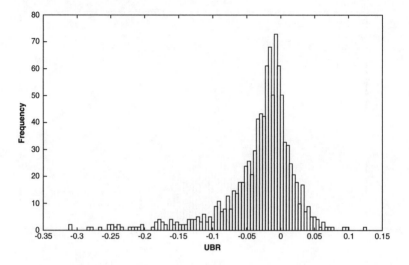

T A B L E   3.2

Moments (centered), quantiles, Jarque-Bera and Kolmogorov-Smirnov statistics against the normal distribution of the distribution in each case

	Mean	Var	Skew	Kurt	Q.25	Q.5	Q.75	J-B test	K-S test
Variations									
MVaR OptMVaR	0.0457	0.0023	1.9464	5.3995	0.0155	0.0355	0.0598	1836.7*	0.6000*
UBR OptMVaR	0.0085	0.0057	−0.0715	5.3974	−0.0213	0.0045	0.0421	1207.1*	0.0950*
MVaR OptUBR	0.0175	0.0024	2.1074	5.8453	−0.0099	0.0062	0.0303	2153.0*	0.1680*
UBR OptUBR	−0.0246	0.0028	−1.8500	5.3904	−0.0409	−0.0131	0.0043	1771.9*	0.2220*

* At 1 percent.

whole ecdf under consideration. Besides, the distribution whose mean is closest to zero and whose behavior is closest to symmetric is the UBR conditional on MVaR optimization.

CONCLUSION

This chapter has examined the stability profile of two higher moments based risk measures, i.e., the MVaR and a UBR deduced from the Bell's utility function. Evidence presented in the two series of tests suggests that the use of a utility-based framework for optimization yields more consistent results between the ex-ante and ex-post properties of optimized portfolios. When the MVaR is taken as the risk metric for optimization, the subsequent MVaR measures for the selected portfolios do not appear to reflect the conditions of the risk minimization program. In other terms, the ex-post behavior of the portfolio is very remote from its ex-ante behavior. This piece of evidence suggests in particular that the use of MVaR for portfolio optimization should be used with great caution if there is no strong evidence of return stationarity.

Clearly, we view this chapter as a descriptive analysis more than a robust comparison test of the two risk measures. The difficulty in comparing the two measures is the matching of the investor profile parameters c (the risk perception) and α (a measure mixing the risk aversion and the risk perception of the investor), which are nonlinear coefficients with respect to the statistical centered moments (variance, skewness, and kurtosis).

Subsequent research in this area should most likely focus on the deepening of the correspondence between the ex-ante and ex-post properties of optimal portfolio allocations. One should probably test dynamic allocations, while controlling for systematic risk exposures, to get better insight of the quality of a risk measure as a predictor of future portfolio risk exposure. We view this chapter as a step toward this direction.

REFERENCES

Arditti, F. (1967) Risk and the Required Return on Equity. *Journal of Finance*, Vol. 22, No. 1, pp. 19–36.

Bell, D.E. (1988) One-Switch Utility Functions and a Measure of Risk. *Management Science*, Vol. 34, No. 12, pp. 1416–1424.

Bell, D.E. (2000) A Contextual Uncertainty Condition for Behavior under Risk. *Management Science*, Vol. 41, No. 7, pp. 1145–1150.

Capocci, D., F. Duquenne, and G. Hübner (2007) Diversifying Using Hedge Funds: A Utility-Based Approach. Working paper, HEC-University of Liège, Liège.

Cornish, E. and R. Fisher, R. (1937) Moments and Cumulants in the Specification of Distributions. *Review of the International Statistical Institute*, Vol. 5, No. 4, pp. 307–320.

Favre, L. and J.-A Galeano. (2002) Mean-Modified Value-at-Risk Optimization with Hedge Funds. *Journal of Alternative Investment*, Vol. 5, No. 2, pp. 21–25.

Galeano, J.-A. and L. Favre (2001) The Inclusion of Hedge Funds in Swiss Pension Fund Portfolios. *Financial Markets and Portfolio Management,* Vol. 15, No. 4, pp. 450–472.

Markowitz, H. M. (1952) Portfolio Selection. *Journal of Finance*, Vol. 7, No. 1, pp. 77–91.

Samuelson, P. (1970) The Fundamental Approximation Theorem of Portfolio Analysis in Terms of Means, Variances and Higher Moments. *Review of Economic Studies*, Vol. 37, No. 4, pp. 537–542.

CHAPTER 4

Using CVaR to Optimize and Hedge Portfolios

Francesco Menoncin

ABSTRACT

It is well known that the risk measure called *value at risk* (VaR) is not coherent (it is not subadditive). Here, we present some results linked to the risk measure called *conditional value at risk* (CVaR), which is, instead, coherent. In particular, we show how to use CVaR (1) for taking into account risk aversion when measuring risk, where we will end up with two new risk measures based upon a so-called distorted probability, and (2) for optimizing and hedging a portfolio, where we will show a numerical example minimizing the CVaR of a portfolio containing Société Générale, S&P500, CAC40, and Nikkei225.

INTRODUCTION

Any investment implying an even very low loss probability is risky. The financial market is arbitrage free if and only if there are no investments with zero loss probability. This implies that any arbitrage-free financial market is risky. In other words, we could say that being risky is the very nature of a financial market. Thus, studying financial markets means studying risk.

Since Markowitz (1952), the notion of risk has been associated to any investment whose return varies around its mean. Nevertheless, according to what we have already stated above, the variability around the mean (the variance) cannot suitably measure the risk. Actually, two investments with a very high gain and a very low loss, respectively, may have the same variance but their risk is of course very different.

The creation of the risk measure called *value at risk* (VaR) was based on the idea of looking just at the left tail of the return distribution.

In 1999 Artzner et al. (hereafter ADEH) presented a paper that lists the (four) properties that any good risk measure must satisfy. They also demonstrated that any good risk measure can be written as a conditional expected value (and vice versa). According to ADEH's definition, VaR is not a good risk measure since it does not verify one of the above-mentioned properties. Nevertheless, another risk measure can be developed on the same idea as VaR but which also verifies all the ADEH's properties: the conditional value at risk (CVaR).

In this contribution, after presenting the main properties of the CVaR, we suggest the creation of two new risk measures by modifying VaR and CVaR according to a so-called distortion function. This allows us to take into account subjective risk aversion while computing these risk measures.

Finally, we will present the computation of a portfolio minimizing CVaR on Société Générale, S&P500, CAC40, and Nikkei225. The choice of the assets is made because of the financial distressed that hit Société Générale during the fourth quarter of 2007. In that way, we can check the ability of CVaR in measuring (and managing) this kind of risks.

MEASURING RISK (COHERENT RISK MEASURES)

During this chapter we will take into account a stochastic payoff x whose density and distribution functions are $f(x)$ and $F(x)$, respectively.[1] According to ADEH any function $\Psi(x)$ can be considered as a *coherent risk measure* if it satisfies all the following axioms:

---

[1] The domain of $f(x)$ is the whole real line.

- *Transitional invariance*. Adding a deterministic payoff (x_0) to the stochastic variable x makes the total risk decrease exactly by the amount x_0: $\Psi(x + x_0) = \Psi(x) - x_0$.
- *Subadditivity*. If we have two payoffs x_1 and x_2, then $\Psi(x_1 + x_2) \leq \Psi(x_1) + \Psi(x_2)$.
- *Homogeneity*. For any real positive number λ we have $\Psi(\lambda x) = \lambda \Psi(x)$.
- *Monotonicity*. If we have two payoffs such that $x_1 \geq x_2$ in any state of the world, then $\Psi(x_1) \leq \Psi(x_2)$.

The so-called representation theorem states the following (see ADEH).

Theorem 4.1: *A risk measure is coherent if and only if it can be represented as*

$$\Psi(x) = -\inf_{P \in \text{Pr}} E^P[x], \qquad (4.1)$$

where Pr is a (subjectively chosen) family of probability distributions.

Since any investor can chose a different probability distributions Pr, then any investor is able to chose a different coherent risk measure.

It is evident from Equation (4.1) that even the (opposite of the) expected value of x is a coherent risk measure. On the contrary, the so widely used standard error is not a coherent risk measure since it does not verify transitional invariance and monotonicity.[2]

SPECTRAL RISK MEASURES

If we want to write Equation (4.1) such that it is more suitable for applications, then we can write the risk measure as

$$\Psi_\phi(x) = -\int_{-\infty}^{\infty} h(x) f(x) x dx \qquad (4.2)$$

where the function $h(x)$ is used for altering the original density function $f(x)$. Nevertheless, $h(x)f(x)$ must be a density function itself, and this means that $h(x)$ must never be negative and must satisfy

$$\int_{-\infty}^{\infty} h(x) f(x) dx = 1 \qquad (4.3)$$

---

[2] If we call $V[x]$ the variance of x, then for any constant k, it immediately follows that $V[x + k] = V[x]$.

Furthermore, in order to take into account a risk aversion, the function $h(x)$ must attribute higher weights to severer losses. This means that $h(x)$ must be nonincreasing in x.

Equation (4.2) is often rewritten in terms of probability (and not in terms of gains or losses). Accordingly, we can apply a variable change by knowing that the probability p is equal to the distribution function [i.e., $p = F(x)$] from which we have $dp = f(x)\,dx$ and $F^{-1}(p) = x$. Thus, we can write Equation (4.2) as $\Psi_\phi(x) = -\int_0^1 \phi(p)F^{-1}(p)\,dp$, where $\phi(p) = h(F^{-1}(p))$.

Given the properties of function $h(x)$, function $\phi(p)$, the so-called spectrum, must never be negative, never increasing, and sum up to 1.[3] Acerbi (2002, Theorem 4.1) shows that any spectral risk measure $\Psi_\phi(x)$ is coherent if and only if the spectrum has the above-mentioned properties.

Many of the most commonly used risk measures can be written as spectral risk measures by suitably choosing a spectrum. Let us now study some special cases.

Value at Risk

In this case the spectrum gives all the weight to the payoff occurring with probability α. In order to give all the weight only to one event for a continuous distribution, the Dirac function is needed.[4] If we set $\phi(p) = \text{Dirac}(p - \alpha)$, then we have

$$\Psi_\phi(x) = -\int_0^1 Dirac\,(p - \alpha)F^{-1}(p)dp = -F^{-1}(\alpha) \qquad (4.4)$$

which is the opposite of the α quantile of the density function of x, better known as VaR_α. Since all the payoffs occurring with probability lower than α are totally neglected, then we incur what is known as *tail risk*.

---

[3] This last condition comes from condition (4.3) with the variable change $p = F(x)$.

[4] The Dirac function Dirac(x) is zero for any x except for $x = 0$, where its value tends toward infinity. The integral on the whole real line of the Dirac function is 1.

Conditional Value at Risk

In this case the spectrum gives a uniform weight to all the payoffs occurring with probability lower than α (and zero to the other payoffs). In this case we can set $\phi(p) = 1/\alpha \, I_{p<\alpha}$, where $I_{p<\alpha}$ is an indicator function whose value is 1 if $p < \alpha$ and 0 otherwise. Thus, we have

$$\Psi_\phi(x) = -\int_0^1 \frac{1}{\alpha} I_{p<\alpha} F^{-1}(p) dp = -\frac{1}{\alpha} \int_0^\alpha F^{-1}(p) dp \qquad (4.5)$$

which coincides with the expected value of x conditional to the fact that x is lower than $F^{-1}(\alpha)$. This risk measure is called *expected shortfall* or CVaR_α.

Risk Aversion Spectrum

As shown in Acerbi (2004), the following spectrum $\phi(p) = \delta e^{-\delta p}/(1 - e^{-\delta})$ for any positive constant δ represents an agent who becomes more and more risk averse as δ increases. It is easy to show that $\lim_{\delta \to 0} \delta e^{-\delta p}/(1 - e^{-\delta}) = 1$ and, in this case, the risk measure $\Psi_\phi(x)$ coincides with the expected value of the payoffs. If an agent is interested only in the expected value, then we can argue that such an agent is risk indifferent. On the contrary, when the parameter δ tends toward infinity, we have

$$\lim_{\delta \to +\infty} \frac{\delta e^{-\delta p}}{1 - e^{-\delta}} = \begin{cases} +\infty & p = 0 \\ 0 & 0 < p \leq 1 \end{cases}$$

which means that all the weight is put on the worst loss (the one occurring with probability zero), which is the only payoff the agent is interested in.

Distorted Risk Measure

In this case the spectrum is set equal to the first derivative of the so-called distortion function [see, for instance, Hürlimann (2006)]

$$.\phi(p) = g'(1 - p) \qquad (4.6)$$

where the prime indicates the first derivative, $g(1-p):[0,1]\to[0,1]$ is nondecreasing and strictly convex with $g(1)=1$ and $g(0)=0$. Given these hypotheses, the first derivative of the distortion function is a coherent spectrum.[5] Thus, the risk measure is

$$\Psi_g(x) = -\int_0^1 g'(1-p)F^{-1}(p)dp \qquad (4.7)$$

If we solve the differential Equation (4.6) with the suitable boundary condition, we obtain $g(1-p) = 1 - \int_0^p \phi(y)dy$.

In the case of the risk aversion spectrum, for instance, we have $g(1-p) = (e^{\delta(1-p)}-1)/(e^\delta-1)$ for the CVaR, we have

$$g(1-p) = \left(\frac{1-p}{\alpha} - \frac{1-\alpha}{\alpha} \right) I_{1-p>1-\alpha}$$

and for the VaR, we have[6]

$$\begin{aligned} g(1-p) &= 1 - \int_0^p \mathrm{Dirac}(y-\alpha)dy \\ &= 1 + Heaviside\,(-p+\alpha) - Heaviside\,(\alpha) \\ &= Heaviside\,(-p+\alpha) = I_{1-p>1-\alpha} \end{aligned}$$

Finally, we underline that the distortion function $g(1-p) = 1-p$ [coinciding with spectrum $\phi(p)=1$] gives back the expected value of x.

The spectra and the distortion functions for VaR_α and $CVaR_\alpha$ are represented in Figures 4.1 and 4.2, respectively.

The link between VaR_α and $CVaR_\alpha$ is given by [as also shown in Acerbi and Tasche (2002)]

$$CVaR_\alpha = \frac{1}{\alpha}\int_0^\alpha VaR_p\,dp$$

and it is graphically shown in Figure 4.3.

---

[5] Since $g'(1-p)$ is always positive, then $\phi(p)$ is positive. Since $g(1-p)$ is convex, i.e., $g''(1-p)$ is positive, then $\phi'(p) = -g''(1-p)$ is negative (and the spectrum is decreasing). Finally, $\int_0^1 \phi(p)dp = \int_0^1 g'(1-p)dp = -\int_0^1 g'(y)dy$, and since $g(1) = 1$ and $g(0) = 0$, the integral is 1.

[6] We recall that the Heaviside function Heaviside(x) is 1 for any nonnegative value of x and 0 for any negative value of x and is defined as the primitive of the Dirac function.

FIGURE   4.1

Spectra of CVaR$_\alpha$ (on the left) and VaR$_\alpha$ (on the right)

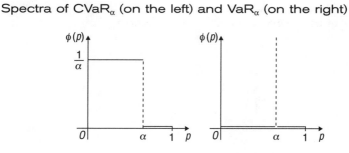

FIGURE   4.2

Distortion functions of CVaR$_\alpha$ (on the left) and VaR$_\alpha$ (on the right)

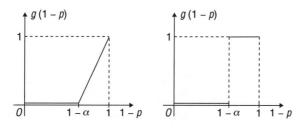

Here are some main futures about the CVaR.

CVaR$_\alpha$ is never lower than VaR$_\alpha$; in fact, when computing CVaR$_\alpha$ all the losses occurring with probabilities between 0 and α are taken into account. Since these losses are worse than the loss occurring with probability α, it follows that CVaR$_\alpha \geq$ VaR$_\alpha$. This property also suggests that measuring risk with VaR can lead to an underestimation of it.

CVaR$_\alpha$ is never increasing in α (which is not true for VaR$_\alpha$). The elasticity of CVaR$_\alpha$ with respect to α is given by

$$\frac{\partial \text{CVaR}_\alpha}{\partial \alpha} \frac{\alpha}{\text{CVaR}_\alpha} = \frac{\text{VaR}_\alpha}{\text{CVaR}_\alpha} - 1$$

Now, since we have already argued that CVaR$_\alpha \geq$ VaR$_\alpha$, then it follows that the above computed elasticity is negative.

F I G U R E   4.3

Value at risk and CVaR as functions of the opposite of the inverse of the cumulative density function

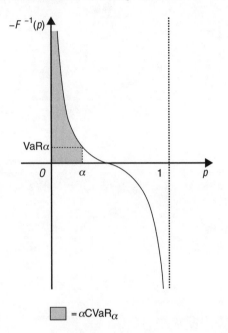

$$\square = \alpha\mathrm{CVaR}_\alpha$$

When the events we are studying are described by a discrete probability distribution, then Equation (4.5) becomes

$$\mathrm{CVaR}_\alpha = -\frac{1}{\alpha k}\left(\sum_{i=1}^{[\alpha k]}\vec{x}_i + (\alpha k - [\alpha k])\vec{x}_{[\alpha k]+1}\right) \qquad (4.8)$$

where k is the number of observations, $\vec{x}$ is the set of all the observations put in increasing order and $[\alpha k]$ is the integer part of αk.

The problem of how to compute CVaR (and VaR) for different density functions of x is studied in Andreev et al. (2005) according to what is presented in Bibby et al. (2005).

PROBLEMS WITH USING VAR

There are two main problems linked to the use of VaR as a risk measure: (1) it is not coherent (it is not subadditive), and (2) it does not take into any account the losses that happen with probability lower than α.

In order to check both these points, we use the following example: On the financial market there is an infinite number of independent and identically distributed (i.i.d.) risky assets on which there exists a default risk such that we may either loose 95 percent of our wealth with probability 3 percent or gain 5 percent. Algebraically, the payoff x is given by

$$x = \begin{cases} -95\% & 5\% \\ 0.03 & 0.97 \end{cases}$$

If we hold an equally weighted portfolio with two of these (i.i.d.) assets, the possible portoflio payoffs (y) are

$$y = \begin{cases} -95\% & -90\% & 5\% \\ 0.0009 & 0.0582 & 0.9409 \end{cases}$$

Now we can ask ourselves which investment is better (between a single asset x and a portfolio y) by using a risk measure. The simplest intuition suggests putting as many assets as possible in a portfolio because the risk of the portfolio will decrease.

Let us use CVaR and VaR at 5 percent. We have

$$\text{CVaR}_{0.05}(x) = -\frac{-95\% \times 0.03 + 5\% \times 0.02}{0.05} = 55\%$$

$$\text{VaR}_{0.05}(x) = -5\%$$

and

$$\text{CVaR}_{0.05}(y) = -\frac{-95\% \times 0.0009 - 90\% \times 0.0491}{0.05} = 8.2\%$$

$$\text{VaR}_{0.05}(y) = 90\%$$

It is important to stress that the VaR at 5 percent confidence level is negative. This means that the highest loss we can incur at the minimum confidence level of 5 percent is actually a gain. Thus, the VaR is not able to detect the big loss that can in fact happen with probability 3 percent (this is the so-called tail risk). The tail risk is avoided when using CVaR since it takes into account all the losses below a given confidence level.

Furthermore, since we have $\text{CVaR}_{0.05}(x) > \text{CVaR}_{0.05}(y)$, then the CVaR suggests we should invest in more than one asset. Instead, the VaR suggests that one asset is better than two since

$$\text{VaR}_{0.05}(x) < \text{VaR}_{0.05}(y)$$

If we continue this exercise by adding more and more assets to the equally weighted portfolio, we obtain Figure 4.4. We see that the CVaR is never increasing while the VaR has a sawtooth behavior, which makes optimization very difficult. Thus, not only is the VaR nonsubadditive, but it is not suitable for portfolio optimization.

F I G U R E   4.4

Conditional value at risk (in bold) and VaR on a number (on the abscissa) of independent and identically distributed (i.i.d.) assets

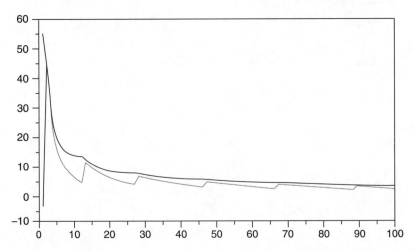

VALUE AT RISK, CVaR, AND THE OPTIMAL CAPITAL ALLOCATION

Let us take into account the case of a financial intermediary that has to keep a given amount of capital (v) for facing the risk on its financial positions. If we call x the payoff on these financial positions, then the total risk (H) born by the intermediary can be measured by the capital itself augmented by a risk measure computed on the losses exceeding the capital (v). Algebraically, we can write

$$H_{\alpha,g}(v)=v-\frac{1}{\alpha}\int_{-\infty}^{-v}g'(1-F(x))f(x)(x+v)dx \qquad (4.9)$$

where $\alpha \in [0,1]$ and g is the distortion function which can stand for an agent risk aversion (as already shown in the previous sections). The less risk-averse agent uses a risk measure given by the (opposite of the) expected value. In terms of the distortion function this means that $g(1-p)=1-p$ [i.e., $g'(1-p)=1$] and so

$$H_{\alpha}(v)=v-\frac{1}{\alpha}\int_{-\infty}^{-v}f(x)(x+v)dx \qquad (4.10)$$

which is the case studied in Rockafellar and Uryasev (2000).

The function $H_{\alpha}(v)$ has nice properties, as shown in the following proposition and in Figure 4.5.

Proposition 4.2: *Given the function $H_{\alpha}(v)$ as in Equation (4.10),*

$$VaR_{\alpha} = \arg\min_{v} H_{\alpha}(v)$$
$$CVaR_{\alpha} = \min_{v} H_{\alpha}(v)$$

Proof: The first and second derivatives of $H_{\alpha}(v)$ are

$$\frac{\partial H_{\alpha}(v)}{\partial \alpha}=1-\frac{1}{\alpha}\int_{-\infty}^{-v}f(x)dx$$
$$\frac{\partial^2 H_{\alpha}(v)}{\partial \alpha^2}=\frac{1}{\alpha}f(-v)$$

F I G U R E   4.5

Risk function whose minimum is CVaR and the minimum
point coincides with VaR

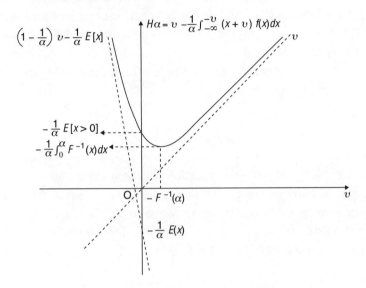

Since the second derivative is positive for any value of v, then equating to
zero the first derivative is a necessary and sufficient condition for a minimum. The value v^* equating to zero the first derivative solves $F(-v^*)=$
$\alpha \Leftrightarrow v^* = -F^{-1}(\alpha)$, which is exactly the VaR$_\alpha$. Now, the optimal value of
H_α is given by

$$H_\alpha(v^*)=v^*-\frac{1}{\alpha}\int_{-\infty}^{-v^*}f(x)(x+v^*)dx=v^*-\frac{1}{\alpha}v^*F(-v^*)$$

$$-\frac{1}{\alpha}\int_{-\infty}^{-v^*}f(x)xdx=-\frac{1}{\alpha}\int_{-\infty}^{-v^*}f(x)xdx$$

which is exactly the CVaR$_\alpha$.

Proposition 4.2 justifies the use of VaR for capital allocation purposes
only if the financial intermediaries are risk neutral or, in other words, they
use the expected value as a risk measure. Nevertheless, when using
expected value, the risk of a financial position is severely underestimated.

This problem can be avoided by the use of function $H_{\alpha,g}(v)$, as defined in Equation (4.9), instead of function $H_\alpha(v)$. The previously stated results are modified as follows.

Proposition 4.3: *Given the function $H_{\alpha,g}(v)$ as in Equation (4.9), if the distortion function g is invertible, then*

$$-F^{-1}(1-g^{-1}(1-\alpha)) = \arg\min_v H_{\alpha,g}(v)$$

$$-\frac{1}{\alpha}\int_0^{1-g^{-1}(1-\alpha)} g'(1-p)F^{-1}(p)dp = \min_v H_{\alpha,g}(v)$$

Proof: The proof follows the same lines than that of Proposition 4.2. Nevertheless, it is convenient to use the following transformation:

$$\int_{-\infty}^{-v} g'(1-F(x))f(x)(v+x)dx = -\int_{-\infty}^{-v}\left(\int_x^{-v} g'(1-F(x))f(x)du\right)dx$$

Now we can invert the order of integration

$$\int_{-\infty}^{-v}\left(\int_{-\infty}^{u} -g'(1-F(x))f(x)dx\right)du = \int_{-\infty}^{-v}\left(\int_{-\infty}^{u} \frac{dg(1-F(x))}{dx}dx\right)du$$

$$= \int_{-\infty}^{-v}(g(1-F(u))-1)du$$

Accordingly, we can rewrite function $H_{\alpha,g}(v)$ as

$$H_{\alpha,g}(v) = v + \frac{1}{\alpha}\int_{-\infty}^{-v}(1-g(1-F(u)))du$$

whose first and second derivatives are

$$\frac{\partial H_{\alpha,g}(v)}{\partial v} = 1 - \frac{1}{\alpha}(1-g(1-F(-v)))$$

$$\frac{\partial^2 H_{\alpha,g}(v)}{\partial v^2} = \frac{1}{\alpha}g'(1-F(-v))f(-v)$$

Since the second derivative is always positive, then equating to zero the first derivative is a necessary and sufficient condition for having a minimum. From the first-order condition, we obtain

$$1 - \frac{1}{\alpha}(1 - g(1 - F(-v^*))) = 0 \Leftrightarrow v^* = -F^{-1}(1 - g^{-1}(1 - \alpha))$$

and after substituting this optimal value into function $H_{\alpha,g}(v)$ we have

$$
\begin{aligned}
H_{\alpha,g}(v^*) &= v^* - \frac{1}{\alpha}\int_{-\infty}^{-v^*} g'(1 - F(x))f(x)(v^* + x)dx \\
&= v^* - \frac{1}{\alpha}v^* \int_{-\infty}^{-v^*} g'(1 - F(x))f(x)dx - \frac{1}{\alpha}\int_{-\infty}^{-v^*} g'(1 - F(x))f(x)x\,dx \\
&= v^* + \frac{1}{\alpha}v^* \int_{-\infty}^{-v^*} \frac{dg(1 - F(x))}{dx}dx - \frac{1}{\alpha}\int_{0}^{1-g^{-1}(1-\alpha)} g'(1 - p)F^{-1}(p)dp \\
&= v^* + \frac{1}{\alpha}v^* (g(1 - F(-v^*)) - 1) - \frac{1}{\alpha}\int_{0}^{1-g^{-1}(1-\alpha)} g'(1 - p)F^{-1}(p)dp \\
&= -\frac{1}{\alpha}\int_{0}^{1-g^{-1}(1-\alpha)} g'(1 - p)F^{-1}(p)dp
\end{aligned}
$$

which completes the proof.

The new functions we have found could be defined as *distorted* VaR (DVaR) and *distorted* CVaR (DCVaR), respectively:

$$\mathrm{DVaR}_\alpha \equiv -F^{-1}(1 - g^{-1}(1 - \alpha)) = \mathrm{VaR}_{1-g^{-1}(1-\alpha)} \qquad (4.11)$$

$$
\begin{aligned}
\mathrm{DCVaR}_\alpha &\equiv -\frac{1}{\alpha}\int_{0}^{1-g^{-1}(1-\alpha)} g'(1 - p)F^{-1}(p)dp \\
&= \frac{1 - g^{-1}(1 - \alpha)}{\alpha}\mathrm{CVaR}_{1-g^{-1}(1-\alpha)}
\end{aligned}
\qquad (4.12)
$$

and they are able to take into account the risk aversion while measuring risk.

OPTIMIZING A PORTFOLIO USING CVAR

Let us take into account a financial market with n risky assets (whose returns are listed in vector μ) and one riskless asset (whose return is r). If we call w the vector containing the portfolio weights on the risky assets and w_G the amount of riskless asset held in portfolio, then the optimal portfolio minimizing CVaR$_\alpha$ can be found by solving the following problem:

$$\min_{w, w_G} \text{CVaR}_\alpha(w, w_G)$$
$$w'\mu + w_G r = \mu_R$$
$$w'1 + w_G = 1$$

where μ_R is the expected return desired on the optimal portfolio and the prime denotes transposition.

If we substitute w_G into the first constraint from the second one, the problem can be rewritten just in terms of w:

$$\min_w \text{CVaR}_\alpha(w)$$
$$w'(\mu - r1) = \mu_R - r$$

Furthermore, since the CVaR$_\alpha$ can be written as the result of a minimization problem, then we can rewrite the problem as

$$\min_{w, v} \left[v - \frac{1}{\alpha} \int_{-\infty}^{-v} (v + x) f(x) dx \right]$$
$$w'(\mu - r1) = \mu_R - r$$

where the variable x now stands for the portfolio return whose density function must now be estimated.

One of the most commonly used techniques for estimating $f(x)$ is the so-called historical simulation: The past returns for k periods are computed (μ), and the possible future returns are estimated by applying these returns to the present value of x (all the returns are assumed to have the same probability). Accordingly, we will have k different states of the world (any of them with probability $1/k$), and the estimation of the integral in the minimization problem can be done as follows:

$$-\int_{-\infty}^{-v}(v+x)f(x)dx \to \frac{1}{k}\sum_{i=1}^{k}\max(-v-x_i,0)$$

The past k returns on n assets can be stored in a $k\times n$ matrix M, and accordingly, the estimated returns on the risky assets (μ) can be computed as $\mu = 1/k\, M'\mathbf{1}$.

The portfolio return in the state of the world i can then be written as, $x_i = w'(M_i' - r\mathbf{1}) + r$, where M_i is the ith row of matrix M. Finally, the optimal portfolio problem can be restated as[7]

$$\min_{w,v,z_i\geq 0}\left[v+\frac{1}{\alpha}\frac{1}{k}\sum_{i=1}^{k}z_i\right]$$

$$z_i \geq -v-w'\left(M_i'-r\mathbf{1}\right)-r$$

$$w'\left(\frac{1}{k}M'\mathbf{1}-r\mathbf{1}\right)=\mu_R-r$$

where the integral has been substituted by its estimation. Gaivoronski and Pflug (2004) study in detail this linear programming framework for optimizing the CVaR of a portfolio. When the distortion function is different from $g'(1-p)=1$, then this approach does not lead any longer to a linear programming problem and more sophisticated approaches must be used.

A NUMERICAL EXAMPLE

By using the framework presented in the previous section, we now study the optimal portfolio (minimizing daily $CVaR_{0.01}$ computed on past 250 days) for an agent who wants to invest in four financial activities: Société Générale, CAC40, S&P500, and Nikkei225 (all the prices are taken from

---

[7] It is of course possible to implement the constraint $w\geq 0$.

January 1, 2003 to April 29, 2008). The two last indexes are put in the portfolio for checking the opportunities coming from an internationally diversified portfolio. CAC40 is taken for having a benchmark to the unique stock in the portfolio. Société Générale was subject to a severe financial fiasco that led to a €3.35 billion (US$4.9 billion) loss in the fourth quarter of 2007 (as can be seen in Figure 4.6). In this section we want to check whether the portfolio minimizing CVaR is able to protect the investor against such kind of distresses (which can be more suitably classified as operational risk rather than financial risk).

The daily returns on the four financial activities are represented in Figure 4.7 where the same scale for the abscissa has been kept in the four parts of the graph in order to make the returns easier to compare. It is evident that Société Générale has a higher volatility with respect to the indexes. Of course, this behavior is common to any asset that is more volatile than any index (made of a mix of assets).

F I G U R E   4.6

Prices (on the left ordinate) and daily returns (on the right ordinate) of Société Générale (January 2003–April 2008)

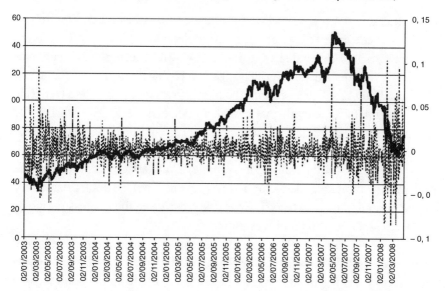

F I G U R E   4.7

Daily returns on the financial assets in portfolio (January 2003–April 2008)

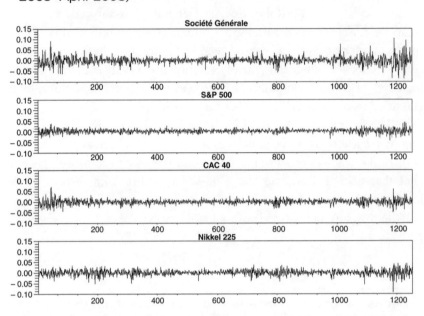

In Table 4.1 the correlations, variances, covariances, and returns on the assets are listed. The highest correlation (0.75) is of course found between Société Générale and its index CAC40. Instead, the three indexes have a very low correlation. The lowest is that between S&P500 and Nikkei225 (0.12). The asset with the highest variance is Socitété Générale (0.084) and the one with the lowest variance is S&P500 (0.021). The annual returns (in the last row of Table 4.1) are quite similar. The highest is that of the Japan index (11.92 percent).

In Figure 4.8 the values of VaR and CVaR at 1 percent are shown. Again, Société Générale is the riskiest, even if Nikkei looks riskier for some periods. The less risky is S&P. We clearly see the distress period of Société Générale around observation 850.

It is evident that VaR and CVaR have a very similar behavior. Nevertheless, CVaR seems to have better explaining capacities during turbulences on the financial market. Let us look at the beginning and the end

T A B L E   4.1

Matrix of correlations, annual variances (on the main diagonal), and annual covariances (in the lower part of the matrix) between the financial activities in the portfolio. On the last row are the annual mean returns (from January 2003 to the end of April 2008)

	Société Générale	S&P 500	CAC 40	Nikkei 225
Société Générale	0.0844499	0.4438139	0.7507625	0.2699321
S&P 500	0.0186907	0.0210015	0.5101723	0.1236737
CAC 40	0.0405387	0.0137376	0.0345251	0.3524455
Nikkei 225	0.0165062	0.0037713	0.0137801	0.0442779
Returns	0.0989100	0.0951412	0.1098058	0.1191782

F I G U R E   4.8

Daily VaR and CVaR at 1 percent for Société Générale (bold), S&P500 (solid), CAC40 (dashed), and Nikkei225 (dotted) from August 2003 to April 2008

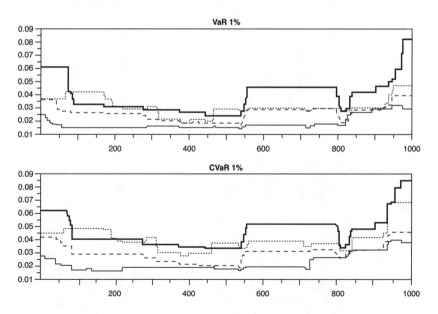

of the period. At the far left, both VaR and CVaR decrease, indicating that the risk is reducing. Nevertheless, CVaR reduces less sharply than VaR. In the same way, on the far right, when the risk increases because of the big volatility (that can be also seen in Figure 4.7), CVaR increases less sharply. This means that CVaR allows financial investors to react more efficiently to the financial market changes and their portfolios can be rebalanced with less sharp changes.

The optimal portfolio weights minimizing CVaR at 1 percent level are shown in Figure 4.9. The expected return we want to obtain from our portfolio (μ_R) is daily set to the mean of the returns on the four assets in portfolio.

F I G U R E   4.9

Optimal asset allocation minimizing CVaR at 1 percent (portfolio weights have been constrained to be positive)

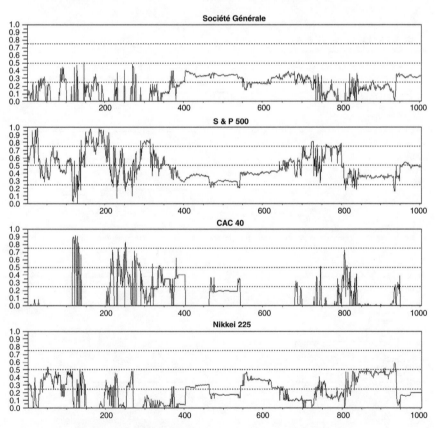

It is evident that the optimal portfolio is dominated by the S&P500 (the asset with the lowest CVaR). CAC40 does not play a crucial role in optimal portfolio since it is highly correlated with Société Générale (and with very close returns). Even during the distress period for Société Générale (observations around 850), the optimal percentage of wealth to invest in it is kept around 25 percent. The main reason for this behavior is that the Société Générale problems arise just when all the financial markets experience an increase in risk.

In Figure 4.10 both the (daily) VaR and CVaR at 1 percent for the optimal portfolio are drawn. Conditional value at risk is of course always higher than VaR, but it is worth highlighting two main features: (1) CVaR has a less sharp behavior with respect to VaR, as already shown in Figure 4.8 (even if here this phenomenon more clearly arises), and (2) there is a period (between observation 300 and observation 350) where the CVaR increases, showing a higher risk, while VaR decreases, suggesting a reduction in risk. During this period, we clearly see the effect of the so-called tail risk. There are severe losses that are neglected by VaR while they are included in the computation of CVaR.

Figure 4.11 shows the (daily) values of VaR and CVaR at 1 percent level for both an equally weighted portfolio and the optimal portfolio. We

F I G U R E   4.10

Daily VaR at 1 percent (bold) and CVaR at 1 percent (solid) of the optimal portfolio

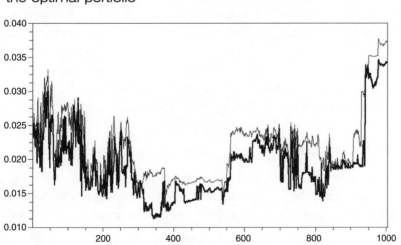

F I G U R E   4.11

Daily VaR and CVaR at 1 percent for an equally weighted
portfolio (bold) and for the optimal portfolio

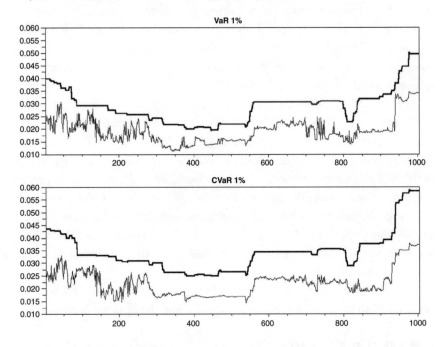

see that the optimization procedure is actually able to keep a low value for
portfolio CVaR with respect to an equally weighted strategy.

Finally, Figure 4.12 shows a comparison between the (daily) returns
on the equally weighted portfolio and the optimal portfolio. As we expected,
the optimal portfolio is less volatile than the equally weighted one. In the
optimal portfolio, both the very high and very low returns are avoided.

The annual mean return of the equally weighted portfolio is 7.07 percent, while the annual mean return on the optimal portfolio is 22.65 percent.

CONCLUSION

In this chapter we have recalled the properties of the coherent risk measures
by also presenting the family of the spectral risk measures to which VaR and
CVaR belong. In particular, we have shown the main disadvantages of

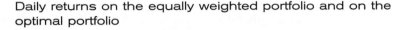

F I G U R E   4.12

Daily returns on the equally weighted portfolio and on the optimal portfolio

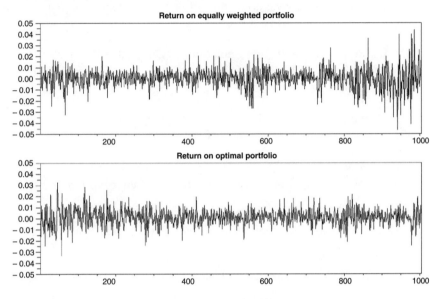

measuring risk by using VaR, which could lead to a nonoptimal portfolio diversification.

By using the so-called distorted probability, we have presented a way for creating a risk measure by also taking into account the investor's risk aversion. Thus, we have presented the DVaR and DCVaR as linear transformations of VaR and CVaR, computed at a particular confidence level.

In the final part, after presenting a numerical procedure for finding the asset allocation minimizing portfolio CVaR, we have applied it to a portfolio containing Société Générale, S&P500, CAC40, and Nikkei225. The numerical results show that the return on the optimal portfolio minimizing CVaR has a much lower volatility than the equally weighted portfolio and the risk reduction is very effective. Furthermore, the mean return on the optimal portfolio is 1,500 basis points higher than the return on the equally weighted portfolio. This allows us to conclude that using CVaR instead of VaR is a very effective way to manage risk.

REFERENCES

Acerbi, C. (2002) Spectral Measures of Risk: A Coherent Representation of Subjective Risk Aversion. *Journal of Banking and Finance*, Vol. 26, No. 7, pp. 1505–1518.

Acerbi, C. (2004) Coherent Representations of Subjective Risk-Aversion. In G. Szego (ed.), *Risk Measures for the 21st Century*. New York: John Wiley & Sons.

Acerbi, C. and D. Tasche. (2002) On the Coherence of Expected Shortfall. *Journal of Banking and Finance*, Vol. 26, No. 7, pp. 1487–1503.

Andreev, A., A. Kanto, and P. Malo (2005) On Closed-Form Calculation of CVaR. Working paper (W–389), Helsinki School of Economics.

Artzner, Ph., F. Delbaen, J.-M. Eber, and D. Heath (1999) Coherent Measure of Risk. *Mathematical Finance*, Vol. 9, No. 3, pp. 203–228.

Bibby, B.M., I.M. Skovgaard, and M. Sørensen (2005) Diffusion-Type Models with Given Marginal Distribution and Autocorrelation Function. *Bernoulli*, Vol. 11, No. 2, pp. 191–220.

Gaivoronski, A.A. and G. Pflug (2004) Value-at-Risk in Portfolio Optimization: Properties and Computational Approach. *Journal of Risk*, Vol. 7, No. 2, pp. 1–31.

Hürlimann, W. (2006) A Note on Generalized Distortion Risk Measures. *Finance Research Letters*, Vol. 3, No. 4, pp. 267–272.

Markowitz H. (1952) Portfolio Selection. *Journal of Finance*, Vol. 7, No. 1, pp. 77–91.

Rockafellar, R.T. and S. Uryasev (2000) Optimization of Conditional Value-at-Risk. *Journal of Risk*, Vol. 2, No. 3, pp. 21–41.

PART TWO

Banking and Insurance Sector Applications

CHAPTER 5

Value at Risk, Capital Standards, and Risk Alignment in Banking Firms

Guy Ford, Tyrone M. Carlin, and Nigel Finch

ABSTRACT

This chapter examines the perplexing question of how to efficiently align the investment decisions of managers in a bank with the risk–return goals of the center of the bank. It argues that the contemporary approach aimed at achieving such alignment, which involves the top-down allocation of some proportion of the total bank's capital against positions taken by managers and then remunerating managers based on the return generated on this capital, serves as a poor mechanism for aligning incentives. This arises because bank capital standards have evolved around the concept of a predetermined solvency standard—conversant with the value-at-risk measure of risk—which has at its core a risk-neutral attitude to risk. If bank stakeholders are risk averse and desire that this risk attitude be captured in bank investment decisions, then risk measures used internally for investment selection and performance measurement must diverge from those used to measure total bank capital. This chapter shows how alternative measures to value at risk serve as better mechanisms for aligning incentives within banking firms.

INTRODUCTION

This chapter examines risk congruence in a large, decentralized banking firm. It considers the troubling question of how to efficiently align the investment decisions of managers in the bank with the risk–return goals of the center of the bank. It is argued that the contemporary approach aimed at achieving such alignment, which involves the top-down allocation of some proportion of the bank's total capital against positions taken by managers, and then remunerating managers based on the return generated on this capital, serves as a poor mechanism for achieving alignment of incentives. Indeed, it is shown that this approach may lead to outcomes that are against the best interests of bank stakeholders whom the center is deemed to represent. Our central proposition is that the risk measure used internally for assessing the risk-adjusted performance of investments made by managers needs to diverge from that used for calculating total bank capital, where the latter is based on achieving a predetermined solvency standard.

The basis of this proposition is that the risk preference function of the center of the bank—which embodies the diverse interests of bank owners, depositors, debt holders, and regulators—does not calibrate with the attitude to risk implicit in the measurement of total bank capital requirements. We argue that the risk preference function of the center of the bank is one that is likely to demonstrate nonsatiety, risk aversion, and a preference for positive skewness in the distribution of bank returns. This is at odds with the attitude to risk implicit in a predetermined solvency standard, which is essentially one of risk neutrality. If banks adopt a policy of spreading their actual capital against risky positions taken by managers—a full capital allocation policy—then this imposes an internal risk standard that may lead managers to make portfolio decisions that are suboptimal for the bank.

The chapter is structured as follows. The second section considers how bank capital requirements have evolved to become directly linked to the concept of a target solvency probability for a bank that is based on a "value-at-risk" methodology for quantifying unexpected losses. The third section considers the relevant risk preference function for a banking firm. The fourth section provides criteria for ranking risk in bank portfolios. The fifth section assesses the risk ranking criteria for compatibility with the risk preference function of the bank. The sixth section identifies the selected risk measures and their key characteristics, and the seventh section provides a practical application of the framework by examining the incentive-compatible properties of the set of risk measures against five risk distributions for a hypothetical credit portfolio. Our conclusions are presented in the final section.

TARGET SOLVENCY AND VALUE AT RISK

Over recent decades, capital adequacy has become the focal point of the prudential regulation of banking firms. Capital is viewed by bank regulators as a key defence against financial system instability and a major source of protection for bank depositors. The requirement that banks hold a minimum level of capital in concert with the risk in their assets and off-balance sheet activities means that capital has also served as a regulator of bank asset growth.[1]

From the perspective of the banking firm, there are two types of capital that must be measured and managed: economic capital and regulatory capital. The Basel Committee of the Bank for International Settlements defines *economic capital* as the capital that a bank holds and allocates internally as a result of its own assessment of risk, while *regulatory capital* is determined by supervisors on the basis of the Basel Accord.[2] Economic capital is based on the notion that future gains and losses on a portfolio of credit exposures, over a specified time horizon, can be described by its probability distribution function. This function forms the basis upon which a bank that owns the portfolio can assign capital that will reduce the bank's probability of failure to a desired confidence level, within a desired time horizon. Economic capital thus defines risk at a common point (confidence level) in the distribution, where the confidence level represents the target solvency standard of the bank.[3] In defining risk

---

[1] The Basel Accord of 1988 imposed an 8 percent capital requirement on assets, adjusted for crude measures of credit risk. In 1995 the Accord was amended to require banks to set aside capital to cover unexpected losses related to market risk. In the market risk amendment, banks were permitted to use their own models to determine the value at risk in their market portfolio, which is the maximum loss that the portfolios are likely to experience with a set probability over a given holding period.

[2] Basel Committee on Banking Supervision (2001b, Section 15).

[3] For example, a bank that holds sufficient economic capital to protect against losses at the 99.97 percent confidence level has a 0.03 percent probability of default, which is about the same solvency standard (default) risk as an AA-rated bond.

in probabilistic terms, economic capital represents a common currency for risk that allows exposures related to credit risk, market risk, and operational risk to be directly compared across the bank.

The solvency standard adopted by a bank forms the link between its internal assessment of risk and the capital structure of its balance sheet. The economic capital of the bank is attributed to the difference between the mean of its loss distribution—expected losses (EL)—and the designated confidence level.[4] In this way economic capital acts to protect the bank against unexpected losses, being downside variations in the expected loss rate. Figure 5.1 shows a graphical representation of economic capital within the context of the distribution of portfolio returns for a bank and assumes a solvency standard equal to the 99.9 percent confidence level.

In 2004 the Basel Committee of the Bank for International Settlements released a revised framework for bank capital measurement and standards, which has become known as Basel II.[5] The revised framework was conceived largely as a response to problems with the original Basel Accord of 1988 and, in particular, to the recognition that banks had

F I G U R E   5.1

Economic capital

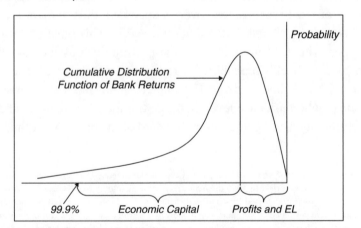

[4] Expected losses are typically offset by some combination of margin income and/or provisions. See Bank for International Settlement (2001a, p.40).

[5] See Bank for International Settlements (2004). An updated version was published in 2005.

become increasingly able to arbitrage regulatory capital requirements and exploit divergences between risks measured under the Accord and the true economic risk in their books.

Under Basel II, banks are permitted a choice between two broad methodologies for calculating their capital requirements for credit risk. One approach requires banks to measure credit risk in a standardised manner, supported by external credit assessments. The alternative approach, which is subject to the explicit approval of the supervisor of the bank in the country of domicile, allows banks to use their own internal estimates of various risk components to determine the capital requirement for a given credit exposure. This approach, known as the *internal ratings-based* (IRB) approach, is based on measures of unexpected losses and expected losses, using risk-weight functions to produce capital requirements to cover for unexpected losses.[6] The IRB approach is a point on the continuum between purely regulatory measures of credit risk and an approach that more fully builds internal credit risk models developed by banks.[7] However, while the revised framework stops short of allowing the results of such credit risk models to be used for regulatory capital purposes, the risk weights in the IRB framework are closely calibrated to those used by "sophisticated" banks in determining their own economic capital requirements. In this regard, for a given target solvency probability, the risk weights in the IRB approach are associated with quantifying the volatility of credit losses over a one-year measurement horizon.[8]

Within the context of this chapter, two important observations can be drawn from the Basel II framework:

1. The IRB approach seeks to make bank regulatory capital requirements for credit risk approximate economic capital requirements.

2. Regulatory capital requirements have evolved to become directly linked to the concept of a target solvency probability for a bank.

---

[6] See Bank for International Settlements (2005, p.48).

[7] See Bank for International Settlements (2005, p. 5).

[8] Bank for International Settlements (2001b, p.60). The committee states (p. 43) that risk weights are implicitly calibrated so that with a specified minimum probability (the target solvency probability) capital will cover total credit losses.

The second observation follows from the first, given economic capital is measured to a specified confidence level based on a predetermined solvency standard. This is reinforced by the Basel Committee, who report that the most important precedent for indexing capital requirements to measures of risk—and thus to an economic capital concept—was the Market Risk Amendment to the Accord of 1988, which embodies a value-at-risk (VaR) methodology to relate capital to a target level of confidence.[9] The calibration of risk weights under the IRB approach for credit risk builds upon the same framework but with modifications to reflect the characteristics of credit risk. This means that unexpected losses, and hence the economic capital held by a bank, is essentially based on a VaR concept of risk.

BANK RISK PREFERENCE FUNCTION

The risk preference function for a banking firm determines the feasible set of portfolios and establishes the relevant risk measures for capital allocation, pricing, and performance measurement. Determining the risk preference function for a bank is complicated by the multiple interests of bank stakeholders—owners, creditors, managers, and regulators—each of whom carry potentially conflicting risk attitudes. In the event that the bank defaults on its debt, some stakeholders may be less concerned with the magnitude of losses than other stakeholders. We can consider that the economic impact of default on owners and managers will be largely invariant to the size of actual losses, with costs to these stakeholders a function of the event of default itself. Managers face loss of employment regardless of the size of default, while losses to owners are capped by the institution of limited liability.[10] In contrast, the economic impact of default on regulators and creditors is more directly related to the size of losses in the event of default. This means risk measures based on the probability of default are likely to be of more relevance to managers and shareholders,

---

[9] Bank for International Settlements (2001a, p.33).

[10] Managers and owners may be concerned with the size of losses if they are to influence the decision to liquidate versus restructure the bank. In the latter case, owners may be able to recover some proportion of their initial investment, and managers may be able to retain their employment, depending on the nature of the restructure and the subsequent fortunes of the bank.

while measures linked to losses in the event of default may be more relevant to regulators and creditors. This has implications for an incentive-compatible risk-adjusted performance measurement framework in the sense that the center of the bank represents stakeholders who may carry different perspectives on risk or tolerance to unexpected losses. It places focus directly on the question of the appropriate risk preference function for the center of the bank.

In this chapter we take the view that capital regulations exist to protect bank depositors and debt holders. This means the relevant risk preference function should be one that reflects a risk-averse attitude towards risk.

RISK RANKING CRITERIA

In order to rank portfolios carrying different risk distributions a risk-ordering mechanism is required. This study employs a stochastic dominance framework because stochastic dominance does not require a full parametric specification of the preferences of decision makers—investment alternatives can be ordered by risk without having to specify the exact form of the utility function of the investor. [11] This suits our needs well given the difficulties in specifying the exact form of the utility function for the center of the bank when it represents a diverse range of stakeholder interests. The central idea of stochastic dominance is that the decision problem can be simplified by sorting out and eliminating dominated alternatives. Stochastic dominance converts the probability distribution of an investment into a cumulative probability curve, which is used to determine the superiority of one investment over another. Stochastic dominance criteria provide a set of rules for making choices among risky assets consistent with the preferences of broad classes of utility functions, obviating the need to know the precise functional characterisation of the objective function. Different orders of stochastic dominance correspond to different classes of utility function. We outline the selection criteria that apply to each order of stochastic dominance below.

---

[11] The contemporary notion of stochastic dominance has its roots in papers by Hadar and Russell (1969), Hanoch and Levy (1969), and Rothschild and Stiglitz (1970).

First-Order Stochastic Dominance

First-order stochastic dominance (FSD) provides a rule for rank-ordering risky portfolios in a manner consistent with the preferences of investors who prefer more wealth rather than less. A portfolio stochastically dominates another portfolio by FSD if investors receive greater wealth from the portfolio in every ordered state of nature. This means the only requirement for FSD is that utility functions are increasing: FSD does not encompass the risk attitude of the investor.

Let F and G represent the cumulative probability distributions of the returns for portfolios X and Y, and let $U(w)$ refer to the utility of w dollars of wealth. Under the FSD selection rule, portfolio X will stochastically dominate portfolio Y if $F_x(w) \leq G_y(w)$ for all w with at least one strict inequality.[12] Alternatively, $[G_y(w) - F_x(w)] \geq 0$ for all w with at least one strict inequality. This means the cumulative probability distribution for portfolio Y always lies to the left of the cumulative distribution for portfolio X. Further, for investors to prefer more wealth to less, the utility function must be increasing monotonically. This implies a positive first derivative for the utility function: $U'(w) > 0$.

Increasing wealth preference can be considered universal for all utility functions and representative of the behavior of the banking firm. Indeed, as mentioned, this includes investors who are risk seekers, risk averters, and those who are risk neutral. As such, a large proportion of the given set of investment alternatives will be members of the FSD admissible set, restricting the practical applicability of the FSD selection rule.

Second-Order Stochastic Dominance

Second-order stochastic dominance (SSD) assumes that in addition to increasing wealth preference, investors are risk averse. Risk aversion can be defined where the utility function of an investor is increasing and concave, implying a positive first derivative and a negative second derivative for the utility function: $U'(w) > 0$ and $U''(w) < 0$.

---

[12] For a proof, see Levy (1998, pp.48–51) or Martin et al (1988, pp.189–191).

Under the assumption of risk aversion, the expected utility of a risky investment portfolio is less than the utility of the expected outcome.

Under the SSD selection rule, portfolio X will dominate portfolio Y if

$$\int_{-\infty}^{w} [G_y(w) - F_x(w)]\, dw \geq 0$$

for all w with at least one inequality.[13] This means that in order for portfolio X to dominate portfolio Y for all risk-averse investors, the accumulated area under the cumulative probability distribution of Y must be greater than the accumulated area for X, below any given level of wealth. Unlike FSD, this implies that the cumulative density functions can cross. Further, a necessary condition for SSD of portfolio X over Y is that the expected value of portfolio X is greater than or equal to the expected value of Y.

The assumption that investors are risk averse provides a stronger utility function constraint than under FSD, and as such, the SSD admissible set is smaller than that under the FSD criterion.[14]

Third-Order Stochastic Dominance

Third-order stochastic dominance (TSD) corresponds to the set of utility functions where[15]: $U'(w) > 0$, $U''(w) < 0$, and $U'''(w) > 0$. The addition of a negative third derivative for the utility function requires the investor to prefer positive skewness in the distribution of portfolio returns (upside returns will have a larger magnitude than downside returns, indicating greater probability in the right tail of the distribution). Using data on the rates of return of mutual funds, Levy (1998) provides empirical evidence that supports the hypothesis that most investors prefer positive skewness and dislike negative skewness.[16] From the perspective of a banking firm, a preference for positive skewness can be interpreted as an unwillingness

---

[13] For a proof, see Levy (1998, pp.69–71) or Martin et al (1988, pp.191–192).
[14] This has been empirically verified by Levy and Sarnat (1970) and Levy and Hanoch (1970).
[15] See Whitmore (1970), Martin et al (1988), and Levy (1998).
[16] See Levy (1998, pp. 89–90).

to accept a small and almost certain gain in exchange for a remote possibility of the bank defaulting on its debt obligations.

Under the TSD selection rule, portfolio X will dominate portfolio Y if and only if the following conditions hold:

$$\int_{-\infty}^{w} \int_{-\infty}^{t} [G_y(w) - F_x(w)] \, dw \, dt \geq 0, \text{ and}$$

$$E_F(x) \geq E_G(x)$$

for all w with at least one inequality.[17] This means a preference for one portfolio over another by TSD may be due to the preferred investment having a higher mean, a lower variance, or a higher positive skewness.[18]

In addition to positive skewness preference, a rationale for a positive third derivative for the investor's utility function is decreasing absolute risk aversion, meaning the higher the wealth of the investor, the smaller the risk premium that the investor would be willing to pay to insure a given loss. While this may be the case for bank owners, this aspect of TSD is less relevant in the current context than the preference for positive skewness. The unwillingness for the investor to accept a small and almost certain gain in exchange for a remote possibility of ruin is a property of TSD that directly conforms to the risk preferences of bank regulators and bank creditors discussed in the preceding section of this chapter.

Bawa (1975) shows that for the entire class of distribution functions and for the class of decreasing absolute risk-averse utility functions, the TSD rule is the optimal selection rule when distributions have equal means. While in cases where distributions have unequal means there is no known selection rule that satisfies both necessary and sufficient conditions for dominance, Bawa shows that the TSD rule may be used as a reasonable approximation to the optimal selection rule for the entire class of distribution functions.

Third-order stochastic dominance represents the most applicable criteria for ranking alternative investment portfolios in the bank setting

---

[17] For a proof, see Levy (1998, pp. 92–96). The symbol t arises from the thrice integration of the expression $E_w[U(w_F)] - E_w[U(w_G)] \geq 0$. It indicates that the cumulative of the cumulative of the cumulative distribution function of F lies above G. See Heyer (2004).

[18] See Levy (1998, p. 97).

given the TSD dominant portfolio embodies risk aversion and positive skewness preference. If bank owners seek to preserve bank franchise value, their utility function will display risk aversion $[U''(w) < 0]$. If bank creditors and regulators are concerned with the size of losses in the event of the bank becoming insolvent, they will demonstrate a preference for positive skewness in bank returns $[U'''(w) > 0]$. Third-order stochastic dominance also applies to the entire shape of the distribution function of bank returns and thus allows for nonnormality in returns. This is important given the nonnormal distribution of returns that characterize many bank portfolios and, in particular, loan portfolios. In contrast, the popular mean-variance criterion is only accurate for ranking portfolios that are normally distributed.

COMPATIBILITY OF RISK MEASURES WITH STOCHASTIC DOMINANCE CRITERIA

In this section we consider the compatibility of risk measures with stochastic dominance criteria. In a recent survey of the risk measurement literature, Albrecht (2003) subsumes risk measures under two broad categories: (1) risk as the magnitude of deviations from a target and (2) risk as a measure of the overall seriousness of possible losses. In the second category, risk is regarded as the capital that must be added to a position to make it riskless. The two categories are linked in the sense that the first can be used as a basis for determining the capital requirement in the second.

With respect to the first category, risk measures can be two sided or one sided. Since the work of Markowitz (1952), variance (standard deviation) has been the traditional two-sided measure of risk. The theoretical arguments against using the mean-variance approach for ranking investments center on the properties of a quadratic utility function (which exhibits increasing and absolute risk aversion) and a normal distribution of returns. These two-sided risk measures assign the same weight to both positive and negative deviations from the expected value, which contradicts the notion that investors view risk as negative deviations from an expected value. Further, variance does not capture kurtosis in the underlying distribution of returns, which is needed if investors wish to incorporate the risk of low probability–high loss events in their assessment of investment alternatives.

Lower partial moments (LPM) are a general class of risk measures where risk is measured in terms of negative deviations from a predetermined loss threshold or target rate of return. For continuous distributions, LPMs are measured as follows:

$$\text{LPM}(n,t) \int_{-\infty}^{t} (t - x)^n f(x)dx \ n > 0,$$

where t is the target rate of return, x are the outcomes of the probability distribution, and $f(x)$ is its density function. The exponential variable n is the degree of the lower partial moment and represents the weight that an investor places on negative deviations from the target. The exponential variable thus allows the LPM to describe below-target risk in terms of the risk tolerance of the investor.

Bawa (1975) provides a proof of the mathematical relationship between lower partial moments and stochastic dominance for risk tolerance levels of $n = 0, 1,$ and 2, with higher orders of n corresponding to greater risk aversion on the part of investors. Fishburn (1977) also provides theoretical support for using lower partial moments to capture the utility functions of specific investors. Specifically, these authors show that LPM_0 is applicable to all utility functions showing nonsatiety ($u' > 0$), and that this is analogous to FSD rules. Further, they show that LPM_1 is consistent with all risk-averse functions ($u' > 0, u'' < 0$), and that this is analogous to SSD rules, while LPM_2 is consistent for all risk-averse functions displaying skewness preference ($u' > 0, u'' < 0, u''' > 0$), and this corresponds to TSD rules.

The findings of Bawa (1975) and Fishburn (1977) are significant in our search for risk measures that are compatible with the risk preference function of the center of the bank because they indicate consistency between specific risk measures and nth-order stochastic dominance criteria. The strong relationship between risk measures based on lower partial moments and stochastic dominance concepts is significant given that stochastic dominance criteria apply to a general class of utility functions and make no assumptions regarding the distribution of portfolio returns. Our earlier conclusion that TSD represents the most applicable criteria for ranking alternative investment portfolios in the bank setting suggests that lower partial moments of order $n > 1$ may be a more relevant family of risk measures for the center of the bank. The key research question is: would risk measures based on higher order lower partial moments lead managers and/or agents in banks to select the portfolios that the center would have them select in the presence of perfect information? In order to address this question, we examine a range of risk measures within the general class of lower partial moments.

Drawing on the findings of Bawa (1975) and Fishburn (1977), we begin with the following definition:

Definition: A *risk measure* $\rho(X)$ is consistent with nth-order stochastic dominance, and consequently expected utility maximization, when portfolios can be ranked by nth-order stochastic dominance. Specifically, for portfolios X_1 and X_2: $X_1 \, SD_{(n)} \, X_2 \rightarrow \rho(X_1) \leq \rho(X_2)$.

This means that if one portfolio X_1 stochastically dominates another portfolio X_2, the risk measure for X_1 will be lower than for X_2 and the expected utility deriving from portfolio X_1 will exceed that from X_2.[19] Further, a risk measure that is consistent with $(n+1)$th-order stochastic dominance is also consistent with nth-order stochastic dominance. This means a risk measure consistent with higher order stochastic dominance will be more applicable than a risk measure consistent with lower order stochastic dominance.

Next, we establish criteria under which a risk measure $\rho(X)$ incorporates losses in the tail of a distribution beyond a specified threshold. Using the definition of the Bank for International Settlements (2000), *tail risk* arises when the probability of returns for one investment has a greater risk of larger losses than another investment, where both distributions have equal means.[20] Tail risk is applicable whenever bank stakeholders are concerned with the size of losses in the event that losses exceeded a predetermined level. We established earlier that bank creditors, depositors, and regulators are more likely to be concerned with the size of losses in the event of default (tail risk), whereas managers and owners are likely to be more concerned with the probability of losses given their personal losses are linked to default itself and are invariant to the size of losses.

---

[19] See Levy (1998, Theorem 3.2) for a proof.
[20] Bank for International Settlements (2000, p. 8).

With respect to a risk measure $\rho(X)$ and the degree of tail risk in the distribution of a portfolio, we put forward the following proposition:

Proposition: *If beyond a specified loss threshold, a portfolio X_1 has lower expected losses than another portfolio X_2, then the risk measure $\rho(X_1)$ should be lower than the risk measure $\rho(X_2)$.*

This requires that our risk measures should differentiate among portfolios in terms of their tail risk. It remains to establish how a risk measure can be categorised in terms of its ability to capture specific degrees of tail risk in a loss distribution.

First, let us consider the most restrictive case. If an investor is concerned only that the *probability of loss* for one portfolio X_1 is less than the probability of loss for another portfolio X_2, then the cumulative distribution function for portfolio X_1 will always lie to the right of the cumulative distribution function for portfolio X_2. In other words, the cumulative distribution functions for the portfolios under consideration should not cross. As discussed earlier, this implies a positive first derivative for the utility function of the investor.

Under these conditions we can say for a risk measure $\rho(X)$, at a given loss threshold (t), that $\rho(X_1) < \rho(X_2)$ if $F_1(x) \leq F_2(x)$, for all x, $x \leq t$, where $F_1(x)$ and $F_2(x)$ are the cumulative distribution functions for X_1 and X_2. Notably, this is consistent with portfolio X_1 dominating portfolio X_2 in terms of FSD principles. Risk measures that fit into this category we denote "Type 1" risk measures.

Next, consider the case of an investor who is concerned not only with the probability of losses, but also the *size of losses* should a certain loss threshold (t) be exceeded. If an investor is concerned that the average losses for portfolio X_1 be less than the average losses for portfolio X_2, for a given loss threshold (t), then the accumulated area under the cumulative distribution function for portfolio X_1 must be less than the accumulated area under the cumulative distribution function for portfolio X_2. Unlike the first case above, this means that the cumulative density functions can cross, and this in turn is consistent with portfolio X_1 dominating portfolio X_2 according to SSD principles. Further, in addition to increasing wealth preference, this implies the investor is risk averse (negative second derivative for the utility function).

Under these conditions we can say for a risk measure $\rho(X)$, at a given loss threshold (t), that $\rho(X_1) < \rho(X_2)$ if

$$\int_{-\infty}^{t} (t-x) f_1(x) dx \leq \int_{-\infty}^{t} (t-x) f_2(x) \, dx \ \text{ for all } x, x \leq t$$

where $f_1(x)$ and $f_2(x)$ are the density functions of X_1 and X_2. Risk measures that fit into this category we denote "Type 2" risk measures.

Finally, consider an investor who perceives a low probability of a large loss to be riskier than a high probability of a small loss, even when expected losses are the same. In addition to increasing wealth preference and risk aversion on the part of the investor, this condition also encapsulates a preference for positive skewness in the portfolio distribution and is consistent with a negative third derivative for the utility function of the investor.

Drawing on this, let two portfolios, X_1 and X_2, have equal means and equal average losses beyond a given loss threshold (t). Furthermore, portfolio X_2 has a small probability of large losses beyond the threshold, while portfolio X_1 has a larger probability of small losses beyond the threshold. If an investor displays a preference for positive skewness in the distribution of portfolio returns, we can say for a risk measure $\rho(X)$, that $\rho(X_1) <$ $\rho(X_2)$ if the following holds:

$$\int_{-\infty}^{t} (t-x)^{(n-1)} f_1(x) dx \leq \int_{-\infty}^{t} (t-x)^{(n-1)} f_2(x) dx \ \text{ for all } x, x \leq t$$

where $f_1(x)$ and $f_2(x)$ are the density functions of X_1 and X_2 and $n > 2$.

This condition employs the lower partial moment of degree $(n-1)$ to penalize large deviations from the loss threshold more than smaller deviations from the loss threshold. This differs from the previous condition, which implicitly assumed that investors have a linear response to losses beyond the threshold. Where $n = 2$, this condition is equal to the previous condition. When $n = 3$, this condition places a quadratic penalty on deviations below the loss threshold[21] and is consistent with portfolio X_1 dominating portfolio X_2 according to TSD principles. Risk measures that fit into this category, where $n = 3$, we denote "Type 3" risk measures.

---

[21] Higher order powers $(n > 3)$ place even larger penalties on wider deviations from the loss threshold. For example, $n = 4$ places a cubic penalty on deviations below the loss threshold.

We summarize each risk measure category in Table 5.1.

T A B L E   5.1

Category of risk measures

Risk Measure Category	Characteristics	Stochastic Dominance Compatibility	Implicit Risk Attitude
Type 1	The investor is concerned with probability of loss beyond a given threshold.	FSD	Nonsatiety
Type 2	Investor is concerned with probability of losses and the average size of losses beyond a given threshold.	SSD	Nonsatiety and risk aversion
Type 3	Investor is concerned with probability of losses, the average size of losses and larger deviations more than smaller deviations from a given threshold.	TSD	Nonsatiety, risk aversion, and positive skewness

RISK MEASURES

The risk measures under consideration are based on statistics of the loss distribution of a portfolio over some predetermined time horizon. These measures are the shortfall probability, VaR, expected shortfall, first-order lower partial moment (LPM_1), and the second-order lower partial moment (LPM_2).

Shortfall probability is the probability that the return on a portfolio will fall below the prespecified target level. Shortfall probability is measured by the zero-order lower partial moment (LPM_0), which is the integral of the unweighted return distribution. Shortfall probability is the relevant risk measure for an investor who is only interested in the probability of falling short of the prespecified target return, ignoring the extent or severity of the shortfall should it eventuate.

Value at risk is defined as the loss that will not be exceeded over a certain time period with a specified confidence level (α). Put differently, the VaR of an investment is the loss that will be exceeded only with a given probability $(1 - \alpha)$ over a specified measurement period. Value at risk is closely related to shortfall probability through the cumulative distribution function. If the VaR is designated as the benchmark for measuring shortfall, the probability that losses exceed the VaR level corresponds to the shortfall risk measure.[22] In terms of our earlier defined criteria, VaR and shortfall probability correspond to Type 1 risk measures.

The determination of economic capital in a bank is consistent with the VaR concept of estimating the distance between expected and unexpected outcome. The VaR confidence level is scaled to the critical threshold level for determining the amount of economic capital deemed necessary to protect the bank against adverse events. In the desire that banks monitor and manage the size of lower-tail outcomes so that the probability of financial distress is low, regulators have adopted VaR as the standard for measuring risk for determining bank capital adequacy. Szegö (2002) notes that the second consultative paper of the new Basel Accord assumes the VaR concept as the risk measure for deriving minimum capital standards and requires in its solution that the risk of each loan must be portfolio invariant.[23] Further, the Accord requires that regulatory capital for each loan must be correlated to its marginal contribution to the VaR.[24]

Expected shortfall is defined as the conditional expectation of loss given that the loss is beyond the VaR level.[25] Thus, by definition, expected shortfall measures losses beyond the VaR level. In terms of our earlier criteria, expected shortfall corresponds to a Type 2 risk measure. If investors (and regulators) are concerned not with the potential loss that would occur at a specified confidence level but rather with the severity of losses beyond the VaR level, the expected shortfall may be considered to be a more suitable measure of risk than the VaR.

The LPM_1 measures the weighted average deviation from the target level. First-order lower partial moment is related to the expected shortfall risk measure in that it provides the expected loss relative to the loss

---

[22] See Schroder (1997) for a mathematical derivation.
[23] See Szegö (2002, p.1258).
[24] See Szegö (2002, p.1259).
[25] Other names for expected shortfall in the literature include *tail conditional expectation, tail* VaR, *conditional* VaR, and *conditional loss*.

threshold or benchmark return. Like expected shortfall, LPM_1 corresponds to a Type 2 risk measure in terms of our criteria.

While LPM_1 and expected shortfall produce the same measure of risk for losses beyond the loss threshold, the LPM_1 risk measure has a significant advantage over expected shortfall, namely, while expected shortfall (like VaR) is usually measured in terms of a specific loss quantile, the LPM_1 can be calculated based on deviations from zero ($t = 0$). This enables the full distribution of losses to be taken into consideration in the risk measure, rather than expected losses beyond the loss threshold. If investors are concerned with all losses (or below target returns) rather than those that are greater than the loss threshold, then the LPM class of risk measures, with $t = 0$, represents more complete measures of risk.

It is worth highlighting the implications of the above from the perspective of external regulatory risk measures. If regulators are concerned only with protection against bankruptcy, then a VaR measure may be appropriate. If regulators, however, are concerned that a bank be sufficiently capitalized to cover the size of losses in the event of bankruptcy (losses beyond the predetermined loss threshold), then expected shortfall is a more relevant risk measure for regulatory purposes. What of smaller losses below the loss threshold, being losses that occur with a less than (α) confidence interval? A regulatory risk measure based on VaR or expected shortfall implicitly assumes that losses that are less than the threshold are self-insured by the bank or that the bank can efficiently recapitalise in the event that it needs to raise equity to cover these unexpected losses. If, however, a bank frequently suffers losses less than the threshold, it may find insurance or recapitalization costly, particularly in times of economic slowdown where loan losses are likely to be larger and equity recapitalisation more expensive.

The lower partial moment class of downside risk measures incorporates all losses into the measure, both above and below the predetermined confidence interval, when the target is set at ($t = 0$). Risk measures that focus either on the probability of losses (VaR) or extreme losses (expected shortfall) fail to capture the likely systemic impact of banks incurring frequent losses below the predetermined loss threshold. If regulators determine that bank capital requirements should be based on either of the above measures of unexpected losses, then they are ignoring the potential for loss in confidence in the banking system if banks do incur frequent unexpected losses below the threshold and subsequently find it difficult to recapitalise. In these circumstances, LPM_1 (or a higher order LPM risk measure) is likely to be more appropriate than VaR or expected shortfall for determining bank capital requirements.

The LPM_2 places a quadratic penalty on deviations below the threshold ($n = 2$). Formally, LPM_2 represents the semivariance or lower partial variance (Markowitz, 1959), and the square root of the lower partial variance represents the downside standard deviation. By placing a larger penalty on larger losses, LPM_2 corresponds to a Type 3 risk measure in terms of our criteria.

Like LPM_1, when the target level from which deviations are measured is set to cover all losses ($t = 0$), LPM_2 captures in the risk measure smaller unexpected losses that are not included in measures based on loss thresholds linked to predetermined confidence intervals (such as VaR and expected shortfall). This means that unlike VaR and expected shortfall, the LPM_2 risk measure does not create an incentive for portfolio managers to take actions that increase the cumulative distribution function for losses that are smaller than the loss threshold. Such actions would increase the risk of the portfolio but would not be captured in risk measures that base losses relative to a loss threshold. Managers may be motivated to take such actions to increase the risk-adjusted return on their portfolios and increase their remuneration where bonuses are linked to such measures. Risk measures that are based on the full distribution of losses should entice such gaming on the part of managers.

EXAMPLE

Table 5.2 presents the probability distributions for five hypothetical credit portfolios and the accompanying risk measures.

The portfolios that form the investment opportunity set have the same expected value, allowing measurement of the risk of the portfolios independently from their expected return. The portfolios increase in risk from A to E in accordance with TSD principles. If managers are remunerated based on the risk-adjusted performance measure (RAPM) for the portfolios under their control, they should be incentivised to select the

T A B L E   5.2

Portfolios and risk measures

	Probability Distributions				
Portfolio				D	E
Market Value					
0					
30				0.4%	0.5%
60	1%	1%	1%		
90			2.5%	0.6%	0.5%
97	5%	7.5%	5%	5%	10%
98	15%	10%	10%	10%	6%
99	30%	32.5%	30%	40%	25%
100	40%	40%	40%	41%	53%
101	5%	5%	5%	2%	4%
102	3%	3%	3%		1%
103	1%	1%	1%		
104					
105					
106			2.5%	1%	
Expected value	98.99	98.99	98.99	98.99	98.99
Risk Measures					
1. $LPM_0(98.99)$	0.210	0.185	0.185	0.160	0.170
2. VaR 99%	38.99	38.99	38.99	8.99	8.99
3. ES 99%	38.99	38.99	38.99	32.99	38.99
4. $LPM_1(98.99)$	0.6379	0.6382	0.8132	0.5284	0.6483
5. $LPM_1(99.01)$	0.6451	0.6451	0.8199	0.5356	0.6542
6. $LPM_2(98.99)$	15.547	15.597	17.519	19.819	24.657

portfolios that have the lowest risk measure in the denominator. Risk measures that fulfil this requirement will be those that increase in size for portfolios that are dominated in accordance with TSD conditions. Our aim is to test for the risk measures that promote congruency between the goals of the center of the bank and the decisions of managers with respect to the selection of credit portfolios. Any risk measures that increase in size from A to E conform to this requirement.

The probability of shortfall (LPM_0) is measured at a loss threshold that is equal to the expected value of each portfolio at $98.99. The results show that this measure is not congruent with SSD or TSD because the lowest risk portfolio according to stochastic dominance principles, portfolio A, has the largest risk measure in terms of shortfall probability. Indeed, a manager who wishes to maximize the risk-adjusted return on a credit portfolio would find portfolio A the *least* attractive investment if shortfall probability is used as an internal risk measure. A second observation is that the evaluation of portfolio risk according to shortfall probability tends to induce behavior on the part of managers that is consistent with a risk-seeking utility function. Perversely, managers will have a risk-based preference to select the least attractive portfolios from the perspective of the center of the bank, given these portfolios generate the highest expected risk-adjusted returns. This arises because the lower partial moment of order $n < 1$ gives less weight to larger deviations from the reference point.

The VaR for each portfolio is measured at a 99 percent confidence level, where the basis for measuring losses is the $98.99 expected value. The results indicate that like shortfall probability, VaR is not incentive-compatible with the risk preference function of the center of the bank. The figures suggest that VaR is not congruent with SSD or TSD criteria because portfolios A, B, and C carry the same VaR metric at the 99 percent confidence level, indicating the portfolios carry the same risk, while these portfolios are increasing in risk in terms of SSD and TSD. Of potentially greater concern is the fact that the VaR for portfolios D and E at the 99 percent confidence level is lower than for portfolios A, B, and C, yet portfolios D and E are the riskiest portfolios in terms of SSD and TSD criteria. This arises because $VaR_{(99\%)}$ fails to capture the greater tail risk in portfolios D and E—both portfolios have a small probability of larger losses than portfolios A, B, and C. Further, the $VaR_{(99\%)}$ fails to identify the greater risk in portfolio E relative to D. These results arise because VaR fails to incorporate losses beyond the predetermined loss threshold (the selected confidence interval).

Expected shortfall (ES) captures losses beyond the VaR level, and in particular, extreme losses that could prove catastrophic for the bank. The ES for each portfolio is measured at the 99 percent confidence level where the basis for measuring losses is the expected value of each portfolio of

$98.99. The results show that ES is not compatible with the ranking of the portfolios according to SSD and TSD, arising because the risk attitude implicit in ES is risk neutrality—ES gives equal weight to loss quantities below the α quantile. This means that it makes no difference as to the dispersion of losses in the left tail of the distribution—if the average of the losses are equal, the ES of the portfolios will also be equal. This clearly runs counter to the characteristics of risk measures that are compatible with TSD. The risk-neutral attitude implicit in the ES measure indicates that like VaR, ES may lead managers to engage in manipulations in the lower tail of the distribution, such that a portfolio with greater tail risk may be misrepresented as one with equal or lower risk. This action may lead to an overstatement of the risk-adjusted return on the portfolio, with the intention to increase the probability or size of bonuses paid to managers.

The LPM_1 is measured at a loss threshold that is equal to the expected value of each portfolio at $98.99. The results show that this measure is not compatible with stochastic dominance principles. Specifically, LPM_1 is inefficient with respect to the risk ranking of portfolios D and E relative to portfolios A, B, and C because LPM_1 fails to recognise the greater tail risk in portfolios D and E—like expected shortfall, LPM_1 embodies a risk-neutral stance with respect to the deviation of losses beyond the threshold. The order of one for the power function means LPM_1 also only captures average losses beyond the threshold and thus does not distinguish between large losses with a small probability of occurrence and smaller losses carrying a large probability of occurrence. This contradicts the assumption of risk aversion and positive skewness preference inherent in risk ordering by TSD. Further, note that a small change in the target threshold from $98.99 to $99.01 results in a change in the risk ordering of the portfolios according to LPM_1 showing the measure is dependent on the choice of target threshold.

The LPM_2 is measured at a loss threshold that is equal to the expected value of each portfolio at $98.99. The results show that LPM_2 is congruent with SSD and TSD. This arises because the LPM_2 risk measure includes all losses that occur beyond the target level (which includes the entire distribution of losses if the target threshold is set at zero), and it places greater weight on larger deviations from the target threshold, even though average losses may be the same. An assessment of the incentive compatibility of LPM_2 rests with consideration of whether the measure is dependent on the target threshold. Threshold dependence in the LPM_1 measure arises because, as discussed, losses are treated equally in the calculation of the LPM_1 regardless of their size. However, if a portfolio F dominates a portfolio G by SSD and $LPM_1(F) = LPM_1(G)$, then it must always hold that $LPM_2(F) < LPM_2(G)$ because the quadratic power function in LPM_2 places a greater weight on larger deviations from the loss threshold. This is where compatibility between SSD and LPM_2 arises: a risk-averse investor will place greater emphasis on larger tail losses than smaller tail losses. We conclude that LPM_2 is not dependent on the target threshold.

CONCLUSION

If regulators or ratings agencies deem that total bank capital should be measured in terms of a target solvency standard, which in turn is based on the probability of the bank defaulting on its debt, then the internal risk measure must diverge from the external measure of risk, where the objective of the internal measure is to achieve a disciplined and consistent analysis of risk based on the entire distribution of potential outcomes. Risk measures that are based on the probability of default display a risk-neutral attitude towards risk, which (questionably) may apply to managers and shareholders but not to regulators and creditors for whom the economic impact of default is more directly related to the size of losses in the event of default. If bank capital exists to protect bank creditors, risk measures used internally for pricing and performance measurement should be based on losses in the event of default, rather than the probability losses.

Shortfall probability, VaR, ES, and LPM_1 are not incentive-compatible risk measures if the risk preference function for the center of the banking firm is characterized by risk aversion. The use of these measures in the dominator of a RAPM may induce managers to select portfolios that are dominated in terms of TSD criteria. Value at risk, ES, and LPM_1 also display dependence on the target threshold, meaning changes in the threshold for these measures can impact on the risk ordering of portfolios. The LPM_2 risk measure is compatible with TSD and provides a risk ordering of portfolios that is incentive compatible. The measure also provides a consistent risk ordering independent of the target loss threshold.

Should we be concerned if the basis for measuring risk within the bank differs from the risk basis for determining external capital? While alignment is desirable, we argue that it is acceptable to use different measures where the objectives differ. It may not be desirable, or possible, for a risk measure to satisfy competing objectives—different measures may be needed to meet the specific requirements under consideration. We have shown that the objectives of insuring against default and aligning incentives do not allow for a common risk measure.

With respect to the internal measurement of risk, we assert that the overriding objective is to use risk measures that align the interests of the diverse group of bank stakeholders—creditors, depositors, managers, owners, and regulators. It does not necessarily follow that the actual allocation of capital across portfolios should be based on these risk measures. Our argument is that a risk-adjusted performance measure that forms the basis for determining bonuses and other forms of compensation to managers must, in the presence of information asymmetries, be incentive compatible with the objective function of the bank. This risk measure need not reflect the actual capital held or allocated against the portfolio, particularly when external capital requirements are based on other objectives, such as achieving a desired external credit rating. The bank can apportion its actual capital against various portfolios in order to insure the portfolios against default, within the predetermined confidence level. However, the apportionment of actual capital held by the bank, when based on risk measures that are not coherent or compatible with TSD principles, may result in investment decisions that are inefficient with respect to the risk preference function of the center of the bank. It is for this reason that we argue that the risk basis for allocating actual capital can and must differ from the risk basis for measuring the performance of managers within the bank.

REFERENCES

Albrecht, P. (2003) Risk Measures. Working paper (No. 03–01), University of Mannheim, Germany.

Bank for International Settlements. (2000) Stress Testing by Large Financial Institutions: Current Practice and Aggregation Issues. Committee on the Global Financial System, Basel, April.

Bank for International Settlements (2001a) The Internal Ratings-Based Approach. Basel Committee on Banking Supervision, Basel, January.

Bank for International Settlements (2001b) Quantitative Impact Study: Frequently Asked Questions. Basel Committee on Banking Supervision, Basel, May.

Bank for International Settlements (2004) International Convergence of Capital Measurement and Capital Standards: A Revised Framework. Basel Committee on Banking Supervision, Basel, June.

Bank for International Settlements (2005) International Convergence of Capital Measurement and Capital Standards: A Revised Framework. Basel Committee on Banking Supervision, Basel, November.

Bawa, V. (1975) Optimal Rules for Ordering Uncertain Prospects. *Journal of Financial Economics*, Vol. 2, No.1, pp. 95–121.

Fishburn, P. (1977) Mean-Risk Analysis with Risk Associated with Below-Target Returns. *The American Economic Review*, Vol. 67, No. 2, pp. 116–126.

Hadar, J. and W. Russell (1969) Rules for Ordering Uncertain Prospects. *American Economic Review*, Vol. 59, No.1, pp. 25–24.

Hanoch, G. and H. Levy (1969) The Efficiency Analysis of Choices Involving Risk. *Review of Economic Studies*, Vol. 36, No.3, pp. 335–346.

Heyer, D. (2004) Stochastic Dominance: A Tool for Evaluating Reinsurance Alternatives. *Casualty Actuarial Society Forum*, Vol. 71, No.4, pp. 95–117.

Levy, H. (1998), *Stochastic Dominance: Investment Decision Making Under Uncertainty.* Boston, MA: Kluwer Publishers.

Levy, H. and G. Hanoch (1970) Relative Effectiveness of Efficiency Criteria for Portfolio Selection. *Journal of Financial and Quantitative Analysis*, Vol. 5, No.,1 pp. 63–76.

Levy, H. and M. Sarnat (1970) Alternative Efficiency Criteria: An Empirical Analysis. *Journal of Finance*,Vol. 25, No.5, pp. 1153–1158.

Markowitz, H. (1952a) Portfolio Selection. *Journal of Finance*, Vol. 7, No.1, pp. 77–91.

Markowitz, H. (1959) *Portfolio Selection: Efficient Diversification of Investments*. New York: John Wiley & Son.

Martin, J., S. Cox, and R. MacMinn (1998) *Theory of Finance: Evidence and Applications*. New York: Dryden.

Rothschild, M. and J. Stiglitz (1970) Increasing Risk: A Definition. *Journal of Economic Theory*, Vol. 2, No.3, pp. 225–243.

Schroder, M. (1997) The Value-at-Risk Approach: Proposals on a Generalisation. In Sue Grayling (ed.), *VaR: Understanding and Applying Value-at-Risk*. London: Risk Publications.

Szegö (2002) Measures of Risk. *Journal of Banking and Finance*, Vol. 26, No.7, pp. 1253–1272.

Whitmore, G. (1970) Third-Degree Stochastic Dominance. *The American Economic Review*, Vol. 60, No. 3, pp. 457–459.

CHAPTER 6

The Asset–Liability Management Compound Option Model: A Public Debt Management Tool[1]

Jorge A. Chan-Lau and André O. Santos

ABSTRACT

This chapter describes the asset-liability management compound option model introduced in Chan-Lau and Santos (2008). The model is useful for public debt management, but also for debt sustainability analysis, and, more generally, for asset-liability management in financial institutions. This model also helps fixed-income investors to establish price benchmarks for sovereign debt.

INTRODUCTION

Public debt management in emerging market countries has witnessed profound changes. In particular, sovereign borrowing has shifted increasingly toward arms-length financing through the issuance of government bonds. The rapid growth of assets under management of institutional investors, especially pension funds, and the implementation of sound macroeconomic

---

[1] This chapter draws from Chan-Lau and Santos (2008).

and fiscal policies in most countries have enabled governments to gain access to international markets and to establish domestic government bond markets successfully.

Sound public debt management should follow six principles.[2]

1. The objectives of debt management should be aligned with those of monetary and fiscal policy.

2. There should be adequate transparency and accountability enforced through the disclosure of relevant risk measures and the allocation of responsibilities.

3. The institutional framework should clarify the legal issues related to debt management, ensure clear roles and responsibilities, and develop an adequate data framework.

4. The debt structures should be easy to monitor and cost efficient, while minimizing liquidity and repayment risk.

5. There should be an appropriate risk-management framework in place that accounts for the contingent liabilities of the government.

6. The debt-management strategy should foster an efficient government securities markets.

Sound public debt management, however, is ultimately an operational issue. Therefore, it is necessary to provide debt managers with practical tools to meet the high standards set by the policy guidelines above. This chapter describes a new tool introduced in Chan-Lau and Santos (2008), the asset-liability management (ALM) compound option model. The rest of the chapter is structured as follows. This chapter's second section explains the advantages of the ALM compound option model over alternative models, and the third section defines a debt repayment capacity measure consistent with the 2001 IMF Government Finance Statistics (GFS) definitions of the government balance sheet and net worth. The fourth section of this chapter presents the ALM compound option model,

---

[2] See International Monetary Fund and International Bank for Reconstruction and Development (2003).

which is used in the fifth section to analyze the risk profile of New Zealand's public debt. Finally, the sixth section indicates how the ALM compound option model can be extended to incorporate jumps, stochastic interest rates, stochastic volatility, lines of credit with embedded options, government guarantees, and other risks. The last section summarizes our conclusions.

CONCEPTUAL FOUNDATIONS OF THE MODEL

The ALM compound option model is based on the pricing model for compound options introduced by Geske (1977). As in the simpler one-period option-based models, the basic intuition underlying the model is that the value of the public sector net worth in a multiperiod setting is equivalent to the value of an option on an option on the total assets the government holds. The compound option pricing model, however, is better suited for analyzing and evaluating the risk profile of a sovereign's public debt than one-period option-based models currently being used or being proposed in multilateral and national agencies.

One-period option-based models, built on the work of Black and Scholes (1973) and Merton (1974), attempt to extend the insights derived from the capital structure of a corporate issuer to a sovereign issuer. The models' implications for the analysis of public debt are hampered by difficulties in the definition and measurement of the net worth of the public sector. For corporate issuers, it is possible to back assets of the firm by using its equity price value and volatility. However, this is not the case for the public sector. In addition, practical public debt management requires examining the cash flow and currency composition structure of the debt profile.[3] The original terms of the debt contracts, hence, are not secondary factors in the risk analysis of a given debt profile. In consequence, one-period approximations may be impractical for applications, technical assistance, or even policy advice.

In the ALM compound option model, the one-period restriction is relaxed as the debt maturity and the timing of the cash flows associated

---

[3] For instance, short-term debt can be rolled over.

to interest rate and principal payments is explicitly accounted for in the model.[4] In this multiperiod setup, the debt issuer has the option to default at every debt repayment period. The decision to default depends on whether the call option on the asset value of the firm held by the debt issuer, or the net worth of the debt issuer, is "out of the money." In the context of public debt management, the net worth of the debt issuer is equivalent to the expected value of the current and future resources available to the debt agency or government to service the debt in a timely manner.

In contrast to one-period models, the value of the call option in any period depends on the value of the call options in subsequent periods. By necessity, the ALM compound option model focuses on the cash-flow aspects of the debt profile from an ALM perspective rather than attempting to stretch the corporate capital structure analogy to a sovereign issuer. The inclusion of the time dimension in the ALM compound option model can help debt managers to identify, to monitor, and to control the risks associated to different fiscal policy stances (Togo, 2007). For instance, debt managers can use the ALM compound option model to assess whether the asset growth rate associated with different primary surplus scenarios is consistent with the asset and liability matching needs.

As in the case of the macroeconomic approach to debt sustainability, the ALM compound option model takes into account the intertemporal nature of the debt structure and defines public debt as sustainable, if the growth and proceeds from total assets are enough to finance future coupon and principal payments. As in the case of option-based models, however, our model improves on the macroeconomic approach, since it uses market information from the market prices of government securities, or other assets and liabilities, to derive the risk-neutral default probabilities of a given debt profile. Finally, the compound option approach is flexible enough to incorporate other extensions, such as stochastic interest rates, stochastic volatility, and jumps, as we explain in detail in the following section.

---

[4] While the intuition builds on the Geske (1977) model, his closed form solution to the two-period problem cannot accommodate realistic debt profiles. Numerical solutions are required, as explained in the section The ALM Compound Option Model.

THE GOVERNMENT BALANCE SHEET AND NET WORTH

The measurement of the repayment capacity of the public sector needs to be consistent with the definition of public sector net worth, as defined in the 2001 IMF GFS Manual. This is accomplished by defining the repayment capacity in terms of the public sector intertemporal budget constraint definition presented in Easterly and Yuravlivker (2000).

The 2001 GFS Manual emphasizes that the public sector net worth should be the "preferred measure" for fiscal sustainability analysis. The 2001 GFS Manual, which is consistent with the United Nations' National System of Accounts, defines *net worth* as the difference between assets and liabilities at market prices and includes both financial and nonfinancial assets and liabilities. Changes in net worth occur as a result of (1) budgetary transactions, such as the collection of taxes, social contributions, grants, and other revenues or the payment of salaries, goods, subsidies, grants, social benefits, interest, depreciation, and other expenses; (2) price effects (holding gains); and (3) changes in the volume of assets and liabilities other than transactions arising from exceptional or normal events (earthquakes, floods, wars, and natural resources discoveries and depletions, etc.) and account reclassifications.

Easterly and Yuravlivker (2000) use a definition of the public sector intertemporal budget that is consistent with the concept of net worth outlined in the 2001 GFS Manual. Table 6.1 shows what asset and liability items are included in the public sector balance sheet, including contingent liabilities arising from deposit insurance, pension fund schemes, and government debt guarantees to the private sector.[5] The public sector intertemporal budget constraint then requires that the present value of the operating balance, which is government expenditures minus revenues—excluding interest revenues and expenses—be less than or equal to the government's net worth.

From the public sector balance sheet, it follows that taxpayers are the government's shareholders. On the one hand, taxes are equivalent to an increase in the participation of taxpayers in the public sector equity

---

[5] Contingent assets, such as credit lines to the private sector, can also be included in the government balance sheet.

T A B L E   6.1

Public sector balance sheet

Assets	Liabilities
Government-owned public goods (infrastructure, schools, health clinics, etc., that generate an adequate ERR and an indirect ERR through tax collection)*	Public external debt
Government-owned capital that is financially profitable (anything for which government can charge user fees to generate adequate ERR).	Public domestic debt
Value of government-owned natural resource stocks (oil, minerals, etc.).	Domestic contingent liabilities (e.g., bank deposit guarantees, net present value of pension schemes, guarantees of private debt).
Expected present value of loans to private sector	Government's net worth

* ERR stands for economic rate of return.

through retained earnings.[6] On the other hand, whenever the government buys good and services or grants subsidies to taxpayers (or to the society, in general), net worth declines accordingly as if dividends were distributed to taxpayers. In the hypothetical case that the government was to be liquidated, the remaining resources after selling the government assets and repaying bondholders and banks would be used to continue providing goods, services, and subsidies to taxpayers. Taxpayers, hence, are the residual claimants or government shareholders.[7]

Because taxpayers are the government shareholders, both the domestic and external debt should be considered in the public sector debt sustainability and asset and liability management analysis. Identifying only domestic bondholders as residual claimants is incorrect and can lead to the underestimation of the health of the government's financial conditions. This problem is compounded by the fact that emerging market countries have reduced substantially the amount of external debt outstanding due to easier market access and increased risk appetite for domestic debt among foreign investors.

---

[6] Indeed, the New Zealand public sector balance sheets include the item "taxpayer fund" in net worth to account for the operating balance in a fiscal year.

[7] Debt restructurings are more complex than this simplified description since bondholders and taxpayers share the restructuring burden. Usually, debt restructuring is conditioned on the adjustment programs as taxes are raised and expenditures reduced.

THE ALM COMPOUND OPTION MODEL
Model Intuition

Debt with multiple payments can be viewed as a compound option, or in other words, as an option on an option. Starting with Black and Scholes (1973) and Merton (1974), it has been recognized that the equity value of a leveraged firm is equivalent to a call option on the value of the firm's assets, where the strike price is associated to the face value of the debt owed by the firm. Geske (1977) and Geske and Johnson (1984) generalize this intuition by allowing multiperiod debt payments. For simplicity, this section focuses on a two-period setting.

Let T_i, $i = 1, 2$ be the payment dates, and for each date, T_i, M_i is the coupon and principal payment due, V_i is the value of the government's assets, and S_i is the value of taxpayer's equity, which is an option on an option. At date T_2, the option not to default is "in the money" if the market value, V_2, is larger than the coupon and principal payments, M_2. At date T_1, this option of not defaulting at date T_2 has a present value equivalent to $C(V_1)$ that depends on the market value V_1 of government's total assets. The government defaults if the present value of the compound option $C(V_1)$ is worth less than the debt payments M_1 at date T_1. Finally, the option of not defaulting at date T_1 has a present value equal to $C(V_t)$ at date t, $t < T_i$, $i = 1, 2$. From the discussion in the section The Governance Balance Sheet and Net Worth, it follows that $S_t = C(V_t)$.[8]

The term structure of default probabilities is enough to capture the default risk of the government. Denote the probability that the government may default before or at date T_i, $I = 1, 2$, by $PD(T_i)$. In our two-period setting the term structure is simply given by $PD(T_1)$ and $PD(T_2)$, and by bootstrapping, it is possible to calculate the one-period forward default probability of default, $PD(T_2|T_1)$, that measures the probability of default between dates T_1 and T_2 conditional on the event of no default at date T_1.

The intuition carries over if the government has both domestic and foreign currency-denominated liabilities. Under a floating exchange rate

---

[8] The compound option model of Geske (1977) requires that the process governing the market value V_t of the government's total assets be continuous at any point in time. In the two-period setting above, this implies that on the first expiration day T_1, the coupon payment M_1 is refinanced by extra retained earnings or new taxes.

regime, the value of the coupon and principal payments in local currency depends on the behavior of the exchange rate.[9] In other words, the compound option is a function of two state variables, the value of the government's assets and the exchange rate. If the public sector debt is denominated exclusively in foreign currency, the two-period setting could be reduced to the compound exchange option of Carr (1998).

If the public sector debt comprises both domestic and foreign-currency-denominated debt, the analysis is more complex. If there is only one debt payment date, the payoff is the difference between the value of the government's total assets and the debt service payment and is equivalent to a spread option.[10] This is not the case in a two-period setting: at date T_1, the value of the option not to default at date T_2, $C(V_1)$, needs to cover both domestic and external debt service payments. Unfortunately, there are no analytical solutions for such an option and Monte Carlo simulation methods should be used.

The Two-Period Case

Geske (1977) and Geske and Johnson (1984) offer an analytical solution to the compound option and, therefore, the value of the taxpayers' equity, S_t. For the public sector, the value, S_t, of the taxpayers' equity at date t is also the price of an option on an option. Under a risk-neutral probability measure, the value of the government's assets, V_t, follows a stochastic differential equation given by

$$\frac{dV_t}{V_t} = r dt + \sigma dW_t, \qquad (6.1)$$

where r is the constant risk-free interest rate, σ is the instantaneous variance of the value of government's total assets, and W_t is a standard Wiener process. The analytical solution for the taxpayers' equity value can then be written as

---

[9] In a fixed exchange rate regime, even though the domestic currency is pegged to a foreign currency, there still exists the exchange rate risk in the different currency composition of the liabilities. For instance, the value of the U.S. dollar or the euro moves against other currencies coupled with some reduction in the net present value of the debt.

[10] See Carmona and Durrleman (2003).

$$S_t = V_t N_2\left(k_1 + \sigma\sqrt{T_1 - t}, k_2 + \sigma\sqrt{T_2 - t}, \rho\right) -$$
$$M_2 e^{-r(T_2-t)} N_2\left(k_1, k_2, \rho\right) - M_1 e^{-r(T_1-t)} N\left(k_1\right),$$ (6.2)

where

$$k_1 = \frac{\ln\left(V_t/\bar{V}\right) + \left(r - \sigma^2/2\right)\left(T_1 - t\right)}{\sigma\sqrt{T_1 - t}},$$

$$k_2 = \frac{\ln\left(V_t/M_2\right) + \left(r - \sigma^2/2\right)\left(T_2 - t\right)}{\sigma\sqrt{T_2 - t}},$$

$$\rho = \sqrt{\frac{T_1 - t}{T_2 - t}},$$

$N_1(.)$ is the standard cumulative normal distribution function, $N_2(.)$ is the standard cumulative bivariate normal distribution function, ρ is a correlation coefficient, and $\bar{V}$ is the value of government's total assets such that

$$\bar{V} - M_1 = \bar{V}N_1\left(k_2 + \sigma\sqrt{T_2 - T_1}\right) - M_2 e^{-r(T_2-T_1)} N_1\left(k_2\right) - M_1.$$ (6.3)

The existence of an analytical solution to the compound option requires that the first coupon payment M_1 be refinanced by the issuance of new equity on the first expiration day T_1. This is equivalent to extra retained earnings or new taxes in a public sector context and implies no drop in the market value V_1 of government's total assets, which remains continuous across T_1.

Along the same lines, analytical solutions to the market values of coupon and principal payments M_1 and M_2 can also be derived from the previous equations and the balance sheet constraint. The value at date t of the coupon and principal payments M_1 at date T_1, $B_{1,t}$, is equal to the sum of its discounted value and the discounted expected value of government's total assets if the coupon payment M_1 is not paid:

$$B_{1,t} = M_1 e^{-r(T_1-t)} N\left(\bar{d}_2\right) + V_t N\left(-\bar{d}_1\right),$$ (6.4)

where

$$\bar{d}_1 = \frac{\log(V_t/M_1) + (r + \sigma^2/2)(T_1 - t)}{\sigma\sqrt{T_1}},$$

$$\bar{d}_2 = \bar{d}_1 - \sigma\sqrt{T_1 - t}.$$

In turn, the value, $B_{2,t}$, at time t of the principal payment M_2 is the sum of its discounted value given that there is no default at T_1 and T_2, the discounted expected value of the government's total assets in case of default, and any payment at time T_1 after the coupon payment M_1 is paid out:

$$B_{2,t} = M_2 e^{-r(T_2 - t)} N_2(k_1, k_2, \rho) + V_t N_2\left(k_1 + \sigma\sqrt{T_1 - t}, -k_2 - \sigma\sqrt{T_2 - t}, -\rho\right)$$
$$+ V_t\left[N\left(-k_1 - \sigma\sqrt{T_1 - t}\right) - N\left(-\bar{d}_1\right)\right] - M_1 e^{-r(T_1 - t)}\left[N\left(-\bar{d}_2\right) - N(k_1)\right]. \quad (6.5)$$

Equations (6.2) to (6.5), which also hold in a multiperiod setting, are used to derive the term-structure of risk-neutral probabilities of default and the one-period forward probabilities of default.[11] The term structure consists of the joint probability $PD(T_2)$ of defaulting either on the first or the second maturity dates T_1 or T_2:

$$PD(T_2) = 1 - N_2(k_1, k_2; \rho), \quad (6.6)$$

and the short-term marginal probability $PD(T_1)$ of defaulting on the first maturity day T_1:

$$PD(T_1) = 1 - N(k_1). \quad (6.7)$$

Finally, the one-period forward probability $PD(T_2|T_1)$ of defaulting on the second maturity day T_2 conditional on not defaulting on the first maturity day T_1:

$$PD(T_2 | T_1) = 1 - \frac{N_2(k_1, k_2; \rho)}{N(k_1)}. \quad (6.8)$$

---

[11] See Delianedis and Geske (2003) for more details.

T A B L E   6.2

Greeks for compound options

$$\partial S_t / \partial V_t = N_2 \left(k_1 + \sigma \sqrt{T_1 - t}, k_2 + \sigma \sqrt{T_2 - t}; \sqrt{(T_1 - t)/(T_1 - t)} \right) > 0,$$

$$\partial S_t / \partial M_2 = -e^{-r(T_2 - t)} N_2 \left(k_1, k_2; \sqrt{(T_1 - t)/(T_1 - t)} \right) < 0,$$

$$\partial S_t / \partial M_1 = -e^{-r(T_1 - t)} N(k_1) < 0,$$

$$\frac{\partial S_t}{\partial r} = \frac{N_2(\cdot)}{N_1\left(k_2 + \sigma\sqrt{T_2 - t}\right)} M_2 (T_2 - t) e^{-r(T_2 - t)} N_1 (k_2) > 0,$$

$$\frac{\partial S_t}{\partial \sigma^2} = \frac{N_2(\cdot)}{N_1\left(k_2 + \sigma\sqrt{T_2 - t}\right)} M_2 e^{-r(T_2 - t)} N_1'(k_2) \frac{\sqrt{T_2 - t}}{2\sigma} > 0,$$

$$\frac{\partial S_t}{\partial T_2} = \frac{N_2(\cdot)}{N_1\left(k_2 + \sigma\sqrt{T_2 - t}\right)} M_2 e^{-r(T_2 - t)} \left[N_1'(k_2) \frac{\sigma}{2\sqrt{T_2 - t}} + r N_1(k_1) \right] > 0,$$

$$\partial S_t / \partial T_1 > 0.$$

Source: Geske (1977).

Geske (1977) also derives the sensitivity of the market value of the tax-payer's equity S_t to changes in the option parameters. Table 6.2 below summarizes his results. The market value S_t rises in response to an increase in the market value of government's total assets V_t and its volatility σ, the risk-free interest rate r, and the two expiration days T_1 and T_2. On the other hand, the market value, S_t, declines as the payments M_1 and M_2 increase.

Multiperiod Extension through Least-Squares Monte Carlo Simulation

We use Longstaff and Schwartz (2001) least-squares Monte Carlo (LSMC) simulation method to solve for the equity value, the term structure of default probabilities, and the one-year forward default probabilities of the multiperiod ALM compound option model.[12] One advantage of using LSMC

---

[12] While an analytical formula for the multiperiod problem can be derived, its numerical solution requires the cumbersome computation of a cumulative multinormal distribution, using numerical integration techniques that do not converge easily.

simulation is that it also helps to estimate the Greeks. The sensitivity of the probabilities of default to the parameters listed above can be obtained through finite differences approximations with an optimal perturbation size.[13]

The LSMC simulation method is based on the idea that least squares can estimate the continuation value of the conditional expected payoff in an American Option. At each small time interval, the option holder compares the continuation value of the option with the payoff from the immediate exercise of the option. The continuation value is given by a projection of the discounted payoffs on a set of orthogonal bases. If the payoff from the immediate exercise of the option is larger than the continuation value, the option holder exercises the option. The procedure is then repeated backward for each Monte Carlo path from the maturity date up to the initial period, as in a dynamic programming exercise in continuous time. Optimal stopping times and continuation values are found for each Monte Carlo path, and the price of the American option is then a simple average of the discounted continuation values.

The LSMC simulation method is not affected by the upward or high bias associated to the use of plain Monte Carlo simulation for pricing American options. The bias arises from the fact that the recursive procedure for estimating the continuation value of the option, which determines whether the option should be exercised, uses information only from the paths for which continuation is an optimal strategy. Plain Monte Carlo simulation, therefore, leads to superoptimal exercising strategies, since it "knows" the future. The upward bias can be solved by interleaving high-bias and low-bias estimators obtained, using stochastic mesh methods, such as the LSMC, where the low-bias estimator is obtained by following a defined stopping rule.[14]

AN EXAMPLE: RISK ANALYSIS OF NEW ZEALAND'S GOVERNMENT DEBT

This section analyzes the debt sustainability and the asset and liability management of the New Zealand Crown, as of end of June 2006 in this section. The New Zealand Crown has used accrual accounting since 1999

---

[13] Glasserman (2004).
[14] See Broadie and Glasserman (2004).

and has implemented the 2001 IMF GFS Manual since 2004. While assets in the New Zealand Crown balance sheets are recorded at their fair value, borrowings are booked at their nominal value. As a result of sound fiscal policy and cautious public debt management, the New Zealand sovereign debt is rated "AA+" by Standard & Poor's and "Aaa" by Moody's.

For the analysis, we obtain annual data on balance sheets, operating balances, domestic and external debts, pension benefits, and accident compensation claims from publications available on the web.[15] In regards to the projections for debt service items, pension benefits, and accident compensation claims, some approximations and assumptions were needed. The results, therefore, only illustrate how the ALM compound option model can be used in debt sustainability analysis and for asset and liability management.

Projections for the debt service (before any currency swap effects), pension benefits, and accident compensation claims are plotted in Figure 6.1 for the first 12 fiscal years. Debt payment dates range from 2007 to 2018 (or 12 fiscal years), while pension benefit and accident compensation claim dates extend from 2007 to 2031 (or 26 fiscal years).[16] The domestic debt consisted of Kiwi and government bonds, treasury bills, and loans while the external debt included U.S. dollar, euro, yen, British pound, Norwegian krona, and Australian dollar-denominated sovereign bonds converted into New Zealand dollar at end of June 2006 exchanges rates. Treasury bills represented most of the short-term debt, which comprises a large share of the debt due by the end of fiscal year 2007.

The New Zealand government has taken a proactive role in its asset and liability management using derivatives transactions such as currency and interest rate swaps, foreign exchange and interest rate futures, and options. In particular, through the use of currency swap arrangements, the government increased the relative share of foreign currency-denominated debt flows and benefited from the strengthening of the domestic currency. The use of currency swaps yielded a net positive fair value of NZ$669.5 million in June 2006.

---

[15] The New Zealand public sector consists of the Core Crown, Crown entities, state-owned enterprises, and intersegment elements.

[16] Quarterly or monthly projections would have been possible also if debt service projections were prepared accordingly.

F I G U R E   6.1

New Zealand: Core Crown debt service, GFS pension
benefits, and ACC claims, end of June 2006 (in billions
of New Zealand dollars)

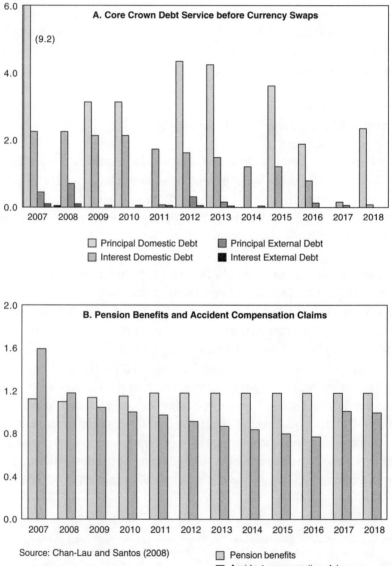

Source: Chan-Lau and Santos (2008)

Contingent liabilities such as pension benefits and accident compensation claims that are partially funded with public resources can affect the probabilities of default. In the case of New Zealand, these contingent liabilities correspond to the Government Superannuation Fund (GSF) and the Accident Compensation Corporation (ACC). The projections in Figure 6.1 were based on publicly available information and incorporate assumptions for years when data were incomplete. As before, the caveat is that current projections are only for illustrative purposes to show how other contractual obligations affect the probabilities of default.

The market value of the government's total assets, V_t, and its volatility, σ, are not directly observable in financial markets and, therefore, need to be estimated. We assume that the risk-free interest rate r over a year is equal to the 7.45 percent LIBOR rate in June 2006. Given the risk-free interest rate, the annual debt service projections M_1 to M_{12} for the period June 2007 to June 2018, and the pension benefit and compensation claim projections for the period June 2007 to June 2031, Equations (6.2), (6.4), and (6.5) can be solved simultaneously for V_t, $\bar{V}$ and σ. As an alternative approach, we use the fair value of total assets V_t in the Core Crown balance sheet and approximate its associated volatility σ by the observed volatility in the Core Crown operational balance excluding financial costs and pension expenses.[17] The fair value of total assets V_t amounted to about NZ$102.3 billion in June 2006 and the maximum likelihood estimate for the standard deviation σ of the annual changes in the operating balance excluding financial costs and pension expenses in the period 2000 to 2006 was equivalent to 19.7 percent.

Movements in exchange rates are an extra risk factor in the balance sheet as total assets move in tandem with the exchange rate and the domestic-currency value of the foreign currency-denominated debt becomes a random variable. To simplify our analysis, we consider only the direct impact of movements in the USD/NZD exchange rate on the foreign-currency-denominated debt. The market value of the exchange

---

[17] The maximum likelihood estimate for the annual volatility of the Core Crown total assets was at about 5.2 percent. The corresponding term structure of default probabilities was flat and equal to zero. This is consistent with the zero default rates over a 10-year period published by Moody's and Standard & Poor's.

rate at end of June 2006 was NZD/USD 1.6494 and the maximum likelihood estimates for its volatility and correlation with total assets were equal to 14.8 and −39.3 percent, respectively, in the period 2000 to 2006.

Table 6.3 summarizes the results from performing 100,000 LSMC simulations for different definitions of contractual obligations—including only debt in one definition and adding pension benefits and accident compensation claims to it in the second definition—under the effects of one-risk and two-risk factors—namely, the Core Crown total asset growth and the NZD/USD floating exchange rate. Figure 6.2 plots the corresponding term structure of default probabilities and the one-year forward probabilities of default. Note that the fair value of the Core Crown debt in Table 6.3 is larger than the booked value in June 2006.

When debt is the only contractual obligation (columns 3 and 5 in Table 6.3), the model successfully approximates the fair values of the Core Crown liabilities and equity. Our associated term structures of probabilities of default in Figure 6.2 are positively sloped over the period 2007 to 2018. However, the rate of increase of the joint probabilities of default declines with time in line with declines in the one-year forward probability of default. When debt is the only contractual obligation, the term structure of

T A B L E   6.3

New Zealand: Core Crown balance sheets, June 2006
(in billions of New Zealand dollars)

			One Risk Factor*		Two Risk Factors†	
	Book Value (1)	Fair Value (2)	Debt (3)	Debt, GFS and ACC (4)	Debt (5)	Debt, GFS and ACC (6)
Assets	102.3	102.3	102.3	102.3	102.3	102.3
Liabilities	62.2	63.3	64.6	60.0	65.1	60.9
Borrowings	34.5	35.6	36.8	—	37.3	—
ACC and GFS	27.7	27.7	27.7	—	27.7	—
Net Worth	40.1	39.0	37.7	42.3	37.2	41.4

*Core Crown total assets as the only risk factor
†Core Crown total assets and exchange rate as risk factors
Source: Authors' calculations.

F I G U R E   6.2

New Zealand: Core Crown probabilities of default, end of
June 2006 (in percentage)

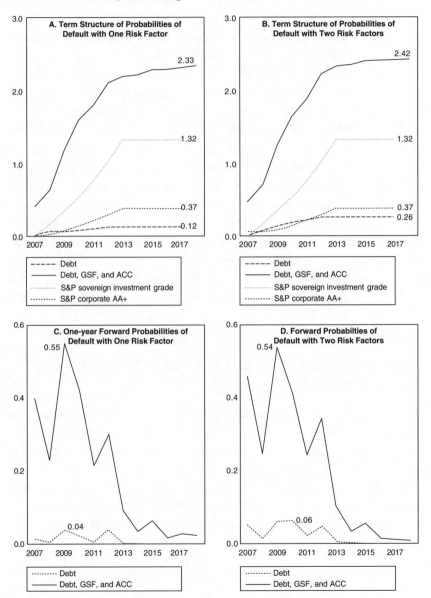

Source: Chan-Lau and Santos (2008)

the probability of default is very close to the term structure of AA+ corporate default rates reported by Standard & Poor's for the period 1981 to 2006.[18] This result suggests that the ALM compound option model is well calibrated.

Adding the exchange rate risk and other contractual obligations to the analysis yields new insights about the debt sustainability of the New Zealand Core Crown. The exchange rate and the fair value of Core Crown total assets have a negative correlation, which has a negative impact on the taxpayer's equity. The negative correlation reduces the total volatility of the Core Crown total assets and the value of the option not to default on both the domestic and foreign debt. Taxpayers lose equity value as Core Crown total assets' volatility declines. Finally, when pension benefits and accident compensation claims are matched by assets in the Core Crown balance sheets, they are exempt from default by the government. However, as part of contractual obligations, the option of not defaulting on pension benefits and accident compensation claims has a positive value for the taxpayer. Therefore, the estimated net worth, including pension benefits and accident compensation claims as contractual obligations (columns 4 and 6 in Table 6.3), is larger than government guaranteed obligations with matched assets.

EXTENSIONS OF THE ALM COMPOUND OPTION MODEL

The ALM compound option model presented above assumes continuous asset prices, constant asset volatility, and a flat term structure of interest rates. These assumptions, while helpful for simplifying the analysis, may not reflect well the main characteristics of events and/or scenarios relevant to public debt managers. For instance, assuming a flat term structure of interest rates may be too restrictive for long-term planning. This section explains possible extensions to the basic ALM compound option model presented above.

---

[18] Standard & Poor's cumulative average sovereign default rates for AA+ borrowers were zero for all years in the period 1975 to 2006.

Discontinuous Market Values

The assets held in the government balance sheet may experience abrupt changes in their market value due to account reclassifications, normal events such as natural resources discoveries and depletions, or exceptional events such as earthquakes, floods, and wars. These price disruptions can be assessed by extending the model to allow for asset dynamics that are governed by jump diffusions, as in Gukhal (2004).

Stochastic Interest Rates

Assuming a flat term structure of interest rates may not be adequate for long-term analysis for at least two reasons. First, the risk-free interest rate, or short-term interest rate, changes through time. Second, under usual business conditions, long-term debt payments should have a higher discount rate due to the time value of money. The ALM compound option model can be extended along the lines of Chen (2003). Chen incorporates a Gaussian short-term interest rate model, consistent with those of Vasicek (1977), Ho and Lee (1986), and Hull and White (1990), to the Geske (1977) model while allowing the short-term interest rate and the asset value to be correlated. Another alternative is to incorporate an arbitrage-free model of the term structure, such as the one proposed by Heath et al. (1992), in the basic Geske (1977) model, and as done by Frey and Sommer (1998).

Stochastic Volatility

One of the main characteristics of asset prices, widely documented in the empirical literature, is that volatility is highly persistent: periods of large price changes tend to be followed by periods of large price changes and vice versa. The time-varying nature of volatility can be built into the ALM compound option model using results available in the literature, as in Buraschi and Dumas (2001).

Lines of Credit with Embedded Options

Governments may have access to lines of credit from banks that contain either explicit or implicit extendible options, that is, options to extend the maturity of obligations coming due in exchange for an additional fee. In other instances, the lines of credit may allow banks to extend the debt maturity in the event that the sovereign faces difficulties repaying the debt coming due, enabling the government to make the necessary fiscal adjustments to repay its debt at a posterior date. The extendible option is valuable when the value of the assets held by the government is less than the face value of its short-term debt obligations and the economic fundamentals are such that it is better for the government and its creditors to avoid default on the short-term debt. The ALM compound option model can incorporate this type of credit lines by building on the analytical solutions on extendible options presented in Longstaff (1990).

Government Guarantees

Government guarantees are equivalent to a put option where the option holder has the right to sell back the underlying asset at par to the government at a predetermined date. In the case of deposit insurance, the latter protects depositors from a fall in the banking system's assets arising, for instance, from an increase in loan defaults by the corporate sector. The fall in the banking system's assets is partially offset by an increase in the deposit insurance guarantee, transferring risks from the corporate and banking sectors to the government. In the government balance sheet, the value of its contingent liabilities increases and reduces net worth—or the market value of taxpayer's equity [see Merton and Bodie (1992) and Draghi et al. (2003)].

Other Sources of Risk

If most changes in government balance sheets result from budgetary transactions, it might be also important to single out the effect of particular risks on the government balance sheet. For instance, if tax revenues are related directly or indirectly to commodity prices, then changes in the latter are an important risk factor for both the market value of government's assets and its net worth. Therefore, by applying Ito's lemma, changes in the market value of assets can be written as a function of commodity prices.

CONCLUSION

Sound public debt management can only be accomplished if debt managers have the needed tools for understanding, measuring, and managing the risks associated to the government balance sheet. This chapter proposes such a tool, the ALM compound option model. The model is useful not only for public debt management but also for debt sustainability analysis and, more generally, for asset–liability management in financial institutions and fixed-income investors interested in establishing price benchmarks for sovereign debt.

The ALM compound option model builds on the options approach to credit risk analysis and the intertemporal macroeconomic approach to debt sustainability. It goes beyond the standard option approach assumption of a single debt payment, however, since it accounts for the fact that sovereign debt profiles involve multiple debt payments. Specifically, our model builds on the compound options model of Geske (1977), where default can be interpreted as an option on an option to buy back the debt at each debt payment date at a discount. The two-period setting of the original model by Geske is extended to a multiperiod setting through the use of the LSMC simulation method introduced by Longstaff and Schwartz (2001).

In contrast to the macroeconomic approach to debt sustainability, the ALM compound option model uses market information, as it incorporates the information contained in the market prices of sovereign debt. Finally, we want to note that the model can be extended easily in a number of directions to incorporate features such as stochastic interest rates and volatility, discontinuous prices, and extendible options.

REFERENCES

Black, F. and M. Scholes (1973) The Pricing of Options and Corporate Liabilities. *Journal of Political Economy*, Vol. 81, No. 3, pp. 637–654.

Broadie, M. and P. Glasserman (2004) A Stochastic Mesh Method for Pricing High-Dimensional American Options. *Journal of Computational Finance*, Vol. 7, No. 4, pp. 35–72.

Buraschi, A. and B. Dumas (2001) The Forward Valuation of Compound Options. *Journal of Derivatives*, Vol. 9, No. 1, pp. 1–10.

Carmona, R. and V. Durrleman (2003) Pricing and Hedging Spread Options. *SIAM Review*, Vol. 45, No. 4, pp. 627–685.

Carr, P. (1998) The Valuation of Sequential Exchange Opportunities. *Journal of Finance*, Vol. 43, No. 5, pp. 1235–1256.

Chan-Lau, J.A. and A.O. Santos (2008) Asset and Liability Management: New Tools and Applications to Public Debt Management. Washington, DC (unpublished).

Chen, R. (2003) *The Extended Geske-Johnson Model and Its Consistency with Reduced Form Models*. Mimeograph, Rutgers University, Newark, NJ.

Delianedis, G. and R. Geske (2003) Credit Risk and Risk Neutral Default Probabilities: Information about Rating Migrations and Defaults. *EFA 2003 Annual Conference Paper* No. 962, Philadelphia, PA.

Draghi, M., F. Giavazzi, and R.C. Merton (2003) Transparency, Risk Management, and International Financial Fragility. *Geneva Reports on the World Economy*, No. 4, London: Center for Economic Policy Research; Geneva: International Center for Monetary and Banking Studies.

Easterly, W. and D. Yuravlivker (2000) *Treasury or Time Bombs? Evaluating Government Net Worth in Colombia and Venezuela.* World Bank, mimeo, Washington, DC.

Frey, R. and D. Sommer (1998) The Generalization of the Geske-Formula for Compound Options to Stochastic Interest Rates is not Trivial—A Note. *Journal of Applied Probability*, Vol. 35, No.2, pp. 501–509.

Geske, R. (1977) The Valuation of Corporate Liabilities as Compound Options. *Journal of Financial and Quantitative Analysis*, Vol. 12, No. 4, pp. 541–52.

Geske, R. and H. E Johnson (1984) The Valuation of Corporate Liabilities as Compound Options: A Correction. *Journal of Financial and Quantitative Analysis*, Vol. 19, No. 2, pp. 231–232.

Glasserman, P. (2004) *Monte Carlo Methods in Financial Engineering*, Berlin: Springer-Verlag.

Gukhal, C.R. (20040 The Compound Option Approach to American Options on Jump-Diffusions. *Journal of Economic Dynamics and Control*, Vol. 28, No. 10, pp. 2055–2074.

Heath, D., R. Jarrow, and A. Morton (1992) Bond Pricing and the Term Structure of Interest Rates: A New Methodology for Contingent Claim Valuation. *Econometrica*, Vol. 60, No.1, pp. 77–105.

Ho, Thomas S. Y. and S. Lee (1986) Term Structure Movements and Pricing Interest Rate Contingent Claims. *Journal of Finance*, Vol. 41, No. 5, pp. 1022–1029.

Hull, J. and A. White (1990) Pricing Interest-Rate-Derivatives Securities. *Review of Financial Studies*, Vol. 3, No. 4, pp. 573–592.

International Monetary Fund and International Bank for Reconstruction and Development. (2003) *Guidelines for Public Debt Management*, International Monetary Fund. Washington, DC.

Longstaff, F.A. (1990) Pricing Options with Extendible Maturities: Analysis and Applications. *Journal of Finance*, Vol. 45, No. 3, pp. 935–957.

Longstaff, F.A. and E.S. Schwartz (2001) Valuing American Options by Simulation: A Simple Least-Squares Approach. *Review of Financial Studies*, Vol. 14, No. 1, pp. 113–147.

Merton, R.C. (1974) On the Pricing of Corporate Debt: the Risk Structure of Interest Rates. *Journal of Finance*, Vol. 29, No. 2, pp. 449–470.

Merton, R.C. and Z. Bodie (1992) On the Management of Financial Guarantees. *Journal of the Financial Management Association*, Vol. 21, No. 4, pp. 87–109.

Togo, E. (2007) Coordinating Public Debt Management with Fiscal and Monetary Policies: An Analytical Framework, Working paper, World Bank Policy Research, Washington, DC.

Vasicek, O. (1977) An Equilibrium Characterization of the Term Structure. *Journal of Financial Economics*, Vol. 5, No.2, pp. 177–188.

CHAPTER 7

A Practitioner's Critique of Value-at-Risk Models

Robert Dubil

ABSTRACT

In this critical mathematical review of the value-at-risk (VaR) research, we show that the focus on distributional simplifications, linear options approximations, variance modeling, and heteroskedasticity does not help the VaR practitioner deal with the efficient loss value sampling faced by a bank with thousands of positions, hundreds of risk factors, various derivatives with nonlinear cross-termed factor exposure, and autocorrelated factor returns with changing implied volatilities and cross-correlations. Our numerical examples bring out issues and point to possible avenues of inquiry.

INTRODUCTION

Most value-at-risk (VaR) literature focuses on value and distribution approximations and mostly ignores the institutional setting of VaR computation: a typical financial institution's portfolio has thousands of positions in many markets and hundreds of risk factors (prices, yields, spreads, volatilities) driving the firm's VaR. As positions are priced daily, the pricing models are readily available and approximations are not necessary.

What becomes critical is an efficient sampling method of the present value space in the multidimensional factor space.

To shape the discussion, we review the VaR fundamentals, starting with a single asset linear in normally distributed returns, and adding complexity step by step: a number of assets, the type of assets (linear/nonlinear in risk factors), and the probability distribution of prices and yields. The distribution assumption often forces the implementation: normal Monte Carlo simulation vs. nonparametric historical bootstrap. We cover the related issues of covariance modeling. We end with the portfolio of positions whose present values are nonlinear in underlying prices (options in stock prices or FX rates) or risk factors (corporate bonds in yields, spreads), with the factors following arbitrary multivariate distributions. We offer theoretical discussion of pitfalls and use numerical examples to illustrate typical results. We focus on the practicalities of implementing VaR in a large bank with an implicit objective to convince the reader that the only realistic alternatives even for a small to medium size institution is a large scale, numerically intensive, nonlinear, revaluation-based, multivariate Monte Carlo simulation or historical bootstrap.[1] The simple (univariate, linear) and intermediate (delta-normal) cases serve as elegant theoretical constructs but are vastly inadequate.

DEFINITION OF VAR

A firm starts with the initial wealth W_0 equal to the value of its portfolio. After a holding period d, it can end up with random wealth $\tilde{W}$. The change in the portfolio value

$$\tilde{P} = \tilde{W} - W_0 \qquad (7.1)$$

is the profit (loss) over the horizon d in today's dollars. We refer to it as the *present value* (PV) function or *profit and loss* (P&L) function. It is a function of J random risk factors, $\tilde{F}, j = 1, \ldots, J$, which may be returns on

---

[1] A Monte Carlo VaR involves estimating parameters from a multivariate distribution of factors, simulating random realizations of the factors, computing PVs, and finding the desired order statistic (95th percentile). In the bootstrap, as the distribution is unknown, the PVs are computed from the historical realizations of the changes in factors.

stocks, commodities, foreign exchange (FX) rates, changes in yields, spreads, implied volatilities, correlations, or other variables with a material impact on the firm's P&L. The P&L of the firm's portfolio is a known, typically numerical, function $P(\cdot)$ of the factors.[2]

$$\tilde{P} = \tilde{P}(\tilde{F}_1, ..., \tilde{F}_J) \tag{7.2}$$

Definition 7.1. In general, *value at risk* (VaR), at a confidence level c, over a given horizon period d, is defined as the critical value P^*, such that the probability that the profit $\tilde{P}$ will be lower or equal to P^* is equal to $C = 1 - c$. That is,

$$C = 1 - c = \text{Prob}\left(\tilde{P} \leq P^*\right) \tag{7.3}$$

There are two givens: the confidence level c, typically equal to 95 or 99 percent, and the time horizon d in years, e.g., one day (1/252), one week (1/52), or two weeks (1/26). The Bank for International Settlements (BIS) requires 10-day 99 percent VaRs with minimum of six months of data.

Value at risk is expressed in dollars, not in probabilities or the number of standard deviations. It allows making statements like "The firm's profit is likely to be above P^* dollars with c percent probability," or "The firm's loss will exceed $|P^*|$ only C percent of the time." Value at risk can be also stated as a critical portfolio value W^*, not its change. The definition can be modified in terms of the probability region for the factors themselves:

$$C = 1 - c = \text{Prob}\left(P\left(\tilde{F}_1, ..., \tilde{F}_J\right) \leq P^*\right) \tag{7.4}$$

This offers the leanest specification for the nonparametric case (a historical bootstrap). In the parametric case, in which the multivariate probability distribution, $\Phi(\cdot)$, and the associated density function, $\phi(\cdot)$, of the factors are given, frequently assumed to be Gaussian and continuous in the factors, one can narrow the definition down to read

$$C = 1 - c = \int ... \int_{P\left(\tilde{F}_1,...,\tilde{F}_J\right) \leq P^*} \phi\left(\tilde{F}_1, ..., \tilde{F}_J\right) d\tilde{F}_1, ..., d\tilde{F}_J \tag{7.5}$$

---

[2] To avoid confusion with $P(\cdot)$, the probabilities of events will be denoted by Prob( ).

This form is a general specification for the Monte Carlo simulation where the pdf function $\phi(\cdot)$ is that of a multivariate normal with a known mean vector and the covariance matrix. The normality assumption delivers a significant simplification at a cost of ignoring well-documented left fat tails in many asset return distributions.

The main feature of the VaR definition is its local focus and one-sidedness. Even though we labor to reconstruct the entire P&L distribution, the VaR percentile statistic is taken from its extreme left tail and ignores the rest of the information.[3] This often leads to unstable VaR estimates given the paucity of data in that region. As most P&L distributions are quite "irregular" in the left tail, it can be beneficial to supplement VaR with another statistic called the *conditional expected loss*, or *expected tail loss* (ETL).

Definition 7.2. The *expected tail loss* (ETL) is the expected loss in a $c\%$ tail event, when the P&L falls below the critical VaR value P^*:

$$ETL = E\left(\tilde{P} \mid \tilde{P} \leq P^*\right) = \int \ldots \int_{P\left(\tilde{F}_1, \ldots, \tilde{F}_J\right) \leq P^*} P\left(\tilde{F}_1, \ldots, \tilde{F}_J\right)$$
$$\phi\left(\tilde{F}_1, \ldots, \tilde{F}_J\right) d\, \tilde{F}_1, \ldots, d\, \tilde{F}_J \tag{7.6}$$

The ETL is slightly more difficult to compute and thus less popular than VaR. The latter is simply read off a sorted table of simulated values or a histogram.

Lastly, for a portfolio of positions whose PVs are all linear in factors (e.g., stocks, commodities), the risk factors are as asset returns. The terminal wealth $\tilde{W}$ becomes

$$\tilde{W} = W_0\left(w_1(1 + \tilde{R}_1) + \ldots + w_J(1 + \tilde{R}_J)\right) \tag{7.7}$$

where $w_1, \ldots, w_J$ are the weights of the initial wealth W_0 invested in each asset and $\tilde{R}_1, \ldots, \tilde{R}_J$ are nonannualized d-period returns on those assets. The P&L function becomes even simpler:

$$\tilde{P} = W_0\left(w_1 \tilde{R}_1 + \ldots + w_J \tilde{R}_J\right) \tag{7.8}$$

---

[3] See the discussion in the section Extreme Value Theory.

The VaR can be defined narrowly as that value P^* for which

$$C = 1 - c = \text{Prob}\left(w_1 \tilde{R}_1 + \ldots + w_J \, \tilde{R}_J \leq \frac{P^*}{W_0} \right)$$

$$= \int \ldots \int_{w_1 \tilde{R}_1 + \ldots + w_J \tilde{R}_J \leq \frac{P^*}{W_0}} \phi\left(\tilde{R}_1, \ldots, \tilde{R}_J \right) d\, \tilde{R}_1, \ldots, d\, \tilde{R}_J$$

(7.9)

A critical return defined as

$$R^* = \frac{P^*}{W_0}$$

(7.10)

can be thought of as the VaR in terms of the return on initial total investment.

While bank regulations do not mandate a VaR definition and/or implementation, they do state that the capital set aside to cover market risks be based on VaR (see the 1996 Amendment to Basel). Many firms also use VaR to allocate business capital and to compute risk-adjusted returns.

DATA

To illustrate the issues that arise in the implementation of each case, we use the same data but vary the composition of the portfolio. The raw data set[4] contains daily closing values for 28 variables in Table 7.1 for the period beginning December 31, 1986 to January 12, 2000.

From the raw data, we compute nonannualized daily and weekly returns for all stocks, FX rates (in dollars per foreign currency), and commodities (in dollars), i.e.,

$$return_t = \frac{price_t - price_{t-1}}{price_{t-1}}$$

(7.11)

and changes in yields for all interest rate, spread and volatility variables, i.e., discrete differentials

$$return_t = yield_t - yield_{t-1}$$

(7.12)

---

[4] The data set was obtained from the Corporate Risk Management group at Merrill Lynch in New York. Special thanks to Erik Banks for the permission to use it and the group analysts for its scrubbing.

T A B L E   7.1

Historical data series description

Category	Series	Description
Equity Indices	eus	S&P 500 stock index
	emx	Banamex bolsa index
	edm	DAX 30 stock index
	ejp	Nikkei 225 stock index
Exchange Rates	xdm	USD/DM FX rate
	xmx	USD/MXN FX rate
	xjp	USD/JPY FX rate
Commodity Prices	coil	WTI oil price
	cgld	Gold price
	cwht	Wheat (spring) price
Interest Rates	ius10	10-year U.S. Treasury yield
	idm10	10-year German Bund yield
	ijp10	10-year Japanese government bond yield
Swap Spreads	sus10s	U.S. swap spread over the 10-year Treasury
	sdm10s	DM swap spread over the 10-year Bund
	sjp10s	JPY swap spread over the 10-year Japanese government bond
	sushy	Average U.S. high yield spread over the 10-year T
Yield Curve Tilts	sus0210	UST 2-year minus UST 10-year yield
	sus3010	UST 10-year minus UST 30-year yield
	sdm0210	DM 2-year Bund minus DM 10-year Bund yield
	sdm3010	DM 10-year Bund minus DM 30-year Bund yield
	sjp0210	2-year Japanese government minus 10-year Japanese government bond yield
	sjp3010	10-year Japanese government minus 30-year Japanese government bond yield
Volatilities	veus	Implied vol on 1m options on S&P
	vedm	Implied vol on 1m options on DAX
	vejp	Implied vol on 1m options on Nikkei
	vecb	Composite CBOE implied vol on 1m options on U.S. stocks
	vius	Implied vol on 1m options on UST 30

The daily return series has 3,400 and the weekly series 680 observations. Tables 7.2 and 7.3 provide summary statistics. Observe that many variables exhibit high kurtosis[5] (fat tails) and the minima fall several std.

T A B L E   7.2

Summary statistics for daily returns series*

	Min	Max	Mean	St. Dev.	Skewness	Kurtosis	1st Percentile	5th Percentile
eus	−0.204139	0.090994	0.000576	0.010170	−2.63	57.57	−0.025408	−0.014340
emx	−0.132990	0.140178	0.001095	0.018072	0.14	10.63	−0.052250	−0.025859
edm	−0.128116	0.075596	0.000547	0.012901	−0.66	11.79	−0.035076	−0.019225
ejp	−0.149009	0.132359	0.000096	0.014046	0.14	12.07	−0.036268	−0.022350
xdm	−0.033974	0.035673	0.000026	0.006736	0.06	5.28	−0.017456	−0.010894
xmx	−0.257312	0.182540	−0.000636	0.010218	−6.40	219.05	−0.026608	−0.008439
xjp	−0.040547	0.079884	0.000145	0.007466	0.85	11.31	−0.017310	−0.010776
coil	−0.331045	0.309707	0.000438	0.025280	−0.57	32.70	−0.064044	−0.034533
cgld	−0.069635	0.076613	−0.000069	0.007463	−0.18	13.94	−0.019750	−0.011974
cwht	−0.115724	0.073937	0.000116	0.014312	−0.17	8.47	−0.038512	−0.021431
ius10	−0.006350	0.003960	−0.000002	0.000614	−0.14	8.91	−0.001625	−0.000910
idm10	−0.003780	0.003260	−0.000001	0.000467	0.47	8.48	−0.001175	−0.000705
ijp10	−0.005330	0.005610	−0.000011	0.000522	0.34	18.59	−0.001325	−0.000720
sus10s	−0.008298	0.008832	0.000000	0.000267	1.97	638.79	−0.000450	−0.000200
sdm10s	−0.003640	0.002620	−0.000001	0.000486	−0.12	6.40	−0.001330	−0.000800
sjp10s	−0.002600	0.001920	−0.000001	0.000391	−0.22	8.02	−0.001205	−0.000600
sushy	−0.009010	0.008250	−0.000001	0.001114	0.09	13.06	−0.003385	−0.001575
sus0210	−0.002960	0.002100	0.000002	0.000358	−0.25	8.29	−0.000940	−0.000560
sus3010	−0.001980	0.001650	−0.000001	0.000201	−0.50	14.45	−0.000605	−0.000290
sdm0210	−0.003460	0.003360	−0.000001	0.000424	−0.14	10.93	−0.001150	−0.000630
sdm3010	−0.003750	0.002940	−0.000009	0.000470	−0.13	9.56	−0.001415	−0.000765
sjp0210	−0.004790	0.005180	−0.000001	0.000441	0.16	21.85	−0.001250	−0.000590
sjp3010	−0.001980	0.001650	−0.000001	0.000201	−0.50	14.45	−0.000605	−0.000290
veus	−4.959898	11.847600	0.001733	0.444737	5.55	161.24	−0.942099	−0.542200
vedm	−126.848100	218.457300	−0.002644	5.030962	19.67	1171.76	−6.496954	−2.845300
vejp	−69.573490	119.819300	0.001466	2.882905	17.27	983.63	−4.331949	−2.059998
vecb	−66.090000	113.820000	0.001741	2.752501	17.02	964.03	−4.145000	−2.019999
vius	−16.488500	16.950500	0.000552	0.750169	2.17	177.23	−1.617101	−0.855300

* Each series runs 3400 observations from 12/31/86 to 1/12/00.

---

[5] Heteroskedasticity is likely responsible for the apparent leptokurtosis.

T A B L E   7.3

Summary statistics for weekly returns

	Min	Max	Mean	St. Dev.	Skewness	Kurtosis	1st Percentile	5th Percentile
eus	−0.153491	0.067215	0.002840	0.020990	−1.04	8.61	−0.051094	−0.034067
emx	−0.181192	0.400000	0.005784	0.047745	0.80	11.27	−0.119961	−0.060752
edm	−0.172059	0.088204	0.002708	0.027758	−0.78	5.98	−0.086418	−0.047008
ejp	−0.103201	0.129066	0.000415	0.029210	0.00	4.86	−0.082176	−0.048334
xdm	−0.075460	0.059385	0.000133	0.015105	−0.10	4.85	−0.040442	−0.022085
xmx	−0.342190	0.065056	−0.003203	0.020672	−8.18	119.82	−0.069491	−0.020882
xjp	−0.062813	0.133637	0.000720	0.016296	1.10	10.31	−0.036505	−0.023397
coil	−0.287335	0.418079	0.001923	0.052385	0.50	11.34	−0.128536	−0.069578
cgld	−0.065380	0.146858	−0.000334	0.017349	0.79	11.72	−0.049659	−0.027497
cwht	−0.118462	0.160251	0.000537	0.030643	0.11	5.44	−0.082323	−0.043293
ius10	−0.008380	0.005030	−0.000008	0.001376	−0.09	5.23	−0.003200	−0.002090
idm10	−0.003570	0.004690	−0.000006	0.001056	0.51	4.59	−0.002540	−0.001445
ijp10	−0.005100	0.005620	−0.000053	0.001150	0.45	6.56	−0.003250	−0.001720
sus10s	−0.001200	0.002200	−0.000002	0.000272	1.02	15.19	−0.000900	−0.000400
sdm10s	−0.002590	0.002600	−0.000005	0.000570	−0.04	5.73	−0.001600	−0.000920
sjp10s	−0.002590	0.002600	−0.000003	0.000577	−0.07	6.11	−0.001700	−0.000920
sushy	−0.009990	0.018390	−0.000003	0.001922	1.31	17.82	−0.004890	−0.002745
sus0210	−0.002930	0.002460	0.000009	0.000716	−0.56	4.57	−0.002260	−0.001255
sus3010	−0.001550	0.001580	−0.000004	0.000381	−0.19	4.73	−0.001120	−0.000665
sdm0210	−0.004130	0.004060	−0.000004	0.000956	−0.23	5.18	−0.002740	−0.001685
sdm3010	−0.005680	0.004780	−0.000045	0.001008	−0.48	8.35	−0.003310	−0.001760
sjp0210	−0.005530	0.005100	−0.000005	0.000938	−0.20	7.69	−0.002520	−0.001460
sjp3010	−0.001550	0.001580	−0.000004	0.000381	−0.19	4.73	−0.001120	−0.000665
veus	−4.032999	9.301500	0.008666	0.833725	2.28	28.56	−1.994499	−1.083699
vedm	−43.703000	91.263800	−0.013221	5.259352	6.78	143.16	−14.663700	−5.172600
vejp	−23.970100	50.056300	0.007329	3.300865	4.63	84.73	−8.653200	−3.590350
vecb	−22.770000	47.550000	0.008706	3.139914	4.54	84.19	−8.219999	−3.440000
vius	−7.977200	13.080000	0.002761	1.304879	1.55	22.05	−2.742100	−1.913600

* Each series runs 680 observations from 12/31/86 to 1/12/00.

deviations below the means. Several series, notably the implied volatilities, exhibit skewness. The tables contain first and fifth percentile statistics, interpolated if falling between data samples.[6] We do not show lag correlations or

---

[6] In the remainder of this chapter, I will show the true order statistics, which are C-percentile uninterpolated values for both normal simulations and historical bootstraps. The differences are insignificant, but illustrate the scarcity of data argument of those who espouse the use of ETL in lieu of VaR.

Q statistics, but we find that several series exhibit autocorrelations at various lags, particularly in daily data.[7]

CASE 1: ONE LINEAR ASSET WITH NORMAL AND NONNORMAL RETURNS

With one asset whose price is observed daily and return is normally distributed, the P&L is linear in and equal to the realization of the factor (return). The VaR defined by Equation (7.9) is simply:

$$C = 1 - c = \text{Prob}\left(\tilde{R} \leq R^*\right) = \int_{-\infty}^{R^*} \phi\left(\tilde{R}\right) d\,\tilde{R} \qquad (7.13)$$

Since $\tilde{R}$ is distributed normally with an annualized mean μ and standard deviation σ, Equation (7.13) can be stated in terms of a standard normal variate z as

$$C = 1 - c = \text{Prob}\left(z < \frac{R^* - \mu\sqrt{d}}{\sigma\sqrt{d}}\right) \qquad (7.14)$$

By picking, from the standard normal with the cumulative distribution function (CDF) $\Phi(\cdot)$, a critical value α, which corresponds to the C percent tail region, i.e., $C = 1 - c = \Phi(\alpha)$, the VaR can be stated explicitly (as a definition):

$$P^* = W^* = W_0 R^* = W_0 (\mu + \alpha\sigma)\sqrt{d} \qquad (7.15)$$

In most implementations the mean is dropped (short horizon), and the definition reduces to

$$P^* = W^* = W_0 \alpha\sigma\sqrt{d} \qquad (7.16)$$

Here, VaR is scaled by time $\sqrt{d}$ making VaR conversions from daily to weekly simple: multiply by the square root of the ratio of times, $\sqrt{5}$ (five business days). However, if daily and weekly covariances are estimated

---

[7] Note that Monte Carlo and historical bootstrap rely on i.i.d. assumptions or model covariances to rectify heteroskedasticity but ignore autocorrelations.

separately, and the data are autocorrelated or nonstationary, then empirically this will not obtain. Value at risk is also scaled by α, making confidence interval conversions simple, e.g., from a 95 to 99 percent multiply by the ratio of αs, e.g., $2.33/1.65$. If we relax normality or independent identically distributed (iid) assumptions, none of the simple equations and conversions materialize.

To illustrate, for each data series, we run separate Monte Carlo simulations with 10,000 samples. Tables 7.4 and 7.5 show the daily and

T A B L E   7.4

Daily univariate Gaussian VaRs and ETLs (10,000 Monte Carlo simulations)

			VaR			ETL		
	Mean	St. Dev.	99%	95%	90%	99%	95%	90%
eus	0.00058	0.01017	−0.02369	−0.01613	−0.01246	−0.02697	−0.02055	−0.01729
emx	0.00110	0.01807	−0.04136	−0.02853	−0.02234	−0.04690	−0.03625	−0.03064
edm	0.00055	0.01290	−0.02918	−0.02074	−0.01618	−0.03335	−0.02591	−0.02205
ejp	0.00010	0.01405	−0.03210	−0.02263	−0.01814	−0.03690	−0.02834	−0.02426
xdm	0.00003	0.00674	−0.01565	−0.01110	−0.00854	−0.01799	−0.01386	−0.01178
xmx	−0.00064	0.01022	−0.02426	−0.01746	−0.01379	−0.02802	−0.02172	−0.01861
xjp	0.00015	0.00747	−0.01683	−0.01227	−0.00944	−0.01951	−0.01514	−0.01295
coil	0.00044	0.02528	−0.05777	−0.04129	−0.03192	−0.06661	−0.05141	−0.04375
cgld	−0.00007	0.00746	−0.01796	−0.01257	−0.00964	−0.02032	−0.01576	−0.01337
cwht	0.00012	0.01431	−0.03305	−0.02387	−0.01834	−0.03761	−0.02954	−0.02522
ius10	0.00000	0.00061	−0.00146	−0.00101	−0.00079	−0.00164	−0.00127	−0.00108
idm10	0.00000	0.00047	−0.00110	−0.00077	−0.00060	−0.00127	−0.00098	−0.00083
ijp10	−0.00001	0.00052	−0.00124	−0.00088	−0.00069	−0.00144	−0.00111	−0.00094
sus10s	0.00000	0.00027	−0.00064	−0.00044	−0.00034	−0.00073	−0.00056	−0.00047
sdm10s	0.00000	0.00049	−0.00115	−0.00080	−0.00062	−0.00132	−0.00100	−0.00085
sjp10s	0.00000	0.00039	−0.00090	−0.00064	−0.00049	−0.00104	−0.00080	−0.00068
sushy	0.00000	0.00111	−0.00253	−0.00183	−0.00144	−0.00294	−0.00228	−0.00195
sus0210	0.00000	0.00036	−0.00084	−0.00059	−0.00045	−0.00098	−0.00074	−0.00063
sus3010	0.00000	0.00020	−0.00048	−0.00033	−0.00026	−0.00055	−0.00042	−0.00036
sdm0210	0.00000	0.00042	−0.00100	−0.00070	−0.00054	−0.00113	−0.00088	−0.00075
sdm3010	−0.00001	0.00047	−0.00109	−0.00079	−0.00062	−0.00124	−0.00098	−0.00084
sjp0210	0.00000	0.00044	−0.00104	−0.00073	−0.00057	−0.00119	−0.00090	−0.00077
sjp3010	0.00000	0.00020	−0.00046	−0.00033	−0.00026	−0.00054	−0.00042	−0.00035
veus	0.00173	0.44474	−1.04794	−0.74191	−0.57084	−1.18257	−0.92997	−0.78844
vedm	−0.00264	5.03096	−11.81575	−8.25566	−6.49043	−13.27852	−10.35275	−8.79719
vejp	0.00147	2.88291	−6.60623	−4.70830	−3.69124	−7.78452	−5.92899	−5.05411
vecb	0.00174	2.75250	−6.42229	−4.55593	−3.51485	−7.40466	−5.74323	−4.86771
vius	0.00055	0.75017	−1.80861	−1.22932	−0.94194	−2.04177	−1.56827	−1.31965

T A B L E   7.5

Weekly univariate Gaissian VaRs and ETLs (10,000 Monte Carlo simulations)

	Mean	St. Dev.	VaR 99%	VaR 95%	VaR 90%	ETL 99%	ETL 95%	ETL 90%	VaR 95%*
eus	0.00284	0.02099	−0.04594	−0.03139	−0.02394	−0.05347	−0.04033	−0.03381	−0.03607
emx	0.00578	0.04775	−0.10639	−0.07302	−0.05525	−0.12002	−0.09308	−0.07819	−0.06380
edm	0.00271	0.02776	−0.06236	−0.04262	−0.03303	−0.07166	−0.05450	−0.04595	−0.04638
ejp	0.00042	0.02921	−0.06860	−0.04834	−0.03673	−0.07913	−0.06094	−0.05133	−0.05060
xdm	0.00013	0.01510	−0.03559	−0.02503	−0.01924	−0.04070	−0.03132	−0.02654	−0.02482
xmx	−0.00320	0.02067	−0.05148	−0.03716	−0.03007	−0.05709	−0.04566	−0.03947	−0.03904
xjp	0.00072	0.01630	−0.03819	−0.02603	−0.02028	−0.04324	−0.03341	−0.02817	−0.02744
coil	0.00192	0.05238	−0.11909	−0.08359	−0.06612	−0.13755	−0.10582	−0.08998	−0.09233
cgld	−0.00033	0.01735	−0.04012	−0.02904	−0.02253	−0.04606	−0.03578	−0.03063	−0.02811
cwht	0.00054	0.03064	−0.07001	−0.04984	−0.03898	−0.08175	−0.06265	−0.05324	−0.05337
ius10	−0.00001	0.00138	−0.00316	−0.00225	−0.00178	−0.00364	−0.00282	−0.00241	−0.00226
idm10	−0.00001	0.00106	−0.00252	−0.00178	−0.00137	−0.00281	−0.00222	−0.00189	−0.00172
ijp10	−0.00005	0.00115	−0.00283	−0.00195	−0.00150	−0.00317	−0.00247	−0.00209	−0.00197
sus10s	0.00000	0.00027	−0.00063	−0.00045	−0.00035	−0.00074	−0.00057	−0.00048	−0.00098
sdm10s	0.00000	0.00057	−0.00134	−0.00095	−0.00073	−0.00154	−0.00118	−0.00101	−0.00179
sjp10s	0.00000	0.00058	−0.00131	−0.00096	−0.00074	−0.00150	−0.00118	−0.00101	−0.00143
sushy	0.00000	0.00192	−0.00450	−0.00319	−0.00243	−0.00507	−0.00398	−0.00336	−0.00409
sus0210	0.00001	0.00072	−0.00165	−0.00117	−0.00091	−0.00191	−0.00146	−0.00125	−0.00132
sus3010	0.00000	0.00038	−0.00087	−0.00062	−0.00049	−0.00099	−0.00078	−0.00066	−0.00074
sdm0210	0.00000	0.00096	−0.00227	−0.00160	−0.00124	−0.00259	−0.00200	−0.00170	−0.00157
sdm3010	−0.00004	0.00101	−0.00238	−0.00170	−0.00133	−0.00269	−0.00211	−0.00181	−0.00177
sjp0210	−0.00001	0.00094	−0.00218	−0.00157	−0.00122	−0.00258	−0.00196	−0.00167	−0.00163
sjp3010	0.00000	0.00038	−0.00088	−0.00063	−0.00049	−0.00101	−0.00078	−0.00067	−0.00074
veus	0.00867	0.83373	−1.91585	−1.37294	−1.05885	−2.16501	−1.69676	−1.45047	−1.65896
vedm	−0.01322	5.25935	−12.17379	−8.56109	−6.68904	−13.82912	−10.68481	−9.11185	−18.46022
vejp	0.00733	3.30086	−7.68973	−5.45983	−4.19956	−8.67103	−6.78577	−5.76244	−10.52808
vecb	0.00871	3.13991	−7.21638	−5.15883	−4.01558	−8.35090	−6.43488	−5.47443	−10.18737
vius	0.00276	1.30488	−3.00074	−2.12445	−1.67147	−3.42672	−2.65766	−2.27045	−2.74884

* Value at risk converted from the 95% daily column in Table 7.6 by multiplying by $\sqrt{5}$.

weekly VaRs and ETL for 99, 95, and 90 percent confidence intervals for portfolios consisting of single $1 linear positions in the underlying factors. For example, a position with $1 exposure per 1-bp move in the 10-year

Bund yield, idm10, incurs a $0.00077 loss 5 percent of the time, and the expected loss in the 5 percent left tail is $0.00098. The normal simulation fails to preserve the fat left tails for nonvolatility series. All the 99 percent VaRs are to the right, and many 95 percent VaRs to the left, of their percentile statistics in Tables 7.2 and 7.3 (simulated vs. historical), and the simulations do not generate the extreme values of the original distributions. The volatility series naturally exhibit kurtosis and right skewness (being bounded below by zero), implying fat right but lean left tails. The normal Monte Carlo exaggerates the left tails showing higher absolute VaRs. For example, the Monte Carlo on *vedm* (most skewed and kurtic), yields the 99 and 95 percent VaRs of -11.81575 and -8.25566 instead of the sample percentile statistics of -6.496954 and -2.845300. The last column in Table 7.5 shows weekly VaRs converted from daily. A comparison with the 95 percent column shows that the conversion does not work very well for many series in our data sample.

Tables 7.6 and 7.7 show the results for historical bootstraps. They preserve the fat left tails. The 95 percent VaR converted from daily looks no worse than in the simulation case.

The comparison of simulations in Tables 7.4 and 7.5 to the historical in Tables 7.6 and 7.7 reveals an 'irregular' behavior of data *precisely* in the region of interest, i.e., in the 5–10th percentile. This is the basis of a body of literature which applies the Extreme Value Theory (EVT) to VaR analysis. The essence of EVT is the modeling of the left tail in lieu of the complete distribution. It relies on limit theorems for order statistics and the maxima of random variables which state that the block maxima generally follow one of three well-specified distributions (Fréchet, Weibull, or Gumbel). The conditional distribution of exceedances (ETLs) can be approximated by the generalized Pareto function. EVT advocates fitting the limit distributions to the left tail to obtain extreme (VaR) or exceedance (ETL) statistics. The advantage is a parsimonious parameterization; the critical disadvantages are no multivariate theory and the inability to handle nonlinear assets. Most authors focus on theory and univariate fitting, and ignore the multifactor aggregation of VaR. See Embrechts et al. (1998), Embrechts (1999), surveys by Smith (1999), and Këllezi and Gilli (2006). Longin (2000) applies EVT to VaR.

T A B L E   7.6

Daily historical bootstrap VaRs and ETLs
(3,400 samples)

	Mean	St. Dev.	VaR			ETL		
			99%	95%	90%	99%	95%	90%
eus	0.00058	0.01017	−0.02545	−0.01437	−0.00944	−0.04249	−0.02313	−0.01737
emx	0.00110	0.01807	−0.05257	−0.02589	−0.01687	−0.07073	−0.04182	−0.03136
edm	0.00055	0.01290	−0.03532	−0.01925	−0.01315	−0.05468	−0.03068	−0.02318
ejp	0.00010	0.01405	−0.03630	−0.02235	−0.01534	−0.04878	−0.03212	−0.02534
xdm	0.00003	0.00674	−0.01753	−0.01090	−0.00762	−0.02245	−0.01512	−0.01215
xmx	−0.00064	0.01022	−0.02680	−0.00847	−0.00499	−0.06011	−0.02231	−0.01445
xjp	0.00015	0.00747	−0.01733	−0.01078	−0.00804	−0.02409	−0.01531	−0.01234
coil	0.00044	0.02528	−0.06407	−0.03456	−0.02368	−0.10673	−0.05704	−0.04281
cgld	−0.00007	0.00746	−0.01980	−0.01199	−0.00792	−0.02925	−0.01769	−0.01378
cwht	0.00012	0.01431	−0.03861	−0.02153	−0.01534	−0.05436	−0.03297	−0.02545
ius10	0.00000	0.00061	−0.00163	−0.00091	−0.00068	−0.00215	−0.00136	−0.00108
idm10	0.00000	0.00047	−0.00118	−0.00071	−0.00051	−0.00151	−0.00101	−0.00080
ijp10	−0.00001	0.00052	−0.00133	−0.00072	−0.00052	−0.00210	−0.00115	−0.00088
sus10s	0.00000	0.00027	−0.00045	−0.00020	−0.00010	−0.00099	−0.00042	−0.00028
sdm10s	0.00000	0.00049	−0.00133	−0.00080	−0.00055	−0.00171	−0.00113	−0.00089
sjp10s	0.00000	0.00039	−0.00122	−0.00060	−0.00041	−0.00157	−0.00096	−0.00072
sushy	0.00000	0.00111	−0.00343	−0.00158	−0.00096	−0.00474	−0.00279	−0.00201
sus0210	0.00000	0.00036	−0.00094	−0.00056	−0.00040	−0.00136	−0.00083	−0.00065
sus3010	0.00000	0.00020	−0.00061	−0.00029	−0.00020	−0.00088	−0.00049	−0.00036
sdm0210	0.00000	0.00042	−0.00116	−0.00063	−0.00044	−0.00174	−0.00099	−0.00076
sdm3010	−0.00001	0.00047	−0.00143	−0.00077	−0.00051	−0.00192	−0.00117	−0.00090
sjp0210	0.00000	0.00044	−0.00125	−0.00059	−0.00040	−0.00184	−0.00101	−0.00075
sjp3010	0.00000	0.00020	−0.00061	−0.00029	−0.00020	−0.00088	−0.00049	−0.00036
veus	0.00173	0.44474	−0.94420	−0.54300	−0.39140	−1.50976	−0.85804	−0.65956
vedm	−0.00264	5.03096	−6.54491	−2.85000	−1.90000	−14.93505	−6.18491	−4.23876
vejp	0.00147	2.88291	−4.43200	−2.06000	−1.35790	−8.78366	−3.99195	−2.81670
vecb	0.00174	2.75250	−4.20000	−2.02000	−1.29000	−8.51118	−3.89694	−2.73979
vius	0.00055	0.75017	−1.62540	−0.85700	−0.59280	−2.67106	−1.43172	−1.06807

T A B L E 7.7

Weekly historical bootstrap VaRs and ETLs (680 samples)

	Mean	St. Dev.	VaR 99%	VaR 95%	VaR 90%	ETL 99%	ETL 95%	ETL 90%	VaR 95%*
eus	0.00284	0.02099	−0.05364	−0.03412	−0.02126	−0.08612	−0.04995	−0.03881	−0.03213
emx	0.00578	0.04775	−0.12821	−0.06079	−0.04461	−0.15286	−0.10065	−0.07648	−0.05789
edm	0.00271	0.02776	−0.08942	−0.04704	−0.03217	−0.10701	−0.06662	−0.05215	−0.04304
ejp	0.00042	0.02921	−0.08776	−0.04834	−0.03520	−0.09536	−0.06680	−0.05364	−0.04998
xdm	0.00013	0.01510	−0.04147	−0.02210	−0.01843	−0.05378	−0.03206	−0.02609	−0.02437
xmx	−0.00320	0.02067	−0.07629	−0.02093	−0.01418	−0.15419	−0.05857	−0.03786	−0.01894
xjp	0.00072	0.01630	−0.03802	−0.02349	−0.01725	−0.04512	−0.03141	−0.02565	−0.02410
coil	0.00192	0.05238	−0.12969	−0.06971	−0.05708	−0.19724	−0.11078	−0.08652	−0.07728
cgld	−0.00033	0.01735	−0.05260	−0.02758	−0.01856	−0.05958	−0.03899	−0.03068	−0.02681
cwht	0.00054	0.03064	−0.08477	−0.04401	−0.03437	−0.10602	−0.06886	−0.05378	−0.04814
ius10	−0.00001	0.00138	−0.00322	−0.00209	−0.00172	−0.00436	−0.00289	−0.00239	−0.00203
idm10	−0.00001	0.00106	−0.00263	−0.00145	−0.00117	−0.00307	−0.00209	−0.00169	−0.00159
ijp10	−0.00005	0.00115	−0.00330	−0.00174	−0.00131	−0.00404	−0.00253	−0.00200	−0.00161
sus10s	0.00000	0.00027	−0.00090	−0.00040	−0.00030	−0.00104	−0.00064	−0.00049	−0.00045
sdm10s	0.00000	0.00057	−0.00175	−0.00092	−0.00064	−0.00205	−0.00134	−0.00105	−0.00179
sjp10s	0.00000	0.00058	−0.00180	−0.00092	−0.00064	−0.00212	−0.00141	−0.00109	−0.00134
sushy	0.00000	0.00192	−0.00515	−0.00275	−0.00196	−0.00684	−0.00418	−0.00321	−0.00353
sus0210	0.00001	0.00072	−0.00240	−0.00126	−0.00084	−0.00270	−0.00178	−0.00139	−0.00125
sus3010	0.00000	0.00038	−0.00119	−0.00067	−0.00049	−0.00128	−0.00092	−0.00074	−0.00065
sdm0210	0.00000	0.00096	−0.00283	−0.00169	−0.00113	−0.00353	−0.00228	−0.00182	−0.00141
sdm3010	−0.00004	0.00101	−0.00350	−0.00176	−0.00112	−0.00431	−0.00268	−0.00206	−0.00172
sjp0210	−0.00001	0.00094	−0.00253	−0.00146	−0.00110	−0.00373	−0.00217	−0.00171	−0.00132
sjp3010	0.00000	0.00038	−0.00119	−0.00067	−0.00049	−0.00128	−0.00092	−0.00074	−0.00065
veus	0.00867	0.83373	−2.33370	−1.08390	−0.75000	−2.93528	−1.67334	−1.28801	−1.21418
vedm	−0.01322	5.25935	−15.48900	−5.20140	−3.46000	−22.30573	−9.64646	−6.84798	−6.37279
vejp	0.00733	3.30086	−8.81000	−3.61070	−2.44000	−12.65445	−6.51275	−4.75593	−4.60630
vecb	0.00871	3.13991	−9.02000	−3.45000	−2.51000	−12.37167	−6.15176	−4.55397	−4.51686
vius	0.00276	1.30488	−2.77770	−1.92610	−1.33660	−4.47748	−2.66747	−2.14801	−1.91631

* Value at risk converted from the 95% daily column in Table 7.8 by multiplying by $\sqrt{5}$.

CASE 2: MANY LINEAR ASSETS WITH NORMAL AND NONNORMAL RETURNS

Let us consider a portfolio of many assets, but keep the PV functions linear in returns (no convex bonds or options). Equation (7.9) applies as the VaR definition. Its first (probability) part is for the unknown return distribution (nonparametric case). The second (integration) is the parametric specification when the probability density function (pdf) $\phi\,(\tilde{R}_1,\ldots,\tilde{R}_J)$ is multivariate normal with a mean vector μ and covariance matrix Σ. In practice, both μ and Σ have to be estimated.

In the normal case, if we denote the vector of portfolio weights by $\mathbf{w}$, since the PV function as a fraction of wealth, $\tilde{R} = \tilde{P}/W_0$ is a weighted sum of normals, it is normal with mean $\mathbf{w}'\mu$ and variance $\mathbf{w}'\Sigma\mathbf{w}$. Using the return definition Equation (7.10), Equation (7.9) can be simplified to a univariate case:

$$C = 1 - c = \int_{-\infty}^{R^*} \phi\big(\tilde{R}\big)d\,\tilde{R} \qquad (7.17)$$

which is just like Equation (7.13), where $\phi(\cdot)$ is the normal pdf with mean $\mu = \mathbf{w}'\mu$ and variance $\sigma^2 = \mathbf{w}'\Sigma\mathbf{w}$. The asset linearity of assets leads to this substantial reduction. In order to derive the VaR statistic P^* implicitly defined in Equation (7.17), we need to estimate the covariance matrix Σ. The number of covariances to be estimated is $J(J+1)/2$, and, for any international bank, the number of factors j tends to be in the hundreds, even before the modeling of *specific* risks (defined as risks associated with issuer names). For the portfolio variance, σ^2, to be positive, the estimated matrix, Σ, must be positive definite. The number of samples must be greater than the number of series and the return factors must not be linear combinations of each other. With so many variables, that is not easily satisfied, but can be alleviated by a diagonal model in which the variability of the return vector $\tilde{R} = (\tilde{R}_1, \ldots, \tilde{R}_J)'$ depends on just one "market" factor:

$$\tilde{R} = \mathbf{a} + \tilde{r}_m\mathbf{b} + \tilde{\varepsilon} \qquad (7.18)$$

where all the elements of the idiosyncratic term, $\tilde{\varepsilon}$, are uncorrelated with each other and the market return, $\tilde{r}_m$, and $\mathbf{a}$ and $\mathbf{b}$ are $J \times 1$ coefficient vectors. The matrix, Σ, reduces to

$$\sum = \sigma_m^2\mathbf{bb}' + \mathbf{Is}_\varepsilon \qquad (7.19)$$

where σ_m^2 is the market variance, $\mathbf{I}$ is a $J \times J$ identity matrix and $\mathbf{s}_\varepsilon$ is a vector of idiosyncratic variances. The problem reduces to $2J+1$ parameters. When one factor is not adequate (e.g., the movements of the yield curve), a generalization involves L common linear factors with uncorrelated idiosyncratic terms. The returns follow:

$$\tilde{R} = \mathbf{a} + \sum_{l=1}^{l=L} \tilde{r}_l \, \mathbf{b}_l + \tilde{\varepsilon} \qquad (7.20)$$

and the covariance matrix is an expression in $L \, J \times 1$ coefficient vectors, $\mathbf{b}_l = 1, \ldots, L$. That is,

$$\Sigma = \sum_{l=1}^{l=L} \sigma_l^2 \, \mathbf{b}_l \, \mathbf{b}_l' + \mathbf{Is}_\varepsilon \qquad (7.21)$$

and the number of parameters to be estimated is reduced to $JL + L + J$. Once the covariance matrix is determined, Monte Carlo simulations rely on a Cholesky decomposition of the covariance matrix into a lower triangular matrix $\mathbf{L}$, such that $\Sigma = \mathbf{LL}'$. The success of the procedure depends on careful handling of the dimensionality. We generate TxJ standard normal variates, arrange them into T J-tuples, $\mathbf{z}_t, t = 1, \ldots, T$, and construct T multivariate samples $R'_{t,.} = (R_t, 1, \ldots, R_t, j)' = \mathbf{Lz}_t, t = 1, \ldots, T$. The PV function for each sample is $P_t = \mathbf{w}'R_{t,.}$. The historical bootstrap is straightforward. We apply the PV function directly to the past return vectors. In either case, the PV function operates on the rows, $R'_{t,.}$, of the matrix of observations:

$$\mathbf{R} = \left| R_{t,.}; t = 1, \ldots, T \right| = \left| r_{t,j}; t = 1, \ldots, T, j = 1, \ldots, J \right| \qquad (7.22)$$

to create a column vector of PVs

$$P = |\, P_t, t = 1, \ldots, T \,| = \mathbf{Rw} \qquad (7.23)$$

from which VaRs are read off as percentile statistics.

To illustrate, we come up with "canonical" examples. Table 7.8 shows the weights (fractions of $1) assigned to each asset class.[8] *P1* is an all-stock

---

[8] Two series *sjp0210* and *sjp1030* were assigned zero weights in all portfolios as they exhibited numerical collinearity in the Cholesky decomposition step of the weekly simulations, but they are left in here as a reminder of the pitfalls of dealing with large numbers of financial variables.

T A B L E   7.8

Canonical portfolio weights

Series	P1	P2	P3	P4	P5	P6	P7	P8	P9	P10
eus	0.250			0.250					0.100	
emx	0.250								0.100	
edm	0.250								0.100	0.500
ejp	0.250								0.100	0.500
xdm	0.250	0.333					0.333		0.200	
xmx	0.250	0.333					0.333		0.200	0.500
xjp	0.250	0.333					0.333		0.200	0.500
coil			0.333	0.250					0.050	
cgld			0.333						0.050	
cwht			0.333						0.050	
ius10		0.333		0.500	0.500	1.000			0.400	
idm10		0.333			0.250				0.300	
ijp10		0.333			0.250				0.300	
sus10s				0.250	0.250	0.750			0.200	
sdm10s					0.250				0.300	
sjp10s					0.250				0.300	
sushy				0.250	0.250	0.250			0.200	0.500
sus0210						−0.100			0.100	
sus3010						0.100			−0.100	
sdm0210									0.100	
sdm3010									−0.100	
sjp0210									0.000	
sjp3010									0.000	
veus								0.333		
vedm								0.333		−0.200
vejp								0.333		−0.200
vecb										
vius										

portfolio equally invested in each stock index.[9] Portfolio *P2* is a multicurrency nonconvex bond portfolio (e.g., invested in foreign bond futures). *P3* is a commodity portfolio. *P4–10* have mixed of assets. *P8* and *P10* have vega exposures, i.e., contain options. The results in Tables 7.9 to 7.12 are unremarkable. All the portfolios, except P8 and P10 with daily data, have

---

[9] A U.S. investor in foreign stocks has index and currency exposure, including a cross term.

T A B L E   7.9

Daily Monte Carlo VaRs and ETLs for "canonical" portfolios
(10,000 simulations)

			VaR			ETL		
	Mean	St. Dev.	99%	95%	90%	99%	95%	90%
P1	0.00046	0.01017	−0.02301	−0.01635	−0.01246	−0.02647	−0.02044	−0.01732
P2	−0.00016	0.00536	−0.01250	−0.00898	−0.00708	−0.01431	−0.01113	−0.00953
P3	0.0006	0.01026	−0.02380	−0.01694	−0.01321	−0.02713	−0.02110	−0.01796
P4	0.00025	0.00662	−0.01483	−0.01071	−0.00828	−0.01719	−0.01336	−0.01138
P5	0.00000	0.00034	−0.00080	−0.00057	−0.00045	−0.00090	−0.00070	−0.00060
P6	0.00000	0.00050	−0.00116	−0.00082	−0.00065	−0.00129	−0.00102	−0.00087
P7	−0.00015	0.00525	−0.01216	−0.00880	−0.00694	−0.01380	−0.01089	−0.00934
P8	0.00018	2.65386	−6.14659	−4.43556	−3.40473	−7.04332	−5.48705	−4.67696
P9	0.00016	0.00514	−0.01187	−0.00822	−0.00652	−0.01363	−0.01046	−0.00887
P10	0.00031	1.55574	−3.60239	−2.56906	−1.99037	−4.08565	−3.21062	−2.73191

T A B L E   7.10

Weekly Monte Carlo VaRs and ETLs for "canonical" portfolios
(10,000 simulations)

			VaR			ETL			VaR
	Mean	St. Dev.	99%	95%	90%	99%	95%	90%	95%*
P1	0.00235	0.02401	−0.05368	−0.03685	−0.02831	−0.06148	−0.04674	−0.03953	−0.03656
P2	−0.00080	0.01099	−0.02626	−0.01897	−0.01495	−0.02935	−0.02357	−0.02019	−0.02008
P3	0.00071	0.02209	−0.04901	−0.03545	−0.02805	−0.05599	−0.04399	−0.03766	−0.03788
P4	0.00119	0.01361	−0.03035	−0.02138	−0.01642	−0.03471	−0.02688	−0.02283	−0.02395
P5	−0.00002	0.00078	−0.00184	−0.00132	−0.00102	−0.00211	−0.00164	−0.00140	−0.00127
P6	−0.00001	0.00112	−0.00262	−0.00188	−0.00145	−0.00302	−0.00236	−0.00200	−0.00183
P7	−0.00078	0.01106	−0.02673	−0.01895	−0.01478	−0.02999	−0.02366	−0.02015	−0.01968
P8	0.00092	2.96472	−7.04994	−4.84010	−3.77075	−8.03692	−6.14484	−5.20560	−9.91821
P9	0.00079	0.01114	−0.02497	−0.01741	−0.01346	−0.02882	−0.02208	−0.01862	−0.01838
P10	0.00150	1.66227	−3.93783	−2.75523	−2.13117	−4.46490	−3.47043	−2.94484	−5.74459

* Value at risk converted from the daily 95% column in Table 7.11 by multiplying by $\sqrt{5}$.

T A B L E   7.11

Daily historical bootstrap VaRs and ETLs for "canonical" portfolios (3,400 samples)

			VaR			ETL	
	Mean	St. Dev.	99%	95%	90%	99%	95%	90%
P1	0.00046	0.01011	−0.03030	−0.01448	−0.01010	−0.04243	−0.02376	−0.01798
P2	−0.00016	0.00529	−0.01339	−0.00734	−0.00534	−0.02286	−0.01201	−0.00911
P3	0.00016	0.01023	−0.02714	−0.01466	−0.01053	−0.04090	−0.02339	−0.01790
P4	0.00025	0.00662	−0.01688	−0.00890	−0.00647	−0.02777	−0.01502	−0.01134
P5	0.00000	0.00034	−0.00088	−0.00053	−0.00038	−0.00119	−0.00076	−0.00060
P6	0.00000	0.00050	−0.00125	−0.00074	−0.00053	−0.00178	−0.00109	−0.00086
P7	−0.00015	0.00527	−0.01337	−0.00725	−0.00535	−0.02263	−0.01194	−0.00908
P8	0.00018	2.68879	−3.33679	−1.52058	−1.04239	−7.87344	−3.32170	−2.28868
P9	0.00016	0.00509	−0.01461	−0.00716	−0.00509	−0.02161	−0.01194	−0.00902
P10	0.00031	1.55824	−1.88355	−0.90670	−0.54920	−5.68031	−2.14400	−1.42946

T A B L E   7.12

Weekly historical bootstrap VaRs and ETLs for "canonical" portfolios (680 samples)

			VaR			ETL			VaR
	Mean	St. Dev.	99%	95%	90%	99%	95%	90%	95%*
P1	0.00235	0.02387	−0.07794	−0.03649	−0.02566	−0.09271	−0.05564	−0.04325	−0.03238
P2	−0.00080	0.01095	−0.03139	−0.01682	−0.01246	−0.04931	−0.02592	−0.02018	−0.01641
P3	0.00071	0.02211	−0.05918	−0.03324	−0.02498	−0.08102	−0.04790	−0.03840	−0.03278
P4	0.00119	0.01356	−0.03566	−0.01845	−0.01473	−0.04599	−0.02761	−0.02203	−0.01990
P5	−0.00002	0.00079	−0.00197	−0.00120	−0.00091	−0.00224	−0.00158	−0.00130	−0.00119
P6	−0.00001	0.00112	−0.00265	−0.00181	−0.00135	−0.00310	−0.00231	−0.00194	−0.00165
P7	−0.00078	0.01101	−0.03095	−0.01670	−0.01253	−0.04933	−0.02593	−0.02024	−0.01621
P8	0.00092	2.94883	−8.76393	−3.07409	−2.05594	−12.19204	−5.55407	−3.97049	−3.40012
P9	0.00079	0.01122	−0.03584	−0.01717	−0.01217	−0.04360	−0.02630	−0.02034	−0.01601
P10	0.00150	1.65814	−4.45009	−1.72932	−1.05031	−8.81597	−3.61058	−2.47155	−2.02744

* Value at risk converted from the daily 95% column in Table 7.11 by multiplying by $\sqrt{5}$.

higher 99 percent and mostly lower 90 percent historical VaRs than normal simulation VaRs. All the VaRs in the 99 percent column of Table 7.12 are higher in absolute value than the correspondent ones in the 99 percent column of Table 7.10; the opposite is true for the 90 percent column. The normal approximation is again not very good. The bootstrap suffers from the scarcity of data in the relevant region. The implications are the following: the Monte Carlo has to rectify the nonstationarity of the variances; the bootstrap has to reduce the interpolation errors. Either the method has large VaR confidence intervals with the relative "goodness-of-fit" or the predictive power of both methods is unclear. See also Hendricks (1996).

THE NONSTATIONARITY OF THE PROBABILITY DISTRIBUTION

The predictive power of the multivariate normal VaR and the historical bootstrap depends on the underlying distribution of the risk factors being constant through time. Yet the standard deviations of financial variables fluctuate dramatically, and evidence suggests that correlations are not stable over time either. Longin and Solnik (1995) show that correlations increase during tail-event crises (contagion effect). One approach to the covariance nonstationarity is to model the changing covariance while assuming that the distribution remains the same. In the univariate VaR, we can compute rolling volatilities over a past window of n days or weeks

$$\sigma_t^2 = \frac{1}{n}\sum_{i=1}^{n} R_{t-i}^2 \qquad (7.24)$$

and then use the last number. We assume that the realized volatility over the last n days will hold for the next n. To improve Equation (7.24), we apply high-frequency data to longer horizon variances, as in Andersen et al. (1998) and Taylor and Xu (1997), or fit GARCH(1,1) to the return series:

$$\sigma_t^2 = \gamma + \alpha R_{t-1}^2 + \beta \sigma_{t-1}^2, \quad \alpha + \beta < 1 \qquad (7.25)$$

Weekly volatilities can be recovered from daily as functions of the fitted parameters α, β, and γ. The advantage is a small number of fitted parameters. The disadvantages are the convergence pitfalls of numerical conditional likelihood maximizations, and the adequacy of the functional form (a claim indefensible for some financial data). Figure 7.1 shows

F I G U R E   7.1

SPX Vol: 30d roll and GARCH(1,1)

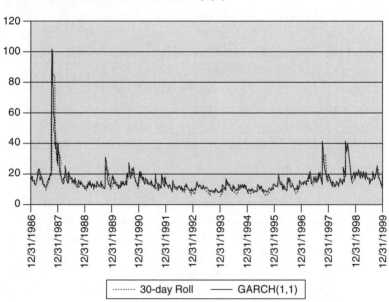

annualized rolling 30-day and in-sample GARCH(1,1)-fitted standard deviations for the *eus* series.[10]

While the shape is great, the levels can deviate. Also, GARCH(1,1) fails in a multivariate setting not only because of the optimizations, but also because each covariance pair requires an estimation of three parameters, resulting in a huge total number of parameters. Ensuring positive definiteness is almost impossible. RiskMetrics offers an alternative in the form of a simplified recursive non-mean-reverting (persistent) exponential model in which each covariance follows:

$$\Sigma_{ij,t} = \beta\Sigma_{ij,t-1} + (1-\beta)R_{i,t-1}R_{j,t-1}, \forall i,j \qquad (7.26)$$

where β is fixed for all return variables and in the i.i.d. case for all data frequencies, $\sigma_{i}^2, t = \Sigma_{ii}, t$. (In RiskMetrics, to fit the data better, $\beta = 0.94$ for

---

[10] The GARCH(1,1) parameters for the entire sample of 3400 observations were
$\gamma = 1.26e-06, \alpha = 0.0808933, \beta = 0.9102993$ showing a high level of persistence $(\alpha + \beta > 0.99)$.

daily, but $\beta = 0.97$ for monthly.) The advantage is that we update today's covariance simply using yesterday's return squared and covariance via the recursive rule of Equation (7.26). The constant β ensures positive definiteness. Hull and White (1998) adapt the updating to GARCH. Another approach is to use implied volatilities as forecasts, which can be "locked in" by hedging with options or volatility swaps, but derivative markets in volatilities and correlations too sketchy. The historical bootstrap benefits from the volatility modeling through a nonparametric randomization, which preserves all the quirks of the left tail of the empirical distribution. As first proposed by Efron (1979), the predictive power of the bootstrap relied on the same i.i.d. assumptions. Berkowitz and Kilian (1996) document extensions. Barone-Adesi et al. (2000) propose to filter a heteroskedastic return series by dividing its ARMA(1,1) residuals by the GARCH(1,1)-fitted standard deviation:

$$R_t = AR(1)R_{t-1} + MA(1)\varepsilon_{t-1} + \varepsilon_t, \quad \varepsilon_t \sim N(0, \sigma_t^2)$$
$$\sigma_t^2 = \gamma + \alpha(\varepsilon_{t-1} - \xi)^2 + \beta\sigma_{t-1}^2$$
$$e_t = \frac{\varepsilon_t}{\sigma_t}$$

(7.27)

drawing the standard residuals from the dataset and rescaling them by the volatility forecasts:

$$\hat{\varepsilon}_{t+1} = e_1\sigma_{t+1}$$

(7.28)

and reconstructing returns, $\hat{R}_{t+1}$, using Equation (7.27) with the estimated ARMA terms, recursively, until all $\hat{R}_{t+t'}, t' = 1, \ldots, T$, have been computed. In the multivariate setting, the correlation is modeled by following the steps for each variable separately, but drawing strips of standardized residuals $(e_t^1, \ldots, e_t^J)$ for the same date. Barone-Adesi and Giannopoulos (2000) and Holton (2003) compare the bootstrap and the simulation.

The equation of motion for variances and its parameters can be subjects of disagreement. Albanese et al. (1997), in a Bayesian setting, propose the inverse Wishart distribution as a natural prior for covariance matrices, and derive solutions for the linear asset case. Glasserman et al. (2000)

forgo variance evolution modeling (in Figure 7.1 the shape is modeled well, but the absolute level can be off) and instead focus on a better choice of the unconditional distribution. They study multivariate t distributions in a Monte Carlo with the focus on a variety of variance reduction techniques.

The variance filtering and heteroskedastic specifications do not extend to the multivariate case to produce a reliable estimation for thousands of factor covariances and are not used by financial institutions. Not a single disclosure note in six randomly picked annual reports for the fiscal year 2000[11] mentions any use of filtering or GARCH. Instead, practical research focuses on numerical PV approximations, finer factor specifications, and better descriptions of the multivariate unconditional distribution and its left tail, both parametric and nonparametric.

CASE 3: NONLINEAR ASSETS

An introduction of even a single nonlinear asset into the portfolio disrupts the entire VaR machinery, and the issue does not disappear through some diversification effect as the number of nonlinear positions grows. This is true for convex bond and mortgage portfolios and both equity and fixed income derivatives. We illustrate these points by applying to a numerical example involving only equity options in three different VaR methods: delta-normal, generalized Taylor series expansion, and full valuation, the latter with two subvariants.

Let us start by considering a portfolio consisting of a short six-month at-the-money straddle on SPX (veus).[12] We assume a Black–Scholes volatility of 16 percent, an interest rate of 6 percent and a dividend yield of 0 percent. The residual delta for the position is -0.18 and gamma 0.0972. The P&L of the position depends on the index, $\tilde{S}$, whose initial value is S_0, the change in the index over the holding horizon is $\Delta \tilde{S}$. The return on the index, $\tilde{R}$, is the single risk factor. We ignore the interest rate and implied volatility risk. $BS_C(\cdot)$ and $BS_P(\cdot)$, the Black–Scholes values of a call and a put, respectively, are functions of the normalized value of the index,

---

[11] Deutsche Bank, Morgan Stanley, UBS, Goldman Sachs, J.P. Morgan Chase, Merrill Lynch.

[12] A short call and short put on one unit of SPX with both strikes at the initial level of the index. As we are only interested in percentage changes, we normalize the index so that its initial level is equal to 1.

$\tilde{S}/S_0 = 1 + \tilde{R}$ with a strike equal to 1. The initial wealth (i.e., position) can then be described as:

$$W_0 = S_0 \left(- BS_C(1) - BS_P(1) \right) \tag{7.29}$$

After a holding period d, the random wealth becomes

$$\tilde{W} = S_0 \left(- BS_C(1 + \tilde{R}) - BS_P(1 + \tilde{R}) \right) \tag{7.30}$$

The P&L function does not simplify to a weighted sum of returns as in Equation (7.8) but is instead

$$\tilde{P} = \tilde{W} - W_0 = S_0 \left(- BS_C(1 + \tilde{R}) + BS_C(1) - BS_P(1 + \tilde{R}) + BS_P(1) \right) \tag{7.31}$$

and requires a revaluation at the new return using the nonlinear functions $BS_C(\cdot)$ and $BS_P(\cdot)$. In order to use the simplified definition [Equation (7.9)], we resort to local approximations. The first uses the delta of the options as a first-order proxy for the value. Combined with the assumptions of normality, this is the *delta-normal method*. We denote the Black–Scholes deltas (evaluated at 1) as Δ_C and Δ_P. The normalized changes in the option values can then be approximated as

$$\begin{aligned}\Delta_C \, \tilde{R} &= BS_C(1 + \tilde{R}) - BS_C(1) \\ \Delta_P \, \tilde{R} &= BS_P(1 + \tilde{R}) - BS_P(1)\end{aligned} \tag{7.32}$$

The PV function can be written in the desired linear form as

$$\tilde{P} = S_0 \, \Delta \, \tilde{R} \tag{7.33}$$

where $\Delta = -\Delta_C - \Delta_P$ is the combined portfolio delta (here equal to zero since $\Delta_C = -\Delta_P$). If, in addition, $\tilde{R}$ follows a normal distribution with an annualized mean μ and standard deviation σ, then, in general, similar to Equation (7.15), the VaR can be defined explicitly as (definition of the delta-normal method)

$$P^* = S_0 \, \Delta \, (\mu + \alpha\sigma)\sqrt{d} \tag{7.34}$$

where the critical value α is taken from the standard normal. The delta method for the nonparametric case offers no such closed-form expression, but relies on the simplified PV function of Equation (7.8) to obtain a vector of P&L values from which to read off the percentile statistics. For a better approximation to the changes in the portfolio value, we apply a higher order Taylor series expansion, using the option Γ. The PV in the *delta-gamma method* is

$$\tilde{P} = S_0 \left(\Delta \, \tilde{R} + \frac{1}{2} \Gamma \, \tilde{R}^2 \right) \tag{7.35}$$

Under normal $\tilde{R}$, it can be shown that the annualized variance of $\tilde{R}^2$ is $2\sigma^4$ and that $\tilde{R}$ and $\tilde{R}^2$ are uncorrelated. The mean of $\tilde{P}$ is $S_0\Delta\mu$ and the variance is $\Delta^2\sigma^2 + 1/2\,\Gamma^2\sigma^4$. Following the argument in Equations (7.13) through (7.15), we obtain the *delta-gamma-normal* VaR approximation, defined as

$$P^* = S_0 \left(\Delta\mu\sqrt{d} + \sqrt{\Delta^2\sigma^2 d + \frac{1}{2}\Gamma^2\sigma^4 d^2} \right) \tag{7.36}$$

The Taylor expansion can also incorporate risk factors, e.g., the changes in the implied volatility of the options in the short straddle. If we denote the return changes as the first risk factor, $\tilde{F}_1 = \tilde{R}$, the changes in the squares of the returns as the second factor, $\tilde{F}_2 = \tilde{R}^2$, and the changes in the volatility as the third factor, $\tilde{F}_3$, then the P&L Equation (7.8) can be expanded to read

$$\tilde{P} = S_0 \left(\Delta \, \tilde{F}_1 + \frac{1}{2} \Gamma \, \tilde{F}_2 + \Lambda \, \tilde{F}_3 \right) \tag{7.37}$$

where Λ is the combined vega of the portfolio (this is the *delta-gamma-vega-normal method*). Proceeding in this manner is fraught with many pitfalls. The implicit noncorrelation of factors (returns and volatilities) grossly distorts the approximation. There is an obvious inconsistency of the changing volatility with models of constant "greeks." The main problem is again the dimensionality, even without the addition of vega. In portfolios of options on many underlyings or sources of risk (e.g., interest rate options), one has to account for the correlations between the underlyings and the second-order cross terms. The general P&L Taylor series approximation can be written as

$$\tilde{P} = \Delta \; \tilde{F} + \frac{1}{2} \tilde{F}' \, \Gamma \, \tilde{F} \qquad (7.38)$$

where Δ is a $J \times 1$ vector of the factor sensitivities, $\tilde{F}$ is a $J \times 1$ vector of the factor realizations, and Γ is a $J \times 1$ matrix of second-order sensitivities. In the normal VaR, for a portfolio of options with just 10 risk factors, this requires 10 delta, 55 gamma, and 55 covariance estimates and the number grows geometrically. With such numerical demands, the Taylor series expansion approach with covariance estimation of square and cross-factor terms is practically never used. Nevertheless, the overriding issue with this method is the fact that it relies on a local approximation to a large deviation problem of VaR.

The choice of the VaR implementation becomes a trade-off between two methods of PV calculation: (1) multivariate PV space sampling and (2) full revaluation, used in a multivariate normal simulation or a historical bootstrap. The first consists of sparse sampling of the portfolio PV as a function of sets of carefully chosen predetermined factor values (scenarios), using the exact valuation model, or first- and second-order approximations, where appropriate. For our short straddle position, we could precalculate a matrix of PVs for five different returns $(-30, -15, 0, 15, 30$ percent) and three volatility changes (down 1 percent, up 2 percent, up 6 percent).[13] This matrix could then be used to interpolate the portfolio P&L in normal simulations or a historical bootstrap. This approach is used when trading systems are fragmented and separate from the VaR calculation engine, so that exchanging vectors of factor realizations for PV changes is not easy. Another reason for the popularity of this approach is that doing 10,000 revaluations for a Monte Carlo can exceed the processing power in the case of complex numerical pricing models for derivatives or mortgage-backed securities. When that is not the case, the preferred method is a full

---

[13] Mark-to-market losses occur in both the up and down scenarios for the index and up scenarios for the volatility; so we sample that region of the distribution more carefully.

revaluation for the simulated sample vectors. The two approaches can be combined: PV sampling used for numerically intensive positions and full revaluation for cash securities and closed-form bonds and options.

For the example of the short straddle position, Figure 7.2 shows the P&L relative to the return on the S&P index. The P&L is computed using three methods: (1) PV sampling for a dense set of index values, using the exact valuation model in Equation (7.31); (2) a delta approximation defined in Equation (7.33); and (3) a delta-gamma approximation defined in Equation (7.35). As can be seen, the delta approximation fails completely, and the delta-gamma proxy is quite inaccurate in the extreme tails, where it actually overstates the true losses, but performs well for a large region of returns between −15 and +10 percent

Note that, like the inclusion of gamma, the inclusion of vega in the Taylor series expansion would cause loss overstatements in extreme tails. Applying a high vega of at-the-money options to the tails where vega is low would show the value to be more convex than it really is. The neglected second cross-derivative of the underlying and the volatility would make things worse.

F I G U R E   7.2

Short SPX ATM straddle

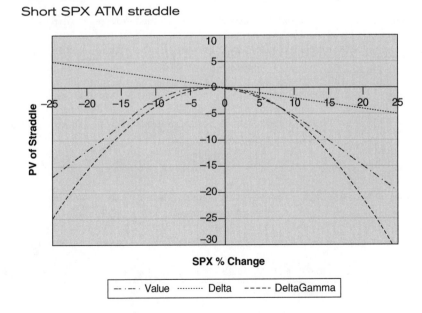

SPX % Change

| Value   Delta   DeltaGamma |

Table 7.13 shows VaR results for the short straddle example. The delta-gamma approximation works quite well, showing errors of less than 2 percent of the true VaRs and less than 8 percent of the true ETLs. For example, for the weekly 95 percent VaR in the historical bootstrap, the delta-gamma approximation of -0.01323 is only 1.77 percent away from its true value of -0.01300, and the 95 percent ETL delta-gamma approximation is 3.42 percent away from its true value of -0.01988. From Tables 7.4 to 7.7, one can see that the VaRs for eus are negative 2.6 to 1 percent for the daily case, and negative 5.3 to 2.1 percent for the weekly case. In these regions, the delta-gamma approximation to the option PV works very well as shown in Figure 7.3. In addition, because only the ETLs include all the extreme realizations, the errors for them are greater than for the VaRs.

T A B L E   7.13

TheVaRs and ETLs for the ATM straddle on SPX

	Mean	St. Dev.	VaR 99%	VaR 95%	VaR 90%	ETL 99%	ETL 95%	ETL 90%	VaR 95%*
				Daily historical bootstrap					
Exact Valuation	−0.00067	0.00300	−0.00820	−0.00403	−0.00263	−0.01633	−0.00756	−0.00541	
Delta-Gamma	−0.00067	0.00349	−0.00825	−0.00402	−0.00262	−0.01755	−0.00780	−0.00553	
				Weekly historical bootstrap					
Exact Valuation	−0.00271	0.00549	−0.02336	−0.01300	−0.00808	−0.03547	−0.01988	−0.01486	−0.00901
Delta-Gamma	−0.00270	0.00574	−0.02443	−0.01323	−0.00813	−0.03758	−0.02056	−0.01523	−0.00899
				Daily normal simulation					
Exact Valuation	−0.00068	0.00199	−0.00735	−0.00465	−0.00343	−0.00852	−0.00616	−0.00508	
Delta-Gamma	−0.00067	0.00202	−0.00760	−0.00468	−0.00338	−0.00905	−0.00631	−0.00514	
				Weekly normal simulation					
Exact Valuation	−0.00271	0.00506	−0.02127	−0.01327	−0.00950	−0.02560	−0.01809	−0.01463	−0.01040
Delta-Gamma	−0.00271	0.00523	−0.02190	−0.01329	−0.00941	−0.02693	−0.01873	−0.01490	−0.01046

* Weekly VaR converted from the daily 95% VaR by multiplying by $\sqrt{5}$.

F I G U R E   7.3

Ten percent OTM strangle–ATM straddle

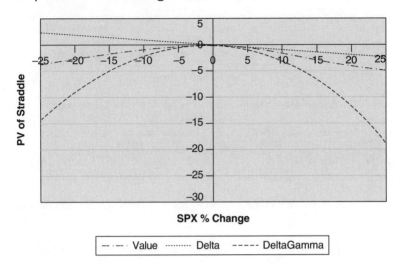

SPX % Change

— · — Value   ········· Delta   ----- DeltaGamma

Let us now turn to the same example of a short at-the-money straddle on the WTI oil series, *coil*, which exhibits more variability. The results
are very different and are summarized in Table 7.14. First of all, the means
and the standard deviations of the PV series are quite different between
the normal simulation and the empirical distribution (even though the
means and standard deviations of the underlying spot oil returns were
identical). This yields VaR and ETL estimates that are quite divergent. The
daily-to-weekly conversion is inadequate. More importantly, the delta-
gamma approximation fails miserably for weekly 99 percent VaRs and
most weekly and some daily ETLs. For example, the 99 percent weekly
VaR under historical bootstrap is -0.10216 using exact valuation, but is
-0.13310 in the delta-gamma approximation, an error of over 30 percent.
Note that the variability of the *coil* series resembles more closely the
(high) variability of many individual U.S. stocks than does that of the SPX
index series, *eus*. Thus, typical results for individual stock portfolios
would be close to those in Table 7.14.

To emphasize the point, that the option approximation based on local
derivatives can fail for any time series, let us return to the example of *eus*. We
add to the short at-the-money straddle a long 10 percent out-of-the-money

T A B L E   7.14

The VaRs and ETLs for the ATM straddle on WTI oil

			VaR			ETL			VaR
	Mean	St. Dev.	99%	95%	90%	99%	95%	90%	95%*
Daily historical bootstrap									
Exact Valuation	−0.00279	0.01008	−0.03727	−0.01321	−0.00782	−0.07499	−0.03159	−0.02072	
Delta-Gamma	−0.00300	0.01426	−0.03979	−0.01342	−0.00784	−0.09783	−0.03668	−0.02326	
Weekly historical bootstrap									
Exact Valuation	−0.01079	0.02122	−0.10216	−0.05028	−0.03261	−0.13488	−0.08377	−0.06249	−0.02954
Delta-Gamma	−0.01197	0.02748	−0.13310	−0.05461	−0.03401	−0.19131	−0.10580	−0.07512	−0.03001
Daily normal simulation									
Exact Valuation	−0.00319	0.00605	−0.02635	−0.01555	−0.01081	−0.03262	−0.02221	−0.01751	
Delta-Gamma	−0.00317	0.00627	−0.02668	−0.01610	−0.01132	−0.03378	−0.02284	−0.01814	
Weekly normal simulation									
Exact Valuation	−0.01257	0.01784	−0.07922	−0.05125	−0.03702	−0.09096	−0.06769	−0.05548	−0.03477
Delta-Gamma	−0.01332	0.02048	−0.09728	−0.05487	−0.03954	−0.11724	−0.07958	−0.06285	−0.03600

* **Weekly** VaR converted from the daily 95 percent VaR by multiplying by √5.

strangle[14] and, again, compare a local delta-gamma approximation to the exact model valuation. Figure 7.3 graphs the values for a range of SPX returns. Table 7.15 shows the VaRs and ETLs. The errors are greater than in Table 7.13, since the PV approximation in the relevant region is not accurate. Here, it is the addition of long options with small local gamma to the short position, which is responsible for the low quality of the delta-gamma approximation. The mix of long and short options is not atypical of many derivative dealers.

---

[14] The position consists of a long at-the-money call, long at-the-money put, short 10 percent out-of-the-money call and short 10 percent out-of-the money put. The index is normalized to 1. Strikes are thus 1, 1, 0.9, and 0.9, respectively.

T A B L E   7.15

The VaRs and ETLs for the short ATM straddle and long 10 percent OTM strangle on SPX

			VaR			ETL			VaR
	Mean	St. Dev.	99%	95%	90%	99%	95%	90%	95%*
Daily historical bootstrap									
Exact Valuation	−0.00032	0.00115	−0.00369	−0.00177	−0.00115	−0.00709	−0.00332	−0.00238	
Delta-Gamma	−0.00034	0.00180	−0.00381	−0.00179	−0.00115	−0.00887	−0.00371	−0.00257	
Weekly historical bootstrap									
Exact Valuation	−0.00131	0.00242	−0.01073	−0.00591	−0.00364	−0.01630	−0.00897	−0.00670	−0.00396
Delta-Gamma	−0.00135	0.00286	−0.01208	−0.00630	−0.00372	−0.01971	−0.01011	−0.00735	−0.00400
Daily normal simulation									
Exact Valuation	−0.00034	0.00084	−0.00311	−0.00204	−0.00151	−0.00387	−0.00272	−0.00224	
Delta-Gamma	−0.00034	0.00086	−0.00325	−0.00205	−0.00152	−0.00399	−0.00279	−0.00227	
Weekly normal simulation									
Exact Valuation	−0.00132	0.00218	−0.00907	−0.00593	−0.00424	−0.01118	−0.00793	−0.00649	−0.00456
Delta-Gamma	−0.00135	0.00235	−0.00994	−0.00621	−0.00435	−0.01252	−0.00860	−0.00691	−0.00458

* **Weekly** VaR converted from the daily 95 percent VaR by multiplying by $\sqrt{5}$.

Contrary to naïve intuition, the inaccuracy of the approximate methods in large portfolios cannot be diversified away. The credit and derivative businesses tend to be highly cyclical. Debt issuers buy interest rate caps when the yield curve is positively sloped expecting their cost of borrowing to go up. Mortgage refinancing generally skyrockets after sharp rate decreases. Stock option trading volumes vary with the popularity of a given equity sector. Foreign exchange options on emerging markets trade more heavily when a geographic sector is in a crisis. Other examples abound. What they all have in common is that rather than diversifying, they concentrate both linear and nonlinear exposures in the financial sector. This in turn leverages the approximation errors as strikes, expiration dates, and credit protection levels, and equity names tend to be bunched together.[15]

SYSTEM IMPLEMENTATION AND CONCLUSION

For almost any size diversified financial institution the VaR system implementation is driven by two choices. The first is the distributional assumption: parametric or nonparametric. The second is the selection of a portfolio revaluation method. If the distribution choice is parametric, almost always it is a multivariate normal, which offers parameter simplicity and has a heuristic appeal. The alternatives like the multivariate t are not well understood and difficult to implement. As we argued in the previous section, in the presence of nonlinear assets, the distribution of the PV function is not known, and closed-form shortcuts cannot be hoped for, even if all factors are Gaussian. In that case, the implementation is a large Monte Carlo simulation of the underlying factors where we choose either a historical period from which to estimate the covariance matrix, appropriately short to represent the current "market regime," or a model of the evolution of volatilities and correlations, like GARCH, or exponential. If the distribution assumption for the factors is nonparametric, i.e., empirical, then the implementation is a historical bootstrap, most likely without volatility filtering, but perhaps with some resampling to increase the number of the samples. We choose a relatively short period on which to base the empirical distribution to remain in the current market regime, in which the covariance structure is assumed constant. In order not to limit the number of samples and subject the estimates to larger standard errors, a re-sampling scheme can be used under the i.i.d assumptions. For example, biweekly samples could be bootstrapped by sampling the history of weekly factor movements with replacement and combining the pairs of successive draws. In this fashion, using T' weekly samples, one could create $T = (T'+1)!/(2(T'-1)!$ biweekly samples. Thus, two years of weekly data would yield 5,406 biweekly samples.

---

[15] Even though in a way it makes the problem more tractable by reducing the number of relevant factors. Some implementations exploit that fact by using clever splining methods to sample PV spaces or in modeling of specific risks.

The second decision is the selection of a portfolio revaluation method. Since the implementing firm may have at any time tens of thousands of positions arranged in portfolios and subportfolios along the firm's business lines, for which low-level as well as aggregate VaRs need to be calculated, this second decision is typically more difficult and costly in terms of system development demands. For cash positions like stocks, commodities, foreign exchange rates, and most bonds, the full revaluation method is very simple. For bonds that are more complicated and all derivatives, which require model valuation and in many instances carry large leveraged risks, the choice is between full revaluation and PV sampling. Approximate methods may be employed for some subportfolios or types of positions. An informal survey of major banks and broker-dealers in New York revealed a great variety of solutions, as of 1999: J.P. Morgan using the RiskMetrics normal simulation, Chase Manhattan using normal simulations with simulated scenarios sent every night to pricing systems for a full revaluation at those scenarios, UBS employing a PV sampling over a matrix of volatilities and underlying changes, old Bankers Trust using a sophisticated spline method for PV approximations, and Merrill Lynch using a historical bootstrap with sparse PV sampling along all factor dimensions. All of these firms describe their methods very parsimoniously in the annual reports, where they also publish aggregate VaR statistics. Several of the firms have merged since; so even fewer methods have survived.

The guidelines for general market risk were first put forth in the 1996 Amendment to the original Basel Accord, affirmed in the new Basel proposals published in January 2001, and adopted by Basel II and the European Union directive. Many large financial institutions have focused on extensions of general market VaR to the so-called specific risk (i.e., due to specific security issuer names), the treatment of hedges and collateral within the portfolio, and the combined market and credit VaR. The inclusion of specific risk increases the number of risk factors by an order of magnitude. The solutions for specific risks typically revolve around factor models, like the sector approach of MSCI Barra for stocks. The issue of collateral is quite complex and is related to the near term credit exposure modeling. A combined model of market and credit VaR is hard to develop, the issues being the legal treatment of many of the credit enhancement techniques and derivative credit exposure modeling.

The academic literature has largely ignored the dimensionality issues in VaR and its numerical challenges (hundreds of factors in general market VaR and more in specific) as well as the PV sampling problems of derivative structures (nontrivial functions of factors), with the riskiest positions concentrated in the most complicated products. We have demonstrated the futility of univariate option approximations of the delta-gamma type, which fail miserably due to their local nature, while VaR operates in extreme left tails, and the misguidedness of variance filtering and heteroschedasticity modeling. Very little good work has been done on improving the nonparametric model sampling, few papers tackle nonnormal multivariate specifications, and progress has stalled in the modeling of EVT-inspired multivariate extreme exceedances. Meanwhile, the role of VaR in practice has expanded from regulation-mandated disclosure to the more important areas of risk-based capital allocation and performance evaluation.

REFERENCES

Albanese, C., A. Levin, and J. Ching-ming Chao (1997) Bayesian Value at Risk, Back-testing and Calibration. Working paper, University of Toronto, Toronto, Ontario.

Andersen, T.G., T. Bollerslev, F. X. Diebold, and P. Labys (2000) Realized Volatility and Correlation. Working paper, New York University, New York.

Barone-Adesi, G., K. Giannopoulos, and L. Vosper (2000) Filtering Historical Simulation. Backtest Analysis. Working paper, University of Westminster, London.

Barone-Adesi, G. and K. Giannopoulos (2000) Non-parametric VaR techniques. Myths and Realities. Working paper, University of Westminster, London.

Berkowitz, J. and L. Kilian (1996) Recent Developments in Bootstrapping Time Series. Working paper, Federal Reserve Board, Finance and Economics Discussion Series, Washington, DC.

Efron, B. (1979) Bootstrap Methods: Another Look at the Jackknife. *The Annals of Statistics*, Vol. 7 No. 1, pp. 1–26.

Embrechts, P., S. Resnick, and G. Samorodnitsky. (1998) Living on the Edge. *Risk*, Vol. 11 No. 1, pp. 96–100.

Embrechts, P. (1999) Extreme Value Theory: Potential and Limitations as an integrated risk management tool. Working paper, Department of Mathematics, ETH Zurich.

Glasserman, P., P. Heidelberger, and P. Shahabuddin (2000) Portfolio Value-at-Risk with Heavy-Tailed Risk Factors. Paine Webber Working Paper Series in Money, Economics and Finance, PW–00–06, Columbia Business School, New York.

Hedricks, D. (1996) Evaluation of Value-at-Risk Models Using Historical Data. *FRBNY Economic Policy Review*, Vol. 2, No. 1, pp. 39–69.

Holton, Glyn A. (2003) *Value-at-Risk: Theory and Practice*. Burlington, MA: Academic Press.

Hull, J. and A. White (1998) Value at Risk When Daily Changes in Market Variables Are Not Normally Distributed. *Journal of Derivatives*, Vol. 5 No. 3, pp. 9–19.

Këllezi, E. and M. Gilli (2006) An Application of Extreme Value Theory for Measuring Financial Risk. *Computational Economics*, Vol. 27, No. 2–3, pp. 207–228.

Longin, F. (2000) From Value-at-Risk to Stress Testing: The Extreme Value Approach. *Journal of Banking and Finance*, Vol. 24, No. 7, pp. 1097–1130.

Longin, F. and B. Solnik (1995) Is the Correlation in International Equity Returns Constant:1960–1990? *Journal of International Money and Finance*, Vol. 14, No. 1, pp. 3–26.

Smith, R.L. (1999) Measuring Risk with Extreme Value Theory. Working paper, University of North Carolina, Chapel Hill, NC.

Taylor, S.J. and X. Xu (1997) The Incremental Volatility Information in One Million Foreign Exchange Quotations. *Journal of Empirical Finance*, Vol. 4, No. 4, pp. 317–340.

CHAPTER 8

Value at Risk for a Microcredit Loan Portfolio: An African Microfinance Institution Case Study

René Azokli, Emmanuel Fragnière, and Akimou Ossé

ABSTRACT

We recently collaborated with an established African microfinance institution. They were able to provide us with a rigorous database of information on more than 250,000 transactions. We first analyzed the database through descriptive statistics. We then developed simple but relevant risk measures to assess credit portfolio risk. This empirical work enabled us to provide management with suggestions on how to better monitor and address the typical credit risks encountered by microcredit organizations.

INTRODUCTION

Our main goal in this article was to develop simple but relevant risk measures to help an African bank specializing in microcredit to better manage its credit risks. This bank does not possess the information technology (IT) resources or capabilities to develop complex credit scoring or value-at-risk (VaR) models.

The collaboration with this bank began one year ago when two of our Geneva Business School of Administration (HEG) students conducted their Bachelor's projects in microcredit lending. Following a successful summer internship at the bank in August 2007, bank management proposed to the HEG professors (and supervisors of the students' projects) to assist them in developing simple credit VaR measures. The risk measures needed to be coded in software available at the bank, such as Microsoft Excel or Access. The analytic approaches also had to be simple enough to be understandable and useful for day-to-day operations, as well as for more strategic issues.

The first step consisted of gathering the data necessary for a statistical analysis and development of VaR measures. Over the years, bank management had stored credit loan information in a very rigorous manner. Thus, in March 2008, they were able to provide us with an Excel file containing data on more than 250,000 transactions.

In the second step, we cleaned and reorganized the database. For the third step, we conducted numerous statistical analyses, based solely on simple descriptions. Our goal was to identify links between the default rate and each variable in the database. We also identified correlations among the variables.

The fourth step was to develop the VaR measures. We first experimented with some logistic regression models, which is the methodology of choice to develop credit scoring functions (see the Literature Review section). However, developing these models requires dedicated statistical packages like SPSS that would not be available in the bank. Moreover, we have found that, in using SPSS, it is not always clear how the resulting VaR measures can be used to create the credit scoring functions. Consequently, we decided to code the VaR measures directly in Microsoft (MS) Access and Excel.

Our final step was to validate the results. Our main concern was to ensure that the entire analysis would be useful for the bank. We also hope that our methodology and results will be relevant for the management of other microcredit structures.

The chapter is organized as follows. In the Literature Review section, we briefly discuss the main academic findings in credit risk analysis for microcredit applications. The Exploratory Data Analysis section presents the credit loans database, as well as the main descriptive statistics. In the Value-at-Risk Modeling section, we illustrate how to use our risk measures to assess credit portfolio risk. The last section concludes and gives ideas for future research.

LITERATURE REVIEW

Over the past several years, many studies have attempted to determine the worldwide social and economic role of microcredit organizations [see, for example, Hartungi (2007), Lelart (2007), and Shankar (2007)], as well as the role of credit scoring methods within financial institutions [see Berger and Frame (2005) and Leonard (1995)].

Microfinance institutions provide small, short-term loans to indigent people. These financial resources are given to individuals (or groups) because they are unable to comply with traditional bank loan requirements (Schreiner, 1999). For example, in Indonesia, Bank Rakyat accepts alternative forms of collateral for loans, such as land titles, bikes, motorbikes, or cattle (Hartungi, 2007).

However, because of their activities, microfinance institutions may face more difficulties than traditional commercial institutions. Shankar (2007) finds that microcredit institutions have higher transaction charges for group formation and credit, direct administrative activities, documentation, disbursement, and monitoring. Charging higher interest rates may make up these internal costs. In addition, Hartungi (2007) finds that public subsidies are needed especially during the start-up phase of a microcredit institution.

Credit risk may seem higher in the microcredit business than in traditional banking. However, empirical data show that the poorest borrowers are often the best repayers (Lelart, 2007). Schreiner (1999) finds this is especially true for women. Nevertheless, the risk of unpaid debts exists, and in some countries, such as Benin, unpaid debts have reached untenable levels (Lelart, 2007).

Furthermore, there is the risk that loan officers, who play a critical role in the decision process, will make errors. Schreiner (1999) shows that this risk increases with the age of the loan: A move from 0–6 months to 148 months increases risk by 3.2 percentage points.

Thus, to make the process more efficient, we need to devise new and better practices and statistical tools. Studies show that one effective method is to first lend small sums to new clients and then and implement a monthly repayment schedule. Borrowers who pay on time every month are likely to be good candidates for larger loans (Hartungi, 2007; Diallo, 2006).

In the United States, small business credit scoring (SBCS) is a new technology used by banks to analyze microcredit institutions. It has been found to provide useful results (Berger and Frame, 2005). Schreiner (2000) confirms that the use of a credit scorecard system for microfinance institutions is a valuable tool in developing countries. In fact, Schreiner (2000) argues that although scorecards can't replace the judgment of loan officers, their predictive power can be used successfully to improve current microcredit practices. Few microlenders have reliable databases for this purpose yet. However, Schreiner (2002) notes that those who do have reliable databases have been able to take advantage of the time and cost savings that result by expanding their businesses. Leonard (1995) notes there are several advantages for credit applications as well, such as shorter approval time, shorter authorization time, and a higher accuracy rate.

Diallo (2006) studied one model of a credit scorecard in Mali. This model uses data analysis of a microfinance institution that provides individual loans in urban areas. The model uses discriminant analysis and logistic regression, and finds that (1) employees are slightly better repayers than independent workers, (2) education and gender have no influence on payments, and (3) single or divorced debtors tend to be higher credit risks. According to Lelart (2007), microfinance in Benin, compared to traditional banks, has increased to about twice the average of countries in the Western African Economic and Monetary Union (UEMOA–WAEMU).

Compared to the academic findings presented in this section, we believe that our contribution here is original because our credit risk analysis is based solely on tools that we developed in spreadsheet and database software that is typically available in any bank.

EXPLORATORY DATA ANALYSIS

Our original data set was extracted from the loan database of an established microfinance institution in Africa. It consisted of 249,709 loans granted by the institution between April 29, 1994 and July 31, 2007. Appendix 1 provides a list of characteristics for each loan. In order to obtain data that are as clean and homogeneous as possible, we applied the following filtering procedure:

- We excluded all loans with missing or aberrant key characteristics (e.g., missing gender or principal amount, year of birth outside the 1926-to-1990 range).
- We excluded mortgage loans and loans to associations.
- We excluded loans whose repayment frequencies were not monthly.
- We excluded loans whose monthly interest rate was different from 2 percent.
- The filtered database consisted of 239,021 loans to individuals, with monthly repayment frequency and a 2 percent interest rate.

The bank had established three categories of "credit status": sound, delinquent, or defaulted. In order to obtain a binomial variable, we merge delinquent and defaulted into a single category called *problem loan*. We note that a loan with at least one payment past due is considered delinquent. The breakdown in our database is as follows: 3.6 percent are problem loans, where 2.4 percent are in default and 1.2 percent are in delinquency.

The first factor we are interested in is gender. In the cleaned sample, females account for 77.3 percent (i.e., 184,794 loans), and males account for 22.7 percent (i.e., 54,227 loans). Within the microfinance world, it is considered well known that loans to males are significantly more risky than loans to females. Indeed, we observe in our sample that 3.1 percent of the problem loans are to females while 5.6 percent are to males.

Age is determined based on client age at the time the loan was granted. We divide this variable into the following four categories: up to 25 years, between 26 and 35 years, between 36 and 45 years, and more than 45 years. As Figure 8.1 shows, the percentage of problem loans decreases as the client's age increases. This suggests that older clients are more responsible and perhaps have more business expertise as well.

The region (or more precisely the city) is also an important variable here, because loans are essentially granted in only three main cities in this country. We thus recode this variable on the following categorical scale:

City 1, City 2, City 3, and Rest (we merge all other neighborhoods and cities into a single variable).

As we mentioned, the average problem loan rate is 3.6 percent. We see from Figure 8.2 that City 1 and City 2 have the smallest problem

F I G U R E   8.1

Problem loan rate by age bucket

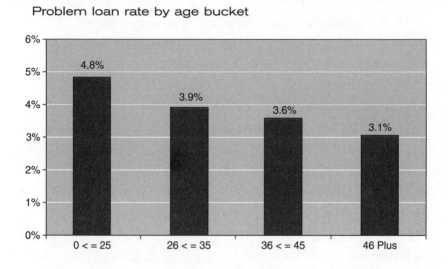

F I G U R E   8.2

Problem loan rate by region

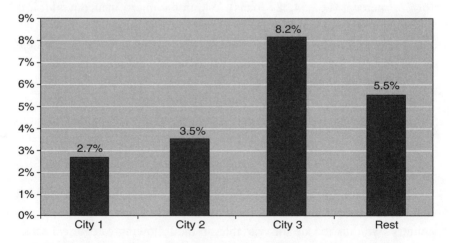

loan rates and that City 3 has the highest default rate. Historically, loans were first granted solely in City 1 and City 2, and only recently did the bank extend its activities to City 3. Moreover, bank headquarters are farthest from City 3 (hence, there is less supervision of loan officers), and the mentality in City 3 is completely different from that in City 1 and City 2. These facts likely explain most of the difference in problem loan rates.

Loan principal is an important factor for assessing the amount of money at risk for the bank. We divide this factor into the following five categories: lower than or equal to 100,000; between 100,000 and 200,000; between 200,000 and 500,000; between 500,000 and 1,000,000; and more than 1,000,000. Figure 8.3 confirms what we expect: The percentage of problem loans increases as loan principal increases. This is obviously related to the well-known criterion of capacity of repayment.

The *credit cycle* factor corresponds to a variable that increases by one each time a given client obtains a new loan. Figure 8.4 indicates a clear positive correlation between the credit cycle and the problem loan rate. Here we can identify some flaws in the credit management process. For example, management should not assume that customers are more solvent as the customer relationship becomes longer. Indeed, customers

F I G U R E   8.3

Problem loan rate by loan principal

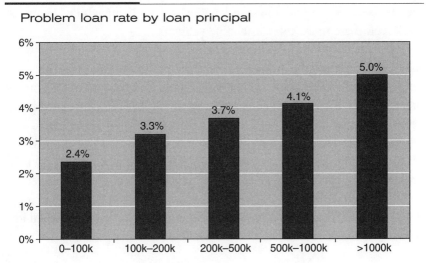

F I G U R E   8.4

Problem loan rate by credit cycle

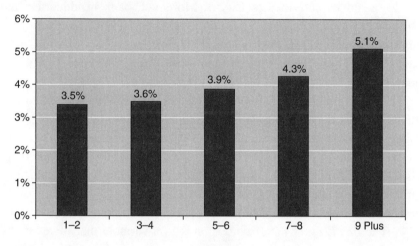

may be aware of this phenomenon and become less risk averse. One danger is that the customer ultimately refinances himself.

We also observe a significant positive correlation between the credit cycle (the number of loans granted so far to a given client) and the amount granted (i.e., the Pearson correlation is 0.47). It appears as if clients tend to receive larger amounts of money each time they obtain a new loan. This may be because the credit manager believes that clients who have a good track record are more solvent than newcomers.

To verify this assumption, we also calculate the correlation between the credit cycle and the amount requested. In this case, the Pearson correlation is quite weak at 0.09, which suggests that clients are not becoming greedier each time they request a new loan. The Pearson correlation between the credit cycle and the ratio between amount requested and amount granted is 0.21, which confirms that management has granted significantly more money to regular clients. This attitude may impact the problem loan rate, as we see that the average amount of money granted for sound loans is XOF 562,921, while the average granted for problem loans is XOF 1,012,274. The maximum exposure to a single creditor should ideally be limited to around XOF 600,000.

The number of repayment periods also seems to impact client solvency. The average number of repayment periods is significantly higher for problem loans (14 months) than for sound loans (11 months). The qualifications of borrowers also provide interesting results regarding the default rate. We divide this criterion into three groups (no education, primary school education, and secondary schools combined with universities and other). Borrowers with no education and those with solely a primary school education on average have a 3.6 percent problem loan rate. The most educated borrowers (roughly 38 percent) have a problem loan rate of 3.7 percent. This is rather surprising, however, since we might have expected education to be negatively correlated with problem loan rates.

We next study the impact of the grace period (a variable period without repayment) on the default rate. We see that the group of clients who benefited from grace periods had on average the highest problem loan rate (9.9 percent for a group of 17,172). The majority of clients with no grace period (a group of 221,849) had a problem loan rate of 3.2 percent. However, we do not retain this variable in the VaR analysis, despite its significance. We have found that most of the loans with grace periods are granted to government contractors, who we do not include in our sample.

Finally, loan maturity also has a significant impact on the problem loan rate. As Figure 8.5 shows, higher maturity is positively correlated with a higher problem loan rate. We note that most of the loans (more than 70 percent) have a 12-month maturity.

We have essentially focused on variables that management can control to some extent. This descriptive analysis shows that these variables all significantly impact the problem loan rate. The next section presents the VaR measures that we derive from this statistical analysis.

VALUE-AT-RISK MODELING

The well-known objective of any value-at-risk (VaR) measure is to provide a tool for estimating the maximum potential loss over a fixed time horizon and with a given confidence level. Many such tools are currently available for credit portfolios, with perhaps the most recognizable being RiskMetrics Credit VaR [see Gupton et al. (1997)].

F I G U R E   8.5

Problem loan rate by loan maturity

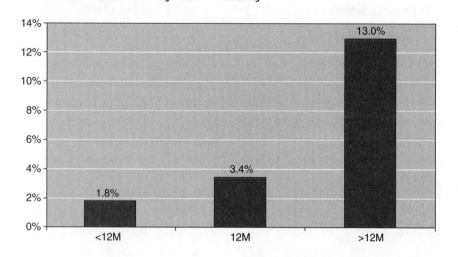

For this article, we adopt an approach based on a "not-so-well-known" indicator of the quality of a loan portfolio. This indicator is computed by dividing the outstanding balance of the problem loans by the outstanding balance of all loans in the portfolio; we refer to this measure as the problem loans ratio (PLR). The PLR takes into account the principal due and the remaining interest payments on each loan. It intuitively measures the percentage of the outstanding portfolio that will be lost if all problem loans default and if nothing is ultimately recovered on any of them. Because the PLR measures the relative size of the problem loans, a higher PLR means a riskier portfolio.

For our database, we compute the PLR at each month's end from September 1994 through July 2007. The evolution of this ratio is depicted in Figure 8.6. After a learning period of two years, the PLR remained well under 0.5 percent until the beginning of 2004. It then steadily increased to the 3 percent level in 2006. The first main reason for this explosion is macroeconomic: The home country of the bank entered a severe economic recession in 2004. The second main reason is managerial: Several months before the recession, the bank decided to relax its lending conditions by quadrupling the maximum exposure allowed to a single client.

F I G U R E 8.6

Monthly evolution of the PLR from September 1994 through July 2007

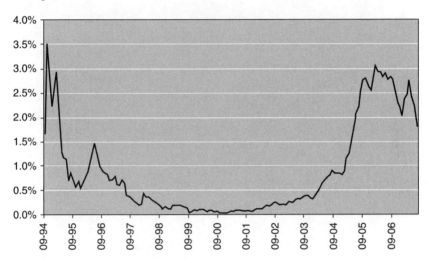

For this analysis, it is more convenient to apply the inverse logistic function to the PLR time series. The inverse logistic function of a quantity (between 0 and 1) is defined as the logarithm of ratio of the quantity with 1 minus the quantity. Figure 8.7 shows the results of this transformation. The trends are more clearly displayed, and we note that, for example, the upward PLR trend began in September 2000, well before the 2004 events.

As Figures 8.6 and 8.7 show, neither the PLR time series nor its transformation are stationary. In our case, we can obtain stationarity by taking the first difference of the transformed times series; we refer to this as the diff-transformed PLR time series. The VaR estimations are performed over the diff-transformed PLR data and subsequently converted into a forecast of the maximum PLR of the portfolio over a one-month horizon.

Note that the risk of loss here corresponds to an unexpected increase of the PLR. We chose the 95 percent confidence level for the empirical tests, and we backtested two VaR estimation methods on the empirical data: the Gaussian and the Cornish–Fisher approximation methods.

The Gaussian method assumes that the normal distribution model can describe monthly changes; VaR can then be computed as the mean plus a scaling factor, multiplied by the standard deviation. The Cornish–Fisher

FIGURE 8.7

Inverse logistic transformation of the PLR time series

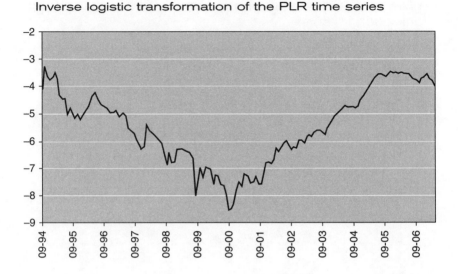

model improves on the Gaussian model by taking skewness and kurtosis into account [see Zangari (1996) for more details on this method].

Backtesting begins at the end of September 1997. We use the most recent 36 diff-transformed PLR figures to estimate the VaR forecasts for the following month. We then compare these forecasts to the actual diff-transformed PLR value at the end of October 1997. This procedure is then repeated for all subsequent months' ends through June 2007.

The results are presented in Figure 8.8, which shows that the Gaussian method performs better than the Cornish–Fisher method (a 3.4 percent failure rate vs. a 7.6 percent failure rate, respectively). This surprising result shows that more sophisticated models may be needed for accurate VaR estimations. However, it provides bank management with usable indications, which was our initial intent.

CONCLUSION

Like all other banks, an African bank specializing in microcredit needs a thorough, systematic, and rigorous credit risk management method to safeguard its assets over the long run. However, because of the limitations on IT and human resources, such a bank must adopt a practical and cost-effective approach.

F I G U R E   8.8

Backtesting for the Gaussian and Cornish–Fisher VaR
estimation methods

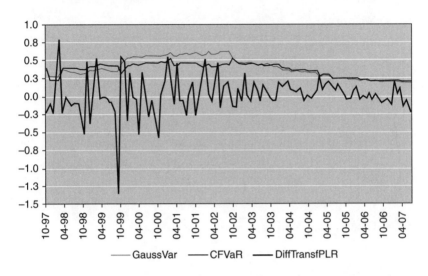

We worked closely with an African bank to develop VaR analyses to better assess its credit risk portfolio. We were able to obtain from the bank a clear-cut and precise database containing more than 250,000 loan observations gathered over the period 1994 to 2007. After cleaning the data, we conducted numerous statistical analyses to understand the main determinants of borrower solvency. Similarly to most research, we observed that each microcredit situation has its own unique cultural, sociological, economical, regional, and managerial characteristics.

Based on the statistical analyses, we adapted VaR measures specifically for the institution. Our developments were motivated by the need to provide the management with simple but sound risk tools. Ultimately, we managed to implement the Gaussian and Cornish–Fisher approximation methods. The main advantage of implementing both was to be able to take into account the dynamic structure of the database information. Our backtesting procedure showed that the Gaussian approach provided better results. We thus concluded that even though we developed simple and relevant VaR measures for the bank's credit risk management, we continue to need more sophisticated approaches.

APPENDIX 1: LIST OF LOAN CHARACTERISTICS IN THE DATABASE

- Gender
- Year of birth
- Level of education
- City of loan origination
- Business creation year
- First year register
- Credit cycle (amount of previous loans, e.g., third loan with the bank means this is the third observation for a given client and that previous loans have been repaid)
- Credit type
- Date of loan request
- Date of approval
- Date of disbursement
- Amount requested by client
- Amount granted to client
- Interest rate (always 2 percent per month)
- Credit status (variable used to code the default variable)
- Number of repayment periods
- Periodicity
- Grace period (period with no repayment just after the loan has been granted)
- Guaranty
- Number and type of arrears
- Number of days of delay
- Main (business) activity
- Family size

APPENDIX 2: PROBLEM LOAN STATISTICS WITH VARIOUS FACTORS

Panel 1: Gender

Group Name	Size	Percentage in the Sample	Problem Loan Rate
Female	179,141	77.3%	3.1%
Male	51,164	22.7%	5.6%

Panel 2: Age

Group Name	Size	Percentage in the Sample	Problem Loan Rate
≤ 25	12,547	5.5%	4.8%
$26 \leq 35$	77,191	33.6%	3.9%
$36 \leq 45$	85,362	37.0%	3.6%
≥ 45	55,205	23.8%	3.1%

Panel 3: Region

Group Name	Size	Percentage in the Sample	Problem Loan Rate
City 1	129,098	55.5%	2.7%
City 2	64,014	27.8%	3.5%
City 3	21,728	9.9%	8.2%
Rest	15,465	6.8%	5.5%

Panel 4: Loan Principal

Group Name	Size	Percentage in the Sample	Problem Loan Rate
0–100 K	30,911	13.2%	2.4%
100 K–200 K	74,291	32.1%	3.3%
200 K–500 K	58,918	25.6%	3.7%
500 K– 1,000 K	30,992	13.5%	4.1%
>1,000 K	35,193	15.5%	5.0%

Panel 5: Credit Cycle

Group Name	Size	Percentage in the Sample	Problem Loan Rate
1–2	121,060	52.5%	3.5%
3–4	63,173	27.4%	3.6%
5–6	28,430	12.4%	3.9%
7–8	11,672	5.1%	4.3%
≥9	5,970	2.6%	5.1%

Panel 6: Qualification

Group Name	Size	Percentage in the Sample	Problem Loan Rate
No formal education	92,924	40.3%	3.6%
Primary education	51,272	22.2%	3.6%
Secondary or higher	86,109	37.4%	3.7%

Panel 7: Maturity

Group Name	Size	Percentage in the Sample	Problem Loan Rate
<12 months	46,975	20.0%	1.8%
12 months	171,569	74.3%	3.4%
>12 months	11,761	5.7%	13.0%

REFERENCES

Berger, A.N. and W.S. Frame (2005) Small Business Credit Scoring and Credit Availability. Working paper, Federal Reserve Bank of Atlanta, Atlanta, GA.

Diallo, B. (2006) Un Modèle de Credit Scoring pour une Institution de Micro-finance Africaine: le cas de Nyesigiso au Mali. Laboratoire d'Économie d'Orléans, Université d'Orléans, Orléans, France.

Gupton, G.M., C. Finger, and M. Bhatia (1997) CreditMetrics Technical Document. Morgan Guaranty Trust Co., New York.

Hartungi, R. (2007) Understanding the Success Factors of Micro-Finance Institution in a Developing Country. *International Journal of Social Economics*, Vol. 34, No. 6, pp. 388–401.

Lelart, M. (2007) Les Mutations dans la Microfinance, L'Expérience du Bénin. Laboratoire d'Économie d'Orléans (LEO), Université d'Orléans, Document de Recherches, Orléans, France.

Leonard, K. J. (1995) The Development of Credit Scoring Quality Measures for Consumer Credit Applications. *International Journal of Quality and Reliability Management*, Vol. 12, No. 4, pp. 79–85.

Schreiner, M. (1999) A Scoring Model of the Risk of Costly Arrears at a Microfinance Lender in Bolivia. Washington University, St. Louis, MO.

Schreiner, M. (2000) Credit Scoring for Microfinance: Can It Work? *Journal of Microfinance*, Vol. 2, No. 2, pp. 105–118.

Schreiner, M. (2002) Scoring: The Next Breakthrough in Microcredit? CGAP Occasional Paper No. 7, Washington, DC.

Shankar S. (2007) Transaction Costs in Group Microcredit in India. *Management Decision*, Vol. 45, No. 8, pp. 1331–1342.

Zangari P. (1996) A VaR Methodology for Portfolios that includes Options. *RiskMetrics Monitor*, Vol.1, No.1, pp. 4–12.

CHAPTER 9

Allocation of Economic Capital in Banking: A Simulation Approach

Hans-Peter Burghof and Jan Müller

ABSTRACT

The approach describes the difficulties implied through consistently equating a bank's allocation of economic capital with an allocation of decision rights in the form of value-at-risk limits. Thereto we model a bank's central planner coping with correlations' uncertainty and learning about the limit addressees' skills. According to the given information and the assumed rationality of the central planner, resulting limit allocations are optimal in a portfolio theoretical sense. The numerical model generates a data set providing evidence concerning this allocation method's superiority compared to others.

INTRODUCTION

Concerning the allocation of economic capital, different categories of analyses can be found in literature. There are comprehensive approaches pointing out major coherences. For example, Froot and Stein (1998) provide a risk management model with the focus on interdependencies between capital structure, capital allocation, and hedging transactions.

Less comprehensive analyses focus on the allocation of economic capital through value-at-risk (VaR) limits. The following gives an oversight concerning related approaches' varieties. To realize an efficient use of the scarce resource economic capital, an allocation of VaR limits has to consider diversification effects. Many models are designed for banks' trading divisions. These divisions represent a convenient example for related analyses since diversification effects, in connection with securities' returns, are a well-explored field and the data are readily available. However, considering portfolios as limit addressees is an oversimplification. This setting equals a portfolio optimization under a VaR constraint, which is adequate when portfolio structure and correlations are given. In context with a bank-wide economic capital allocation limit addressees are not represented in first instance through certain portfolios but rather decision makers, steadily adjusting their portfolios while trying to anticipate the market. The business sections' complexity makes management by delegation inevitable. As a result, exact correlations are unknown to the allocating central planner.

One category of approaches analyzes market mechanisms as a possible allocation method. Stoughton and Zechner (2004) focuses on shareholder value maximization through economic capital allocation. In this context, also an institute's optimal overall amount of economic capital is an issue as well as possibilities of how to determine hurdle rates of certain institute's divisions, which makes the approach also relatively comprehensive. As an adequate allocation mechanism for economic capital, a form of an internal market is identified. First, internal market solutions seemed promising. By contrast, distortions stemming from the decision makers' limited liability and the exclusion of a systematic consideration of diversification effects in a portfolio optimizing sense indicate the opposite.

Furthermore, there are analytical approaches considering the allocation of economic capital as a mere optimization problem. So does Burmester et al. (1999), providing a corresponding general definition concerning economic capital allocation problems. An analytical approach focusing on the optimization problem is also presented by Straßberger (2002). Despite several improvements, compared to Burmester et al. (1999), the approach's mere analytical argumentation seems to be limitative. Straßberger (2002) assigns a certain profit function to each economic capital's addressee. These functions define coherences between the sizes of assigned VaR limits and resulting profits. This enables solving the optimization problem through

Lagrangian optimization. Unfortunately, by assuming certain profit functions, the vital problem of correlations' uncertainty is completely factored
out from optimization issues.

Approaches basing on numerical models may be more adequate concerning aspects of VaR limit allocations. At least if diversification effects
are central, a numerical example is quite illustrative. Dresel et al. (2002)
point out the impact of correlations' instability resulting from traders' independent decision making. It focuses on the increase of VaR limits' utilization ratio. The phenomenon of herding among traders and its impact on
VaR limit systems have been analyzed by Burghof and Sinha (2005), while
Beeck et al. (1999) analyze the transformation of annual VaR limits into
limits for shorter time periods and the impact of fixed, dynamic, and loss-
restricting limits.

The present approach integrates aspects of different analyses from
above and combines them with new ones. In the model, the bank consists
of a number of traders representing the bank's business units. A central
planner assigns value at risk limits to the different traders. Thereby, a
characteristic feature is the understanding of the limit addressees as
autonomous decision makers, which additionally are different in their per-
formances. As a result, diversification effects as performance outlooks no
longer exclusively relate to securities' returns. In contrast to common
portfolio optimization problems, correlations as expected returns are
unknown to the central planner.

Against this background, the following describes the difficulties
implied through equating an allocation of VaR limits with an allocation of
decision rights. Thereto, the present approach models a bank's central
planner coping with correlations' uncertainty and learning about the
addressees' skills. According to the given information and the assumed
rationality of the central planner, resulting limit allocations are optimal in
a portfolio theoretical sense. The numerical model generates a data set
providing evidence concerning this allocation method's superiority compared to others.

The chapter's second section describes the whole model and is sub-
divided into three parts. The first contains remarks on the central planner's
learning ability. The description of the limit allocation as an optimization
problem provides the second subsection. Further content is the objective
function's consistence. In this context the correlations' uncertainty and its

implications for the implementation of portfolio optimization will be pointed out in detail. Remarks concerning the functionality of the actual solving algorithm can be found within the third subsection.

THE MODEL

The bank is designed as a group of 30 traders and a central planner. The institute's daily business volume and ability to take risks respectively, is restricted by a given amount of economic capital which as well defines the bank's daily VaR limit. By assigning VaR limits to the traders the economic capital is allocated among them through the central planner. The banks economic capital is allocated newly in front of every trading day.

Concerning VaR computation, the delta-normal method[1] is applied throughout the model. Assuming jointly normal distributed returns assures VaR being a coherent[2] risk measure. Using the delta-normal method yields a drastically eased portfolio VaR computation that saves simulation time for the key aspects of the present analysis. A further simplification is gained through generally assuming means of zero. Standard deviations as correlations are estimated through a 75-day simple moving average.

The trading activity is modeled as follows. At the beginning of each day a trader has to decide whether to go long or short. In the model, this decision making is simulated with individual probabilities of success. According to those probabilities, the trader succeeds in anticipating the market. The choice concerning which security he should trade in is neglected. Every trader is assigned to one specific Dow Jones Industrial Average (DJIA)-stock. The trade volumes are given by the traders' VaR limits which are always used to full capacity. Infinite divisibility of shares is assumed. At the end of the trading day the position is closed in any case. Hence, other trading strategies, for example holding a position for several days or making no investment, are excluded. Similarities concerning the bank's and the traders' design can be found in Beeck et al. (1999). For the model's movements in stock prices, the discrete daily returns of the thirty

---

[1] See Jorion (2001, p. 219 et seq and p. 255 et seq) for a description of the delta-normal method.
[2] See Artzner (1999) for coherency issues.

stocks of the DJIA were collected for the year 2003. The DJIA was chosen to provide the model with well-known data.

The Central Planner's Learning Ability

The central planner has an idea about the performance outlook concerning every trader. Information asymmetries disturb the information flow between the traders and the central planner. In order to base the limit allocation on future data, in reality performance outlooks are often debated in joint nego-tiations. However, traders tend to exaggerated positive outlooks if these out-looks are decisive concerning their VaR limits' sizes. Corresponding to other budgeting problems, high limits are equated with high status and importance. Incentive systems for truthful reporting in the first instance blow up complexity and additionally lack in performance. In our theoretical model, the corresponding information gathering by the central planner is illustrated through Bayesian updating which is described by the following.

The prior used by the central planner concerning the occurrence of skills in the model world is identical with the model's actual occurrence of skills among all traders (Figure 9.1). This fact eases the modeling by avoiding unnecessary bias. The skills of a trader are represented by a spe-cific probability of success p. The distribution of skills p is described through a transformation of the generalized beta density function.[3]

F I G U R E   9.1

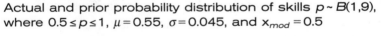

Actual and prior probability distribution of skills $p \sim B(1,9)$, where $0.5 \le p \le 1$, $\mu = 0.55$, $\sigma = 0.045$, and $x_{mod} = 0.5$

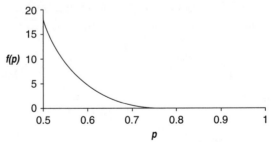

---

[3] See Johnson et al. (1995, pp. 210 and 211) for a description of the generalized beta density function.

$$f(p) = \frac{1}{B(\alpha, \beta)} \frac{(p - \underline{p})^{\alpha-1}(\overline{p} - p)^{\beta-1}}{(\overline{p} - \underline{p})^{\alpha+\beta-1}} \tag{9.1}$$

where $\underline{p} \le p \le \overline{p}$; $\alpha, \beta > 0$. In the model, the function is shaped by the parameters $\alpha = 1$ and $\beta = 9$. It is defined on the interval $[0.5, 1]$. Insertion in the formula above yields the following density function.

$$f(p) = 4608(1 - p)^8 \tag{9.2}$$

where $0.5 \le p \le 1, \alpha = 1, \beta = 9$.

In the model, values of $p < 0.5$ remain disregarded. This seems quite adequate since the imaginable worst case is displayed through a completely uninformed trader, which according to the law of large numbers is inevitably provided with the minimal probability of success of 50 percent. Hence, a probability of success smaller then fifty percent implies a trader qualified to make wrong decisions deliberately. This would relate to insider information issues, which are not part of the present analysis. By contrast, the scenario of a trader without a clue whether to go long or short is common since the distribution's mode is 0.5. The chosen distribution meets the demand of being plausible. This is sufficient since it just has to yield a selection of traders which are different concerning their skills. Which distribution form is chosen in detail is not that vital. Though, it should be mentioned that present modeling corresponds to a bank doomed to make profit just by doing business long enough. However, the present questions' related conclusions will not be biased through this fact. There just has to be used an identical model configuration if the model is used as a basis to compare different limit allocation methods.

Each trader of the model bank is determined by a draw $p_i \sim B(1,9)$ from the cumulative beta distribution function.[4]

$$F(p) = \frac{\int_{\underline{p}}^{\overline{p}} \left((p - \underline{p})^{\alpha-1}(\overline{p} - p)^{\beta-1}(\overline{p} - \underline{p})^{-(\alpha+\beta-1)} \right) dp}{B(\alpha, \beta)}, \tag{9.3}$$

where $\underline{p} \le p \le \overline{p}$; $\alpha, \beta > 0$.

---

[4] See Johnson et al. (1995, p. 211) for a description of the cumulative beta distribution function.

Insertion of $\underline{p} = 0.5, \overline{p} = 1$, $\alpha = 1$ and $\beta = 9$ leads to the subsequently presented cumulative distribution function.

$$F(p) = 1 - (2 - 2p)^9 \qquad (9.4)$$

The subsequent transformation of the cumulative beta distribution yields the bank's employees throughout the model.

$$p_i = 1 - \frac{1}{2}(1 - \zeta_i)^{\frac{1}{9}} \qquad (9.5)$$

where $i = 1, \ldots, 30$ and $\zeta_i \sim U(0,1)$.

Table 9.1 contains the corresponding 30 draws. The framed traders denote the extremal values.

As mentioned above, the specific values of p_i are unknown to the central planner. This leaves the possibility of estimating these parameters which is modeled through Bayesian updating. Thereby the estimates' accuracy develops according to the law of large numbers. The Bayesian updating represents a certain learning ability of the central planner which is assumed to act rational.

In the numerical model, the central planner distinguishes between $n = 1,000$ types of traders. Hence, the interval $[0.5,1]$ of all possible p values is divided into n equal segments on the scale of $\Delta p = 0.0005$. The prior probabilities θ_j $(j = 1, \ldots, n)$ concerning the occurrences of the

T A B L E   9.1

The bank's traders, represented through the draws' outcomes $p_i \sim B(1,9)$, where $i = 1, \ldots, 30$, $0.5 \le p_i \le 1$, $\mu_{Bank} \approx 0.555$, and $\sigma_{Bank} \approx 0.046$

trader	1	2	3	4	5	6	7	8	9	10
$p_i \approx$	0.5465	0.5101	0.5895	0.5065	0.5606	0.5986	0.5173	0.5465	0.53	0.5147
trader	11	12	13	14	15	16	17	18	19	20
$p_i \approx$	0.6321	0.5219	0.5188	0.5549	0.5405	0.582	0.505	0.5094	0.5760	0.5969
trader	21	22	23	24	25	26	27	28	29	30
$p_i \approx$	0.5234	0.6123	0.5362	0.7113	0.513	0.5955	0.5775	0.5058	0.5849	0.5402

specific types of traders are again computed via the cumulative beta distribution function.

Through customization of the function $F(p)$, the occurrences θ_j of the traders' types can be computed as follows.

$$\sum_{j=1}^{n} \theta_j = (1.001 - 0.001j)^9 - (1 - 0.001j)^9 \tag{9.6}$$

The centers of the n intervals of length Δp represent the types' specific probabilities of success p_j which can be computed through the following term.

$$\sum_{j=1}^{n} p_j = \frac{1}{2} - \Delta p \left(\frac{1}{2} - j \right) \tag{9.7}$$

where $n = 1,000$, $\Delta p = 0.0005$.

Figure 9.2 illustrates the knowledge of the central planner concerning each trader at the beginning of the first trading day.

Hence, the planner knows only the occurrences θ_j of the several types of traders serving as prior probabilities at the start of the Bayesian inference process and their corresponding probabilities of success p_j. Throughout the graph, P and L denote profit and loss.

F I G U R E   9.2

Each trader's probability structure at the beginning of the first trading day, which is known to the *central planner*

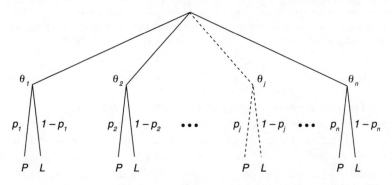

At the end of the first day, there is new information regarding which trader made a profit or a loss. In a first step, this information allows an inference concerning the type a trader belongs to. In order to give a detailed example, this process is shown by picking one trader who generated a profit. In this case, every θ_j in the structure is adjusted by the following two terms, which are based on Bayes' theorem.

$$\overset{n}{\underset{j=1}{\theta_j}} \to \overset{n}{\underset{j=1}{prob(j|P)}}_j = \frac{\theta_j p_j}{\sum\limits_{j=1}^{n} \theta_j p_j} \tag{9.8}$$

where $n = 1,000$, $P = $ profit.

By contrast, if the trader caused a loss, the term changes as displayed by Formula 9.9.

$$\overset{n}{\underset{j=1}{\theta_j}} \to \overset{n}{\underset{j=1}{prob(j|L)}}_j = \frac{\theta_j(1 - p_j)}{\sum\limits_{j=1}^{n} \theta_j(1 - p_j)} \tag{9.9}$$

where $n = 1,000$, $L = $ loss.

Thus, the terms yield a trader's probabilities of belonging to type j under the condition that this trader made a profit or a loss. Since in the model there is new information every day, these computations take place in an according frequency while the input value for the shown adjustment process is always its outcome of the day before. Concerning the example, the input values of the second day are represented through $prob_{j=1}^{n}(j|P)_j$ and $prob_{j=1}^{n}(j|L)_j$ respectively.

The focus is again on the picked trader i which generated a profit. The estimate's computation concerning his probability of success p^e_i is achieved by using $prob_{j=1}^{n}(j|P)_j$. Finally, there is taken the sum of all products between the types' probabilities of success and the corresponding adjusted occurrences displayed by the structure.

$$p_i^e(P) = \sum_{j=1}^{n} p_j prob(j|P)_j = \sum_{j=1}^{n} p_j \frac{\theta_j p_j}{\sum\limits_{j=1}^{n} \theta_j p_j}, \tag{9.10}$$

where $n = 1{,}000, P = $ profit. If the trader causes a loss, the term changes
as follows.

$$p_i^e(L) = \sum_{j=1}^{n} p_j \, prob(j|L)_j = \sum_{j=1}^{n} p_j \frac{\theta_j(1-p_j)}{\displaystyle\sum_{j=1}^{n} \theta_j(1-p_j)} \qquad (9.11)$$

where $n = 1{,}000, L = $ loss.

According to the law of large numbers, the Bayesian inference process
converges to probability p_j of type j, which is closest to the trader's actual
probability of success p_i. Hence, accuracy of the estimates rises with the
number of days and inferences respectively and with the size of the variable
n standing for the number of distinguished types of traders. Since the inference process begins with the start of a simulation, the analysed bank always
corresponds to a just founded one. This fact could be modified by firstly
assuming perfect knowledge of the central planner concerning the traders'
skills as a result of a longstanding banking activity. Bias is generated through
randomly replacing traders through further draws from $B(1, 9)$ after also randomly chosen time intervals. Thereby different fluctuation rates could be
modeled. Finally, the necessity to implement this adjustment depends on the
particular analysis the model is used for.

Figure 9.3 gives an impression of the unadjusted Bayesian inference mechanism's functionality. The squares denote the top trader with
$p_{24} = 0.7113$, the triangles represent the worst trader with $p_{17} = 0.505$, while
the circles belong to the average trader with $p_{30} = 0.505$. For exemplary reasons only, these three candidates are highlighted. After a certain number of
days, a ranking among the traders corresponding to their p_i^e values becomes
apparent. Through Bayesian inferences, the ranking of their actual probabilities of success p_i is reproduced. If the model does not include a certain fluctuation among the bank's traders as mentioned above, the ranking's accuracy
simply depends on the number of trading days the simulation is ran.

Optimization Problem

Economic capital is a scarce expensive resource for the bank. Its scope
defines the institute's business volume since it has to be provided in order
to absorb consequences of business dealings' failures and hence, to prevent

F I G U R E   9.3

Exemplary p_i^e results generated through Bayesian updating

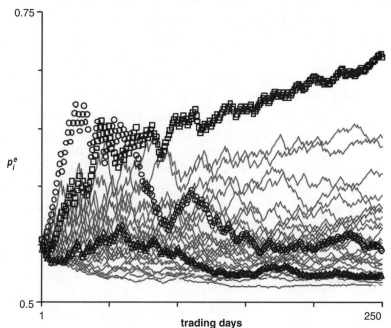

bankruptcy. Regulation demands certain minimum buffers depending on the related sizes and kinds of business transactions. Thereby, a certain provision is a necessary condition for doing business. For the central planner this implicates the possibility of directing the institute through particular limit assignments. Through decreasing or increasing divisions' limits, the corresponding divisions' business volumes can be reduced or expanded. However, deciding which limit adjustments have to be undertaken in detail is not trivial.

Throughout this approach, assigning VaR limits is considered as an allocation of decision rights and hence, as a form of delegation. Normally there is no particular investment project but an entity, trying to anticipate the market through more or less myopic decision making, especially in the case of an equity trader. Forecasting future cash flows which may result from a certain limit assignment appears impossible against this background. In the case of VaR limits the complexity is additionally increased since the resource to be allocated varies in its amount which stems from diversification effects. Finally, from a strict theoretical point of view, VaR limit adjustments always require to be considered in connection with the whole institute's portfolio of divisions and VaR limits respectively. Therefore, in order to assure a comprehensive consideration of diversification effects, the present approach is more closely related to portfolio optimization.

The assignment of VaR limits has to induce maximum institute's returns. The term of the present objective function therefore corresponds to a return to economic capital ratio, already well known under the name of return on risk adjusted capital (RORAC). Commonly the RORAC's denominator corresponds to the relating actually caused VaR. By contrast, the present denominator is substituted through the corresponding assigned VaR limit. This adjustment yields a direct performance measurement of the scarce resource's use and hence, a remedy against VaR limits' low rates of utilization.

$$\mathrm{E}\left[\frac{R_{t+1}}{VL_{t+1}}\right] \to \max$$

such that

$$\mathbf{vl_{t+1}} = vl_{i,\,t+1}(i = 1, ..., n) \mid vl_{i,\,t+1} \in \Re^n \qquad (9.12)$$

$$VL_{t+1} = EC_{t+1}$$

$$\mathrm{VAR}_{t+1} = \sqrt{\mathbf{var_{t+1}^T C_{t+1} var_{t+1}}} \le \sqrt{\mathbf{vl_{t+1}^T C_{t+1} vl_{t+1}}} = VL_{t+1}$$

$$\mathbf{var_{t+1}} = var_{i,\,t+1}(i = 1, ..., n) \mid var_{i,\,t+1} \le vl_{i,\,t+1}$$

Vectors and matrices are not italicized. Boldface indicates vectors and matrices as a whole. Otherwise their single elements are meant. Small letters denote vectors, while capital letters indicate matrices.

Note that E signals an expected value maximization referring to the upcoming day $t + 1$. The $RORAC_{t+1}$ is defined as the bank's return R_{t+1} divided by the given overall VaR limit VL_{t+1} in the denominator. In order to solve the problem, several conditions have to be kept. Firstly, the maximization has to be induced through implementation of a certain VaR limit allocation displayed by vector $\mathbf{vl_{t+1}}$ which consists of real numbers.

Furthermore, the overall limit has to correspond to the provided amount of economic capital. The allocation has to induce an institute's overall value at risk VAR_{t+1}, which does not exceed the overall limit VL_{t+1}.

Consequently, the last constraint excludes violations of each addressees limit. The vector of the traders' caused VaRs is described by the vector $\mathbf{var_{t+1}}$ while $var_{i,\,t+1}$ denotes one of its tuples.

Before going into detail, firstly a superficial but comprehensible description of the basic methods used in context with the optimization is given. The optimization of an expected value belongs to the wider field of stochastic programming.[5] The optimization procedure requires a sample of random data which is set up in order to simulate the upcoming business day of the model bank a certain number of times. In other words, a discrete probability space[6] $(\Omega, \mathbf{A}, P)^m$ is spanned up providing random data for m simulations. The random data's scope includes stock prices and certain variables used to simulate the trader's daily decision making. The bank's expected RORAC of the upcoming day is maximized based on this sample's random data. Since the model is meant to simulate a bank during a certain period of time and an optimization is accomplished each modeled business day, the number of new samples to be set up accords to the number of simulated days. During one single optimization, the sample remains unchanged through all iterations. This proceeding is known as exterior method and shrinks the optimization problem to a deterministic one. Hence, for its solution, a deterministic algorithm can be applied which will be described in chapter 2.3. The whole approach is known under the name of sample average approximation (SAA),[7] which is here used in connection with an exterior method. The SAA itself is also called sample path or stochastic counterpart method.

Previous to the solving algorithm, the mere calculation procedure of the expected bank's RORAC for a given set of traders' VaR limits is explained by the following.

---

[5] For stochastic programming, see, e.g., Birge and Louveaux (1997), Marti (2005), and Shapiro (2003).

[6] See, e.g., Birge and Louveaux (1997, p. 49 et seq) for probability space issues.

[7] See Shapiro (2003, p. 353 et seq) for SAA issues.

$$E\left[RORAC_{t+1}\right]=E\left[\frac{R_{t+1}}{VL_{t+1}}\right]=\frac{1}{m}\cdot\sum_{h=1}^{m}\frac{\sum\limits_{i=1}^{n}R_{h,\,i,\,t+1}}{VL_{t+1}}$$

$$=\frac{1}{m}\cdot\sum_{h=1}^{m}\frac{\sum\limits_{i=1}^{n}r_{h,\,i,\,t+1}\cdot V_{h,\,i,\,t+1}}{VL_{t+1}}$$

$$=\frac{1}{m}\cdot\sum_{h=1}^{m}\frac{\sum\limits_{i=1}^{n}-vl_{i,\,t+1}\cdot\varepsilon_{h,\,i,\,t+1}\cdot\sqrt{\Delta t}\cdot z_{h,\,i,\,t+1}^{-1}(\alpha,\,S)}{VL_{t+1}}$$ (9.13)

where $r_{h,\,i,\,t+1}=\sigma_{i,\,t+1}\cdot\varepsilon_{h,\,i,\,t+1}\cdot\sqrt{\Delta t}$,

$$V_{h,\,i,\,t+1}=\frac{-vl_{i,\,t+1}}{\sigma_{i,\,t+1}\cdot z_{h,\,i,\,t+1}(\alpha,\,S)}\ ,\ \varepsilon_{h,\,i,\,t+1}\sim N(\mu,\,\Sigma)\ \text{and}$$

$$vl_{t+1}=vl_{i,\,t+1}(i=1,\,...,\,n)\,\big|\,vl_{i,\,t+1}=vl_{i,\,t+1}$$

The denominator always corresponds to the bank's overall VaR limit VL_{t+1}. In the numerator, the bank's return is simulated, which consists of the n traders' summed returns $R_{h,i,t+1}$. Such a fraction is produced throughout every simulation's iteration. Getting the expected RORAC furthermore requires the simple addition of all generated fractions and their division by the number of the simulation iterations m. In order to get one trader's return $R_{h,i,t+1}$, a stock's rate of return $r_{h,i,t+1}$ has to be multiplied by the position's market value $V_{h,i,t+1}$ the trader is holding. For the detailed composition of $r_{h,i,t+1}$ and $V_{h,i,t+1}$ see the second last row of formula 9.13. The rate of return $r_{h,i,t+1}$ is generated through a geometric Brownian motion, which means the multiplication of the stock's standard deviation $\sigma_{i,t+1}$ a multivariate standard normal distributed random number $\varepsilon_{h,i,t+1}$ and a square root of the corresponding time increment $\sqrt{\Delta t}$. Each position's market value $V_{h,i,t+1}$ results from the transformation of the commonly used term for delta-normal VaR calculations. The numerator consists of the VaR-limit $vl_{i,t+1}$ and the product between standard deviation $\sigma_{i,t+1}$ and quantile $z_{h,i,t+1}(\alpha,\,S)$ in the denominator.

The quantile's absolute value $|z_{h,i,t+1}(\alpha, S)|$ depends on the underlying confidence level $1 - a$. For the present analyses, a confidence level of 99 percent is applied leading to a quantile's absolute value of $|z_{h,i,t+1}(\alpha, S)| \approx 2.33$. Since the traders can open up long and short positions, the quantile $z_{h,i,t+1}(\alpha, S)$ changes its sign in correspondence. Which positions will be taken during the following trading day is unknown to the central planner. This fact is integrated into the simulations required for expected value computations. Subsequently there is given a description of the states S leading to a positive or negative quantile value. These states S occur during simulation and are induced through particular combinations of random numbers.

$$
\begin{aligned}
z_{h,i,t+1}(\alpha, S) < 0 \quad \forall \quad S & \left|
\begin{array}{l}
\overbrace{\varepsilon_{h,i,t+1} > 0 \wedge \zeta_{h,i,t+1} < p^e_{i,t+1}(\psi_{i,t})}^{\text{profit}} \quad \vee \\[4pt]
\underbrace{\varepsilon_{h,i,t+1} < 0 \wedge \zeta_{h,i,t+1} > p^e_{i,t+1}(\psi_{i,t})}_{\text{loss}},
\end{array}
\right. \\[16pt]
z_{h,i,t+1}(\alpha, S) > 0 \quad \forall \quad S & \left|
\begin{array}{l}
\overbrace{\varepsilon_{h,i,t+1} < 0 \wedge \zeta_{h,i,t+1} < p^e_{i,t+1}(\psi_{i,t})}^{\text{profit}} \quad \vee \\[4pt]
\underbrace{\varepsilon_{h,i,t+1} > 0 \wedge \zeta_{h,i,t+1} > p^e_{i,t+1}(\psi_{i,t})}_{\text{loss}},
\end{array}
\right.
\end{aligned}
\tag{9.14}
$$

where $\zeta_{h,i,t+1} \sim U(0,1)$ and $\psi_{i,t} \sim U(0,1)$.

$\varepsilon_{h,i,t+1}$ is the already known multivariate standard normal distributed random number used in context with the geometric Brownian motion and, hence, defines whether the stock price increases or decreases. $\zeta_{h,i,t+1}$ as $\psi_{i,t}$ denote uniform distributed random numbers. The first one determines, whether a certain trader generates a profit or loss throughout the m simulations. In contrast the second decides whether the trader generates a profit or a loss during the models "real" trading action. Since the real trading results drive the skills estimators' values $P^e_{i,t+1}$, these depend at the same time on $\psi_{i,t}$. The operator $\vee$ separates two different states S which both lead to the same quantile sign, but once the result is a profit and once a loss.

Search Algorithm

Still missing is an explanation of the search process concerning the maximum $E[RORAC_{t+1}]$ inducing VaR limit allocation $\mathbf{vl}_{t+1}$ which represents the solution to the optimization problem. The corresponding technical procedure to track down the solution is described by the following.

Firstly, there is set up a subproblem through modification of the original optimization problem.

$$E\left[\frac{R_{t+1}}{VAR_{t+1}}\right] \rightarrow \max$$

such that   (9.15)

$$\mathbf{vl}_{t+1} = vl_{i,\,t+1}(i = 1, ..., n)\,\Big|\,vl_{i,\,t+1} \in \Re^n$$

$$VAR_{t+1} > 0$$

Instead of the bank's given overall VaR limit VL_{t+1}, now the bank's overall value at risk VAR_{t+1} is used as denominator. Furthermore, there is only one constraint demanding the tuples of the VaR limit's vector $\mathbf{vl}_{t+1}$ to be real numbers. Hence, for technical reasons, this problem neglects risk-taking constraints, which normally result in the model from a limited amount of economic capital. This reduced objective function focuses on identifying the size ratios between the VaR limits of vector $\mathbf{vl}_{t+1}$ that induce maximized expectations concerning the return to VaR ratio. The mere calculation of one objective function's value for a given VaR limit allocation is displayed subsequently.

$$E\left[RORAC_{t+1}\right] = E\left[\frac{R_{t+1}}{VAR_{t+1}}\right]$$

$$= \frac{1}{m} \cdot \sum_{h=1}^{m} \frac{\displaystyle\sum_{i=1}^{n} R_{h,\,i,\,t+1}}{VAR_{h,\,t+1}}$$

$$= \frac{1}{m} \cdot \sum_{h=1}^{m} \frac{\displaystyle\sum_{i=1}^{n} r_{h,\,i,\,t+1} \cdot V_{h,\,i,\,t+1}}{VAR_{h,\,t+1}}$$ (9.16)

$$= \frac{1}{m} \cdot \sum_{h=1}^{m} \frac{\displaystyle\sum_{i=1}^{n} -vl_{i,\,t+1} \cdot \varepsilon_{h,\,i,\,t+1} \cdot \sqrt{\Delta t} \cdot z_{h,\,i,\,t+1}^{-1}(\alpha,\,S)}{|z(\alpha)| \cdot \sqrt{\displaystyle\sum_{i=1}^{n}\sum_{j=1}^{n} V_{h,i,t+1} \cdot V_{h,j,t+1} \cdot \rho_{h,ij,t+1} \cdot \sigma_{i,t+1} \cdot \sigma_{j,t+1}}}$$

The original problem's RORAC relates the overall returns to the overall VaR limit of the bank. By contrast, the present subproblem's RORAC results from relating the returns to the corresponding VaR. Hence, in comparison to the original optimization problem, the numerator remains unchanged, while the denominator is substituted.[8] The closest insight to this substituted part gives the last row's term's denominator consisting of the common portfolio VaR formula. It indicates that during a simulation of m iterations also m different correlation matrices $\rho_{h,j,t+1}$ are required. To be precise, during one optimization the correlations' absolute values stay the same, but their signs change according to the traders' decisions of whether taking long or short positions. However, correlations' uncertainty is represented sufficiently through this proceeding for the model's purposes. The correlations' absolute values only change between the optimizations corresponding to the latest stock price movements.

The present problem's solution can be identified through the following abstractly illustrated search algorithm (Figure 9.4). Note that the solution is denoted by $\mathbf{vl}^*_{t+1}$.

Functionality of the subproblem's search algorithm

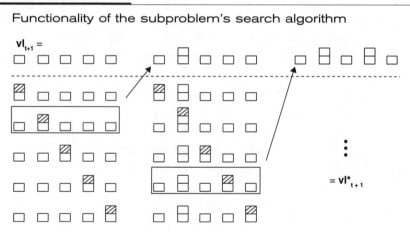

---

[8] For a closer look at the numerator, see formula 9.13.

Every square element displays a trader's VaR limit. For descriptive reasons, the number of traders is reduced to five. The allocation in the left upper corner above the dotted line represents the starting point. Through adding the striped limit extensions in the described manner, the five new allocations beneath the dotted line are generated. Subsequently, according to Formula 9.16, each resulting allocation is tested in a simulation with m iterations concerning which of them yields the highest expected bank's RORAC. In the example, the framed allocations include this attribute and hence serve as input data for the following optimization iteration, while every column denotes one optimization's iteration. If the initial limit extension of size Δvl does not result in at least one allocation outperforming the inputted one, Δvl is adjusted through simple bisection. Subsequently, each of these five new allocations is again tested in a simulation. If this still does not yield an improvement, the bisecting process is continued until a certain stopping criterion is reached (in this case $\Delta vl < \$1,000$). Note that in order to approach the true problem's solution, an extension's adjustment process accordant $\Delta vl \to 0$ would be necessary. Hence, for time reasons, the procedure only yields a solution's estimator of adequate accuracy. As stopping criterion concerning the optimization algorithm itself, an expected RORAC's improvement rate smaller then one percent is used. Also note that the values of the stopping criteria base on experiences and do not stem from optimization processes themselves. Finally, they result from accuracy-time trade-off considerations.

As mentioned, the key feature of the subproblem's solution is the revelation of the VaR limits' size ratios which ought to be provided in order to realize expectations' maximization concerning the institute's return to VaR ratio. Also note that risk taking constraints were neglected so far. The subproblem's solution now has to be transformed into one additionally feasible for the original optimization problem. The corresponding search problem is described subsequently.

$$\mathbf{vl}^*_{t+1} \to \mathbf{vl}^*_{t+1} \ \Big| \ E\Big[VAR_{t+1}\big(\mathbf{vl}^*_{t+1}\big)\Big] = EC_{t+1}$$

such that

$$\Lambda_{t+1} \in \mathfrak{R}^n \text{ and}$$

$$\mathbf{vl}_{t+1} = vl_{i,t+1}(i = 1, ..., n) \ \big| \ vl_{i,t+1} \in \mathfrak{R}^n$$

(9.17)

Hence, a limit allocation vl^*_{t+1} is searched which induces an expected overall value at risk VAR_{t+1} equating the institute's provided economic capital EC_{t+1}. In the present model, an expected VAR_{t+1} smaller then EC_{t+1} would inevitably imply a worse solution to the problem. This stems from the marginal utility of taking risk that never becomes negative in the chosen model setting. Hence, increased risk is always accompanied by an increased expected return. The solutions transformation is realized through the element wise product of vector vl^*_{t+1} and scalar Λ_{t+1}, which has to be a real number. Thereby, the size ratios between the VaR limits, which are responsible for the induction of a maximized expected RORAC, remain unchanged.

Therefore, in order to solve the above-mentioned search problem, the particular scalar Λ_{t+1}, has to be identified. This identification is realized through a binary search algorithm applied to the interval (0, 2).[9] During the binary search process, every interim solution's VaR limit allocation vl_{t+1} is backtested with regard to EC_{t+1} and the applied confidence level of 99 percent. The binary search continues until one allocation induces an institute's VaR, which overshoots the value of EC_{t+1} in exactly 1 percent of all cases. Until then, depending on whether the rate of overshooting exceeds or falls below one percent, the limits are decreased through a lower or increased through a higher scalar Λ_{t+1}. Note that the backtesting includes the simulation of the whole model bank. Hence, also the decision making and its resulting diversification effects are considered. The following denotes the term for the institutes VaR computation during the backtesting of one interim solution vl_{t+1}.

$$
VAR_{h,\,t+1}^{m} = |z(\alpha)| \cdot \sqrt{\sum_{i=1}^{n}\sum_{j=1}^{n} V_{h,i,t+1} \cdot V_{h,j,t+1} \cdot \rho_{h,j,t+1} \cdot \sigma_{i,t+1} \cdot \sigma_{j,t+1}} \,,
$$

$$
\text{where } V_{h,i,t+1} = \frac{-vl_{i,\,t+1}}{\sigma_{i,\,t+1} \cdot z_{h,\,i,\,t+1}(\alpha,\,S)} \text{ and} \tag{9.18}
$$

$$
vl_{t+1} = vl_{i,\,t+1}(i = 1,\,...,\,n)\,\big|\, vl_{i,\,t+1} = vl_{i,\,t+1}
$$

One interim allocation vl_{t+1} is tested in connection with m different portfolio constellations resulting from the simulated traders' decision

---

[9] For an explanation of the binary search algorithm, see, e.g., Knuth (1998, pp. 409–426).

making. The allocation causing a number of overshootings (one over-shooting is denoted through $VAR_{h,t+1} > EC_{t+1}$) equal to $m/100$ denotes the solution. Finally, for the VaR calculation itself, the common formula for portfolio VaR computations is applied, as displayed through Equation (9.18).

Figure 9.5 illustrates the optimization's results concerning six trading days. In example, the leftmost curve displays the interim solutions of the first trading day's optimization. Its highest point indicates the day's optimization's stopping point and, hence, the point when the improvement rate fell below 1 percent. The corresponding VaR limit allocation $\mathbf{vl}^*_{t+1}$ $|E[VAR_{t+1}(\mathbf{vl}^*_{t+1})] = EC_{t+1}$ is then used for the upcoming "real" trading day. The first day's optimization yields an expected RORAC's increase from below 0.38 up to 0.55 percent corresponding approximately to a 45 percent improvement. The low starting points of the curves stem from first using the allocation from the solution of the day before. Except for the first day's curve, where an allocation consisting of equal limits was used as an origin. Without an adjustment to the upcoming days attributes, these previous allocations yield relatively low expected RORACs. Altogether the applied algorithm required 67 optimization iterations to accomplish six days.

F I G U R E   9.5

Exemplary results of the subproblem's search algorithm

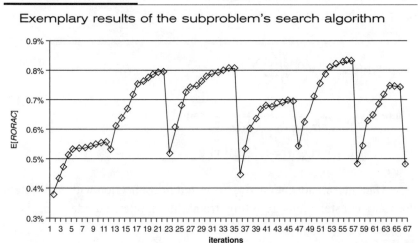

Figure 9.6 gives a further impression of what actually happens during runtime of numerical analyses based on the present model. It displays the first 50 days' results concerning the limit allocations. Again the highlighted limits denote the best (cuboids), worst (pyramids) and average (cylinders) trader as in Figure 9.3. The average trader number 30 appears interesting since he is provided with relatively high VaR limits during the first 50 days, which is surprising since he just has an average probability of success. However, during the first 50 days, he was quite successful, which leads to relatively high estimators p^e_{30} as could be seen in Figure 9.3. Hence, in his case, the optimization process yielded high limits, while the top trader (cuboids) did not yet entirely reach his skills' corresponding rank in the allocation process.

CONCLUSION

Table 9.2 shows the means of thousand simulation outcomes per distinguished allocation method. An economic capital of $100,000 was allocated daily among 10 traders throughout all simulations and methods. The results are arranged according to each method's generated bank's rate of profit to provided economic capital (RORAC 1).

RORAC 2 measures the rate of profit to used economic capital, while VaR is the annual average bank's value at risk. How much economic capital was finally used in average describes the limit utilisation. The next

F I G U R E   9.6

Exemplary illustration of the limit allocations during the first 50 trading days

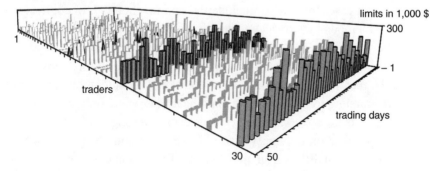

T A B L E   9.2

Means of 1,000 simulation outcomes per allocation method

Allocation Method	RORAC 1	RORAC 2	VaR	Limit Utilisation	Invested Capital	Return	ROI	Confidence Level 1	Confidence Level 2
M1	3.0%	9.8%	30 769$	30.8%	2 511 666$	763 342$	30.4%	100.00%	99.10%
M2	3.7%	4.4%	83 354$	83.4%	3 117 794$	923 402$	29.6%	99.41%	99.12%
M3	3.9%	4.7%	83 333$	83.3%	3 118 339$	993 548$	31.9%	99.46%	99.11%
M4	4.6%	9.9%	45 740$	45.7%	3 792 221$	1 147 965$	30.3%	100.00%	99.10%
M5	5.1%	9.1%	55 702$	55.7%	4 242 019$	1 277 528$	30.1%	99.97%	99.10%
M6	5.5%	10.0%	54 779$	54.8%	4 519 667$	1 387 050$	30.7%	99.98%	99.11%
M7	6.2%	10.7%	58 407$	58.4%	3 897 237$	1 573 849$	40.7%	99.96%	99.11%

two columns provide the annual average of invested capital and the annual returns. They are used to compute the return on investment. Finally, the last two columns show whether the confidence level of 99 percent was kept (1) on the aggregated bank level and (2) on the traders' level.

The number of compared alternatives is restricted to versions that can be derived from recomposing and leaving out different central efficiency criterions met by the potentially superior method number seven. Table 9.3 gives an overview concerning these criterions and their combinations in the allocation methods.

Since certain criterions depend on others, there are only seven instead of 16 different methods to be analyzed. C2 and C4 require C1. Furthermore, C3 requires C4. The following gives an explanation and discussion of the two tables' results.

M1 represents the simplest allocation procedure. The economic capital is equally divided among the traders. Note that this proceeding is also chosen in all cases that do not include the optimization C4. In contrast to M1 these methods include a consideration of diversification effects.

The next three methods M2 to M4 take care of the diversification effects C1 but neglect diversification effects C2. The results show that among the mentioned three methods an additional consideration of C4 and C3 corresponding to M2 and M3 cannot beat M4, where only the diversification effects C1 are considered. This is caused through the fact that M2 as M3's optimization implicitly assumes traders without the possibility of going short, which differs from the "real" trading action in the model. This

T A B L E   9.3

Efficiency criterions in the context with the allocation of economic capital and their combinations in different allocation methods

Allocation Method	Criteria C1 Diversification Effects Stemming from Returns' Correlations	Criteria C2 Diversification Effects Stemming from Traders' Autonomous Decision Making	Criteria C3 Learning Ability of the Central Planner	Criteria C4 RORAC-Optimization
M1	–	–	–	–
M2	X	–	–	X
M3	X	–	X	X
M4	X	–	–	–
M5	X	X	–	X
M6	X	X	–	–
M7	X	X	X	X

fact induces limit allocations where one single trader, whose share provides the highest positive returns throughout the simulations of the upcoming trading day, gets the major part of the economic capital. Shares with mainly negative returns can not serve as investments anymore. This negative effect outshines the remaining diversifying potential of these traders and shares. As a result, there are unbalanced allocations with relatively high VaRs but low RORACs and returns. This finding emphasizes the requirement of a sophisticated modeling of the different existing diversification effects in connection with a RORAC-optimization. If this modeling of diversification effects falls below a certain quality level a RORAC-optimization's benefit deflagrates and a plain consideration of C1 in the form of M4 becomes the dominant strategy although the distorting implicit only-long assumption concerning the trading behavior holds there too.

Methods M5 to M7 provide such a specific consideration of diversification effects as recommended above. However, method M5 seems to provide a counterproof. Although taking care of both diversification effects C1 as C2, an additional consideration of C4 is still worse then a complete coverage of diversification without any other feature as provided by M6. At least the improvement rate of RORAC 1 from M5 to M6 is only a third of the corresponding rate from M2 to M4. That M6 still beats M5, although considering all diversification effects, may be caused by the parameters' similarity of the underlying shares which all stem from the Dow Jones Industrial Average Index. If these shares would be extremely different concerning their volatilities and correlations, the optimization would be associated with a much higher potential for improvement. Also note that in such a setting an equal division of the economic capital among the traders corresponding to M6 would be a much worse and inadequate solution as in the present setting with very similar shares. In contrast to method M5 the last method M7 outclasses M6. M7 combines the optimization C4 with the learning ability C3. M7 clearly represents the superior assigning procedure compared to rest.

The simple mean analysis is meant to serve in the sense of an acceptance test concerning the presented simulation based approach. The results' explanation and discussion show that the model setting is free of inconsistencies. It can be used to produce comprehensive data sets for further analyses of variance and covariance. In this context the following summarizes the potential independent variables: allocation method, frequency of allocation, risk measure, number of entities, and traders, respectively; the rate of job change and the use of the central planner's learning ability, respectively; and homogeneity vs. heterogeneity concerning the underlying businesses of the limit addressees in the bank, which can be regulated through using underlying shares with certain volatility and correlation levels. The adjustment of these variables and further analyses of dependent variables corresponding to the variables described in Table 9.2 provide an adequate procedure to extract relevant statements concerning the grade of sophistication a bank's allocation of economic capital should provide from efficiency aspects.

REFERENCES

Artzner, P. (1999) Coherent Measures of Risk. *Mathematical Finance*, Vol. 9, No. 3, pp. 203–228.

Beeck, H., L. Johanning, and B. Rudolph (1999) Value-at-Risk-Limitstrukturen zur Steuerung und Begrenzung von Marktrisiken im Aktienbereich. *OR-Spektrum*, Vol. 21, No. 1–2, pp. 259–286.

Birge, R. B. and F. Louveaux (1997) *Introduction to Stochastic Programming*. New York: Springer.

Burghof, H.-P. and T. Sinha (2005) Capital Allocation with Value-at-Risk—The Case of Informed Traders and Herding. *The Journal of Risk*, Vol. 7, No. 4, pp. 47–73.

Burmester, C., Hille, C. T., and Deutsch, H.-P. (1999) Risikoadjustierte Kapitalallokation: Beurteilung von Allokationsstrategien über einen Optimierungsansatz. In R. Eller, W. Gruber, and M. Reif (eds.), *Handbuch Bankenaufsicht und Interne Risikosteuerungsmodelle*. Stuttgart, Germany: Schäffer-Poeschel.

Dresel, T., R. Härtl, and L. Johanning (2002) Risk Capital Allocation Using Value at Risk Limits if Correlations between Traders' Exposures Are Unpredictable. *European Investment Review*, Vol. 1, No. 1, pp. 57–64.

Froot, K.A. and J. C. Stein. (1998) Risk Management, Capital Budgeting and Capital Structure Policy for Financial Institutions: An Integrated Approach. *Journal of Financial Economics*, Vol. 47, No. 1, pp. 55–82.

Johnson, N.L., S. Kotz, and N. Balakrishnan (1995) *Continuous Univariate Distributions*. New York: Wiley.

Jorion, P. (2001) *Value at Risk*. New York: McGraw-Hill.

Knuth, D. E. (1998) *The Art of Computer Programming. Volume 3: Sorting and Searching*. Reading, MA: Addison-Wesley.

Marti, K. (2005) *Stochastic Optimization Methods*. Berlin, Germany: Springer.

Shapiro, A. (2003) Monte Carlo Sampling Methods. In A. Ruszczynski and A. Shapiro (eds.), *Stochastic Programming, Handbooks in Operations Research and Management Science*. Amsterdam, Netherlands: Elsevier.

Stoughton, N. M. and J. Zechner. (2004) Optimal Capital Allocation in Banking. Working paper, University of Vienna, Vienna.

Straßberger, M. (2002) *Risikokapitalallokation und Marktpreisrisikosteuerung mit Value-at-Risk-Limiten*. Lohmar and Cologne, Germany.

CHAPTER 10

Using Tail Conditional Expectation for Capital Requirement Calculation of a General Insurance Undertaking

João Duque, Alfredo D. Egídio dos Reis, and Ricardo Garcia

ABSTRACT

In this chapter we develop a solvency model to estimate the necessary economic capital of a real insurance undertaking operating solely in the automobile branch, applying the tail conditional expectation risk measure. The model assumes a one-year time horizon static approach with an unchanged asset and liability structure for the company. After discussing the main factors affecting the whole of the insurance activity and their influence on the assets and liabilities on the real insurance undertaking used in the study, we calculate its necessary economic capital by using the Monte Carlo simulation technique to generate the probability distribution of the possible future profit and losses with impact on the company's fair value. This chapter introduces an application of a set of techniques that are usually applied to manage asset and liability risks to capital requirements. With a simulated exercise applied to a real insurance under-taking we show its feasibility, its advantages, and how useful it may be for investors, regulators, and remaining stakeholders when the technique is explored in depth.

INTRODUCTION

The determination of the economic capital requirement to ensure, with high probability, the development of operations, even in adverse environments, is a primary question, due to the role of insurance undertakings in the economy.

In this chapter we develop a solvency model to estimate the necessary economic capital for a real portfolio of a particular insurer, using a set of specific risk analysis tools that have been widely used for different purposes and aims. It allows us to calculate the economic capital requirement for an insurance undertaking, in order to face adverse situations with a chosen high probability, given its current asset and liabilities structure and considering a one-year time horizon.

We limit our study to the automobile branch, identifying the main assets, liabilities, and operations that cause uncertainty on the economic value of the insurer under study. We measure the causes of uncertainty by the impact on the economic results and enhance the interest and practical applications of the model to the insurance industry.

Here we only consider stocks and bonds as manageable assets, while for liabilities we will account for premium and claims reserves. The stocks and bonds considered are those that the insurance undertaking actually shows in the balance sheet and the simulations are based on the assumption that they are kept constant within the time interval under study. As far as the reserves are concerned, they relate to the underwriting of insurance contracts and respective claims settling.

There are several types of risks in the insurance activity that affect assets, liabilities, or both. In this chapter we model the equity risk, interest rate risk, credit risk, reserve risk, and the premium risk, determining the exposure of the assets and liabilities to the different types of risks.

We suggest the capital requirement to be determined based upon the tail conditional expectation (simply, TCE) risk measure, assuming a (future) simulated profit and loss distribution for the company, which in turn, is estimated by means of Monte Carlo simulation.

We assume that in the case of ruin before the end of the period, the insurance undertaking has the ability to provide additional capital to ensure the continuity of its activities. We consider a static approach, stressing the need for a periodic reevaluation, since it is not expectable that, within a reasonable time horizon, neither the asset and liabilities structure nor the future profit and loss distribution remains unchanged. Furthermore, for the sake of simplicity, we assume that the fair value of the insurer's liabilities equals the *best estimate*, i.e., the market value risk margin is null.

Thus, we present VaR and TCE risk measures, define the risk factors affecting the whole of the insurance industry and the particular insurance undertaking studied, model their individual and aggregate behavior and detail the simulation procedures. Finally, these procedures are applied to a non-life insurer operating in the motor branch and are used to calculate its economic capital requirement. The importance of these sorts of risk measures to compute capital requirement is enhanced by the newly proposed regulations for the insurance industry in the European market, under the program Solvency II. For more details, please see Linder and Ronkainen (2004).

The body of this chapter is divided into five sections. In the next section we formulate the solvency model, introducing the individual risk factors involved, their modeling and simulation procedures. In this chapter's third section, we develop our application under the assumptions considered. In the fourth section, we show the results of our application and calculate the capital requirement for the period, risk by risk, and for the aggregate. Finally, in the last section we present the main conclusions.

THE MODEL

Value at Risk and Tail Conditional Expectation

The value at risk [simply, $\mathrm{VaR}_\alpha (X)$ or VaR_α] is defined as the quantile of order α of the probability distribution of the random variable X that represents the future results (profit and losses) of the insurer. That is, $\mathrm{VaR}_\alpha = \inf [x \in \Re | F_X(x) \geq \alpha]$, where $F_x (x)$ is the distribution function of X. The tail conditional expectation, denoted as $\mathrm{TCE}_\alpha (X)$ or simply TCE_α, is defined as $\mathrm{TCE}_\alpha (X) = E[X | X < \mathrm{VaR}_\alpha(X)]$. That is, while with the VaR we are interested in knowing how much can a firm lose within a certain

time horizon, under certain set of considerations, the TCE allow us to estimate the expected loss whenever the occurred loss is greater than the VaR
(assuming that the VaR is negative). Therefore, it seems that TCE is a
more conservative but safer risk measure to adequately protect the insurance undertaking industry, their shareholders and remaining stakeholders.

Considering the advantages of the TCE over the VaR as presented by
Artzner (1999) and Lynn Wirch and Hardy (1999), this will be the chosen
risk measure to determine the necessary economic capital. Nevertheless,
since VaR is nowadays the most commonly used risk measure and we
need the VaR for the computation of the TCE, we will present both risk
measures for comparative purposes.

Modeling the Individual Risks

As far as *equity risk* is concerned, it is defined as the risk associated with
stock price returns fluctuation, assuming a well-diversified insurer's portfolio. If this is the case, we may then consider the Sharpe (1964) and
Lintner's (1965) capital asset pricing model (CAPM). Assuming a capital
market in equilibrium and that a set of assumptions is fulfilled [see, for
instance, in Elton et al. (2007)], the expected rate of return of the portfolio will then be given by

$$E\left(R_p\right) = R_f + \beta_p\left(E\left(R_m\right) - R_f\right)$$ (10.1)

where R_f stands for the risk-free rate of return, R_m is the market rate of
return, and β_p represents the N assets portfolio beta that equals
$\beta_p = \Sigma_{i=1}^{N} w_i \beta_i$, with each individual beta component determined by
$\beta_i = \sigma_{im}/\sigma_m^2$, denoting σ_{im}, the covariance between the rate of return of
stock i and the market rate of return; σ_m^2 stands for the equity market variance, and w_i is the weight of stock i in the portfolio.

Considering a portfolio with a large number of assets, we can
assume, without loss of accuracy, that $\sigma_p \cong \beta_p \sigma_m$ [see, for instance, in
Elton et al. (2007)]. In order to estimate the parameters β_i, we use the
market model.

For simulation purposes we assumed that the simulated instantaneous market rate of return follows a geometric Brownian motion, whose

dynamics are given by the equation $d \ln S_t = (\mu - \sigma^2/2) dt + \sigma dW_t$, where S_t is the stock market price level at time t, W_t a standard Brownian motion, μ is the *drift* constant, σ is the volatility, and $dW_t = Z(dt)^{1/2}$ is the increment of W_t, $W_t \sim Normal$ $(0;\ dt)$; and Z is standard normal random variable. For practical purposes the above stochastic process is discretized in short time intervals, say $\Delta_t = k/p$, where p is the number of increments and k the chosen time horizon. Thus, the simulated stock price level at $t + \Delta t$ will be given by

$$S_{t+\Delta t} = S_t \cdot \exp\{(\mu - \sigma^2/2)\Delta t + \sigma z\sqrt{\Delta t}\} \qquad (10.2)$$

In order to model the pricing behavior of the debt instruments that are significant for the assets side of the balance sheet of the insurance undertaking, we need to consider both the credit risk and the interest rate risk.

Starting with the *credit risk*, we use the J.P. Morgan's (1997) CreditMetrics to model the credit risk of the debt instruments under consideration.

The credit spreads are extracted from the companies *rating* scores. The better the issuer's rating, the less the credit spread required and, consequently, the larger the discounted value of the debt. The model assumes that if the market value of the issuer's debt follows beyond a given threshold, the entity will enter into default. This reasoning is extended in a way that will allow us to determine a relationship between the assets value and the issuer's rating. We assume that the rate of return of the issuer's asset follows a normal distribution in the case of a single credit or a multivariate normal distribution for a portfolio of credits. For the simulation procedure of the assets rate of returns we generate a set of correlated (pseudo-) normal random values and a new rating, and its respective credit spread is assigned, if necessary.

The analysis is even refined considering scenarios for default. The credit rates of recovery are highly volatile, which means that, for each scenario of default, we simulate a value for the credit recovery rate assuming a beta distribution with parameters in accordance with the credit's level of the subordination. If the debt is simulated to default, then the credit value will equal the simulated rate of recovery times the nominal value of the credit. Otherwise, the issuer's credit risk considering the simulated rating is added up to the respective risk-free discount rate in order to estimate the value of the debt instrument.

In order to model the debt *interest rate risk*, we use simulated zero coupon bonds with maturity equal to the duration of each bond portfolio, as suggested by J.P. Morgan and Reuters (1996).

We assume that the daily short-term interest rate behavior follows a modified one-period one-factor, short-term interest rate model of Cox et al. (1985) (CIR model) suggested by Fisher et al. (2002), whose parameter estimation method is easier to implement. The notation, the parameter estimation, and the simulation procedure are according to those proposed by these authors.

The short-term interest rate behavior is assumed to follow the stochastic dynamics given by

$$dr(t) = (b - a \cdot r(t))dt + \sigma\sqrt{r(t)}dW(t) \qquad (10.3)$$

where b, a, and σ are positive constants and $W(t)$ is a standard Brownian motion. As far as bond prices for the several maturities are concerned, these are assumed to value $\{p(t, r(t), T)\}$ defined by

$$p(t, r(t), T) = A(t, T)e^{-B(t,T)r(t)} \qquad (10.4)$$

where

$$A(t, T) = \left[\frac{2he^{(a+h)(T-t)/2}}{2h + (a+h)(e^{(T-t)h} - 1)} \right]^{2b/\sigma^2}$$

$$B(t, T) = \left[\frac{2(e^{(T-t)h}) - 1}{2h + (a+h)(e^{(T-t)h} - 1)} \right]$$

$h = \sqrt{a^2 + 2\sigma^2}$, t is the time moment when the value is determined, and T is the maturity.

The implicit *yield* curve of the CIR model is estimated from

$$r(t, T) = -\frac{\log(p(t, r(t), T))}{T - t} \qquad (10.5)$$

If Equation (10.3) holds, it means that the process is not directly observed, since it is developed under the risk-neutral probability measure. However, as we need to simulate the stochastic interest rate process under the real world probability measure, an acceptable market estimate for a can be $\tilde{a}$ [see Fisher et al. (2002)]. The parameters b, $\tilde{a}$, and σ can be empirically determined using market data. The estimation method for the parameters b, $\tilde{a}$, and σ is based upon the martingales estimation functions as presented in Fisher et al. (2002). The actual short-term interest rate, $r(0)$, and the estimates of $\hat{b}$ and $\hat{\sigma}$ are then used to estimate a, assuming that market prices (p_i^M) equal the theoretical prices (p_i) for i, $i = 1,\ldots,n$, zero coupon bonds, with maturity T_i at time zero $(t = 0)$. The estimate for a is then obtained by $\underset{a}{\text{Min}} \sum_{i=1}^{n} (p_i - p_i^M)^2$.

Short-term interest rates have to be simulated using the estimate $\tilde{a}$, instead of a, since we are interested in generating real world scenarios for $r(t)$, as in Fisher et al. (2002). Given a time discretization into equally time spaced instants, we split the time interval $[0,T]$ into N equal time intervals: $\Delta = T/N$. Then, we simulate the future values of the short-term interest rate, r_n, using the recursion method, for $n = 1,\ldots,N$, with the starting point $r(0)$ according to

$$r_n = r_{n-1} + \left(\hat{b} - \hat{\tilde{a}} r_{n-1} \right) \Delta + \hat{\sigma} \sqrt{r_{n-1}} \Delta \tilde{W}_n \tag{10.6}$$

With the yield curve, considering the credit risk, and using the inverted version of Equation (10.5) it is then possible to determine a simulated future value of each bond, given both credit and interest rate risks. The difference between the simulated future value of each bond and its present (discounted) value corresponds to the simulated result (gain or loss) of holding each bond for the one-year time period.

The *reserve risk* is related to the risk of adverse development of the claims reserve. It corresponds to an estimate of the total cost that the insurer will have to bear in order to settle all claims occurred until the end of the year, whether they have been reported or not. This is a net value, after the deduction of all payments already done concerning those claims.

Define I_{ij} as the incremental payments made in the development year j regarding claims occurred in the year I, and $R = \Sigma_{(i,j) \in \Delta} I_{i,j}$ is the total reserve. Here, Δ represents the set of indexes associated to the total future incremental payments displayed in the usual development matrix, i.e., $\Delta = \{(i,j) : 0 \leq i \leq N; N - i + 1 \leq j \leq N + 1\}$, N is the observed development period, and we assume the claims development stops at $N + 1$. For more details please see Taylor (2000). We will use a generalized linear model (simply, GLM), where the variables I_{ij} are considered to be independent and identically distributed (i.i.d.), whose distribution belongs to the exponential family, described in McCullagh and Nelder (1989).

A GLM is characterized by a random component and a systematic component. Regarding the first component, consider a set of independent random variables (r.v.)s $Y_i, i = 1, 2, \ldots, n$, with density $f(y_i | \theta_i, \phi)$, where θ_j is the canonical shape of a location parameter and ϕ is a scale parameter. As for the random component, consider a matrix $X_{(n \times p)}$, whose elements x_{ij}, are the n observations of p explanatory variables $X_j, j = 1, \ldots p$. The ith observation of these variables generates a linear predictor (linear combinations of the explanatory variables) η_i, given by $\eta_i = \Sigma_{j=1}^{p} x_{ij} \beta_j, i = 1, \ldots, n$, where the $\beta_j, j = 1, \ldots, p$, are unknown parameters, to be estimated from the data.

The two components relate each other through $\mu_i = h(\eta_i) = h(z_i^T \beta)$ and $\eta_i = g(\mu_i)$, where h is a monotonous and differentiable function; $g = h^{-1}$ is the link function; $\mathbf{z}_i$ is a vector of dimension p, function of the vector of explanatory variables, say, x_i; $\eta_i = E(Y_i)$, and $\text{Var}(Y) = \phi V(\mu_i)/w_i$, where w_i is a constant and $V(\mu_i)$ the variance function.

Then, consider a triangle of development of incremental payments I_{ij}, with $0 \leq i \leq N, 0 \leq j \leq N + 1$. Suppose $w_{ij} = 1, \forall i, j$, thus we have $V(I_{i,j}) = \phi \cdot V(\mu_{i,j})$. The variance function has the following shape $V(\mu_{i,j}) = \mu_{i,j}^{\zeta}, \zeta \geq 0$. The link function and the linear predictor are given by

$$\eta_{i,j} = \ln \mu_{ij} = \mu + \alpha_i + \beta_j \tag{10.7}$$

where α_i denotes the effect caused by the occurrence period i, β_j the effect caused by the development period j, and μ the global average.

The estimates for the future incremental payments $(I_{i,j}, j \geq n - i + 1)$ are given by $\hat{\mu}_{i,j} = \exp\{\hat{\mu} + \hat{\alpha}_i + \hat{\beta}_j\}$, where $\hat{\mu}, \hat{\alpha}_i$, and $\hat{\beta}_j$ are estimates of the maximum *quasi*-likelihood. In order to avoid the over parameterization, the constraints $\alpha_0 = \beta_0 = 0$ are introduced. Estimate $\hat{R}$ is obtained through $\hat{R} = \Sigma_{(i,j) \in \Delta} \hat{\mu}_{ij}$. The standard error (SE) of $\hat{R}$ will be

$$SE\left(\hat{R}\right) = \sqrt{E\left\{\left(R - \hat{R}\right)^2\right\}}$$

$$= \sqrt{\sum_{(i,j)\in\Delta} A\hat{Q}E\left(\hat{\mu}_{i,j}\right) + \sum_{\substack{(i,j)\in\Delta \\ (x,y)\in\Delta \\ (i,j)\neq(x,y)}} \left\{\hat{\mu}_{i,j}\hat{\mu}_{x,y}Cov\left(\hat{\eta}_{i,j},\hat{\eta}_{x,y}\right)\right\}}$$

$$A\hat{Q}E\left(\hat{\mu}_{i,j}\right) = \hat{\phi}\cdot\hat{\mu}_{i,j}^{\zeta} + \left\{V\left(\hat{\mu}\right) + V\left(\hat{\alpha}_i\right)\right.$$

$$+ V\left(\hat{\beta}_j\right) + 2\left\{Cov\left(\hat{\mu}, \hat{\alpha}_i\right) + Cov\left(\hat{\mu}, \hat{\beta}_j\right)\right.$$

$$+ Cov\left(\hat{\alpha}_i, \hat{\beta}_j\right)\}\} \cdot \hat{\mu}_{i,j}^2$$

Renshaw and Verrall (1998) proposed a stochastic version of the *chain ladder* method, which assumes that the incremental payments follow an *over-dispersed Poisson* distribution and a linear predictor with shape as in Equation (10.7) and a logarithmic link function. (In this GLM the parameter ζ of the variance function assumes the value *1*, but the scale parameter ϕ is estimated instead of being predetermined. The model has the following assumption: $E(I_i,j) = \mu_{i,j}, V(I_{ij}) = \phi V(\mu_{ij}) = \phi\mu_{ij}, \zeta = 1$, $\phi > 0, i = 0,\ldots,n; \Sigma_{i=0}^{N-j}I_{ij} \geq 0$, and $0 \leq j \leq N$.

In the model the scale parameter is estimated using the approximation of the generalized Pearson's statistic proposed by McCullagh and Nelder (1989). The model fit is done with two tests: (1) Wald's nullity test of the linear predictor parameter and (2) the global significance test using the scale *quasi*-deviance statistic. In addition, we will analyze the graphical representation of Pearson residuals using a normal probability plot and the graphical representation of the residuals against the adjusted values $\hat{\mu}_i$ and against each of the explanatory variables of the linear predictor.

We will simulate the possible values of R, using a bootstrap method in association with the over-dispersed Poisson GLM. The bootstrap method requires the existence of a set of observations of independent and identically distributed (i.i.d.) random variables. However, the $I_{i,j}$ do not satisfy this assumption since they depend on the parameters; therefore, we will use the Pearson's residuals of the model, $r_{i,j}, 0 \leq i \leq N, 0 \leq j \leq N - i$, since they can be considered as *observations* of the random variables. The residuals $r_{0,N}, r_{N,0}$, and $r_{0,N+1}$ will be dropped since by definition they are equal to zero, as exposed by Pinheiro et al. (2003). The new triangle of residuals will be converted in a pseudo-data triangle I_{ij}^{bs} using $I_{ij}^{bs} = r_{i,j}^{bs}\sqrt{\hat{\mu}_{i,j}} + \hat{\mu}_{i,j}$ with

$r_{i,j}^{bs}$, satisfying $\{(i,j):0\le i\le N,0\le j\le N-i\}\cup\{(i,j)=(0,N+1)\}$ and $\hat{\mu}_{i,j}$ as the estimated values.

We will apply the over-dispersed Poisson *GLM* to the pseudo-data triangle in order to obtain the reserve estimate, called *pseudo-reserve*. We use the notation $\hat{R}_{(b)}^{bs}, 1\le b\le B$, for the pseudo-reserves and $\hat{R}$ for the original estimate. This process is repeated a large number of B times. As far as the computation of the SE is concerned, we'll have to add to the standard deviation of the Bootstrap results, say $\hat{\sigma}_{bs}(\hat{R})$, a volatility measure of the stochastic process inherent to the over-dispersed Poisson GLM. According to England and Verral (1999), this is $\hat{\phi}\cdot\hat{R}$, where $\hat{\phi}$ is an estimate of the scale parameter. Finally, we obtain the SE of the bootstrap estimates for $\hat{R}$, $S\hat{E}_{bs}(\hat{R})=\sqrt{\hat{\phi}\cdot\hat{R}+[n/(n+p)]\hat{\sigma}_{bs}^2(\hat{R})}$.

Given that the total reserve is a sum of the random future payments, its estimate should equal the discounted value of the incremental future payments, discounted with an appropriate rate; therefore, the claims reserve is also subject to interest rate risk. In this chapter we will use the risk-free interest rate as an approximation to the appropriate discount rate for liabilities. We will simulate the risk-free interest rate term structure in one year's time using the CIR model as explained in the preceding section. The difference between the expected value of the discounted reserve today and the discounted value of the simulated reserve within one year will be the result associated of the development of the claims reserve (including the corresponding interest rate risk).

Premium risk is associated with the premium reserves. In motor insurance contracts are usually done on an annual basis and premiums are received upfront. Insurers are required to build premium reserves to cover future claims of the set of policies in force. Premium risk is the risk that those reserves are not sufficient to face these future payments.

To calculate the risk, it is necessary to model the future annual claim payments. To find the distribution of the aggregate claims cost in the time interval, say $(0,t]$, we use the well-known *collective risk model*; for details please see, for instance, Bowers et al. (1997). Under this model the aggregate claims cost is written as a random sum of individual claims, denoted $S(t)$:

$$S(t) = \sum_{i=0}^{N(t)} X_i \tag{10.8}$$

where $X_0 \equiv 0$ and where X_i is the ith individual random claim and $N(t)$ is the number of claims in $(0,t]$. $\{N\ (t), t \geq 0\}$ is a stochastic counting process, $\{X_i, i = 1,2,...\}$ is a sequence of i.i.d. random variables, with common distribution function $G(x)$, and independent of $N(t)$; therefore, $\{S(t), t \geq 0\}$ is a compound process.

In the classical model $N(t)$ follows a Poisson distribution. In the application we test both a Poisson and a negative binomial distribution using the classical χ^2 test. For the claim amount distribution we use both the χ^2 and the Kolmogorov tests, for gamma, Pareto, and lognormal distributions. For details, see Klugman et al. (1998).

Once the distributions are chosen, we simulate the process given by Equation (10.8). For each simulated path we first generate a number $N(t) = n$, then generate the n values $X_i = x_i, i = 1,...,n$. The premium risk for the set of policies in force, considering its remaining time, is calculated from the difference between the aggregate claims cost and the expected premium reserve. For the sake of simplicity and since the duration of the premium reserves in the automobile insurance is usually less than six months, we will neglect the interest rate risk of premium reserve.

For the *aggregation of risks* we assume that the joint distribution of risks follows a multivariate distribution belonging to the elliptic distribution family, as in Embrechts et al. (1999) and Embrechts et al. (2003). Thus, the dependence between risk factors is measured by their linear correlation coefficients, and it will be so in the simulation procedures, whenever applicable.

APPLICATION
General Considerations

Based on the statistical and financial information of an insurance undertaking at December 31, 2002, we modeled the five risk factors earlier explained. All the necessary technical information, the prospectus related to the insurer bond portfolio, the historical bond and stock prices, stock index figures, and interest rates were collected from Bloomberg delivery information system. Given the lack of information to study the joint behavior of the major risk factors, we assumed that all risks were independent, with the exception of the equity and interest rate risks for which we studied their correlation. For confidential issues all monetary values related to the real insurance undertaking used in this study are *masked*.

Equity risk

The stock portfolio held by the insurer under study is composed of 11 listed companies from a single Eurozone country. Therefore, we chose the main representative stock index for that country as a *proxy* of its relevant market portfolio with impact on the stocks' systematic risk. When estimating the stocks *beta* coefficients using the market model, we used daily closing prices from January 2, 1998 to December 31, 2002 adjusted for dividends, stock splits, and other price factors. We tested all regression equations for their global significance (*F* test) and for all the individual parameters (*t* test) rejecting the null hypothesis at 5 percent significance level for all the cases. The results are presented in Table 10.1

The average and standard deviations of the stock index instantaneous rate of return for the same time interval were, respectively, 3.59 and 18.46 percent per annum, and the linear correlation coefficient between the instantaneous short-term interest rate and the instantaneous stock index rate of return was positive but small, and not statistically significant.

Then, using the process given by Equation (10.2), we ran 5,000 simulations for the one-year stock index daily figures, assuming a *time step* = 1/260 per year. From the stock index simulated paths we could then estimate the simulated one-year portfolio returns for the real insurance undertaking stock portfolio, according to the estimated CAPM parameters. The random component of the simulation process was based on the generation of standard normal independent r.v.s. As a proxy for the risk-free interest rate we used a one-year maturity German Treasury bill yield, observed at December 31, 2002.

T A B L E   10.1

Estimates of the individual and portfolio betas

Stock	#1	#2	#3	#4	#5	#6	#7	#8	#9	#10	#11	Port. *Beta*
Beta	0.43	0.83	0.75	0.85	0.48	0.72	0.95	1.76	1.24	1.12	1.30	0.81

Interest Rate and Credit Risks

We started by dividing the insurer's bond portfolio (entirely composed by Eurozone bonds) into three subportfolios regarding the issuer's type: government bonds; bonds issued by banks and other financial institutions; and a single bond issued by one telecommunications company. These three groups were those actually observed within the real portfolio of the insurance undertaking that we are studying. Then, we estimated the weighted Fisher–Weil duration for each subportfolio. The risk-free yield curve was extracted from a series of German zero coupon bonds (coupon strips) with different maturities, ranging from 1 to 27 years, and whose prices were observed at December 31, 2002. Any intermediate maturity yield was estimated by linear interpolation. For the three- and six-month maturities we used the German Treasury bill yields observed at December 31, 2002 for these maturities.

Bond cash flows were discounted by using a discount rate that adds the corresponding risk-free maturity to the relevant credit spread, estimated in accordance to the industry sector and the issuers' rating of the bond. Credit spreads are regularly supplied by J.P. Morgan and could be found in www.riskmetrics.com. The credit spread for German Treasury bill and bonds was assumed to be negligible and, therefore, null.

In order to simplify the simulation of the bond portfolio, we assumed that the interest rate and the credit risk of holding any of the mentioned subportfolios was similar to the risk of holding an equivalent zero coupon bond with analogous duration.

Then we simulated the three zero coupon bond prices using the interest rate model explained in this chapter's second section. As a proxy for the risk-free short-term interest rate, we used the German Treasury bill yield with three months maturity. In the estimation process of the parameter we used the market prices of German Treasury bills maturing in 3 and 6 months' time and the market prices of coupon strips of German Treasury bonds maturing in one, two, three, four, five, six, seven, eight, and nine years' time. Historical parameters were estimated using historical data from January 1, 1998 to at December 31, 2002 and the results were $\hat{\bar{a}} = 3.0411$, $\hat{b} = 0.1068$, $\hat{a} = 2.9210$, and $\hat{\sigma} = 0.0947$.

We started by using Equation (10.6) to simulate the daily behavior of the risk-free short-term interest rate. The random component of the stochastic process was based on the generation of standard normal independent variables. After, we simulated the prices of the three zero coupon bonds using Equation (10.4) considering no credit risk. Then, from Equation (10.5), we calculated the corresponding risk-free yield, and the whole process was repeated 5,000 times, having generated 5,000 values for the one-year risk-free yield.

Afterwards, we applied the Credit Metrics model considering each actual subportfolio average credit rating (Table 10.2) in order to incorporate the credit risk spread into the simulations. Credit ratings were collected from Standard and Poor's, and based upon the J.P. Morgan (www.riskmetrics.com), we built a rating transition probability matrix for the one-year time frame.

In order to estimate the correlation coefficient matrix for the three subportfolios, we used several proxies: the Dow Jones Euro Stoxx Bank Index rate of return as proxy for the banks and financial institutions bond portfolio; the bond itself for the telecom company bond; and the German coupon strip with 2.5 years maturity for the government bonds portfolio, whose duration was 2.71. The correlation matrix among the three subportfolios of bonds is shown in Table 10.3, and all the figures are significant at a 5 percent level.

As a result, we manage to generate, a set of correlated standard normal r.v.s from a set of independent standard normal r.v.s by applying the Cholesky decomposition, as in Horn and Johnson (1990).

Adding up the simulated credit spread to the simulated risk-free yield for all zero coupon bonds, we found the appropriate yield considering the credit risk. From this latter risky yield and inverting Equation (10.5), we got

T A B L E   10.2

Rating and duration of the bond's portfolio

Portfolio	Rating	Duration
Government bonds	AAA	2.71
Bonds issued by banks and other financial institutions	AA	5.08
Bonds issued by telecommunication firms	A	2.05

T A B L E   10.3

Variance–covariance matrix of asset rate of return proxies

	Governmental	Bank and Financial Institutions	Telecommunication Company
Governmental	**0.00052**	−0.00253	−0.00197
Bank and financial inst.	−0.00253	**0.06446**	0.04020
Telecom. company.	−0.00197	0.04020	**0.16080**

the future value of each zero coupon yield, taking into account both interest rate and credit risks. Whenever the simulated rating was considered a default, we assumed the bond value to equal the credit recovery rate (simulated by a beta distribution) times the face value of the bond. The process ends up by comparing each simulated value to its initial price in order to calculate the annual rate of return for each zero coupon bond and then by multiplying this rate of return by its respective market value at December 31, 2002.

Reserve Risk

Our insurer' portfolio was recent and not yet stable. Thus, in order to apply any stochastic methods to the claims payments we had to exclude the occurrences for 1997 and 1998, because we know that the payment pattern of those years was significantly different. We applied the Renshaw and Verral's (1998) model to the claims payments matrix, occurred between 1999 and 2002. We did the *quasi-deviance* scale test and concluded that the model was globally significant. We also did the individual parameter test and concluded they were significant with one exception, the parameter associated with the effect of the occurrence year of 1999. One possible economic reason might be the fact that in this year claims were almost fully developed. Nevertheless, given that the matrix is not fully stable and that we only considered four occurrence years, we decided to keep this parameter in the model. The above results are presented in Tables 10.4 and 10.5.

The SE of the total reserve was 14 percent, which is a value that we find acceptable since the matrix is not fully stable. The graphical rep-

T A B L E   10.4

Estimates of the parameters of the over-dispersed Poisson's model

			Test of the Nullity of the Parameters		
Parameter	Estimate	Standard Error	W	$\chi^2_{(1)}$ at 5%	Conclusion
U	15.4555	0.0737	44,025.29	3.84	Statistically significant
β_1	−0.8152	0.0828	97.01	3.84	Statistically significant
α_1	0.1298	0.0932	1.94	3.84	Not statistically significant
β_2	−2.2827	0.1890	145.84	3.84	Statistically significant.
α_2	0.2337	0.0933	6.27	3.84	Statistically significant
β_3	−2.8761	0.3637	62.54	3.84	Statistically significant
α_3	0.5434	0.0979	30.83	3.84	Statistically significant
β_4	−2.3506	0.2836	68.70	3.84	Statistically significant

T A B L E   10.5

Scale deviance test

H0: Model Is Adequate		
Scale deviance (D^*)		3.02
n		16
p		8
$\chi^2_{(n-p)}$	At 2.5%	15.50
$D^* <$	$\chi^2_{(n-p)}$ at 2.5%: $\Rightarrow$	Accept H0

resentations of the residuals against each of the explanatory variables do not seem to show any systematic standards. As a conclusion, the over-dispersed Poisson model has an acceptable fit to the data.

We then applied a bootstrap procedure associated with the validated model to the paid claims matrix. We simulated 5,000 paid claims matrices and calculated 5,000 values for undiscounted value of the claims reserve. We simulated 5,000 times the risk-free interest rate term structure in a one-year period and determined the discounted value of the simulated claims reserve in December 31, 2003. We got the reserve risk results subtracting the simulated values at December 31, 2003 from the expected value of the discounted claims reserve at December 31, 2002 (for claims occurred 1999 and 2002). Regarding the bootstrap results, the SE of the estimated reserve is 15 percent, in line with the results of the analytic model. The graphical representations of the residuals against each of the explanatory variables did not evidence any systematic pattern.

Premium Risk

First we fit the distribution of the number of claims per year of the whole portfolio, based on data consisting the number of claims occurred per policy in the last year. We applied the chi-square test (with a 5 percent significance level) to the mentioned Poisson and negative binomial distributions. The parameters of the distributions were estimated by maximum likelihood estimation (MLE).

From Table 10.6 we can see that the Poisson distribution was clearly rejected. The negative binomial was accepted, with a p-value of 24.3 percent. Assuming that the number of claims follows a negative binomial, we determined the parameters of the distribution of the number of claims for the set of policies in force at December 31, 2002, $\alpha = 58,211$ and $p = 0.925$, corresponding to the sum m idd negative Binomial, where m is the number of policies in force at that date.

Next, we studied, using a chi-square test, at 5 percent level, the fit for the individual claim amount distribution based on a list of total cost, claim by claim, of all the claims occurred and reported in 2002. We tested a lognormal,

T A B L E   10.6

Distributions for the number of claims per policy

Distribuition	Parameters	Estimates	p-value	Degrees of Freedom
Poisson (λ)	λ	0.066	0.000	2
Negative binomial (α, p)	α, p	0.809, 0.925	0.244	3

Pareto, and a gamma distribution. We use the MLE for the lognormal and both the moment and ML estimates for the Pareto and gamma.

From Table 10.7 we see that the gamma distribution was clearly rejected as well as the Pareto with ML estimation. The distribution that better fits the data is the Pareto, with parameters estimated by the moments method (MME), however with just one degree of freedom. The lognormal was rejected, but if we exclude its tail (claim amounts above €30,000) one observes that this distribution has a better fit than the Pareto. Hence, we also performed the chi-square test to a lognormal distribution truncated at 30,000 with a Pareto tail. The latter distribution gives a p-value of 20 percent, and the χ^2 has two degrees of freedom.

In addition, we performed Kolmogorov tests, at 5 percent level, for the distributions lognormal, Pareto, and truncated lognormal with Pareto tail. All distributions were accepted. Based on the results of both tests, we chose the lognormal distribution with Pareto tail to model the individual claim amounts. Results are shown in Table 10.8

T A B L E   10.7

Distributions for modeling the individual claim amount

Distribution	Parameters	Estimates	p-value	Degrees of Freedom
Lognormal, MLE	μ	6.702	0.007	2
	σ	1.346		
Pareto, MME	α	2.051	0.192	1
	k	2,357.180		
Pareto, MLE	α	0.194	0	2
	k	4.670		
Gamma, MME	α	0.025	0	2
	β	89,374.516		
Gamma, MLE	α	7.483	0	2
	β	299.604		
Lognormal, MLE,	μ	6.702	0.199	2
Truncated at 30,000 with	σ	1.346		
Pareto tail, MME	α	2.051		
	β	2,357.180		

T A B L E   10.8

Results of the Kolmogorov Test

Distribution	Test Statistic	Critical value (5%)	Conclusion
Lognormal, MLE	20.75%	33.84%	Accepted
Pareto, MME	16.33%	33.84%	Accepted
Lognormal, MME, truncated at 30,000, with Pareto tail, MME	20.75%	33.84%	Accepted

Assuming that the number of claims followed a negative binomial distribution and that individuals claims amounts followed a lognormal distribution with the "Pareto tail", we simulated, using equation (10.8), 5,000 values for the aggregate total cost of claims of the policies in force at December 31, 2002, considering the remaining time that they will be in force. We deducted from the expected value of premium provision, the simulated values and achieved the results of the premium risk (suffiency/insuffiency of premium provision).

Aggregation of Risks

For the aggregation of risks and calculation of the VaR and TCE, the global results for the insurer will be the result of the aggregation of all individual risk factors. We considered, risk by risk, each of the simulated values, obtaining 5,000 possible global results for the next year. Results are shown in the next section.

RESULTS

In this section, we present the results from our application, considering the VaR and the TCE measures for one-year time horizon and different alpha levels. We start by presenting the individual analysis for each risk factor and we conclude with the aggregated results for the entire portfolio of assets and liabilities of the company.

T A B L E   10.9

Equity risk results (euros)

Level	95.0%	97.5%	99.0%	99.5%
VaR	−21,437	−29,686	−39,189	−43,119
TCE	−31,885	−38,571	−45,432	−50,258

Equity Risk

Starting with the equity risk we see from Table 10.9 that the results are in line with the expectations, given the model in use and the parameters estimates. Taking into account the reduced exposure to the stock market and the simulated results, the equity risk does not seem to be a menace to this particular insurer's solvency. The worst VaR loss scenario in a one-year time period with a 99.5 percent level is €43,119, and the corresponding TCE is an expected loss of €50,258. This is quite small in relative terms as we will see later in this section after comparing these figures with the reserve and premium risks.

Interest Rate and Credit Risks

Table 10.10 shows that both interest rate and credit risks are also small for the modeled bond portfolio. In the worst VaR loss scenario in a one-year period with a 99.5 percent level, the figures are all positive expressing no defaults and no significant losses in the bond portfolio. Additionally, as the governmental bond portfolio (a high rating and low duration portfolio) was of much higher significance the total bond portfolio doesn't seem strongly affected by interest rate or credit risk.

However, when the TCE is computed, we experience a potential capital loss in terms of both corporate bonds portfolio. As we see, the TCE measure for the simulated figures in a one year period with a 99.5 percent level is negative either for the portfolio of bonds issued by the banks and other financial institutions (−€75,536) and for the bond portfolio issue by the telecommunications company (−€54,387). Even though, the total

T A B L E   10.10

Interest rate and credit risk results (euros)

Statistics	Governmental Bonds	Bonds Issued by Banks and Other Financial Institutions	Bonds Issued by the Telecommunications Company
VaR			
95.0%	429,139	84,444	29,883
97.5%	428,076	83,523	29,604
99.0%	426,668	82,561	29,206
99.5%	425,892	25,619	18,346
TCE			
95.0%	427,684	67,355	20,294
97.5%	426,694	50,734	10,846
99.0%	425,490	2,164	−17,093
99.5%	424,638	−75,536	−54,387

bond portfolio is still positive in this scenario because of the strong weight of the governmental bond portfolio. The negative results shown in the TCE measure are the result of the simulated bond ratings downgrading with a consequent raise in the required credit spreads.

Reserve Risk

Analyzing Table 10.11, we can observe that there is some reserve risk arising from the most adverse development scenarios. The reserve risk follows approximately a normal distribution and even though it is the second more severe single risk factor; it does not have a heavy tail.

Premium Risk

From Table 10.12 we see that the premium risk is the single risk factor that presents future results more severe to the insurer. This is due to the heavy tail of the estimated distribution.

T A B L E   10.11

Reserve risk results (euros)

Level	95.0%	97.5%	99.0%	99.5%
VaR	-1,944,351	-2,409,572	-2,771,884	-2,931,341
TCE	-2,488,839	-2,743,515	-3,005,122	-3,158,818

T A B L E   10.12

Premium risk results (euros)

Level	95.0%	97.5%	99.0%	99.5%
VaR	-1,510,020	-1,916,298	-2,658,329	-3,146,273
TCE	-2,503,282	-3,319,229	-4,950,018	-7,020,996

Determination of the Aggregate VaR and TCE

From Table 10.13 we observe that the TCE is expectedly more conservative as a risk measure than VaR, by presenting capital requirements (clearly) higher. Taking TCE as risk measure at December 31, 2002, the insurance undertaking would need, at the confidence level of 99.5 percent, an economic capital of € 7,201,006, to be solvent.

The difference between VaR and TCE becomes more significant as the confidence level increases, this is due to the heavy tail of the global profit and loss distribution and the influence of the premium risk heavy tail. TCE is much more sensitive to heavy tailed distributions. The study of such distributions requires very special techniques and care, which discussion is beyond the scope of this work.

CONCLUSION

The model presented had the objective of showing that it is possible to build up a solvency model that determines the economic capital requirement using the risk measure TCE, based upon the main risk factors that

T A B L E   10.13

Insurance undertaking's aggregate results (euros)

Level	95.0%	97.5%	99.0%	99.5%
VaR	−1,988,506	−2,488,230	−3,493,925	−3,981,377
TCE	−3,061,498	−3,920,409	−5,471,164	−7,201,006

affect the insurance activity and the balance sheet structure of an insurance undertaking at a given time, for a selected time horizon.

In order to build up the model, it is necessary to identify the assets, liabilities, and operations that generate value and the risks that affect them, as well as the dependences among them. This procedure will lead to a more sound knowledge of the whole activity and structure of an insurance undertaking.

The construction and application of a solvency model for the automobile branch allowed observing that the results obtained depend heavily on the estimates of the involving parameters and on the data used in the estimation. The construction of a solvency model like this one will force insurance companies to invest considerably in human resources training and information technology and on the access to databases with relevant and accurate information. Also important and sensitive are the correlations between risks for the calculation of capital requirements, since the benefits of an increased diversification might result in a considerably lower capital need.

As far as the model practical results are concerned, we conclude that the insurer had a conservative investment portfolio with limited interest rate and credit risks. Given the estimates of the parameters and the reduced exposure to the stock markets, the equity risk did not seem to influence the insurer's solvency. Nevertheless, by considering the volatility observed in stock markets in recent years, it is possible that the actual future results became less favorable than the simulated ones.

From the joint application of the over-dispersed Poisson model with the bootstrap procedure, we concluded that the reserve risk is material to solvency of the insurance undertaking. Individually, the more potentially demanding risk is the premium risk, since the total aggregate claims cost distribution has a heavy tail, as we have already underlined at the end of the preceding section. As we noticed, heavy tail distributions need special care and an accurate estimation is not an easy task. An improper fit can lead to *unfair* capital requirement calculation, either excessive or defective.

Finally, we remark that this is a static approach that assumes the maintenance of the current asset and liabilities structure, not taking into account new business underwriting. Thus, this analysis should be conducted periodically. In addition, we should point out that the TCE risk measure could be shown to be a lot more conservative than the VaR risk measure.

ACKNOWLEDGMENTS

The first author thanks ADVANCE and ISEG, Technical University of Lisbon, and gratefully acknowledges partial support from FCT.

The second author thanks CEMAPRE and ISEG, Technical University of Lisbon, and gratefully acknowledges partial financial support from FCT-Fundação para a Ciência e Tecnologia (Programme FEDER/POCI 2010).

The third author acknowledges the support from ISP-Instituto de Seguros de Portugal (Portuguese Insurance and Pension Fund Supervision Authority).

REFERENCES

Artzner, P. (1999) Application of Coherent Risk Measures to Capital Requirements in Insurance. *North American Actuarial Journal*, Vol.2, No.2, pp. 11–25.

Bowers, N.L., H.U. Gerber, J.C. Hickman, D.A. Jones, and C.J. Nesbitt (1997), *Actuarial Mathematics*, Shaumburg, IL: The Society of Actuaries

Cox, J., J. Ingersoll, and S. Ross (1985) A Theory of the Term Structure of Interest Rates. *Econometrica*, 2nd edition, Vol.53, No.2, pp. 373–407.

Elton, E., M. Gruber, S. Brown, and W. Goetzmann (2007) *Modern Portfolio Theory and Investment Analysis*, 7th edition, New York: John Wiley & Sons.

Embrechts, P., A. McNeil, and D. Straumann (1999) Correlation: Pitfalls and Alternatives. *RISK*, Vol.12, No. 5, pp. 69–71.

Embrechts, P., F. Lindskog, and A. McNeil (2003) Modelling Dependence with Copulas and Applications to Risk Management. In S. Rachev (ed.), *Handbook of Heavy Tailed Distributions in Finance*. New York: Elsevier.

England, P. and R. Verral (1999) Analytic and Bootstrap Estimates of Prediction Errors in Claims Reserving. *Insurance: Mathematics and Economics*, Vol.25, No.3, pp. 281–293.

Fischer, T., A. May, and B. Walther. (2002) Simulation of the Yield Curve: Checking a Cox–Ingersoll–Ross Model. Preprint No. 2226, Stochastik und Operations Research, Technische Universität Darmstadt, Darmstadt.

Horn, R. and C. Johnson (1990), *Matrix Analysis.* Cambridge, MA:Cambridge University Press.

J.P. Morgan and Reuters (1996) Risk Metrics, Technical Document, 4th edition. Morgan Guaranty Trust Company, New York.

J.P. Morgan (1997) CreditMetrics, Technical Document. J.P. Morgan & Co Inc., New York.

Klugman, S., H. Panjer, and G. Wilmot (2008) *Loss Models, From Data to Decisions*, 3rd edition. New York: John Wiley & Sons.

Linder, U. and V. Ronkainen (2004) Solvency II, Towards a New Insurance Supervisory System in the EU. *Scandinavian Actuarial Journal*, Vol. 104, No. 6, pp. 462–474.

Lintner, J. (1965) Security Prices, Risk and Maximal Gains from Diversification. *The Journal of Finance,* Vol. 20, No. 4, pp. 587–615.

Lynn Wirch, J. and M. Hardy. (1999) A Synthesis of Risk Measures for Capital Adequacy. *Insurance Mathematics and Economics*, Vol. 25, No. 11, pp. 337–347.

McCullagh, P. and J. Nelder (1989) *Generalised Linear Models*, 2nd edition, London: Chapman and Hall.

Pinheiro, P., J. Andrade e Silva, and M. Centeno (2003) Bootstrap Methodology in Claims Reserving. *The Journal of Risk and Insurance*, Vol. 70, No. 4, pp. 701–714.

Renshaw, A. and R. Verrall. (1998) A Stochastic Model Underlying the Chain Ladder Technique. *British Actuarial Journal*, Vol. 4, No. 19, pp. 903–923.

Sharpe, W. (1964) Capital Asset Prices: A Theory of Market Equilibrium under Condition of Risk, *The Journal of Finance*, Vol. 19, No.3, pp. 425–442.

Taylor, G. (2000) *Loss Reserving: An Actuarial Perspective.* Kluwer, MA: Kluwer Academic Press.

CHAPTER 11

Economic Capital Management for Insurance Companies

Rossella Bisignani, Giovanni Masala, Marco Micocci

ABSTRACT

The loss ratio (LR) for insurance companies is defined as the ratio of incurred claims and earned premiums for a specified class of insurance (CoI). The company then may estimate its capital requirement for that particular CoI by using value at risk (VaR) or conditional VaR (CVaR) of the LR distribution at a specified probability value. The overall objective of the company is to evaluate the aggregate capital requirement through a weighted sum of marginal capital requirements for all the classes of insurance. Nevertheless, this procedure may tend to over-estimate the aggregate capital requirement because it does not take into consideration the real dependence among the different classes of insurance. In other words, perfect dependence does not allow considering diversification effects.

INTRODUCTION

In this chapter, we present a model for estimating the economic capital for non-life insurance companies; the model takes into account real dependences among losses coming from different classes of insurance (CoI).

The main purpose is determining the diversification benefit considering a real dependence structure through a copula approach. Our analysis is based on the calculation of loss ratios (LR) that represent the ratio of incurred claims and earned premium for a specified CoI. We collected data from main Italian non-life insurance companies for the period 1998 to 2004, and then we built semiannual LRs of a hypothetical representative insurance company for the following five classes of insurance:

1. Accident
2. Land vehicles
3. Goods in transit
4. Fire and natural forces
5. Motor vehicle liability

Through a best-fitting analysis, we determined for each class of insurance the probability distribution of its LR. For each CoI we quantify its economic capital using risk measures like value at risk (VaR) and conditional value at risk (CVaR) at a confidence level of 95 and 99 percent [we note that CVaR is a coherent risk measure, which is an important property for risk management purposes; see Rockafellar and Uryasev (2002)].

Traditionally, the aggregate capital charge is obtained by summing the capital charges for each class of insurance. Nevertheless, this approach does not take into consideration diversification and hence tends to overestimate the capital charge. In this chapter, we propose a copula-based model that permits us to consider correlations. The empirical correlations coming from rough data have been modified on the base of some coherency elements (indeed, we have very few data for estimating correctly empirical correlations). In particular, the empirical values of the correlation coefficients have been compared with their "logical" and intuitive levels. The logical values of the correlation coefficients depend on the definition of the CoI; a deep analysis of the technical structure of each class of insurance permits us to individuate three qualitative levels of correlation among the several CoI:

- High degree (with a correlation coefficient equal to 0.75)
- Medium degree (with a correlation coefficient equal to 0.45)
- Low degree (with a correlation coefficient equal to 0.20)

The empirical values of the correlation coefficients have been compared with their "logical" values. In some cases this comparison has substantially confirmed the empirical value; in other cases the empirical correlation coefficients have been forced to levels that are more reasonable (the "logical" values). The numerical example shows that real correlation model leads to a lower capital charge.

We conclude the analysis with the construction of an efficient frontier based on a CVaR constraint. The chapter is structured as follows: The second section gives an overview of some basic results about copula functions; the third section introduces LRs and risk measures; the fourth section presents the numerical example; and the fifth section presents our conclusions.

COPULA FUNCTIONS AND DEPENDENCE STRUCTURES

Definition 11.1. An *n-dimensional copula* is a multivariate distribution function C, with margins uniformly distributed in $[0, 1]$ that satisfies the following properties:

(i) $C: [0, 1]^n \rightarrow [0, 1]$.

(ii) C is grounded and n-increasing.

(iii) C has margins C_i satisfying

$$C_i(u) = C(1, \ldots, 1, u, 1, \ldots, 1) = u \; \forall u \in [0, 1] \; (i = 1, \ldots, n)$$

The most important result is the following, which is due to Sklar (see Nelsen, 1998, and Meneguzzo and Vecchiato, 2004).

Theorem 11.1. Let F be an n-dimensional distribution, with marginals F_i. Then there exists an n-copula C such that $F(x_1, \ldots, x_n) = C(F_1(x_1), \ldots, F_n(x_n))$. *If the marginals F_i are continuous, then the copula C is unique. Besides, if the density function exists, it will be given by*

$$f(x_1, \ldots, x_n) = c(F_1(x_1), \ldots, F_n(x_n)) \cdot \prod_{i=1}^{n} f_i(x_i), \; with$$

$$c(u_1, \ldots, u_n) = \frac{\partial^n C(u_1, \ldots, u_n)}{\partial u_1 \cdots \partial u_n}$$

The previous representation is called the *canonical representation* of the distribution. Sklar's theorem is then a powerful tool to build n-dimensional distributions by using one-dimensional distributions, which represent the marginals of the given distribution. Dependence among marginals is then characterized by the copula C.

We describe now some important multivariate copulas.

- The *Gaussian copula*. Its parameters are the correlation matrix $\mathbf{R}$.
  - The Gaussian copula is given by $C_{\mathbf{R}}^{Ga}(u_1,\ldots,u_n) = \Phi_{\mathbf{R}}^n$ $(\Phi^{-1}(u_1),\ldots,\Phi^{-1}(u_n))$, where $\Phi_{\mathbf{R}}^n$ denotes the standardized multivariate normal distribution with correlation matrix $\mathbf{R}$ and Φ^{-1} is the inverse of the standard univariate normal distribution. The density of the normal copula is

  $$c_{\mathbf{R}}^{Ga}(u_1,\ldots,u_n) = |\mathbf{R}|^{-\frac{1}{2}} \cdot \exp\left(-\frac{1}{2}\zeta^T \cdot \left(\mathbf{R}^{-1} - I\right)\cdot \zeta\right)$$

  where $\zeta = (\Phi^{-1}(u_1),\ldots,\Phi^{-1}(u_n))$. Finally, we can generate random numbers from the Gaussian copula through the following algorithm:

    ◦ Find the Cholesky decomposition $\mathbf{A}$ of the correlation matrix $\mathbf{R}$.
    ◦ Simulate n independent random variates $\mathbf{z} = (z_1,\ldots,z_n)$ from the standard normal distribution.
    ◦ Determine the vector $\mathbf{x} = \mathbf{A} \times \mathbf{z}$.
    ◦ Determine the components $u_i = \Phi(x_i)$ $i = 1,\ldots,n$. The resultant vector is $(u_1,\ldots,u_n)^T \sim C_{\mathbf{R}}^{Ga}(u_1,\ldots,u_n)$.

- The *Student's t copulas*. Its parameters are the correlation matrix $\mathbf{R}$ and the degrees of freedom υ.
  - It is the copula of the multivariate Student's t distribution. Let X be a vector with an n-variate standardized Student's t distribution with υ degrees of freedom, and covariance matrix $\upsilon/(\upsilon - 2)\mathbf{R}$ (for $\upsilon > 2$). It can be represented in the following way: $X := \sqrt{\upsilon}/\sqrt{S}\,Y$, where $S \sim \chi_\upsilon^2$ (the chi-square distribution) and the random vector $Y \sim N_n(0, \mathbf{R})$ are independent. The copula of vector Y is the Student's t copula with υ degrees of freedom. The analytical representation is the following: $C_{\upsilon,\mathbf{R}}^n$ $(u_1,\ldots,u_n) = t_{\upsilon,\mathbf{R}}^n(t_\upsilon^{-1}(u_1),\ldots,t_\upsilon^{-1}(u_n))$, or equivalently,

$$C_{v,\mathbf{R}}^{n}\left(u_{1},\ldots,u_{n}\right)=\int_{-\infty}^{u_{1}}\int_{-\infty}^{u_{2}}\cdots\int_{-\infty}^{u_{n}}\frac{\Gamma\left(\dfrac{v+n}{2}\right)\cdot\left|\mathbf{R}\right|^{-1/2}}{\Gamma\left(\dfrac{v}{2}\right)\cdot\left(v\cdot\pi\right)^{\frac{n}{2}}}\cdot$$

$$\left(1+\frac{1}{v}u^{T}\cdot\mathbf{R}^{-1}\cdot u\right)\,du_{1}\,du_{2}\,\cdots\,du_{n}$$

where $\mathbf{R}_{ij}=\Sigma_{ij}/\sqrt{\Sigma_{ii}\cdot\Sigma_{jj}}$ for $i,j\in\{1,\ldots,n\}$ are the correlations. We also indicate $t_{v,\mathbf{R}}^{n}$ the multivariate cumulative distribution function (CDF) of the random vector $\sqrt{v}\cdot Y/\sqrt{S}$, where the random variable $S\sim\zeta_{v}^{2}$ and the random vector Y are independent. Besides, t_{v}, (CDF of the standard univariate Student distribution) denotes the margins of $t_{v,R}^{n}$. Finally, the t copula has the following density:

$$c\left(u_{1},\cdots,u_{n};\mathbf{R},v\right)=\frac{\Gamma\left(\dfrac{v+n}{2}\right)\cdot\left[\Gamma\left(\dfrac{v}{2}\right)\right]^{n}\cdot\left(1+\dfrac{1}{v}\omega^{T}\cdot R^{-1}\cdot\omega\right)^{-\frac{v+n}{2}}}{\sqrt{\left|\mathbf{R}\right|}\cdot\Gamma\left(\dfrac{v}{2}\right)\cdot\left[\Gamma\left(\dfrac{v+1}{2}\right)\right]^{n}\cdot\displaystyle\prod_{i=1}^{n}\left(1+\dfrac{\omega_{i}^{2}}{v}\right)^{-\frac{v+1}{2}}}$$

where $\omega_{i}=t_{v}^{-1}(u_{i})$. If we choose a Student's t copula, the degree of freedom v can be evaluated with a log-likelihood estimator. Having chosen the marginals, this can be accomplished through a maximum likelihood estimation (MLE). Let us denote with F_{i} the cumulated distribution function of the marginals; we already know that the probability density of our multivariate distribution is given by

$$f_{v}\left(x_{1},\ldots,x_{n}\right)=\frac{\partial^{n}}{\partial x_{1}\cdots\partial x_{n}}C_{v,\mathbf{R}}^{n}\left(F_{1}\left(x_{1}\right),\ldots,F_{n}\left(x_{n}\right)\right)$$

where $C_{v,\mathbf{R}}^{n}$ is the chosen copula and v is the degree of freedom. The likelihood function is defined as $L\left(v\right)=\prod_{j=1}^{h}f_{v}(x_{1,j},\ldots,x_{n,j})$, where h is the number of data in our sample. The maximum likelihood method states that the value $v = v_{max}$ at which the likelihood function reaches its maximum can be assumed as a good estimator of the parameter v we want to estimate. We can alternatively maximize the so-called log-likelihood function: $l(v) = \log L(v) = \sum_{j=1}^{h} \log f_v(x_{1,j}, \ldots, x_{n,j})$, which can be written as

$$l(v) = \sum_{j=1}^{h} \log \left[\frac{\partial^n}{\partial u_1 \cdots \partial u_n} C_v(u_1, \ldots, u_n) \Big|_{u_1 = F_1(x_{1,j}), \ldots, u_n = F_n(x_{n,j})} f_1(x_{1,j}) \cdots f_n(x_{n,j}) \right]$$

Some simplifications give

$$l(v) = \sum_{j=1}^{h} \log \left(\frac{\partial^n}{\partial u_1 \cdots \partial u_n} C_v(u_1, \ldots, u_n) \Big|_{u_1 = F_1(x_{1,j}), \ldots, u_n = F_n(x_{n,j})} \right) +$$
$$+ \sum_{j=1}^{h} \left(\log f_1(x_{1,j}) + \cdots + \log f_n(x_{n,j}) \right)$$

As the second sum in the last expression does not depend on the parameter v, we only have to maximize the modified log-likelihood function:

$$\hat{l}(v) = \sum_{j=1}^{h} \log \left(\frac{\partial^n}{\partial u_1 \cdots \partial u_n} C_v(u_1, \ldots, u_n) \Big|_{u_1 = F_1(x_{1,j}), \ldots, u_n = F_n(x_{n,j})} \right)$$

with respect to the parameter v. Nevertheless, we can choose several degrees of freedom and then compare then different results. Finally, we can generate random numbers from the Student t copula through the following algorithm:

○ Find the Cholesky decomposition $\mathbf{A}$ of the correlation matrix $\mathbf{R}$.

○ Simulate n independent random variates $\mathbf{z} = (z_1, \ldots, z_n)$ from the standard normal distribution.

○ Simulate a random variate s from χ_v^2 distribution, independent of $\mathbf{z}$.

- ○ Determine the vector $\mathbf{y} = \mathbf{A} \times \mathbf{z}$.
- ○ Set $\mathbf{x} = \sqrt{\upsilon} / \sqrt{s} \ \mathbf{y}$.
- ○ Determine the components $u_i = t_\upsilon (x_i) \ i = 1, \ldots, n$. The resultant vector is $(u_1, \ldots, u_n)^T \sim C_{\upsilon, R}^n$.

LOSS RATIO MODELING AND RISK MEASURES

We build for each CoI the LR in the following way:

$$LR_{i,t} = \frac{IC_{i,t}}{EP_{i,t}} \qquad i = 1, \ldots, 5$$

where $IC_{i,t}$ represents incurred claims and $EP_{i,t}$ represents earned premium during the period $(t; t+1)$ for the class of insurance i. We then define the aggregate LR as $LR_t = \sum_{i=1}^{5} \xi_i \cdot LR_{i,t}$, where the weights ξ_i are all equal to 0.20; the choice of ξ_i has the aim of highlighting the role of correlations in the economic capital valuation; their sum is equal to one; in this way they represent the composition quotas of the earned premiums of the selected company.

As already said, the calculation of the economic capital of the company is based on the aggregate LR of the company; it is obvious that it should take into consideration correlations among the five CoI. At this purpose, we use a dependence structure given by copula functions. We compare results obtained with the Gaussian copula and the Student t copula (with several degrees of freedom). We perform then a Monte Carlo simulation with N scenarios. The simulation steps are the following (see Tang and Valdez, 2005):

1. Estimate the parameters of the marginal distributions (LR distribution for each class of insurance).
2. Estimate the correlation matrix.
3. Generate N random correlated LRs $\widetilde{LR}_{i,j}$ (with $i = 1, \ldots, 5$ and $j = 1, \ldots, N$) from the selected copula.
4. Determine for each scenario the aggregate LR $\widetilde{LR}_j = \sum_{i=1}^{5} \xi_i \cdot \widetilde{LR}_{i,j}$.

5. Determine the statistics of the N-vector we obtained; in particular we determine some risk measures such as VaR and CVaR.

Let us fix a confidence level $\alpha \in (0, 1)$. The VaR and CVaR values for the loss random variable X at probability level α with CDF $F_X(x)$ will be defined as $\text{VaR} = \min \{\zeta \in \mathbb{R} : F_X(\zeta) \geq \alpha\}$ and $C\text{VaR} = E[X \mid X > \text{VaR}]$.

In the first definition, VaR turns out to be the left endpoint of the nonempty interval consisting of the values ζ such that $F_X(\zeta) = \alpha$. Besides, we deduce that the probability that $X \geq \text{VaR}$ equals $1 - \alpha$. Consequently, CVaR is seen as the conditional expectation of the loss associated with X relative to that loss being equal to VaR or greater.

The discretized version of the CVaR is the following:

$$CVaR = VaR + \frac{1}{N \cdot (1 - \alpha)} \cdot \sum_{j=1}^{N} \left[X_j - VaR \right]^+$$

The algorithm for the simulation in the independence case is similar to the previous one and may be obtained by eliminating step 2 and by substituting into step 3 the "generate N random independent LRs $\widetilde{LR}_{i,j}$ (with $i = 1, \ldots, 5$ and $j = 1, \ldots, N$)." In the independence context, the risk measures (VaR and CVaR) should reach their lower bound; this is equivalent to consider the so-called independence copula: $C(u_1, \ldots, u_n) = \prod_i^n u_i$. The upper bound is reached when we consider perfect dependence among classes of insurance. In this last case, the aggregate VaR (or CVaR) is just the sum of VaR for each class of insurance (the random vectors LR_i are then called *comonotonic*): $\text{VaR}_c = \sum_{i=1}^{5} \text{VaR} (LR_i)$.

Performing the numerical application, we will show that risk measures that consider real correlations stay between a lower bound (independence case) and an upper bound (perfect correlation). In this framework, a diversification benefit can be assessed by comparing the real correlation state with the perfect correlation state. We can estimate it as $DB = \text{VaR}_c - \text{VaR}$. In our numerical example, diversification benefit is expressed in a percent form and then transformed into monetary form (by considering the aggregate earned premiums).

NUMERICAL EXAMPLE

We collected data of incurred claims and earned premiums for five classes of insurance from some of the most important Italian non-life insurance companies for the period 1998 to 2004. As already said in this chapter's first section, the five classes of insurance are

1. Accident
2. Land vehicles
3. Goods in transit
4. Fire and natural forces
5. Motor vehicle liability

Mixing these data in a proper way, we have built an "average" insurance company Z. Figure 11.1 shows the historical series of the semi annual LRs of each CoI in the described period (1998 to 2004).

F I G U R E   11.1

Historical series of LRs

We determined for each class of insurance the best-fitting distribution using standard tools (such as @Risk). We found the distributions presented in Table 11.1.

The empirical correlation matrix of the CoI may be estimated using the historical series of the LR; we obtained the following correlation matrix displayed in Table 11.2:

Nevertheless, empirical correlations are not reliable in general, based on the few data we have at our disposal. Consequently, we decided to compare empirical correlations with the "logical" values of the coefficients we previously described to eliminate some false correlations. This comparison deals to the matrix shown in Table 11.3.

The degrees of freedom υ (that individuate the best Student copula) are calculated with a log-likelihood estimation that gives $\upsilon = 3$ (Figure 11.2). The following graph represents graphically the log-likelihood vs. degrees of freedom:

T A B L E   11.1

Best fitting distributions for the LRs of the five CoI

Col	μ	σ	Skewness	κ	Distribution	Parameter 1	Parameter 2
1	0.5707	0.0282	−0.6564	2.2195	logistic	0.5736	0.0158
2	0.4129	0.0206	0.6131	1.9537	pareto	16.6554	0.3884
3	0.5622	0.1211	−0.2755	2.0898	logistic	0.5683	0.0687
4	0.5984	0.0682	0.0783	2.7571	ext value	0.5658	0.0627
5	0.8953	0.0865	−0.0112	1.3307	exponential	0.1155	

T A B L E   11.2

Empirical correlation matrix for the LRs of the five CoI

ρ	1	2	3	4	5
1	100%	71%	73%	20%	92%
2	71%	100%	26%	8%	85%
3	73%	26%	100%	45%	61%
4	20%	8%	45%	100%	12%
5	92%	85%	61%	12%	100%

T A B L E   11.3

Coherent correlation matrix for the LRs of the five Col

ρ	1	2	3	4	5
1	100%	0%	0%	20%	75%
2	0%	100%	0%	0%	45%
3	0%	0%	100%	0%	45%
4	20%	0%	0%	100%	0%
5	75%	45%	45%	0%	100%

F I G U R E   11.2

Estimation of degrees of freedom of Student copula

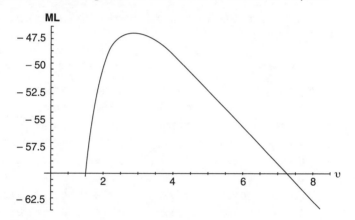

To quantify the capital requirement and the diversification benefit, we perform a Monte Carlo simulation with 100.000 scenarios. We consider the Gaussian copula and the Student copula with 10, 3, and 1 degrees of freedom, respectively. The degree of freedom of the Student copula influences the tail dependence of the distribution. A low degree of freedom leads to high tail dependence, while if we consider $\upsilon \rightarrow \infty$, the Student copula tends to the Gaussian copula, which has no tail dependence. The student copula with one degree of freedom is also called the Cauchy copula. Results coming from the adoption of the different copula dependence structures are then compared with results coming from the independence and the comonotonic assumptions.

As already said, we assume that the different classes of insurance are equally weighted, in order to estimate efficiently correlation effects. The correlations used are those shown in Table 11.3. Table 11.4 shows the results obtained performing the Monte Carlo simulation.

We may appreciate the diversification benefit by comparing the results of the various copulas with those deriving from the comonotonic assumptions (Table 11.5).

Table 11.6 shows the results of a simplified sensitivity analysis performed by supposing that all the coefficients of the correlation matrix are equal to $0, 0.1, 0.2, \ldots, 1$. As intuitive, both the risk measures are increasing functions.

T A B L E   11.4

Statistics and risk measures of the company using several copula functions

	Independent	Gauss	Student T10	Student T3	Cauchy	Sum
Mean	0.6090	0.6093	0.6080	0.6080	0.6087	
Standard dev.	0.0389	0.0481	0.0474	0.0480	0.0482	
Skewness	0.5791	0.7927	0.8786	1.1140	1.4892	
Kurtosis	4.3377	4.7055	5.1431	6.6535	8.8490	
VaR 95%	0.6774	0.6958	0.6937	0.6938	0.6955	0.7442
CVaR 95%	0.7027	0.7312	0.7286	0.7357	0.7449	0.8027
VaR 99%	0.7178	0.7534	0.7504	0.7596	0.7747	0.8383
CVaR 99%	0.7429	0.7872	0.7865	0.8060	0.8271	0.8979

T A B L E   11.5

Relative differences of VaR and CVaR with the comonotonic assumption

Saving	Independent	Gauss	Student T10	Student T3	Cauchy
VaR 95%	8.98%	6.51%	6.79%	6.78%	6.54%
CVaR 95%	12.46%	8.91%	9.23%	8.35%	7.20%
VaR 99%	14.38%	10.13%	10.49%	9.39%	7.59%
CVaR 99%	17.27%	12.33%	12.41%	10.23%	7.89%

T A B L E   11.6

Value at risk and CVaR vs. correlation

	VAR 95%	CVAR 95%	VAR 99%	CVAR 99%
Independent	0.6774	0.7027	0.7178	0.7429
10%	0.6854	0.7226	0.7428	0.7867
20%	0.6931	0.7376	0.7634	0.8117
30%	0.6988	0.7430	0.7695	0.8163
40%	0.7071	0.7550	0.7823	0.8392
50%	0.7148	0.7658	0.7974	0.8517
60%	0.7207	0.7754	0.8078	0.8715
70%	0.7291	0.7823	0.8124	0.8728
80%	0.7369	0.7932	0.8246	0.8869
90%	0.7435	0.7986	0.8323	0.8878
Sum	0.7442	0.8027	0.8383	0.8979

Finally, we built the efficient frontier in the plane LR–CVaR. It is obtained solving the following optimization problem:

$$\text{Max } E\left(\sum_{i=1}^{5} \xi_i \cdot LR_i \right)$$

$$CVaR = \tau$$

$$\sum_{i=1}^{5} \xi_i = 1$$

This problem consists in maximizing the expected aggregate LR (varying the weights ξ_i, which must sum up to one) with a fixed conditional VaR level τ. We then represent graphically the efficient frontier in Figure 11.3.

The efficient frontier may be used to manage the total risk of the company and to individuate the best composition of the insurance business among the various CoI line in correspondence of a specified economic capital requirement (CVaR).

CONCLUSION

Insurance companies face the problem of estimating economic capital requirements for risk management and solvency purposes. In this chapter, we show that an approach consisting in ignoring real correlations among

F I G U R E   11.3

Efficient frontier LR–CVaR

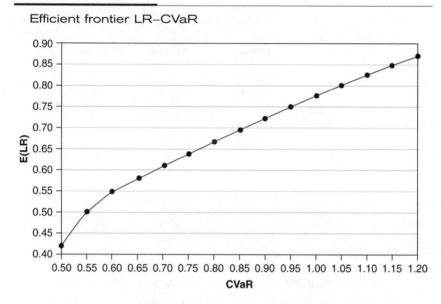

the several classes of insurance can lead to overestimating consistently the economic capital. A dependence structure given by copula functions turns out to be the optimal tool for managing correlations among the classes of insurance of the company. Besides, we take into account a coherent risk measure, the CVaR, for constructing an efficient frontier [see Rockafellar and Uryasev (2002)] that may be used to optimize the relation between expected LR and economic capital (represented by CVaR).

REFERENCES

Meneguzzo, D. and W. Vecchiato (2004) Copula Sensitivity in Collateralised Debt Obligations and Basket Default Swaps Pricing and Risk Monitoring. *Journal of Future Markets*, No 1, pp. 37–70.

Nelsen, R. B. (1998) *An Introduction to Copulas*. Springer: New York.

Rockafellar, R. T. and S. Uryasev (2002) Conditional Value-At-Risk for General Loss Distributions. *Journal of Banking & Finance*, Vol. 26, No 7, pp. 1443–1471.

Tang, A. and E. Valdez. (2005) Economic Capital and the Aggregation of Risks Using Copulas. Working paper.

CHAPTER 12

Solvency II: An Important Case in Applied VaR

Alfredo D. Egídio dos Reis, Raquel M. Gaspar, and Ana T. Vicente

ABSTRACT

Value at risk (VaR) is an extremely popular risk measure and many financial companies have successfully used it to manage their risks. Recent developments toward a general single European financial regulation have led to a great increase in the use of VaR. At least, for the European bank and insurance industry, VaR is no longer an optional risk management tool, but it became mandatory. In this chapter we focus on the insurance business and discuss the use of VaR as it has been proposed in the context of the Solvency II (undergoing) negotiations. Our goals are, on the one hand, to present the underlying assumptions of the models that have been proposed in the quantitative impact studies (QIS) and, on the other hand, to suggest alternative VaR implementations, based upon estimation methods and firm specific characteristics. Our suggestions may be used to develop internal models as suggested in Solvency II context. Finally, we analyze the case of a Portuguese insurer operating in the motor vehicle branch and compare QIS and internal model VaR implementations. In our concrete application, (one-year horizon) capital requirements are similar under the two alternatives, allowing us to conclude for the robustness of the models proposed in QIS.

INTRODUCTION

Insurance is a risky and a risk business, and insurance companies' role, in the economic activity as institutional investors, is increasingly important. On the one hand and given the purpose of its business, an insurer is a *risk taker* by selling insurance. So, to be able to survive in their industry, insurers need to make sure they are able to satisfy the responsibilities assumed toward their clients. To fulfill that purpose an insurer needs not only to appropriately evaluate the risks at stake charging appropriate insurance premiums but also to calculate the amount of capital that should be kept in order to face other losses that, in some situations, can be quite adverse. Naturally, such capital requirements are based on risk taking and depend upon the concrete nature and amount of risks a specific insurer covers. Risks that can be associated with the insurance firm core activity are many times called *insurance risks.* Examples of such risks are the following: possible wrong assessment of the risks insured (premiums charged may not be enough to cover the assumed responsibilities), defaults from their clients (in paying agreed future premiums); or counterparty risk from reinsurers (other entities whom they sold their risks to and may default on their contracts leaving the insurance company with the original obligations they thought they no longer had since they had been resold).

On the other hand, an insurer is an *investor* and a natural player on financial or capital markets. As with any investor, an insurer's portfolio typically consists of various assets of different types with different risk profiles. The assets portfolio of an insurer include all types of products, from simple deposits to stocks, bonds, investment funds units, real estate investments, and various types of derivative products on a variety of possible underlying. These risks should also be accessed, both in nature and in amount, and taken into account when computing capital requirements. These are risks that do not result directly from the insurer's core activity but from the fact that cash flows resulting from that activity are invested in risky financial products. Therefore, they are globally called *market risk.*

The insurance sector carries significant importance in Europe. On voluntary, as well as on statutory basis, it provides cover against various risks facing the citizens, corporations, and other organizations. In addition, collecting long-term savings of millions of Europeans, it is the largest institutional investor on European Union (EU) stock exchanges. An appropriate prudential framework for insurance is therefore of extreme importance. Recent catastrophic events—whether natural or man-made—have highlighted the significance of having a stable and solvent insurance sector.

The previous EU solvency system, introduced in the 1970s, was conceived in a period when the general economic features, as well as insurance practices, were different. Capital requirements of insurance undertakings were determined based on simple ratios that were calculated as percentages of risk exposure measures (e.g., technical provisions, premiums or claims). Nowadays, insurance companies are faced with a different business situation with increasing competition, convergence between financial sectors as well as international dependence. At the same time insurance, asset, and risk management methods and techniques have been significantly refined. The recent economic downturn and volatile financial markets have also put the insurance sector solvency and risk management under significant pressure.

The inadequacy of the old solvency system started to be discussed in 1998, when the European Commission acknowledged the need of "enhancing consumer confidence by promoting full financial market integration while ensuring high levels of consumer protection" [European Commission (1998)] and initiated several changes to the existing directives, leading the European control authorities (of the insurance business) into the development of a new solvency project. For further details, on the background and international context of the new project, we refer to Linder and Ronkainen (2004).

The new European Solvency Project was organized in two phases: In the first phase, known as *Solvency I*, fundamental arrangements were specified, a general framework was defined, and several studies were ordered by the European Commission. The most well-known studies are the KPMG (2002) study and what became known as the Sharma (2002) Report. For a survey on all studies ordered by the European Commission and their recommendations, see Eling et al. (2007). This first phase ended during 2003, and its recommendations became effective as of January 2004.[1] In a second phase, called *Solvency II*, these fundamentals are being developed into specific rules and guidelines. This project follows in spirit the so-called Basel II agreement, established and already in application in the European banking industry. The solvency working group is, thus, moving toward convergence of insurance and banking regulatory systems. Still, a significant difference between the two is that Solvency II focuses more heavily on a holistic risk management approach rather than on management of single risks independently. The Solvency II project is not yet established, as it is still under scrutiny by different supervisory authorities in each EU country and changes may still occur. In fact, this input capacity was specifically sought by the EU as part of the regulatory development process. [See European Commission (2003).]

Value at risk (VaR) has emerged as a key instrument and will continue to be so. This study discusses the use of VaR, as it has been proposed in the context of the Solvency II, and it is organized as follows. In the next section, we make a summary presentation of the Solvency II project and discuss the possibility insurance companies have of developing their own internal models when computing capital requirements. In this chapter's third section, we do a critical presentation of the standard method for capital requirement calculation suggested in Solvency II and put into practice by the third quantitative impact study (QIS3).[2] We highlight the standard method assumptions and propose alternatives that could be useful in building internal models. In the fourth section, we consider the case of an insurer operating in the Portuguese motor branch. For this concrete insurer we compute (one year) capital requirement both directly applying the QIS3 rules and through an internal model that takes into account our suggestions. In the last section we finish the work by addressing final remarks and criticisms on the models used and results obtained.

---

[1] Solvency I addressed many of the coordination issues across regulatory bodies and provided an initial rules-based set of capital requirements (see EU Directive 2002/13/EC for non-life insurers and EU Directive 2002/83/EC for life insurers).

[2] Several quantitative impact studies have been put in place by the Comité Européen des Assurances (CEA) by request of the Committee of European Insurance and Occupational Pension Supervision (CEIOPS). Their purpose is to study the impact of the introduction of Solvency II rules.

SOLVENCY II AND QIS3

Traditional European solvency systems, monitored by control authorities in each country, were based on solvency margins and technical reserves for each branch. Even in the current system, Solvency I, the solvency level depends only on the amount of premiums or claims, and there is no relation with capital requirements and risk taken.

Solvency II aims to be a major improvement over the previous schemes. For the first time a solvency scheme acknowledges the important role insurers play in the world financial markets and has the ambition of taking into account the financial market risk associated with insurers' investments—the *market risk*. In addition, Solvency II also acknowledges the business of risk is risky in itself, classifying and taking into account various insurance risks: *underwriting risk, counterparty risk*, and *operational risk*. Similarly to its banking industry counterpart, the Basel II project, Solvency II has been structured along three main objectives, called the *three pillars*. *Pillar I* defines the financial resources that a company needs to hold in order to be considered solvent. Two thresholds are defined, the first called the *solvency capital requirement* (SCR), and another lower threshold called the *minimum capital requirement* (MCR). The SCR level is a first action level, that is, supervisory action will be triggered if resources fall below its level. The MCR is a severe action level by the control authority, which can include company closure to new business. While Pillar I focuses on quantitative requirements, *Pillar II* defines more qualitative requirements and supplements the first. For instance, it defines the framework of intervention of the supervisory authority. Finally, *Pillar III* addresses issues such as risk disclosure requirements, transparency, and free access to information.

In this chapter our main focus is on the quantitative aspects of Solvency II, and thus on Pilar I, and, in particular, in evaluating the SCR. For the calculation of the SCR, Solvency II proposes a standard (simple) model but encourages the development of internal models that would provide a better adequacy to the kind, spread, and amount of risks taken by each insurer. This is underlined by Ronkainen et al. (2007). Still, as mentioned in Liebwein (2006), any internal model alternative would have to accomplish legal requirements, provide greater added value to shareholders when risk management processes are included, and be subject to approval by the control authorities.

On what concerns technical reserves, i.e., those directly connected with *insurance risks*, the premium reserves and the reserves for pending claims must be computed separately. In the absence of an active market, the technical reserves must be estimated and a risk margin must be added. For the estimating procedure a probability distribution of the cash flows must be estimated; the mean value of this distribution will then be used as an estimate. This is known as the *best estimate*. The risk margin works as loading and intends to cover the volatility of the risk factors, the uncertainty of the best estimate, the risk associated with the insurance portfolio of the company, and natural estimation errors, from the model and its parameters. It is also used to compute a market value for the insurer or branch. The best estimate will be used as an approximation of the future costs that the insurer is expected to cover, and this will be the basis of the computation of its capital needs. For such calculation the insurer must have reliable and organized past loss data to allow the use of proper statistical methods. For instance, claim payments of accidents occurring in one year develop along one or more future years. Typically, we need to fill out an empty triangle with properly estimated values.[3] The discounted sum of the estimated claim payments of each occurrence year will be our estimate for the loss reserves for that year. There are several methods to compute the future payments; the most popular is the so-called *chain ladder*. For more details on this and other methods, please see Taylor (2000). Further discussion on this subject can also be found in Mack (1994) and Verral (1994).

Market risk can be computed, in a more straightforward way, from market quotes. These risks are also not related with each insurance firm; instead, they are related to specificities of particular classes of assets. So, one can think of general rules that may apply to such classes of assets and that should be implemented by all firms.

Whether implied from market quotes or estimated, future uncertainty should be evaluated using a *risk measure*. Although the European

---

[3] An example is shown in Table 12.3 with the data of our application. There, we can see, for instance, that losses that occurred in 2001 can develop until 2006 or even longer, which needs to be estimated as well. Along each line, we have payments for losses that occurred in each starting year; here the values are incremental payments.

working parties suggest the use of both the VaR *measure* and the *conditional tail expectation measure*, also known as *tail* VaR; at the moment only the VaR measure is considered as a standard .[4]

Definition 12.1. Let X be a random variable representing the values of an asset or a return rate for instance. The *value at risk,* denoted as VaR_α, is defined as

$$VaR_{\alpha \times 100\%} = \inf\{x \in \mathbb{R} : \Pr(X > x) \le \alpha\} \qquad (12.1)$$

In the following, we critically present the standard model proposed by the Committee of European Insurance and Occupational Pension Supervision (CEIOPS), as it stands in the latest quantitative impact study (QIS3) and discuss possible alternatives for implementing VaR, whenever we feel it is appropriate.

One first point we would like to make is that the VaR measure makes no assumption concerning the distribution of the random variable we are interested in computing the quantile. Thus, various approaches exist, some called *parametric* and based upon assumptions about the underlying distributions—the most commonly used is the Gaussian distribution—others based upon empirical distributions. This last approach requires collecting (usually historical) past information on the random variable we are interested in and observing the appropriate quantile and, thus, is known as an *historical* approach to VaR. Both parametric and historical approaches to implementing VaR have their own advantages and disadvantages. On the one hand, any parametric model requires parameter estimation, which require choosing the appropriate estimation method and evaluating the ability of the model to explain the data. Furthermore, many

---

[4] In any situation, we will stick to the use of VaR as it is the only risk measure considered as standard in the context of Solvency II. We notice, however, that VaR as a risk measurement has been quite criticized, in the financial literature. A subtle technical problem is that VaR is not subadditive. That is, it is possible to construct two portfolios, A and B, in such a way that VaR $(A + B) >$ VaR$(A) +$ VaR(B), which contradicts the idea of diversification. A theory of *coherent risk measures* exists outlining the properties we would want any measure of risk to possess. As opposed to VaR, tail VaR is a coherent risk measure. For further details on this subject we refer to the canonical paper on the subject: Artzner et al. (1999).

of the variables in which we are interested are far from the most well-known parametric distributions (and clearly far from Gaussian), indicating a historical approach could be best. The historical approach to determining VaR is a nonparametric approach that requires no direct estimation. On the other hand, however, and especially because we are concerned with extreme events, the amount of historical information one may need to collect in order to capture well the tail behavior of a distribution can be substantial. In addition, we may want to consider the possibility that some extreme events that have not yet occurred in the past may occur in the future. This advocates in favor of parametric methods. Probably the sensible attitude is to use either both methods—choosing the worst-case scenario—or a mixture of them. For a detailed discussion on various VaR implementations, we refer to Linsmeier and Pearson (1996) and Jorion (2001).

As we will see, the standard model, as proposed in QIS3, relies considerably on a parametric Gaussian implementation of VaR. We propose, instead that, provided there is enough information on the relevant variables—which is typically the case, at least on what concerns financial data—that an historical approach will be more accurate evaluating VaR. The QIS3 computations rely considerably on the following VaR result for normally distributed random variables.

Result 12.1. *Suppose you have N random variables, X_n for $n = 1, 2, \ldots, N$, all normally distributed with mean zero and variance σ_n. Let $Y = \Sigma_{n=1}^{N} w_n X_n$ define a linear combination of the random variables X_n, where the w_n's are constants. We denote shortly by $VaR(X_n)$ the VaR of order a of each random variable. Then the VaR of Y,*

$$\mathrm{VaR}(Y) = \sqrt{\sum_{i,j=1}^{N} \rho_{ij} w_i w_j \, \mathrm{VaR}(X_i) \mathrm{Var}(X_j)} \qquad (12.2)$$

where all VaR are computed for the same probability a.

For the remainder of this section we discuss in detail the implementation of both alternatives. The various risks are divided according to their nature into *market risk, counterparty risk, underwriting risk,* and *operational risk*. The final assessment of the *capital requirement* is obtained by a risk aggregation, considering all the above-mentioned risks.

We aim at applying the methods here discussed to an insurer operating in the motor branch. Therefore, we focus, as far as insurance risks are concerned, on risks specific to that branch. In addition, we do not include in our study catastrophe risk as appropriate data would be hard to find and its complexity is beyond the scope of our application. As far as market risks are concerned, we refrain from discussing the impact of two important classes of assets in capital requirements: risk management assets (such as derivatives) and real estate assets. Both these classes of assets were absent from our concrete insurer portfolio but deserve special attention in QIS3. For details on how to include risks of these types of assets not mentioned in this study, we refer to CEIOPS (2007a; 2007b; 2007c).

Market Risk

When evaluating market risk we are mainly concerned with measuring the impact that changes in the market value of various assets have in the overall investments that insurers do when applying the cash flows of its activity, in risky financial markets. The standard approach suggested in QIS3 relies on two key assumptions: (1) financial returns are normally distributed and (2) such a distribution is static, i.e., it does not evolve over time. Both these assumptions have been widely studied in the financial literature, and enough evidence has been found allowing us to clearly reject any of them. See, for instance, Cont (2001). Moreover, capital requirements are computed assuming a static portfolio, i.e., that a portfolio does not change over time. Good risk management practice, however, requires rebalancing the portfolio periodically. There is a clear inconsistency in accessing risk (via capital requirements) assuming a static portfolio when good risk management leads to a dynamic portfolio. The best we can suggest to overcome this difficulty is to periodically reevaluate the capital requirement estimation; with a periodicity similar to the periodicity with which each firm changes their portfolio. We now look deeper into each asset class, present the QIS3 standard model suggestion, and propose our alternative. For exact formulas concerning the QIS3 approach, we refer to CEIOPS (2007a; 2007b; 2007c).

As far as *equity risk* is concerned, QIS3 divides it into specific and systematic risk. As the first type of risk can be eliminated in a well-diversified portfolio, QIS3 considers it as concentration risk (and not equity risk). Having to deal only with the systematic part of equity risk, QIS3 relies on two indexes: a *Global index* that includes all stocks from European countries and other global markets, and a second index called *Others index*, where the remaining countries should be included as well as any nonquoted stocks (irrespective of their country). Based upon collected historical information and assuming a Gaussian distribution with mean zero for each index returns, QIS3 estimated each index $VaR_{99.5\%}$ obtaining -32 and -45 percent, for the Global and Others indexes, respectively. In addition, QIS 3 suggests the use of a correlation of 0.75 between the two indexes and equation to take into account the diversification effect across indexes.[5]

An insurer is exposed to *interest rate risk* via all assets and liabilities whose value is sensitive to changes in the term structure of interest rates. Example of such assets and liabilities are fixed-income investments, insurance liabilities, and loans. The QIS3 standard model assumes that default-free interest rates (also known as *zero rates*) maturing each year from 1 to 20 years are independent variables. For each of these variables, QIS3 estimates VaR, with both $\alpha = 0.005$ and $\alpha = 0.995$, assuming that changes in rates of any maturity are normally distributed with mean zero. Even though the independence across maturities and the Gaussian assumption are questionable, the proposed standard method allows considering the risk of various movements of the term structure taking into account that rates with different maturities have different volatilities. In addition, computing two quantiles for each variable makes sense as an insurer may be more exposed to the risk of interest rates increasing or decreasing. Finally, when implementing the standard method each insurer must decompose the payoffs of each interest rate sensitive asset or liability to match the yearly maturities up to 20 years.[6]

---

[5] To the best of our knowledge, only the Global index volatility was estimated based upon quarterly data on the MSCI Developed Markets index, from 1970 to 2005. The Others index volatility and correlation between both indexes are ad hoc values suggested in QIS3.

[6] The QIS3 recommends for maturities longer than 20 years that the 20-year VaR be used.

Table 12.1 presents QIS3 VaR estimates for changes in zero rates of different maturities.[7]

Currency risk arises from the level of volatility of currency exchange rates. An insurer is exposed to that risk whenever she directly invests in foreign currencies or when some of her assets or liabilities are denominated in a currency other than its home currency. Once again, the standard model in QIS3 assumes that changes in exchange rates follow a Normal distribution with zero mean. Supposing quotes are in a (Foreign/Home) form, whenever a foreign currency depreciates the mentioned ratio increases. So, provided we subtract the liabilities to the assets denominated in foreign currency (i.e., we consider only the net asset value), adverse movements are measured by VaR with $\alpha = 0.005$. QIS3, considered only the variation of the euro relative to a index of foreign currencies and estimates, therefore, only one which turned out to be of 20 percent.[8]

Spread or *credit risk* is part of the risk an insurer is exposed to via its investments in financial markets. It is associated with the credit worthiness of some financial products issued by corporations. The typical example are corporate bonds whose value is lower than a (otherwise equivalent) government bond because it may happen that the corporation fails to pay some of the coupons or capital. Credit risk can be measured by the difference in yields between corporate and government bonds.

T A B L E   12.1

Value at risk for changes in zero rates of several maturities (QIS3 estimates)

VaR\T	1	2	3	4	5	6	7	8	9	10–15	16	17	18	19	20+
$\alpha = 0.005$	0.94	0.77	0.69	0.62	0.56	0.52	0.49	0.46	0.44	0.42	0.41	0.40	0.39	0.38	0.37
$\alpha = 0.995$	−0.51	−0.47	−0.44	−0.42	−0.40	−0.38	−0.37	20.35	20.34	20.34	20.33	20.33	20.32	20.31	20.31

[7] These estimates were obtained using German monthly zero coupon rates, from 1- to 10-year maturities since 1972 and also extracted from daily data European swaps with 1, 5, 10, 15, 20, 25, and 30 years, since 1997.

[8] This estimation was performed using monthly exchange rate quotes toward the euro from 1958 to 2006, excluding the Bretton-Woods period (1992 to 2001). The foreign currencies considered were the U.S. dollar, the British pound, the Japanese yen, the Swedish crone, the Swiss franc, and the Australian dollar.

Such a difference is called the *credit spread*. Clearly, in the same way interest rates vary across maturities also credit spreads will do so, originating what is known as a *credit curve* or *credit spread terms structure*. Moreover, naturally, credit spreads vary across ratings: products with less credit risk (higher rating) will have lower spreads than those with lower credit worthiness (lower rating). The QIS3 standard approach takes both these facts into account and analyzes various pairs of (duration,[9] credit rating class). Nonetheless, credit spreads of each pair are taken as independent random variables. For an insurer the risk is that their investments will be worth less due to a decrease in credibility, which is the same as an increase in credit spreads. Thus, the appropriate figure we are looking for when trying to access this risk is a VaR with $\alpha = 0.995$. Table 12.2 presents such a VaR for some combinations of duration and/or credit class.[10]

The last risk we must refer to before aggregating all market risks is *concentration risk*. In QIS3, the definition of concentration risk is

T A B L E   12.2

Value at risk for assets with different durations and credit spreads (based upon QIS3 calibrations)

VaR$_{99.5\%}$	2	4	6	8	10	12	14
AAA or AA	0.5%	1%	1.5%	2%	2.5%	3%	3.5%
A	2.06%	4.12%	6.18%	8.24%	10.30%	12.36%	14.42%
BBB	2.25%	4.50%	6.75%	9%	11.25%	13.05%	15.30%
BB	6.78%	13.56%	20.34%	27.12%	27.12%	27.12%	27.12%
B	11.2%	22.4%	33.6%	33.6%	33.6%	33.6%	33.6%
CCC	22.4%	44.8%	44.8%	44.8%	44.8%	44.8%	44.8%
Unrated	4%	8%	12%	16%	20%	24%	28%

---

[9] Here we refer to the *Fisher-Weil duration measure* that can be interpreted as an *average* payment time of a cash-flow stream paid at several points in time. For further detail we refer to Weil (1973).

[10] Quantitative impact studies are not presented as in Table 12.2. Instead, they present two separate functions: a function dependent upon the rating class and an independent function that depends upon duration alone. The final VaR measure is then obtained multiplying the two functions. We believe Table 12.2 allows a better understanding of the risks at stake and refer to CEIOPS (2007c) for further details.

restricted to the risk regarding the accumulation of exposures with the same counterparty, also called *name*. It does not include other types of concentrations such as geographical concentration and industry sector concentration. All entities belonging to the same group are interpreted as the same name. An ad hoc concentration threshold is defined based upon the credit rating of each product: for products with A or higher rating the threshold is 5 percent for the insurer total assets value while for products with lower rating is 3 percent. QIS proposes an excess expose measure based upon those thresholds and VaR corrections that should be pre-formed when the insurer's assets are not well diversified enough. Most insurers do have well diversified portfolios, so it is quite common to obtain zero concentration risk. This is the case in our case study, we refer to CEIOPS (2007a) for calibration details and actual VaR corrections. Finally, to compute the *overall market risk* VaR, QIS3 simply suggests the use of Equation (12.1) with an ad hoc correlation matrix[11] and takes into account each asset class weight in terms of the total assets considered in the market risk analysis.

We now briefly discuss an alternative to the QIS3 standard VaR, for measuring all market risks. In the case study we will use this alternative as our *internal model*. Our suggestion relies on two main ideas: (1) to consider the historical approach to VaR when evaluating market risks and (2) to use information each insurer has easy access to; its own current portfolio composition. The historical approach to VaR is considered by many authors as "the simplest and most transparent method of calculation" (Dowd, 2005). It involves running the current portfolio across a set of historical asset values and to build a historical return distribution to obtain the relevant percentile (the VaR). The key aspect here is that we do not assume a normal distribution of asset returns. Moreover, using the insurer specific portfolio composition, we focus on the exact risks the insurer takes and not all the risk it could take. The first main drawback that could be pointed out is the requirement for a large market database and the computationally intensive calculations. This is hardly a problem in the concrete case of market risks as long financial time series are typically available. The second drawback depends

---

[11] The exact correlation matrix suggested in QIS3 is presented in Table 12.4, where it is compared with an alternative matrix estimated considering our case study insurer-specific portfolio.

upon the complexity of the insurer portfolio and can be overcome with a good computer program. Our suggestion for computing market risk takes into account the current issuer portfolio and, for each risk class, can be summarized in the following five-step procedure:

1. Collect as much historical information as possible on the market value of any product subject to that risk. Denote the collection of all such products by $W_p = (w_1, \ldots, w_N)$ where w_n for all $n = 1, \ldots, N$ are the weights of a specific asset or liability.[12]

2. Use those weights to build a time series of the collection value. Let $V_n(t)$ be the market price of a specific asset or liability at some past date t. Then, current collection value at the same date, $V_p(t)$, is given by $V_p(t) = \sum_{n=1}^{N} w_n V_n(t)$.

3. From that time series deduce the time series of collection value returns, R_p. For data with high frequency the actual returns may be well approximated by log returns,

$$R_p(t) = \frac{V_p(t+1) - V_p(t)}{V_p(t)} \approx \ln\left(\frac{V_p(t+1)}{V_p(t)}\right) \qquad (12.3)$$

4. Assume the annual returns are given by $R_p^a(t) = \Delta^{-1} \times R_p^\Delta(t)$, where D denotes the periodicity of the data expressed in years and built a time series of annual returns.

5. Using the series of annual returns, determine the appropriate VaR for the risk under analysis observing the appropriate quantile from the historical distribution.

To aggregate the total market risk, estimate the correlations between each type of risks from the various time series determined in step 5. Then, using the estimated correlations and the previously obtained VaR for each risk, we apply Equation (12.2) and obtain the SCR for market risk using.

We note that our internal model approach to estimate market risk is similar, at least in spirit, to the ideas underlying the QIS3 proposal. To be more concrete, when dealing with *interest rate risk*, we recommend

---

[12] We take assets to have a positive weight and liabilities to have a negative one.

considering several points of the interest rate term structure and computing the VaR for each of them. The difference is that we believe the relevant points should be chosen taking into account the durations of the assets and liabilities exposed to interest rate risk in the insurer current portfolio. For *credit spread risk*, we also suggest grouping the products according to their rating and duration. However, taking a historical VaR approach would mean estimating a VaR for each pair (duration, rating) based upon past yield changes. Finally, we notice that using this approach it makes no sense to define a concentration risk, as we have not considered both the systematic risk of each product and its actual total risk.[13] We now go on analyzing *insurance risks*, i.e., risks that are more related to an insurer's core activity.

Counterparty Default Risk

This is the risk of default of a counterparty to risk mitigation contracts like reinsurance and financial over-the-counter (OTC)[14] derivatives. In terms of the amounts at stake, reinsurance counterparty risk tends to be the most important. In our case study, it is also the only one. Here we analyze only reinsurance counterparty risk. If case of default from a reinsurance counterparty, the insurer will incur in replacement costs (RC), which can be evaluated as the sum of the technical reserves of the ceded reinsurance plus the extra (previously paid) premium minus any recoveries. The QIS3 assumes zero recovery in case of default and estimates probabilities of default (PD) for different reinsurance rating classes. The rating classes are the same as those in Table 12.2, except that the first two, AAA and AA, come separated and the last two come merged. The figures in a decreasing rating scale are 0.002, 0.01, 0.05, 0.24, 1.2, 6.04, and 30.41 percent, respectively. The VaR for this risk is computed in three steps: (1) calculation of the so-called Herfindahl index,[15] (2) calculation of capital requirement per counterparty,

---

[13] Due to space restrictions, we do not describe in detail our approach to each of the market risks. Instead, we present the main steps and refer to Vicente (2008) for further details.

[14] Over-the-counter (OTC) derivatives are bilateral contracts traded outside exchanges and thus subject to counterparty risk.

[15] The Herfindahl index is a measure of the size of firms in relationship to the industry and an indicator of the amount of competition among them.

and (3) aggregation. The final formula for the VaR depends on an implicit correlation of counterparty default. In our case study, the correlation is 1 and the formula is given by $VaR = RC \times \min\{100 \times PD; 1\}$. We refer to CEIOPS (2007a) for details on this method or on how the QIS3 handles derivative related counterparty risk. Given the complexity of counterparty risk modeling we suggest no internal model to the QIS3 approach.

Underwriting Risk

This sort of risk arises directly from the nature of the insurance activity. In the case of non-life insurance, it basically includes premium risk and the reserve risk.[16] On what concerns premium and reserve risk, the QIS3 standard approach relies on two measures: a premium volume measure (PVM) and a reserve volume measure (RVM) and in evaluating the variations of such measures to compute their volatilities. For the *premium risk* the QIS3 suggestion is either to directly observe the PMV from the insurer's estimate of the premiums for next year, net of reinsurance, or to consider an increase of 5 percent on the actual net premiums. Even though 5 percent is an ad hoc, lack of information makes this second option quite used in practice. This will also be the option we will choose for our case study. The QIS3 then suggests to obtain the PVM volatility, σ^{pr}, by the well-known Bühlmann and Straub's credibility formula: $\sigma^{pr} = \sqrt{c\sigma_I^2 + (1-c)\sigma_M^2}$, where σ_I is the insurer's sigma, σ_M is the market sigma, and c is a constant dependent upon the sample size n ($c = n/(n+4)$ if $n \geq 7$ and $c = 0$ otherwise).[17] The QIS3 uses a fixed value of 10 percent for σ_M and suggests σ_I to be computed by (historical) estimation, calculating a (weighted) sample standard deviation of the loss ratio annual claims cost over premiums net of reinsurance. For the *reserve risk*, their suggestion is to use the figure for the loss reserves from the insurer's last year balance sheet as RVM. This is an amount supervised by the control authorities. The QIS3 computes the RVM volatility, σ^{res}, first computing the volatility of the line of business *third-party liabilities* and of the *other classes* and then aggregating it. The

---

[16] Catastrophe risk (Cat risk) is also considered as underwriting risk. However, as previously mentioned, we do not analyze this risk in the context of this study.

[17] See Bühlmann and Gisler (2005) for more details on the credibility formula.

QIS3 recommends the use of 12.5 and 7.5 percent, respectively, for the two mentioned volatilities. Finally, the *overall underwriting* VaR is obtained using the sum of the volume measures $VM = PVM + RVM$ and using the following formula:

$$\text{VaR} = VMf(\sigma) \quad \text{with} \quad f(\sigma) = \frac{e^{\left\{N_{99.5\%}\sqrt{\ln(\sigma^2+1)}\right\}}}{\sqrt{\sigma^2+1}} - 1 \quad (12.4)$$

where $N_{99.5\%}$ stands for the 99.5 percentile of a standard normal distribution and σ is an overall volatility given by $\sigma^2 = (PVM \times RVM \times \sigma' \times \sigma^{res})/VM^2$. The function $f(\sigma)$ implicitly assumes that the underwriting risk follows a lognormal distribution and, for a small and medium size σ, gives roughly 3σ.

Next, we discuss alternative procedures, that may be used an internal model, to evaluate the underwriting risk. For *premium risk* we consider a sum of loss and expense ratios, called *combined ratio* (CR), $CR = LR + ER$. The loss ratio (incurred losses and loss-adjustment expenses divided by net earned premium) is added to the expense ratio (underwriting expenses divided by net premium written) to determine the company's combined ratio. The CR is a reflection of the company's overall premium profitability. A CR of less than 100 percent indicates premium profitability, while anything over 100 indicates an underwriting loss. The expense ratio (ER) tends to be relatively constant over time, so most of the premium risk is, in fact, associated with the loss ratio that should be properly evaluated. Our suggestion is to follow El-Bassiouni's (1991) model, where loss ratio (LR) is assumed to follow a lognormal distribution.

The proposed model can be understood as a linear regression model on the logarithm of the LR, $Y_{it} = \ln(LR_{it}) = \lambda_i + \beta_t + \bar{\omega}_{it}$, with i and t the insurer and year indexes. The expected value Y_{it} is given by λ_i, while $\beta_t \sim N(0;\ \theta_2)$ and $\bar{\omega}_{it} \sim N(0; \theta_1/RP_{it})$ with RP_{it} the received premiums. Note that, to estimate an insurer LR, all the LRs of other insurers in the same branch are used. The model has $(n+2)$ parameters that need to be estimated. Its (stepwise) estimation is a mix of data estimation and simulation. With these estimates and the distribution assumed we simulated 5,000 values for Y_{it} and built the empirical distribution. The $\text{VaR}_{99.5\%}(LR)$ is then used to compute the VaR for overall risk $\text{VaR}_{pr} = (\text{VaR}\ (LR) + ER - 100)\ RP$. As far as the *reserve risk* is concerned, we follow Hersterber et al. (2003). In some sense the computations are related to those of the best estimate for the loss reserving, but they go further by computing an (estimated) distribution for the future liabilities, since we should estimate a maximum value for reserves under that distribution. For that we use the bootstrap resampling technique to simulate the residues obtained from the chain-ladder method. Finally, we produce an estimate distribution of reserves. The VaR for this risk will be the difference between that 99.5 percent percentile of the estimated distribution and its mean value.[18] The VaR that evaluates the *overall underwriting risk* will be the result of the aggregation of the premium risk and the reserve risk using the formula in Equation (12.2).

Operational Risk

Operational risk arises with potential losses from a group of misconducts of internal systems, procedures, human resources, external events, legal risk, and others. For this risk we follow fully the QIS3 lines, i.e., we consider the same approach in our internal model. By its nature it is not easy to make an allocation of this risk among all possible different branches. The QIS3 considers information along major branches like life, non-life and health insurance. For our application, we only need information on the non-life branch. Based upon studies on operational misconducts in non-life insurance QIS3 suggests a calculation formula for this risk, underlining however that it is not definite, as it needs further developments. The QIS3 computes the solvency operational capital requirement, $SCR^{operational}$, as the minimum between two risk figures: (1) 30 percent of what they call the SCR^{basic} and (2) 2 percent of either gross technical reserves or gross premiums, whichever is bigger. The basic SCR results from the aggregation of the market, counterparty and underwriting VaRs using Equation (12.2) and assuming correlations of 0.25, 0.25, and 0.5 between the pairs (market, counterparty), (market, underwriting), and (counterparty, underwriting), respectively. Operational risk assessment is complex and reliable information hard to obtain, so we propose no internal models concerning this risk.

---

[18] For more details on the procedures concerning the underwriting risk, we refer to Vicente (2008), where all details can be found.

Final Capital Requirements and Risk Margin

The final solvency capital requirement (SCR^{final}) for the period under analysis is the sum of the SCR^{basic} and the SCR^{operational}. Under the *Swiss Solvency Test*, the solvency of periods other than the one we are interested in, called *run-off* periods, should also be considered in building up a prudential *risk margin*. Given our main goal—discuss the use of VaR in the context of Solvency II—we refrain from explaining the exact risk margin computations that are non-VaR related.

CASE STUDY

In this section we illustrate the ideas previously presented and compute the solvency capital requirements for the case of a Portuguese insurer operating in the motor branch. From now on we refer to this insurer as the *Insurer*. We present in parallel the results from QIS3 standard model and the IM proposed by the authors. Our analysis is a static one (thus, limited) and based upon the Insurer information at the end of 2006. We note that the data from the automobile insurance includes some other additional, but smaller, covers. We have decided not to work the models for the different lines of business because were not quite sure on the reliability of the separation. Figure 12.1 presents the composition of the Insurer's assets and liabilities.

F I G U R E   12.1

Assets and liabilities of the Insurer

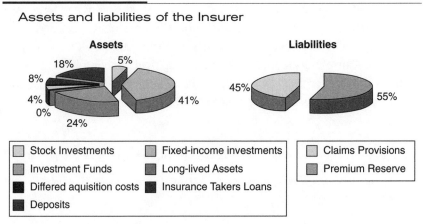

Market Risks

The Insurer "portfolio," i.e., the amount of assets or liabilities that is exposed to market risk, represented 70.5 percent of its total assets and 54.6 percent of its total liabilities. We note that the same asset, for instance corporate bonds in foreign currencies, exposes the Insurer to several market risks at the same time: interest rate risk, credit spread risk and currency risk. This, together with the fact that risk (and risk measures) are nonadditive (due to the diversification effects), makes it far from trivial to present the proportion of each risk class on the total portfolio market risk.

Table 12.3 compares the QIS3 and the IM VaR results. For the IM estimates we have used daily market data, from the previous five years[19] on all possible portfolio products. The analysis can be easily extended to a longer data series.[20] All information—stock quotes, bonds technical information and quotes, interest rate quotes and exchange rates—was extracted from the Bloomberg, L.P. information system. The deviations column in Table 12.3 shows the difference between the QIS3 and IM VaR estimates both in absolute terms and measured in percentage of the QIS3 results. We start by noticing that the IM VaR results can be considerably higher or lower. For instance, the IM currency risk VaR is 42.1 percent lower and the IM interest risk VaR is 32.5 percent higher than the QIS3 VaRs. These deviations, however, partially compensate each other and the final SCR^{market} in the IM is only 9.4 percent higher than according to QIS3. The Insurer exposure to *equity risk* was mainly (95 percent) due to investments in stocks belonging to QIS3 Global index. However, 17.5 percent of those investments are in home stocks, which clearly lead to a nonperfect correlation of the portfolio with the Global index and, consequently, to a higher risk. This is clearly a concentration risk not captured by QIS3 because it does not consider geographical concentration. The IM captures this higher risk, producing a higher equity VaR estimate. As far as *interest rate risk* is concerned the Insurer risk was that of an increase in

---

[19] For a few stocks that were not listed during the entire period, the information was somewhat shorter.

[20] It is far from clear whether going further into the past would be more accurate in estimating future risks, which is really what we are trying to assess.

TABLE 12.3

Market risk QIS3 vs. IM comparison

		QIS3			Internal Model (IM)			Deviations (IM-QIS3)	
		VaR	Percent Asset Class	Percent Overall Portfolio	VaR	Percent Asset Class	Percent Overall Portfolio	VaR Dev	Percent of QIS3 VaR
Equity	Global (95%)	2,108,575							
	Other (5%)	144,472							
	VaR	2,113,519	31%	2.8%	2,308,447	33.4%	3.0%	194,928	9.2%
Interest Rate	Assets	3,012,414			3,682,230			Assets	
	Liabilities	−658,332			−562,716			Liabilities	
	VaR	2,354,082	15%	3.2%	3,119,514	20.0%	4.2%	765,432	32.5%
Currency	VaR	848,494	20%	1.1%	491,162	11.6%	0.6%	−357,332	−42.1%
CreditSpread	VaR	544,989	3.4%	0.70%	544,989	3.4%	0.70%	0	0%
Concentration	VaR	0	0%	0%	—	—	—	—	—
SCRmarket		3,563,370		4.80%	3,897,404		5.20%	334,034	9.4%

287

interest rates. The differences are a direct result of the difference in the way VaR is estimated under QIS3 under our IM.

Table 12.3 illustrates such differences, and we note that for maturities between 2 and 14 years the IM model predicted higher VaRs. Most of the interest rate sensitive products had durations within that interval, which justifies the increase of 32.5 percent of the QIS3 VaR (Figure 12.2).

The Insurer was exposed to *currency risk* both because of direct investments in foreign currency and because it had investments in products denominated in foreign currencies. The exposure was, however, only in the following currencies: GBP (38 percent), CHF (32 percent), SEK (17 percent), and NOK (13 percent). The lower VaR produced by the IM can easily be understood as all these currencies are strong currencies with low variation relative to the euro. Despite that, the QIS3 approach fixed a 20 percent depreciation to compute the VaR. The absence of *credit spread risk* difference results from having adopted, for the IM, the standard approach proposed in QIS3. In our Insurer case 65.2 percent of credit sensitive investments were rated AAA or AA, 30.3 percent A, and the remaining BBB. So, to some extent, this exposure was too small to justifying the development of an IM alternative.

Table 12.4 compares the correlations used by the QIS3 and IM for aggregating all market risk. We note that the QIS3 numbers are not based upon estimations while the IM are. The QIS3 suggested matrix gives higher correlations than what seems realistic.

F I G U R E   12.2

Comparison of QIS3 and IM VaR for interest rate changes

— QIS3   — Internal Model

T A B L E   12.4

The QIS3 vs. IM estimated correlations between the various market risks

QIS 3	Equity	Interest Rate	Currency	Credit Spread	IM	Equity	Interest Rate	Currency	Credit Spread
Equity	1				Equity	1			
Interest Rate	0	1			Interest Rate	−0.033	1		
Currency	0.25	0.25	1		Currency	−0.064	0.045	1	
Credit Spread	0.25	0.25	0.25	1	Credit Spread	0.079	−0.154	−0.007	1

Insurance Risks

Table 12.5, below, presents the results concerning the *underwriting risk*. To estimate the premium risk in the IM, we have used premium and loss data on 20 Portuguese insurers during 20 years. Starting values for the parameters were $\theta_1^{(0)} = 0.0539$ and $\theta_2^{(0)} = 0.0125$. After four additional steps, we reached the final values of $\theta_1^{(4)} = 1.019.543€$ and $\theta_2^{(4)} = 0€$. The final 20 values for the λ_i can be seen in Vicente (2008); $\lambda_{14} = 4.2969$ is the value for the Insurer. From there we got the values for the mean and variance of $\hat{E}[Y_{2006}] = 4.297$ and $\hat{V}[Y_{2006}] = 0.189$. Concerning reserve risk there was available a triangle of data from 2001 to 2006 with the occurrence year and the corresponding claim payment developments, see Table 12.6.

Because we have insufficient data for the estimation of the correlation coefficients, we use as an estimate the average of the coefficients of the Portuguese insurers in the motor branch. The standard deviations are calculated with the data of received premiums and loss reserves. The final results for the premium risk and the reserve risk are shown in Table 12.5. More details on the procedure can be found in Vicente (2008). The main difference between the QIS3 and the IM underwriting risk evaluation is due to the fact that the IM uses basically information of the Portuguese instead of the European market, as the QIS3 does. This application concerns with the motor insurance and is known that Portuguese drivers have a loss rate greater than that of the European counterpart, giving support to using Portuguese data only.

T A B L E   12.5

Underwriting risk, QIS3 vs. IM comparison

		QIS3		IM	Deviation	
Premium Risk	PMV	58,610,179	RP	51,549,852		
	σ_I	49.8%	LR	120.03%		
	σ_M	10.0%	ER	25.46%		
	C	0.667	VaR	23,448,828		
	σ^{pr}	41%				
Reserve Risk	RMV	28,972,444	Mean	14,615,425		
	σ^{res}	12.5%	RES	27,483,984		
			SE	5,339,722		
			VaR	12,868,559		
Underwriting Risk	VM	87,582,623				
	σ	10.70%	$\rho_{pr, res}$	0.3789		
	$f(\sigma)$	0.3133				
SCR^{underwriting}		27,395,091		28,805,711	1,410,620	5.15%

T A B L E   12.6

Matrix of the incremental paid claims

	1	2	3	4	5	6
2001	7,792,345	2,262,154	166,760	393,132	206,338	86,268
2002	9,545,760	4,324,696	768,550	613,266	240,614	
2003	11,879,234	5,522,645	646,284	571,696		
2004	13,804,560	4,993,800	1,230,524			
2005	15,336,473	7,390,653				
2006	18,170,211					

On what concerns counterparty risk and operational risk we followed fully the QIS3 directives. Our Insurer had only one reinsurance contract and no financial derivatives. As the reinsurer was rated A by Standard and Poor's, its estimated probability of default was considered to be of 0.05 percent. The replacement cost was €6,079,915, and thus, the final $SCR^{counterparty} = 303,996€$. For operational risk, we got the following values for the pairs (gross premiums, gross technical reserves) as (55,660,560; 51,549,852) and (39,026,522; 51,549,852) for the QIS3 and the IM, respectively.

Across all insurance risks the main difference between the two models is in the way they handle the underwriting risk. Not surprisingly, it is here that we find bigger SCR discrepancies.

CONCLUSION

Table 12.7 summarizes the quantities for the two approaches we worked out for the different risks. The structures of the two methods are similar, allowing for a risk-to-risk comparison. On a quick look, we find that the capital requirements are quite similar, although the IM gives (slightly) higher requirements. Given a company value of about €50 million at the end of 2006, the Insurer remain solvent under any of the proposed approaches. However, we must say that the models used have obvious limitations. The analysis is not dynamic; for instance, it assumes that the business structure remains unchanged, that there are no new insurance contracts, and that the asset structure is the same. In addition, the IM is quite simplified in order to ease the calculations and adapt to the information available, which quite often is limited. Finally, the QIS3 approach is not yet settled, and it is expected soon that a new project, called QIS4, will be launched by CEIOPS.

T A B L E   12.7

SCR, QIS3 vs. IM

	QIS 3	IM	Deviations
SCR^{market}	3,563,370	3,897,404	9.40%
$SCR^{counterparty}$	303,996	303,996	0%
$SCR^{underwriting}$	27,395,091	28,805,711	5.10%
SCR^{basic}	28,144,636	29,627,565	5.30%
$SCR^{operational}$	1,113,211	1,030,997	27.40%
SCR Final	**29,257,847**	**30,658,562**	**4.80%**

Besides that, there are risks not developed like Cat risk, by its complexity [e.g., see the model by Lescourret and Robert (2006)]. In addition, as we said earlier, operational risk needs a better development. The possibility of a derivatives market was not considered here and could serve as risk mitigation. Also, we made the (usual) assumptions concerning probability distributions fit for some random factors, such as the lognormal for the LR, without enough supporting data.

As a final remark we must say that a great step has been taken concerning risk assessment for insurers and that the official model proposed by the European control bodies can be the model built by the insurer herself, although subject to approval. This is in fact encouraged.

ACKNOWLEDGMENTS

The first author thanks CEMAPRE and ISEG, Technical University of Lisbon, and gratefully acknowledges partial financial support from FCT-Fundação para a Ciência e Tecnologia (Programme FEDER/POCI 2010).

The second author thanks ADVANCE and ISEG, Technical University of Lisbon and gratefully acknowledges support from FCT under grant PTDC/MAT/64838/2006.

The third author acknowledges the support from ISP-Instituto de Seguros de Portugal (Portuguese Insurance and Pension Fund Supervision Authority).

REFERENCES

Artzner, P., F. Delbaen, J.-M. Eber, and D. Heath (1999) Coherent Measures of Risk. *Mathematical Finance,* Vol. 9, No. 3, pp. 203–228.

Bühlmann, H. and A. Gisler (2005) *A Course in Credibility Theory and its Applications*, New York: Springer.

Committee of European Insurance and Occupational Pensions Supervisors (2007a) QIS3—Technical Specifications, *CEIOPS Consultive Document,* CEIOPS-FS–11/07, Frankfurt, Germany.

Committee of European Insurance and Occupational Pensions Supervisors (2007b) QIS3—Callibration of the Underwriting Risk and MCR, *CEIOPS Consultive Document,* CEIOPS-FS–14/07, Frankfurt, Germany.

Committee of European Insurance and Occupational Pensions Supervisors (2007c) QIS3—Callibration of Credit Risk, *CEIOPS Consultive Document,* CEIOPS-FS–23/07, Frankfurt, Germany.

Cont, R. (2001) Empirical Properties of Asset Returns: Stylized Facts and Statistical Issues. *Quantitative Finance,* Vol. 1, No. 2, pp. 223–236.

Dowd, K. (2005). *Measuring Market Risk,* 2nd edition. Hoboken, NJ: John Wiley & Sons.

El-Bassiouni, M.Y. (1991) A Mixed Model for Loss Ratio Analysis. *ASTIN Bulletin,* Vol. 21, No. 2, pp. 231–238.

Eling, M., H. Schmeiser, and J.T. Schmit (2007) The Solvency II Process: Overview and Critical Analysis. *Risk Management & Insurance Review,* Vol. 10, No. 1, pp. 69–85.

European Commission (1998) Financial Services: Building a Framework for Action, Communication of the Commission. Working paper, Brussels.

European Commission (2003) Design of a Future Prudential Supervisory System in the EU—Recommendations by the Commission Services. Working paper, Brussels.

Jorion, P. (2001) Value at Risk: *The New Benchmark for Managing Financial Risk,* 2nd edition. MA: McGraw-Hill Trade.

KPMG (2002) Study into the Methodologies to Assess the Overall Financial Position of an Insurance Undertaking from the Perspective of Prudential Supervision. Brussels.

Lescourret, L. and C. Robert (2006) Extreme Dependence of Multivariate Catastrophic Losses. *Scandinavian Actuarial Journal,* Vol. 2006, No. 4 (2006), pp. 203–225.

Liebwein, P. (2006) Risk Models for Capital Adequacy: Applications in the Context of Solvency II and Beyond. *The Geneva Papers,* Vol. 31, No. 2, pp. 528–550.

Linder, U. and V. Ronkainen (2004) Solvency II, Towards a New Insurance Supervisory System in the EU. *Scandinavian Actuarial Journal*, Vol. 104, No.6, pp. 462–474.

Linsmeier, T. and N. Pearson (1996) *Risk Measurement: An Introduction to Value at Risk*, University of Illinois at Urbana: Champaign, IL.

Mack, T. (1994) Measuring the Variability of Chain Ladder Reserve Estimates. *Casualty Actuarial Society Forum*, Vol. 1, No. 2, pp. 101–182.

Ronkainen, V., L. Koskinen, and R. Berglund (2007) Topical Modelling Issues in Solvency II. *Scandinavian Actuarial Journal*, Vol. 2007, No. 2, pp. 135–146.

Sharma, P. (2002) Prudential Supervision of Insurance Undertakings. Report of the Conference of the Insurance Supervisory Services Conference, London.

Taylor, G. (2000) *Loss Reserving: An Actuarial Perspective*. Kluwer, MA: Kluwer Academic.

Verrall, R.J. (1994) Statistical Methods for the Chain Ladder Technique. Vol. 2, No. 2, pp. 393–446.

Vicente, A.T. (2008) *Requisitos de Capital e Solvência II. Uma Aplicação ao Seguro Automóvel*, Master Thesis, ISEG, Technical University of Lisbon.

Weil, R. (1973) Macaulay's Duration: An Appreciation. *Journal of Business,* Vol. 46, No. 4, pp. 589–592.

PART THREE

Portfolio Management

CHAPTER 13

Quantile-Based Tail Risk Estimation for Equity Portfolios

John Cotter and Kevin Dowd

ABSTRACT

We present two quantile-based tail risk measures: value at risk and expected shortfall. We then use extreme value theory applied to portfolios of equity returns to estimate these risk measures at very high confidence levels. In particular, we fit the fat-tailed generalized Pareto distribution to extreme returns and compare the associated risk measures to those from the normal distribution that underpins much of portfolio theory.

INTRODUCTION

Portfolio performance (as we have seen all too clearly in recent times) is driven by extraordinary rather than ordinary events. Average daily returns tend to be near zero, but we know on any one day that extreme and large returns can occur. Take an investment for the year 2001 as an example: we know that the large negative returns of the market around September 11 dominated equity markets overall performance for this year. More recently, 2007 and 2008 have seen a number of institutions reporting so-called 25 sigma events—losses said to be equivalent to the market moving 25 standard deviations.[1] Investors in equity markets clearly need to protect themselves against these extreme events and their associated returns. As the recent losses indicate, this is no easy task, but a first attempt is to try and adequately model the tail risks associated with their investments. This chapter addresses this issue by estimating two quantile-based tail risk measures Value at risk (VaR) and expected shortfall (ES) for a selection of equity portfolios and very high—that is to say, extreme—confidence levels).

Our first quantile-based risk measure is VaR that represents the maximum loss for a given probability. Although it has many applications and is intuitively appealing (See Dowd, 2005, for a discussion), VaR has been criticized as a risk measure on the grounds that it does not satisfy the properties of coherence and, most particularly, because it is not subadditive (Artzner et al. 1999; Acerbi, 2005). The failure of VaR to be subadditive can lead to undesirable outcomes: the use of VaR takes no account of the magnitude of possible losses exceeding VaR and can therefore leave the investor heavily exposed to very high losses. Most important, however, is that using VaR can have strange diversification effects with related portfolio implications in that the sum of individual asset VaRs can be less than the portfolio VaR.

The second quantile-based risk measure we use is ES that estimates the average loss assuming the VaR quantile has been breached. This measure is subadditive and consequentially represents a coherent risk measure. The ES measure is closely related, but not identical to, the tail conditional expectation (TCE), which is the probability-weighted average of losses exceeding VaR.[2] Unlike the VaR, the ES is coherent (and hence subadditive as well) and so satisfies many of the properties we would desire a

---

[1] A widely publicized example was in August 2007, when the CFO of Goldman Sachs, David Viniars explained the very large losses on their flagship GEO hedge fund by saying that "We are seeing things that were 25-standard deviation moves, several days in a row" (reported in the Financial Times, August 13, 2007).

[2] For more on these risk measures and their distinguishing features, see Acerbi and Tasche (2001) or Acerbi (2005). We do not consider the TCE further in this chapter because it is equivalent to the ES, where the density function is continuous, and where it differs from the ES, it is not coherent.

priori from a "respectable" risk measure.[3] The ES is bigger than the VaR and, more importantly, takes account of the magnitude of losses exceeding the VaR. Both measures are applied to the tails of a probability distribution as in Figure 13.1, where VaR analyzes returns up to a predefined threshold, α, and ES is the average of the losses beyond the probability level, α.[4] (Note that Figure 13.1 illustrates a distribution of returns with high α threshold levels.)

Using these risk measures we use two approaches to model the tail behavior. First, we use extreme value theory (EVT) that statistically captures the tail of a distribution of returns. The literature is supportive of this approach as it adequately models the shape of financial returns and, in particular, the fat-tailed property associated with market outcomes spanning many different asset classes in both spot and derivative markets.[5]

F I G U R E   13.1

Lower and upper tail extreme returns for a distribution of returns

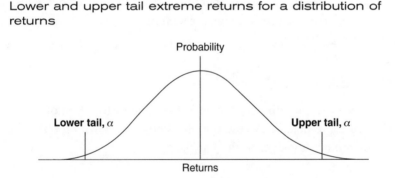

_____

[3] Loosely speaking, let X and Y represent any two portfolios' P/Ls over a given forecast horizon, and let $\rho(.)$ be a measure of risk. The risk measure $\rho(.)$ is subadditive if it satisfies $\rho(X + Y) \leq \rho(X) + \rho(Y)$. Subadditivity is the most important criterion we would expect a "respectable" risk measure to satisfy. It can be demonstrated that VaR is not subadditive unless we impose the empirically implausible requirement that returns are elliptically distributed. Given the importance of subadditivity, the VaR's nonsubadditivity makes it very difficult to regard the VaR as a respectable measure of risk.

[4] We use α interchangeably for our risk measures to represent either (high) quantiles or (low) probabilities throughout the text.

[5] The literature is extensive first giving support for fat-tailed asset returns for different assets and across markets, for example, currencies and equities, and second advocating the use of EVT in modeling this feature (Koedijk and Kool, 1994; Longin, 1996; Cotter, 2001; ibid., 2004; ibid., 2005; and Cotter and Dowd, 2006).

Second, we benchmark the EVT approach by providing risk measures underpinned by the commonly assumed Gaussian distribution. This distribution is prominent throughout finance and in particular in portfolio theory (for example, mean-variance analysis). Studies examining tail behavior [e.g., Danielsson and DeVries (1997)] have shown that the Gaussian distribution is thin-tailed relative to the empirical features of financial data, thereby leading to an underestimation of associated risk measures. The underestimation increases as you move further out the tail (Cotter, 2007).

The outline of the chapter is as follows. In the next section, we describe the risk measures that are estimated. This is followed by detailing the modeling procedure of EVT and the associated quantile-based risk measures. The fourth section of this chapter has a discussion of the data. We use a selection of equity portfolios from Asian markets. Next, our empirical findings detail the modeling of tail behavior using EVT on the equity data coupled with a presentation and discussion of our extreme quantile-based risk measures. Finally, a summary is given in the concluding section.

RISK MEASURES

Our risk measures are directly obtained from the distribution of extreme returns [for more details and their applications see Dowd (2005)]. For a given low probability level α, the VaR is

$$\text{Var}_\alpha = q_\alpha \tag{13.1}$$

where q_α is the relevant quantile of the probability distribution.

Our second risk measure, the ES, is the average of the losses beyond the low probability level, α. In the case of a continuous distribution, the ES is

$$ES_\alpha = \frac{1}{1-\alpha} \int_\alpha^1 q_p \, dp \tag{13.2}$$

Using the ES measure implies taking an average of quantiles beyond the threshold in which tail quantiles have an equal weight.

As both measures are tail dependent, we calculate them separately for upper and lower tail realizations representing long and short trading positions, respectively.

MODELING PROCEDURE

We discuss our use of EVT to model the tail returns and then show how EVT is used to estimate our risk measures. Many studies have examined the modeling of tail returns [see Mandelbrot (1963) for an early example]. Given the existence of fat-tails, the EVT approach is supported to model tail returns in an unconditional setting. Extreme value theory analyzes tail outcomes only and allows for three separate classifications of the tail distributions. We apply the peaks-over-threshold (POT) approach based on the generalized Pareto distribution (GPD) to describe tail behavior.[6] Begin by assuming that equity returns represent the realizations of a random variable X over a high threshold u. More particularly, if X has the distribution function $F(x)$, we are interested in the distribution function $F_u(x)$ of exceedances of X over a high threshold u:

$$F_u(x) = P\{X - u \leq x \mid X > u\} = \frac{F(x+u) - F(u)}{1 - F(u)} \qquad (13.3)$$

As u gets large, which happens as you move further and further out the tail, then the distribution of exceedances tends to a GPD:

$$G_{\xi,\beta}(x) = \begin{cases} 1 - (1 + \xi x / \beta)^{-1/\xi} & \\ 1 - \exp(-x / \beta) & \end{cases} \quad \text{if} \quad \begin{matrix} \xi \geq 0 \\ \xi < 0 \end{matrix} \qquad (13.4)$$

---

[6] Alternatively, extreme tail returns could be modeled parametrically by generalized extreme value (GEV) theory or using semiparametric methods and related estimators such as the Hill or Picklands estimators. Asymptotically the approaches are analogous. We prefer to use the parametric POT approach over semiparametric estimators; and we prefer the POT over the GEV approach because it (generally) uses one less parameter and because the GEV approach does not utilize all extreme returns if extremes occur in clusters. We present only salient features of the literature and for more comprehensive discussions refer the readers to Embrechts et al. (1997) or Beirlant et al. (2004).

where

$$(x) \in \begin{cases} (0, \infty) \\ [0, \beta / \xi] \end{cases} \text{ if } \begin{matrix} \xi \geq 0 \\ \xi < 0 \end{matrix}$$

and the shape ξ and scale $\beta > 0$ parameters are estimated conditional on threshold u (Balkema and de Haan, 1974; Embrechts et al., 1997, pp. 162–164).

Note that the shape parameter ξ sometimes appears in GPD discussions couched in terms of its inverse, a tail index parameter α given by $\alpha = 1/\xi$. One advantage of EVT is that we can distinguish between different types of tail behavior based on parameter values and in this sense the shape parameter is especially important. Thus, a negative ξ is associated with very thin-tailed distributions that are rarely of relevance to financial returns, and a zero ξ is associated with other thin tailed distributions such as the Gaussian or normal. However, the most relevant for our purposes are heavy-tailed distributions associated with $\xi > 0$. Market returns such as equity indexes are in fact heavy tailed [see Cotter, (2004)]. The tails of such distributions decay slowly and follow a "power law" function. Moreover, the number of finite moments is determined by the value of ξ: if $0.25 \leq \xi \leq 0.5$ (or, equivalently, $\alpha \geq 2$), we have infinite second and higher moments; if $\xi \leq 0.25$ (or $\alpha \geq 4$), we have infinite fourth and higher moments; and so forth. Thus, α indicates the number of finite moments. Evidence generally suggests that the second moment is probably finite, but the fourth moment is more problematic [see, e.g., Loretan and Phillips (1994)].

The GPD parameters can be estimated by maximum likelihood methods. The log-likelihood function of the GPD for $\xi \neq 0$ is

$$l(\xi, \beta) = -n(\ln(\beta) - (1 + 1 / \xi) \sum_{i=1}^{n} \ln(1 + \xi x_i / \beta) \tag{13.5}$$

where x_i satisfies the constraints specified for x. If $\xi = 0$, the log-likelihood function is

$$l(\beta) = -n(\ln(\beta) - \beta^{-1} \sum_{i=1}^{n} x_i \tag{13.6}$$

Maximum likelihood (ML) estimates are then found by maximizing the log-likelihood function using suitable (e.g., numerical optimization) methods.

Assuming that u is sufficiently high, the distribution function for exceedances is given by

$$F_u(x) = 1 - \frac{N_u}{n}\left(1 + \xi\frac{x-u}{\beta}\right)^{-\frac{1}{\xi}} \qquad (13.7)$$

where n is the sample size and N_u is the number of observations in excess of the threshold (Embrechts et al., 1997, p. 354).

In order to estimate the risk measures we rely on our tail return distribution of exceedances. Taking the αth quantile of this distribution—which is also the VaR at the (high) confidence level α—it is then obtained by inverting the distribution function and adjusting for the mean return u:

$$\text{VaR}_\alpha = u + \frac{\beta}{\xi}\left[\left(\frac{n}{N_u}p\right)^{-\xi} - 1\right] \qquad (13.8)$$

For its part, the ES is then given by

$$ES_\alpha = \frac{q_p}{1-\xi} + \frac{\beta - \xi u}{1-\xi} \qquad (13.9)$$

We now turn our attention to the application of this modeling approach and the associated risk measures. We begin by providing some preliminary details of the portfolios chosen for analysis.

DATA DESCRIPTION

Daily log returns of portfolios of equities using market indexes are analyzed from January 1985 through December 2000. The indexes chosen and their abbreviations are Nikkei 225 Stock Average (Nikkei), Hang Seng (Hang Seng), Singapore Straits Times (Singapore), Bangkok S.E.T. (Bangkok), Jakarta SE Composite (Jakarta), and Kuala Lumpur Composite

(Kuala Lumpur). The first three represent diversified portfolios from leading Asian markets, and the latter represent equities from markets most affected by the Asian crises of 1997–1998.

Time-series plots of the returns series are provided in Figure 13.2 displaying volatility clustering and the existence of large spikes (extreme returns). These extreme returns incorporate financial crises such as the October 1987 crash, the Asian crises in October 1997, and the increased (mostly downside) volatility in 2000. For the most part—the exception being the Jakarta index—the extreme negative returns tend to be larger than positive ones, which suggests that the lower tail risk measures may also be larger.

F I G U R E   13.2

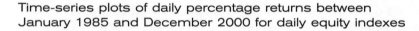

Time-series plots of daily percentage returns between January 1985 and December 2000 for daily equity indexes

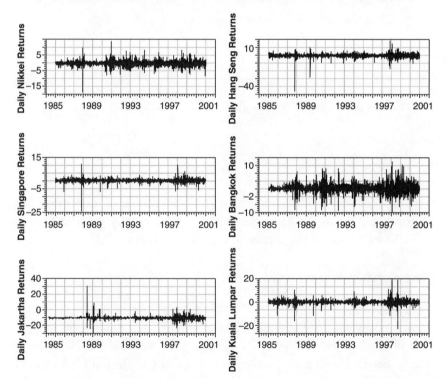

Further characteristics of the returns series are provided by the summary statistics in Table 13.1. The first moment values indicate that expected returns are positive but close to zero, and the second moment values suggest daily volatility in excess of 1 percent. The Nikkei exhibits the lowest levels of average unconditional risk, whereas both Jakarta and Kuala Lumpur have the highest standard deviations. Very long tails both for upside and downside distributions are evident for all series from MinDev (MaxDev) that counts the number of standard deviations minimum (maximum) observed returns are from the mean. These statistics indicate—again, with the Jakarta being the exception—that empirical returns have a longer negative tail than positive tail.[7] All series exhibit excess skewness and excess kurtosis, and the Jarque-Bera results indicate that they are clearly nonnormal. Given this finding of excess skewness, we will present separate tail quantile risk measures for long and short trading positions.

The Q–Q plots of the observed distributions against the normal distribution are presented in Figure 13.3, and these indicate the magnitude of

T A B L E   13.1

Summary statistics for daily equity indexes

Index	Mean	Standard Deviation	MinDev	MaxDev	Skew	Kurt	J-B
Nikkei	0.004	1.34	−12.04	9.28	−0.17	13.01	17453
Hang Seng	0.061	1.79	−22.71	9.61	−3.56	81.66	1084852
Singapore	0.027	1.45	−20.18	10.68	−2.11	57.05	510688
Bangkok	0.015	1.71	−5.87	6.62	0.12	8.95	6177
Jakartha	0.044	1.68	−13.45	23.99	3.97	110	2003473
Kuala Lumpur	0.019	1.71	−14.17	12.19	−0.26	34.6	173703

Notes: The mean and standard deviation are presented in percentages. The number of standard deviations the minimum return (MinDev) and the maximum return (MaxDev) are from the mean exhibit the length of the empirical distribution. The skewness (Skew) statistic and kurtosis (Kurt) for a normal distribution have values of 0 and 3, respectively. Normality is examined with the Jarque-Bera (J-B) test statistic, which has a critical value of 3.84. All skewness, kurtosis and normality coefficients are significant at well below the 5 percent level.

---

[7] The findings for the Indonesian market are affected by the deregulation that took place at the end of 1988 where a single day's return was in excess of +40 percent.

F I G U R E   13.3

The Q–Q plots of daily equity indexes returns: the quantiles
of the observed distribution against the normal distribution
(straight line) for the daily series

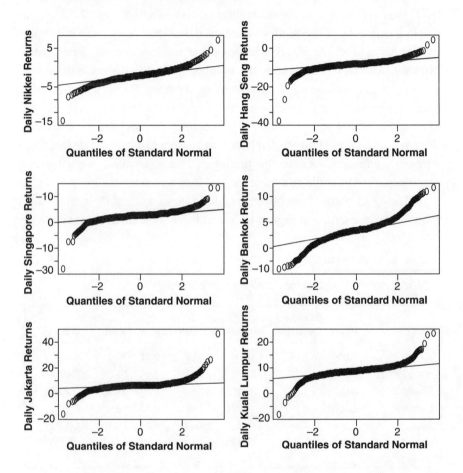

extreme values located at the tails of the distribution. The fact that the tail
regions of these plots have steeper slopes than the more central regions is
clear evidence that Gaussianity underestimates the weights of the respective empirical tails and would underestimate the likelihood of extreme
returns occurring.

EMPIRICAL FINDINGS

We then fitted the GPD to our equity portfolios and used these to generate the risk measures in which we are interested. The GPD parameters are given in Table 13.2 for both tails of the distribution. In order to obtain these, a key issue is to determine where the respective tails begin. We estimated the points where the tails begin using a simple method that identifies possible threshold values and then, after fitting the GPD, determines their relative goodness of fit. The threshold values are identified using the Q–Q plots, which provide natural threshold values at the points where the tails become steeper than the more central observations. After fitting the GPD, we produce tail plots that determine the goodness of fit of the GPD fits; an example of this is the Nikkei GPD fit given in Figure 13.4. This shows that a lower tail threshold of 1.5 and an upper tail threshold of 2.3 implying a good fit for the GPD, which is reflected in the fact that the tail

T A B L E   13.2

Generalized Pareto distribution parameter estimates for daily equity indexes

Index	Tail	Beta	Threshold	Exceedences	Tail	Beta	Threshold	Exceedences
	Lower Tail				Upper Tail			
Nikkei	0.06	0.96	1.50	399.00	0.14	0.85	2.30	375.00
	(0.04)	(0.06)			(0.06)	(0.07)		
Hang Seng	0.34	1.07	2.20	251.00	0.24	1.10	3.00	127.00
	(0.08)	(0.11)			(0.11)	(0.16)		
Singapore	0.48	0.93	2.50	115.00	0.31	1.03	3.00	77.00
	(0.13)	(0.14)			(0.14)	(0.19)		
Bangkok	0.11	1.15	1.30	625.00	0.16	1.17	1.60	470.00
	(0.05)	(0.07)			(0.06)	(0.09)		
Jakartha	0.27	1.22	2.00	192.00	0.17	0.91	2.20	176.00
	(0.09)	(0.14)			(0.09)	(0.10)		
Kuala Lumpur	0.29	1.15	2.00	255.00	0.40	1.01	2.40	187.00
	(0.07)	(0.11)			(0.10)	(0.12)		

Notes: Extreme value parameters, the tail index (tail) and scale (beta) are estimated via maximum likelihood methods with standard errors in parentheses. The number of exceedances and the associated threshold values are also given.

F I G U R E   13.4

Tail plot of Nikkei index returns. This plot shows the tail
realizations after fitting the GPD. The region where a straight
line is recorded implies a good fit for the GPD

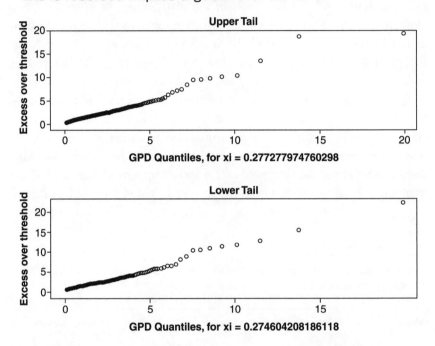

plot is linear around these thresholds.[8] Also, note that the threshold size
impacts the number of exceedences because higher thresholds are associated with smaller numbers of exceedances.

Turning to the GPD parameters, the findings are in line with previous studies on equity markets. The tail indexes are positive which is
indicative of fat tails, and the scale parameters are approximately one.
There are only two exceptions where the tail index is not significantly
positive, and this occurs for the lower tail of the Nikkei and the upper tail
of the Jakarta index. The fattest tail in density mass is recorded for the
Singapore index on a long position and the Kuala Lumpur index on a short
position. For most cases, the magnitude of the tail parameters supports the
existence of a second moment but not necessarily the fourth moment.

---

[8] Similar findings occur for the other markets.

Our two risk measures are given in Table 13.3 and these are predicated on very low confidence levels or probabilities. These probabilities have associated waiting periods of 100 days, 1,000 days, and 10,000 days,

T A B L E   13.3

Extreme quantile-based risk measures of daily equity indexes

Index		Q.99	Q.999	Q.9999	Q.99	Q.999	Q.9999
VaR		Lower Tail			Upper Tail		
Nikkei	Extreme value	3.81	6.50	9.56	3.70	6.90	11.36
		(0.10)	(0.31)	(0.70)	(0.11)	(0.46)	(1.28)
	Gaussian	3.11	4.14	4.98	3.12	4.14	4.99
		(0.05)	(0.08)	(0.10)	(0.05)	(0.08)	(0.10)
Hang Seng	Extreme value	4.84	11.75	26.94	4.40	8.81	16.44
		(0.19)	(1.14)	(4.61)	(0.13)	(0.68)	(2.48)
	Gaussian	4.10	5.47	6.59	4.22	5.59	6.71
		(0.06)	(0.09)	(0.11)	(0.06)	(0.09)	(0.11)
Singapore	Extreme value	3.72	10.10	29.38	3.70	7.91	16.56
		(0.13)	(1.14)	(6.67)	(0.08)	(0.67)	(2.88)
	Gaussian	3.34	4.45	5.36	3.39	4.50	5.41
		(0.05)	(0.08)	(0.10)	(0.05)	(0.08)	(0.10)
Bangkok	Extreme value	4.91	8.94	14.11	5.07	9.89	16.86
		(0.15)	(0.56)	(1.45)	(0.17)	(0.73)	(2.12)
	Gaussian	3.97	5.28	6.35	4.00	5.31	6.38
		(0.06)	(0.09)	(0.11)	(0.06)	(0.09)	(0.11)
Jakarta	Extreme value	4.31	10.20	21.14	3.68	6.94	11.72
		(0.18)	(0.93)	(3.46)	(0.11)	(0.47)	(1.48)
	Gaussian	3.86	5.14	6.29	3.95	5.23	6.29
		(0.06	(0.08	(0.11	(0.06)	(0.09)	(0.11)
Kuala Lumpur	Extreme value	4.75	11.14	23.64	4.46	11.33	28.46
		(0.19)	(1.00)	(3.72)	(0.17)	(1.18)	(5.68)
	Gaussian	3.95	5.25	6.33	3.99	5.29	6.37
		(0.06)	(0.09)	(0.11)	(0.06)	(0.09)	(0.11)
Nikkei	Extreme value	4.97	7.82	11.06	5.07	8.81	14.01
		(0.19)	(0.47)	(0.95)	(0.24)	(0.79)	(1.93)
	Gaussian	3.57	4.51	5.30	3.57	4.51	5.31
		(0.06)	(0.08)	(0.10)	(0.06)	(0.08)	(0.10)
Hang Seng	Extreme value	7.84	18.34	41.43	6.29	12.07	22.10
		(0.57)	(2.62)	(9.05)	(0.33)	(1.43)	(4.33)

T A B L E   **13.3** (Continued)

Index		Q.99	Q.999	Q.9999	Q.99	Q.999	Q.9999
VaR		Lower Tail			Upper Tail		
	Gaussian	4.72	5.97	7.02	4.83	6.08	7.14
		(0.06)	(0.09)	(0.12)	(0.07)	(0.09)	(0.12)
Singapore	Extreme value	6.63	18.91	56.02	5.52	11.65	24.21
		(0.48)	(3.74)	(16.86)	(0.33)	(1.60)	(5.58)
	Gaussian	3.84	4.85	5.71	3.88	4.90	5.76
		(0.06)	(0.08)	(0.10)	(0.06)	(0.08)	(0.10)
Bangkok	Extreme value	6.64	11.16	16.96	7.13	12.87	21.18
		(0.31)	(0.93)	(2.10)	(0.38)	(1.32)	(3.26)
	Gaussian	4.55	5.75	6.76	4.58	5.78	6.79
		(0.06)	(0.09)	(0.11)	(0.06)	(0.09)	(0.11)
Jakarta	Extreme value	6.84	14.89	29.85	5.08	8.98	14.72
		(0.48)	(1.99)	(6.17)	(0.25)	(0.89)	(2.35)
	Gaussian	4.44	5.61	0.04	4.52	5.69	6.69
		(0.06)	(0.09)	(0.01)	(0.06)	(0.09)	(0.11)
Kuala Lumpur	Extreme value	7.50	16.52	34.14	7.49	18.88	47.26
		(0.52)	(2.15)	(6.79)	(0.62)	(3.19)	(12.16)
	Gaussian	4.53	5.73	6.74	4.57	5.77	6.77
		(0.06)	(0.09)	(0.11)	(0.06)	(0.09)	(0.11)

Notes: Standard errors are in parentheses. The statistical approaches of EVT and the Gaussian distribution and related risk measures of VaR and ES are described in the text.

representing intervals of approximately half a year, 4 years, and 40 years, respectively. For example, the loss of 9.56 percent is recorded for the 99.99 percent probability level for the Nikkei index, and we would (if the model is 'correct' and correctly calibrated) expect that this would be exceeded on a single day's return once every 40 years. For comparison, Table 13.3 also includes Gaussian estimates. The EV estimates take account of the most important feature of equity returns, namely, the fact that they are fat-tailed property, whereas the Gaussian estimates ignore this. We see that the extreme value estimates dwarf Gaussian measures, and this is especially so at very low probability levels that correspond to longer waiting intervals.

We see that the VaR and ES estimates give broadly similar pictures. First looking at the VaRs, the findings indicate that Nikkei is the safest market and that Kuala Lumpur exhibits the most extreme returns. For example, the extreme risk of the Kuala Lumpur index is more than twice that of the Nikkei. The EVT estimates are reasonably similar across trading position. The table reports the largest quantile occurring for lower tails realizations on the Singapore index and for upper tail returns on the Kuala Lumpur index. For the EVT estimates there is substantial but not consistent deviations in the risk measures for long and short trading positions. For example, at the 99 percent level the lower tail measures tend to be larger than upper tail values, but this trend reverses when we focus on the lower probability levels. Moreover, the deviations from long to short positions tend to widen for lower probability levels. In contrast, the Gaussian estimates remain near symmetrical (only deviating due to the relatively small daily average returns).

Note also that our confidence in the findings vary considerably for the extreme value findings but less so for the Gaussian ones. While all standard errors tend to increase for larger risk measures, this is particularly so for the extreme value estimates. The lowest level of precision is recorded for the ES on the Kuala Lumpur index at the 99.99 percent level and on a short trading position. Precision levels in the Gaussian estimates are much narrower. This finding for extreme value estimates is to be expected given the relatively small sample size analyzed for the tail values, and this reduces further as you move out the tail.

CONCLUSION

This chapter examines extreme risk in equity portfolios. Overall portfolio performance is driven by a few exceptional trading days that dwarf the outcomes from much of the remaining trading period. These exceptional trading days give rise to large and extreme returns, and these are of interest in this chapter. Two statistical approaches are applied: EVT that models tail returns only and the Gaussian distribution that underpins much of portfolio theory and related modeling. Two separate quantile-based risk measures—VaR and ES—are developed using the two modeling approaches.

We first identify the fat-tailed property of the equity portfolios. Using a POT extreme value approach, we find that the portfolio tail returns are adequately modeled with the fat-tailed GPD. We identify the portfolio of equities from Kuala Lumpur as being prone to the most extreme returns, giving the largest risk measures, in contrast to the relative safe Japanese market. There is no consistency as to whether lower tail risk measures are systematically greater than upper tail ones. Our risk measures are much smaller if we apply the relatively thin tailed Gaussian distribution compared to the GPD estimates. However, the precision of our estimates indicates a greater level of variability for the GPD estimates.

The findings have implications for portfolio management and the use of risk management techniques that manage the exposure resulting from extreme risk. For instance, any hedging strategy seeking to protect against extreme movements in the underlying markets should incorporate methodologies that assume that returns do not belong to a Gaussian distribution. Here a nonlinear approach to derive the hedging strategy incorporating fat-tails is needed.

ACKNOWLEDGMENTS

Cotter's contribution to the study has been supported by a University College Dublin School of Business research grant.

REFERENCES

Acerbi, C. (2005) Coherent Representations of Subjective Risk-Aversion. In G. Szego (ed.), *Risk Measures for the 21st Century*, New York: Wiley, pp. 147–207.

Acerbi, C., and D. Tasche (2001) Expected Shortfall: A Natural Alternative to Value at Risk. *Economic Notes*, Vol. 31, No. 2, pp. 379–388.

Artzner, P., F. Delbaen, J. M. Eber, and D. Heath (1999) Coherent Measures of Risk. *Mathematical Finance,* Vol. 9, No. 3, pp. 203–228.

Balkema, A.A. and L. de Haan (1974) Residual Lifetime at Great Age. *Annals of Probability,* Vol. 2, No. 2, pp. 792–804.

Beirlant, J., Y. Goegebeur, J. Segers, and J. Teugels (2004) *Statistics of Extremes: Theory and Applications*. Hoboken, NJ: John Wiley & Sons.

Cotter, J. (2001) Margin Exceedences for European Stock Index Futures Using Extreme Value Theory. *Journal of Banking and Finance*, Vol. 25, No. 8, pp. 1475–1502.

Cotter, J. (2004) Downside Risk for European Equity Markets. *Applied Financial Economics*, Vol. 14, No. 10, pp. 707–716.

Cotter, J. (2005) Tail Behaviour of the Euro. *Applied Economics*, Vol. 37, No. 2005, pp. 1–14.

Cotter, J. (2007) Varying the VaR for Unconditional and Conditional Environments, *Journal of International Money and Finance*, Vol. 26, No. 4, pp. 1338–1354.

Cotter, J. and K. Dowd (2006) Extreme Spectral Risk Measures: An Application to Futures Clearinghouse Margin Requirements. *Journal of Banking and Finance*, Vol. 30, No. 12, pp. 3469–3485.

Danielsson, J. and C.G. DeVries (1997) Tail Index and Quantile Estimation with Very High Frequency Data. *Journal of Empirical Finance*, Vol. 4, No. 2, pp. 241–257.

Dowd, K. (2005) *Measuring Market Risk*, 2nd edition. Chichester, UK: John Wiley & Sons.

Embrechts, P., C. Kluppelberg, and T. Mikosch. (1997). *Modelling Extremal Events*, Berlin, Germany: Springer.

Koedijk, K.G. and C.J.M. Kool (1994) Tail Estimates and the EMS Target Zone. *Review of International Economics*, Vol. 2, No. 2, pp. 153–165.

Longin, F.M. (1996) The Asymptotic Distribution of Extreme Stock Market Returns. *Journal of Business*, Vol. 63, No.3, pp. 383–408.

Loretan, M. and P.C.B. Phillips. (1994) Testing the Covariance Stationarity of Heavy-Tailed Time Series. *Journal of Empirical Finance*, Vol. 1, No. 2, pp. 211–248.

Mandelbrot, B. (1963) The Variation of Certain Speculative Prices. *The Journal of Business*, Vol. 36, No. 4, pp. 394–419.

CHAPTER 14

Optimal Mixed-Asset Portfolios

Juliane Proelss and Denis Schweizer

ABSTRACT

In general, monthly return distributions of alternative assets are not normally distributed. This means that every portfolio optimization in the mean-variance framework that includes alternative assets is likely to be suboptimal, because those investments have return distributions for which variance does not capture all risks adequately. As a result, higher moments must be taken into account. In this chapter, we estimate the efficient frontier for portfolios consisting of numerous alternative assets as well as traditional asset classes like equities and bonds, where the risk measure of choice is conditional value at risk (CVaR). This enables us to incorporate the characteristics, especially downside risk, of the higher moments in the optimization procedure. It is now possible for mixed-asset portfolios containing the majority of alternative investments to illustrate the previously unknown effects of skewness and excess kurtosis on the efficient frontier.

INTRODUCTION

Alternative investments have gained a great deal of public attention recently with announcements such as "commodities boom,"[1] "publicly-listed REITs around the world reached US$764 billion, up 25 percent from the previous year,"[2] "private equity firepower hits $2 trillion,"[3] and "hedge funds spot 'unbelievable' chance."[4] This has been especially true in light of the beginning of the subprime crisis, which turned into a liquidity crisis. The also affected alternative investments.

While we observe a trend toward alternative investments, these are not new inventions. The first hedge fund was issued in 1949, the first (modern) trade of standardized commodity futures contracts occurred with the formation of the Chicago Board of Trade (CBOT) in 1948, and the first venture capital firm was formed in 1946. The question is why alternatives are attracting such attention now, considering there have been many failures and crises [e.g., the collapse of long-term capital management (LTCM) in 1998] also.

We identify two major, interconnected reasons for the increased attention to alternative investments. First, we observe that expanding globalization causes greater correlation among international financial markets. It thus becomes more difficult to structure a well-diversified portfolio with international stocks and bonds as the sole diversifier of domestic financial assets. Second, worldwide changes in regulation and accounting standards encourage diversification as a means to improve the portfolio risk–return profile. Consequently, investors are searching for return drivers with a low or even negative correlation with traditional assets, such as alternative investments, to enhance their risk-adjusted portfolio performance.

Alternative investments offer investors exposure to risk–return profiles that are often not replicable by traditional assets for regulatory reasons. Mutual funds and traditional investors face prohibitions or limitations on their use of strategies such as leverage, investments in risky assets like derivatives, and short selling. Furthermore, most alternative

---

[1] FT.com, In Depth, March 27, 2008.
[2] Ernst & Young, Global REIT Report: REIT Market Review 2007.
[3] Financial News Online, March 3, 2008.
[4] Deborah Brewster, FT.com, March 27, 2008.

investments involve a level of complexity that requires special skills and long-term experience. Regulatory authorities have acknowledged the advantages of further diversification with laws such as Basel II, which encourages diversification, and the ERISA Act, which opens up the possibility of using certain alternative investments.

Surprisingly, while alternatives are becoming a substantial part of a mixed institutional portfolio, there is very little literature available about how to incorporate such investments. Investors need answers to questions like

1. To what extent should institutional investors move into alternative asset classes to achieve the goal of enhanced risk-adjusted performance?

2. What does an optimal allocation involving alternative investments look like?

These questions are not easily answered. We may conclude that the observed asset allocation is no longer optimal under the current market and regulatory environment as we identify portfolio allocation changes such as the trend toward alternative investments[5] or out of domestic stocks and fixed income [Greenwich Associates (2007)]. However, it is important to determine what an optimal portfolio allocation that accounts for recent diversification changes looks like.

We first consider two major points: (1) Which alternative asset classes should be included in a mixed-asset portfolio and (2) in what proportion? Both questions are essential, because the assets included in a strategic asset allocation determine the diversification potential and, consequently, the portfolio return variability, which is the major determinant of portfolio performance [Hoernemann et al. (2005)].

To assess which alternative investments are the most efficient portfolio diversifiers, we must consider the risk–return characteristics as well as the other factors unique to commodities, hedge funds, private equity, and real estate investment trusts (REITs). Using those characteristics, we aim to identify an adequate asset allocation model that is flexible enough

---

[5] In this chapter, we consider commodities, hedge funds, private equity (venture capital and buyouts), and REITs as alternative investments.

to incorporate return characteristics of alternative investments. In this way we can determine how much to allocate to alternative investments. Note that if the chosen model does not sufficiently capture the risk–return characteristics, the suggested mixed-asset optimal portfolio may include only alternative assets (Terhaar et al., 2003).

To the best of our knowledge, the literature up to now has focused on (1) the effects of including only one alternative investment class in a traditional mixed-asset portfolio or (2) in case of including more than one alternative investment, the tendency to make the model too inflexible or it does not capture the risk–return profiles adequately [e.g., Schneeweis et al. (2002), Conner (2003), Huang and Zhong (2006), Hoecht et al. (2006), and Winkelmann (2004)]. Consequently, we have not found a satisfactory answer to the allocation question in the literature.

In this chapter, we first review the risk–return characteristics of alternative investments to determine which should be considered in a mixed-asset portfolio allocation. We also adjust the risk–return profiles of the chosen alternative investments for selected biases. Based on those return characteristics, we suggest a model that is flexible enough to incorporate a variety of alternative investments as well as traditional investments (stocks and government bonds). We then compute an optimal strategic mixed-asset allocation using conditional value at risk (CVaR) as a risk measure to account for the special characteristics of alternative investments. We compare our results with a traditional mean-variance optimal allocation to identify potential misallocations.

RISK–RETURN PROFILES OF ALTERNATIVE INVESTMENTS

We have known since Markowitz's (1952) seminal paper on portfolio theory that diversification can increase portfolio expected returns while reducing volatility. However, investors should not blindly add another asset class to their portfolios without carefully considering its properties in the context of the portfolio. An added asset class may not improve the risk–return profile, and may even worsen it. Therefore, our first step is to assess which alternative asset classes (commodities, hedge funds, private equity–venture capital, and real estate) can be effective portfolio diversifiers.

Following Kat (2007), we examine (1) the expected return of the asset class, (2) the variation of the returns around its mean, as well as the higher moments of the return distribution, (3) the correlation with traditional assets in the existing portfolio, and (4) the liquidity of the asset class, as well as any fees. We also identify a benchmark to serve as a representative approximation for the asset classes. Note that before we determine whether to include any given asset class, we identify potential biases in the return time series that may affect the risk–return profile, and we make any necessary adjustments.

Commodities

Compared to other asset classes, the existence of a commodity risk premium remains an ongoing question. The literature provides mixed evidence. For example, Bodie and Rosansky (1980) and Gorton and Rouwenhorst (2005) find stocklike historical returns for unleveraged commodity futures indexes. On the other hand, Erb and Harvey (2006), Kat (2007), and Kat and Oomen (2007) find no evidence of time-persistent risk premiums for single commodities (except for energy commodities).[6] These results may be explained by the fact that a well-diversified portfolio of commodities offers a reliable source of returns, which Erb and Harvey (2006) refer to as the *diversification return*.

Unlike the risk premium discussion, the literature is consistent about the second through fourth moments of the return distribution of commodities (namely, variance, skewness, and kurtosis). Researchers such as Erb and Harvey (2006), Gorton and Rouwenhorst (2005), and others show that most single commodity return distributions are positively skewed and have a kurtosis greater than 3, which is also referred to as *positive excess kurtosis* or *leptokurtosis*. This means there is a higher probability of high positive returns compared to a normal distribution. At the same time, the excess kurtosis implies the existence of high extreme risks. The reasoning is that commodity market shocks are generally associated with price spikes. However, that is not the case for well-diversified commodity portfolios, whose return distributions often follow a normal distribution.

---

[6] Energy is considered a subgroup of commodities, which normally include only natural gas, crude oils, unleaded gasoline, and heating oil.

Single commodity returns have a low or negative correlation with nonrelated commodities. This favorable characteristic makes it possible to structure a well-diversified commodity portfolio. Additionally, the generally positive correlation of most single commodities with inflation makes them a good investment during periods of high inflation. Finally, and most importantly for the diversification of a traditional portfolio, commodities often exhibit a correlation of close to zero with bonds and equity [see, for example, Bodie and Rosansky (1980), Gorton and Rouwenhorst (2005), Georgiev (2006), and Idzorek (2006), among others].

Thus far, *diversified* commodity portfolios meet all the criteria necessary to be considered effective portfolio diversifiers. However, the question remains of how best to gain exposure to commodities. The liquidity and any possible fees must be considered.

We believe that the commodity futures index with the largest invested capital is a suitable proxy for a diversified commodity portfolio.[7] Therefore, we include the S&P Goldman Sachs Commodity Index (GSCI) Commodity Total Return Index[8] in the mixed-asset portfolio optimization [Doyle et al. (2007)]. The liquidity of this investable index is generally high. Furthermore, the fees for passive products on the index are low. However, the investor bears the default risk of the issuer, because investable indexes are usually structured as bearer bonds.

Hedge Funds

Like most alternative investments, hedge funds are a very heterogeneous asset class. This results from the high variability of instruments like derivatives, short selling, using leverage, as well as a host of even more complex investment strategies that hedge funds can take advantage of. Depending on the single hedge fund's strategy, these possibilities can be used to a greater or lesser extent and are the reason why hedge funds have special risk–return characteristics. For more details on the different strategies and how they influence a hedge fund strategy's return distribution, see, e.g., Brooks and Kat (2002).

---

[7] See Fabozzi et al. (2007) for a detailed discussion of different ways to gain exposure to commodities and the corresponding benchmarks.

[8] In line with the literature, we find that total return indexes best replicate an investment in a diversified commodity portfolio, as investors must generally collateralize the investment.

Many empirical investigations find statistically and economically significant persistence in the performance of hedge funds relative to their benchmarks [see Jagannathan et al. (2006), Le Sourd (2007) and others]. However, those figures are often subject to biases, so the risk premium may be lower and the variance underestimated. Brown et al. (1999), for example, find no evidence of a consistent risk premium for unbiased hedge fund time series. The differences in the risk premium estimates can often be explained by differing research periods and the use of different databases [for a detailed discussion and survey, see Eling (2007)].

Hedge fund substrategy return distributions also tend to exhibit significant negative skewness and leptokurtosis. This is because many substrategies are based on nonlinear investments like derivatives and nontraditional asset classes like credit derivatives. They may also follow investment strategies with high event risk or invest in illiquid assets like distressed securities [see, for example, Ackermann et al. (1999), Alexiev (2005), Amin and Kat (2003), Anson et al. (2007), and others].

Although there are additional risks associated with the higher moments, there are also compensations. For example, the low or negative correlation among several substrategies makes it possible to structure a well-diversified hedge fund portfolio with more favorable moment characteristics. Hedge fund managers are not subject to the same level of restrictions as mutual fund managers [see Kahan and Rock (2007)]. Therefore, their strategies may also exhibit low correlation with bonds and equity and offer institutional investors the opportunity to gain exposure to the risk–return profiles of nontraditional investment instruments or strategies.

Nevertheless, the cost of gaining exposure to hedge funds should not be underestimated. The management fee is usually about 2 percent p.a., and the incentive fee can be as much as 20 percent or even higher [see Cottier (2000), Ang et al. (2005)]. Because of their sophisticated investment approaches, hedge funds often have long lock-up periods as well, which can range from an average of one year to as long as five years [see, for instance, Dyment and Heavey (2003)]. Note also that there are, in general, minimum investment requirements in the range of US$100,000 to 500,000.[9]

---

[9] Alternatives to single hedge fund investments are investable index products and diversified funds of hedge funds. While the minimum investment for funds of hedge funds is usually much lower than for single hedge funds, there are additional management fees (about 1.5 percent p.a.) and incentive fees (about 10 percent).

In summary, the discussion of consistent performance persistence remains ongoing, and some hedge fund substrategies exhibit unfavorable statistical return distribution characteristics (negative skewness combined with positive excess kurtosis). However, they still offer institutional investors access to new return drivers that may have low correlations with those in their existing portfolios. This makes them a promising asset class for mixed-asset portfolios.

We identify the Credit Suisse/Tremont Hedge Fund Index (CS/T) as a good proxy for the hedge fund asset class. The index is representative of the market, ensures minimum reporting, disclosure, and transparency requirements for included funds, and, most importantly, is the only capitalization-weighted index [see Amenc et al. (2005) and Eling (2006)]. However, before we can add the CS/T to our optimization, we must address several potential data biases.

Some hedge fund strategies exhibit autocorrelation in their returns, due primarily to illiquidity and smoothed returns [see, e.g., Getmansky et al. (2004) and Avramov et al. (2007)]. Positive autocorrelation causes the standard deviation of hedge fund return distributions to be underestimated, which can cause an overallocation of hedge funds [Kat (2003)]. We control for this potential bias in our investigation.

Furthermore, hedge fund indexes are often subject to other biases, such as backfilling or survivorship. The CS/T has no backfilling bias, so we focus on controlling for survivorship. Depending on the investigation period, calculation method, and database used, survivorship bias estimates range from 0.12 percent [Ackermannet al. (1999)] to 6.22 percent [Liang (2002)]. The average for the CS/T database is about 2.5 percent p.a., or 0.21 percent per month [Eling (2006)], so we reduce the CS/T hedge fund index returns by this amount.

Private Equity

Private equity as an asset class exhibits very low transparency. Each private equity fund has some unique characteristics, and the target companies of the private equity funds are generally not publicly traded. Consequently, the lack of available data hinders a comparison with other asset classes on an aggregate level [Schmidt (2004)]. Empirical research in private equity usually calculates returns by using reported cash flows and the appraised values of unrealized investments.

Several researchers have attempted to quantify the risk–return characteristics of private equity on a fund level or on an individual portfolio company level [see Gompers and Lerner (1997), Moskowitz and Vissing-Jørgensen (2002), Cochrane (2005), and Kaplan and Schoar (2005) among others]. However, these studies have some drawbacks. Most analysis is conducted with data from data vendors, which rely on self-reporting. These studies also do not provide a consensus of the reported returns, so annual returns range from −1.5 to 17.0 percent p.a. Additionally, the reported returns are subject to biases induced by the inclusion of unrealized and realized investments, and, e.g., different accounting treatment.

In their latest study, Phalippou and Gottschalg (2007) conclude that the dramatic growth in private equity cannot be attributed to genuinely high past net performance. They find an average underperformance of 3 percent p.a. for private equity funds with respect to the S&P 500. While there is disagreement about the existence of a risk premium for private equity, the literature has found consistent evidence of positive skewness and positive excess kurtosis in the return data.

So although the literature offers no ultimate conclusion on private equity returns, the correlation is an important property that should be considered. Private equity returns exhibit a low to negative correlation with bonds and a low correlation with equity [see Chen et al. (2002)]. Thus, we can infer that private equity should be included in a portfolio to enhance the risk–return profile if investors are willing to assume some risk [see, for instance, Lamm and Ghaleb-Harter (2001), Schmidt (2004), and Ennis and Sebastian (2005)]. The costs of a private equity investment, however, should not be underestimated. The annual management fees usually range between 1.5 and 2.5 percent p.a. with an additional incentive fee (carry) of usually about 20 percent [see, e.g., Metrick and Yasuda (2007)].[10]

---

[10] An alternative to single private equity funds are funds of funds, which charge an additional 1 percent management fee and a 10 percent incentive fee, like their counterparts in the hedge fund industry.

In summary, even without high past returns, the return drivers for private equity differ from those of traditional asset classes, and they have positive correlation benefits. Therefore, we consider venture capital and buyouts as the two major private equity strategies in the mixed-asset portfolio optimization.

Note that the heterogeneity and lack of data for private equity make it hard to identify a suitable benchmark. We use the return time series CepreX U.S. Venture Capital and CepreX U.S. Buyout from CEPRES[11] for the following reasons: (1) The database is based on (partially) audited reports and precise cash flow information of the private equity investment funds. Thus, accurate financial calculations are possible, and no bias or noises are induced due to subjective accounting treatment of unrealized or realized investments, and (2) the indexes are transaction-based and are available on a monthly frequency. These advantages prevail despite the fact that the return time series cannot be reported contemporaneously because of insufficient monthly transactions.

Real Estate

Before analyzing the diversification properties of REITs, we briefly examine whether REITs are 1) representative of the real estate market, 2) more suitable as a substitute for stocks, or 3) an asset class of their own. There is evidence that common factors affect both return series of REITs and direct real estate, as well as REITs and stock market time series [see, e.g., Myer and Webb (1993), Barkham and Geltner (1995), Li and Wang (1995), and Ling and Naranjo (1999)].

However, the literature has found that the sensitivity of REIT returns to the stock market declined significantly in the 1990s, which Clayton and MacKinnon (2000) attribute to the growth and maturity of the REIT market. They show further that the relationship between REITs and direct real estate strengthened in the 1990s. This is a valuable insight for us, because our sample time period begins in the 1990s.

Clayton and MacKinnon (2000) conclude that, in the short term, both REITs and direct real estate have a place in optimal portfolios.

---

[11] For more information, see http://www.centerofprivateequityresearch.com/.

Nevertheless, in the long term, only one should be included, because one is a substitute for the other. There is also evidence that REITs are a "unique" asset class with price behaviour unequal to stocks, fixed-income securities, direct real estate, or combinations thereof [see, e.g., Liang and McIntosh (1998) and Stevenson (2001)]. Based on these results, we conclude that REITs are a reasonable, but incomplete, proxy for the real estate market.

However, although we may conclude that stocks are unequal to REITs and therefore REITs are no substitute for stocks, this does not imply they are a good portfolio diversifier. We will need to assess the return and risk characteristics of this asset class.

The literature reports annualized mean returns for REITs of between 11.6 and 17.9 percent, and standard deviations ranging from about 13.3 to 14.1 percent [Myer and Webb (1993); Jinliang et al. (2005); Cotter and Stevenson (2007)]. Regarding the higher moments, we find mixed results. Myer and Webb (1993) found no significant skewness or kurtosis using an equally weighted equity REIT index; Cotter and Stevenson (2007), however, do report significant negative skewness and excess kurtosis for different research periods.

To summarize, we find that REITs offer a significant risk premium, which makes them an interesting asset class. However, the higher moments of the REIT return distribution must be considered, as they can pose an additional source of risk.

An adequate risk premium is one side of the coin, but diversification potential is the other. The literature provides evidence that the correlation among REITs with bonds is low or even negative. However, the correlation with U.S. equity is not. As a result, the evidence about the diversification advantages of REITs in mixed-asset portfolios is inconclusive, and often depends on the research period.

For example, Kuhle (1987) finds no significant benefits from including REITs in a stock portfolio. Other researchers have found that REITs can be beneficial in mixed-asset portfolios, and can improve the risk-adjusted performance [see, e.g., Mueller et al. (1994), Mull and Soenen (1997), Hudson-Wilson et al. (2004), and Lee and Stevenson (2005)]. They may also enhance the efficient frontier [see Chen et al. (2005) and Chiang and Ming-Long (2007)]. Thus, most evidence suggests that REITs are a good diversifier in a mixed-asset portfolio.

We also find that REITs are a unique asset class, and differ significantly from stocks. Because they are publicly traded, gaining exposure is fairly easy, fees tend to be low, and liquidity tends to be high. Therefore, we include REITs in our mixed-asset portfolio optimization.

As a proxy for REITs, we use the FTSE/NAREIT Equity REITS—Total Return Index, because it provides REIT returns using transaction data, which are therefore representative of market value. The index includes leverage of about 50 percent, which we find beneficial since real estate investments are often leveraged. Therefore, NAREIT volatility reflects higher and more realistic return volatility.

DATA SET DESCRIPTION

We have discussed the risk–return profiles and the potential advantages of including several alternative investments in a mixed-asset portfolio. We also highlighted data biases in the hedge fund return distributions that might affect a portfolio optimization if not properly accounted for. We now turn to our empirical investigation of alternative investments in a mixed-asset portfolio. We use two major traditional asset classes and four alternative asset classes.

We include U.S. equity, as represented by the S&P 500 Composite–Total Return Index (U.S. Equity), and U.S. government bonds, represented by the JPM United States Govt. Bond–Total Return Index (U.S. bonds). As a proxy for the alternative investments, we include the S&P GSCI Commodity Total Return Index (Commodities) for a diversified exposure to commodities, the Credit Suisse/Tremont Hedge Fund Index (hedge funds) for a multi-strategy hedge fund exposure, the FTSE/NAREIT Equity REITS–Total Return Index (REITs) for a diversified exposure to U.S. REITs, and the CepreX U.S. Venture Capital (USVC) and the CepreX U.S. Buyout (USBO) to proxy for an exposure to venture capital and buyout funds.

Our sample consists of 151 monthly index returns from December 1993 through June 2006, with a January 1998 inception date. Because the USVC and the USBO indexes are transaction-based, the observation period will end in June 2006. The sample includes several international market crises, such as the 1994 bond market crash, the 1997 Asian crisis, the 1998 Russian and LTCM crisis, the 2000/2001 Nasdaq crash, and the September 11 terrorist attacks. Our data set includes both up and down markets, and therefore satisfies the recommendations for robustness of Capocci and Hubner (2004) and for reliability of Fung and Hsieh (2000).

As mentioned in the previous subsection, raw data from data vendors can suffer from several biases. In order to obtain an unbiased data set, we correct the raw time series accordingly. This is important because the data feeds the models, and if the input data is biased, the implications will be as well.

First, as noted previously, hedge fund returns are subject to survivorship bias, so we reduce the hedge fund returns by 2.5 percent per annum, or 0.21 percent per month. Second, return series of some hedge fund strategies and private equity often display autocorrelation.

To test for first-order autocorrelation, we apply the portmanteau test of Ljung and Box (1978). Interestingly, we do not find significant first-order autocorrelation for hedge funds, which is not unusual for a diversified hedge fund portfolio [see, e.g., Eling (2006)]. However, we do find significant negative first-order correlation for the USBO and USVC return time series. This is probably a result of the index construction, because these transaction-based indexes do not rely on appraised or managed unrealized interim values. We use the method of Geltner (1991) to adjust for this autocorrelation because it distorts the standard deviation.

Table 14.1 reports the descriptive statistics of the bias-adjusted time series. During our sample period, USBO and USVC had the highest average monthly returns, at 3.80 and 3.12 percent, respectively. USBO and USVC also had the highest observed maximum returns, 62.52 and 67.46 percent, respectively, and the lowest minimum monthly returns, −27.94 and −21.02 percent, respectively. As a result, we find that USBO and USVC exhibit the highest observed standard deviations, 0.1033 and 0.0976, respectively.

Skewness and kurtosis are additional potential sources of risk and return. While USVC and USBO show the highest observed skewness (generally a favorable return distribution characteristic), both also exhibit the highest kurtosis, which is not desirable because it indicates a high probability of extreme risks. Thus, both exhibit the highest returns and the highest observed risk.

T A B L E   14.1

Descriptive statistics of the biased adjusted monthly
return distributions

	S&P 500	JPM Government Bonds	NAREIT	S&P GSCI	CepreX U.S. Buyout	CepreX U.S. Venture Capital	CS/T Hedge Fund Index
Mean	0.0091	0.0048	0.0119	0.0095	0.0380	0.0312	0.0067
Median	0.0128	0.0060	0.0147	0.0093	0.0204	0.0182	0.0062
Maximum	0.0978	0.0427	0.1039	0.1579	0.6252	0.6746	0.0832
Minimum	−0.1446	−0.0449	−0.1458	−0.1392	−0.2794	−0.2102	−0.0776
Standard deviation	0.0418	0.0135	0.0378	0.0573	0.1033	0.0976	0.0224
Skewness	−0.5821	−0.4009	−0.4885	0.0634	1.7332	2.4969	0.1143
Kurtosis	3.6602	3.7949	4.3940	2.9173	10.8262	17.0303	5.2286
Jarque-Bera	11.27*	8.02†	18.23*	0.14	460.96*	1395.41*	31.58*

* and † indicate statistical significance at the 1 and 5 percent levels, respectively, based on monthly returns.

Table 14.1 reports the arithmetic mean, median, maximum, minimum, standard deviation, skewness, and kurtosis of the monthly return
distributions from January 1993 through July 2006. The return time series
is from the CS/T Hedge Fund Index, and has been corrected for the survivorship bias. Therefore, the annual return has been reduced by 2.5 percent. The return time series of the U.S. BO and U.S. VC have been
adjusted for first-order autocorrelation using Geltner (1991). The AR(1)
coefficients for USVC and USBO are –0.434 and –0.409. Both are significant at the 1 percent confidence level. We use the Jarque-Bera [1980] test
to test for the assumption of normally distributed monthly returns.

United States bonds (0.48 percent), followed by hedge funds (0.67
percent), exhibit the lowest average monthly returns, and the lowest maximum monthly returns (4.27 and 8.20 percent, respectively). However,
they also exhibit the lowest risk, as measured by the highest observed
minimum monthly returns (−4.49 and −7.76 percent) and standard deviations (0.0135 and 0.0224). While U.S. bonds have a low kurtosis, they
also have a negative skewness. In contrast, the hedge fund index shows
positive skewness with higher kurtosis.

Real estate investment trusts have higher returns and comparably
lower standard deviations (0.0378). However, they exhibit negative return

distributions, as measured by a high negative skewness (–0.4885) and a high positive kurtosis (4.3940) when compared to U.S. equity and commodities.

As can be seen from Table 14.1, the results of the Jarque-Bera test show that the null hypothesis of a normally distributed return distribution can be rejected at a 1 percent level for U.S. equity, REITs, USBO, USVC, and hedge funds (as well as 5 percent level for U.S. bonds). Note that the risk–return characteristics of commodities are the only ones we consider here for which the normality hypothesis cannot be rejected. For all other asset classes, we find evidence that the return distributions do not follow a normal distribution. Therefore, variance as a risk measure does not sufficiently describe the return distribution of these asset classes. Moreover, relying on a mean-variance framework while ignoring the higher moments will not cover the risk–return profile adequately. As a result, we must consider higher moments in our model when the investors do not have quadratic utility functions.

However, we know that portfolio optimization is about not only risk–return characteristics but also diversification. To gain more insight into the diversification potential of the asset classes, we calculate the correlation matrix in Table 14.2, which reports the correlations among asset classes based on monthly returns.

According to the correlation coefficients, U.S. bonds have the highest diversification potential. In most cases, it has the lowest correlation

T A B L E 14.2

Correlation matrix

	CepreX U.S. Buyout	S&P GSCI	CS/T Hedge Fund Index	JPM Government Bonds	NAREIT	S&P 500	CepreX U.S. Venture Capital
Buyout	1.000	0.137	0.068	−0.118	−0.077	0.139	0.025
S&P GSCI	0.137	1.000	0.021	0.042	0.150	0.036	−0.040
CS/T hedge fund	0.068	0.021	1.000	−0.056	0.222	0.098	0.063
JPM government bonds	−0.118	0.042	−0.056	1.000	0.035	−0.077	−0.085
NAREIT	−0.077	0.150	0.222	0.035	1.000	0.100	0.019
S&P 500	0.139	0.036	0.098	−0.077	0.100	1.000	0.078
Venture capital	0.025	−0.040	0.063	−0.085	0.019	0.078	1.000

with all other asset classes, and negative correlations with USVC, USBO, hedge funds, and U.S. equity. Furthermore, it has only a low positive correlation with commodities and REITs.

CepreX U.S. Venture Capital also has very positive diversification characteristics. It is negatively correlated with commodities and U.S. bonds, and it has a low positive correlation with USBO, hedge funds, and REITs. CepreX U.S. Buyout has a comparable diversification potential. In comparison to USVC, it has a lower correlation with U.S. bonds and REITs and a higher correlation with commodities, hedge funds, and U.S. equity. Note that the 0.222 correlation between REITs and hedge funds is the highest, followed by the 0.150 correlation between REITs and commodities. The correlation of hedge funds with all asset classes is positive, except for U.S. bonds. This characteristic is favorable for diversification in portfolios with an interaction with U.S. bonds.

After reviewing the descriptive statistics of the return distributions and correlations for all asset classes, we cannot determine a priori that one is a substitute for another. Therefore, we consider all asset classes in the portfolio construction. The next section presents a framework for an optimal portfolio construction that accounts for the distribution characteristics. We compare the results with the mean-variance framework in order to assess the influence of the higher moments.

METHODOLOGY

In the early 1950s, Harry M. Markowitz developed the theoretical basis for efficient portfolio theory. The theory is based on the idea that portfolio risk as a whole is smaller than the sum of the risks of the single assets. Variance, or rather standard deviation, was used to measure risk, and the diversification advantage was defined by the correlation or covariance of the assets in the portfolio. Lower correlations were associated with higher diversification potential. Markowitz's portfolio optimization aims for the combination of assets that will result in an expected portfolio return with the lowest portfolio risk as measured by variance.[12]

---

[12] For further details, see Markowitz (1952).

To implement this approach, we consider two traditional asset classes $(1, ..., m)$, and five alternative asset classes $(m + 1, ..., n)$, with the previously described proxy indexes. Formally, for each point in time, we have a vector $\rho = (\rho_1, \rho_2, ..., \rho_n)$ of expected asset returns of the n asset classes. Investors are free to choose what percentage to invest in each asset class, as described by the portfolio vector $x = (x_1, x_2, ..., x_n)$.

In this optimization, we impose some standard assumptions from finance theory, such as a budget constraint and short-selling restrictions. Mathematically, this means the portfolio weights must sum to 1 and cannot be negative. Furthermore, we impose a minimum diversification constraint of 30 percent for the alternative asset classes only. Thus, no alternative asset class portfolio weight x_i may exceed 30 percent.

This restriction aims to avoid having the portfolio dominated by a single alternative asset class. We do not impose this restriction on the traditional asset classes because we want to include alternative asset classes only if they clearly add value to the portfolio construction.

The expected portfolio return equals $E[\theta] = \sum_{i=1}^{n} x_i \rho_i$. Assume a given minimal expected portfolio return $\bar{\mu}$ and that the investor uses variance as the measure for risk. We thus need to solve the following optimization problem:

$$\min_{x} \text{var} (\theta)$$

Subject to

$$E(\theta) = \sum_{i=1}^{n} x_i \rho_i \geq \bar{\mu}$$
$$1 = \sum_{i=1}^{n} x_i$$
$$0 \leq x_i \leq 1 \text{ for } i = 1, ..., m$$
$$0 \leq x_i \leq 0.3 \text{ for } i = m + 1, ..., n$$

This procedure is based on the assumption that an asset's risk can be fully described by its variance or standard deviation. However, variance only measures symmetrical variability around the mean, and so it cannot correctly measures the risk of assets with asymmetrical distributed returns such as significant skewness.

Variance also does not measure extreme risks (fat tails or leptokurtosis). Yet, we find both significant skewness and excess kurtosis in most of the asset classes shown in Table 14.1. Consequently, we find that the classical mean-variance framework using variance as a risk measure cannot capture all risks in a mixed-asset class optimization that includes alternative investments.

In addition to the variance, we use CVaR, a new measure that is especially appropriate for capturing negative tail risks. This risk measure has been applied in a mixed-asset portfolio optimization. It was found to capture extreme risk better than mean variance, which may significantly underestimate tail losses, especially for low-volatility portfolios [Krokhmal et al. (2001); Agarwal and Naik (2004)].

Following the literature, we find that CVaR accounts better for the return characteristics observed in most of the alternative asset classes. We next provide a short summary of CVaR as a risk measure.

Figure 14.1 shows a return distribution with high extreme risks. We observe a concentration of extreme negative returns at −15 percent. We can use alpha quantiles to express the probability of exceeding a certain loss. For example, a loss greater than −14, −6.5, and 2.5 percent occurs with a probability or alpha of 0.1, 1, and 5 percent, respectively. By using this measure, risk-averse investors can derive a return or loss limit also referred to as value at risk (VaR), which will not be exceeded in alpha percent of all observations.

F I G U R E   14.1

Conditional value at risk vs. VaR

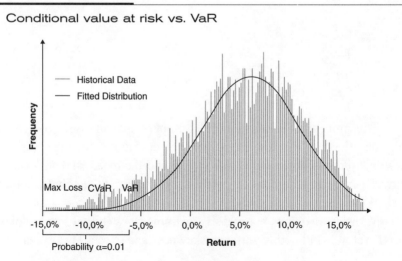

Consider a risk-averse investor who invests in an asset with a return distribution equal to that shown in Figure 14.1. In 1 percent of all observations, the investor realizes a return below the VaR, which in our case equals −6.5 percent. While the VaR seems to capture most risks, it does not account for losses below −6.5 percent, especially not for the concentration of extreme negative returns at −15 percent. If the investor incorrectly assumes that the distribution of returns in Figure 14.1 is normal, he would implicitly assume that the probability of a −15 percent loss is significantly lower, and he may allocate a higher amount to the risky asset than desirable.

However, why is that? In the case of a normal return distribution, VaR has the advantage that losses beyond the α-quantile decrease very quickly. However, that is generally not true for nonnormal return distributions such as those of REITs, hedge funds, and private equity. In those cases, losses beyond the VaR can be so great as to become unacceptable. However, CVaR can account for losses beyond the α quantile, since it is defined as the expected average return below the VaR.

In the example shown in Figure 14.1, CVaR at the 1 percent level equals −9.5 percent. This means that for returns below −6.5 percent, investors can expect a 9.5 percent loss. For a comparable normally distributed return distribution (with identical mean return and standard deviation), CVaR at the 1 percent level would equal about −7 percent. Using CVaR, instead of VaR or the standard deviation, would provide the investor with a more realistic picture of the potential extreme risks involved, because the tail of the return distribution is explicitly considered.

Therefore, following Kaplanski and Kroll (2002), we find that CVaR is an adequate risk measure to model nonnormal return distributions, such as those of most alternative investments.[13]

Using CVaR as the risk measure changes the optimization problem as follows:

$$\min_{x} \text{CVaR}\left(\Theta\right)_{\alpha} = \left| \left(\int_{0}^{\alpha} \text{VaR}_{\Theta} d\Theta \right) \middle/ \alpha \right|$$

---

[13] For a more detailed discussion of risk measures, see also Ortobelli et al. (2005) and Wu and Xiao (2002). For more information on CVaR, see also Artzner et al. (1999), Rockafellar et al. (2006), and Embrechts et al. (2003).

subject to

$$E(\theta) = \sum_{i=1}^{n} x_i \rho_i \geq \bar{\mu}$$
$$1 = \sum_{i=1}^{n} x_i$$
$$0 \leq x_i \leq 1 \text{ for } i = 1, \ldots, m$$
$$0 \leq x_i \leq 0.3 \text{ for } i = m + 1, \ldots, n$$

The curve that represents the dependence of the optimal value of this problem on parameter $\bar{\mu}$ is the boundary of the feasible set of mean-CVaR return pairs. This boundary forms the CVaR efficient frontier, where investors cannot reduce the risk measured by CVaR for a chosen expected return, or do not receive more expected return for a given level of CVaR. Thus, only the optimization problem defined in the target function changes.

Instead of minimizing variance, CVaR is minimized to better account for the return distribution characteristics of the asset classes. We use both variance and the CVaR in our optimization and compare the mixed-asset portfolios resulting from the two optimization procedures.

EMPIRICAL RESULTS

Following this procedure, we estimate the mean-variance and the mean-CVaR efficient ($\alpha = 5\%$) frontiers. For both frontiers, we impose the restrictions that all portfolio weights must be positive and that all alternative investment weights cannot exceed 30 percent. The traditional asset classes U.S. equity and U.S. bonds are subject to a short-selling restriction only, so we can assess whether alternative assets are appropriate substitutes for traditional assets.

Figure 14.2 shows the mean-variance efficient frontier (top chart) in comparison to the CVaR efficient frontier (bottom chart) for the mixed-asset portfolios. The ordinate shows the expected monthly return of the efficient portfolios; the abscissa shows the risk of the respective portfolio measured by standard deviation and by CVaR.[14]

---

[14] Note that the value for CVaR is usually positive. In financial analysis, the loss is often shown in absolute values.

F I G U R E   14.2

Efficient frontiers for mean-variance and mean-CVaR
optimization

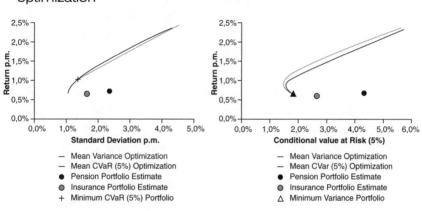

For comparability, we add two proxy portfolios: (1) a typical pension fund portfolio composed of 55 percent U.S. equities, 40 percent U.S. bonds, and 5 percent REITs[15] and (2) a typical insurance company portfolio composed of 35 percent U.S. equities, 60 percent U.S. bonds, and 5 percent REITs.[16] Interestingly, the portfolios of the average pension fund and insurance company do not lie on the efficient frontier regardless of the risk measure. They thus forgo expected returns and/or bear higher than necessary risks.

Note that the frontiers of the mean-variance and mean-CVaR optimization shown in the mean-standard deviation diagram are close to being congruent (see Figure 14.2, left chart). Thus, the mean-CVaR optimization results in a similar efficient frontier as the direct mean-variance optimization, if we use standard deviation as the risk measure. However, if we plot the result of the mean-variance optimization in the mean-CVaR diagram,

---

[15] Surveys report a composition of 48 to 61 percent equity, 25 to 40 percent fixed income to bonds, 4 to 6 percent equity real estate, 5 to 6 percent money market equivalent, and 5 to 14 percenty other (such as alternative investments) [Mercer (2006); GreenwichAssociates (2007); Herrero (2007); WatsonWyattWorldwide (2007)].

[16] Surveys report a composition of 25 to 30 percent equity, 47 to 48 percent fixed income to bonds, 0 to 16 percent equity real estate, 2 to 46 percent money market equivalent, and 0 to 23 percent other (such as alternative investments) [Herrero (2007)].

the frontiers are no longer "congruent" (see Figure 14.2, right chart). The frontier of the mean-variance optimization is clearly below the mean-CVaR frontier. This illustrates that standard deviation does not capture extreme risks adequately. Thus, classical mean-variance leads to an over-allocation to risky assets, increasing the downside risk to an unnecessarily high level.[17] Note also that as the riskiness of the portfolios increases, the optimal portfolios derived from the mean-CVaR and the mean-variance optimization converge somewhat, since most money is allocated to the assets with the highest returns, independent of the level of riskiness.

Considering the minimum-CVaR (5 percent) portfolio weights [1.0 percent return, 1.5 percent CVaR (5 percent), and 1.4 percent StD], we find that U.S. bonds and hedge funds are the most important portfolio stabilizers, with portfolio weights of 49 and 24 percent, respectively. For further diversification U.S. equity, USVC, USBO, and REITs have minor portfolio weights of between 5 and 8 percent. Hence, we do not include commodities in the minimum-CVaR portfolio or in any of the efficient mean-CVaR portfolios (see Figure 14.3, right chart).

Comparing the minimum-CVaR portfolio weights with the portfolio weights of an efficient equal return (return-equivalent) portfolio derived from the mean-variance optimization, we find that U.S. bonds (53 percent) have the highest proportion. CepreX U.S. Buyout, USVC, and U.S. equity exhibit comparable portfolio weights of 5 to 7 percent each.

The return-equivalent portfolio weights ultimately differ from the minimum-CVaR (5 percent) portfolio for three components: commodities, hedge funds, and REITs. In contrast to the minimum-CVaR (5 percent) portfolio, the allocation to commodities equals 2 percent. Furthermore, the allocation to REITs is 13 percent, larger than for the minimum-CVaR (5 percent) portfolio, while the allocation to hedge funds is 15 percent, about 9 percent lower than for the minimum-CVaR (5 percent) portfolio.

Thus, we may conclude that mean-variance optimization fails to properly capture the higher moment characteristics. We find that REITs

---

[17] This conclusion holds even in light of the argument of Cheng and Wolverton (2001) since the CVaR efficient frontier converges strongly to the mean-variance efficient frontier when using variance as a risk measure. Variance also measures upside potential, unlike the CVaR, which is solely a downside risk measure.

F I G U R E   14.3

Portfolio weights for the frontier portfolios for the mean-
variance optimization and the mean-CVaR optimization

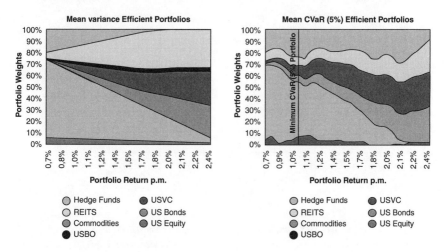

have more unfavorable higher moment characteristics and higher extreme
low returns in comparison with hedge funds. But the mean-variance optimization ignores these higher moment characteristics. The allocation is
higher than for the mean-CVaR optimization. In contrast, hedge funds
have more favorable higher moment characteristics, resulting in higher
allocations when CVaR is the risk measure of choice (see Figure 14.3).

Figure 14.4 shows that the resulting higher moment estimates of the
minimum-CVaR portfolio differ from the return-equivalent, and exhibit
higher positive skewness (which investors usually desire) and positive
excess kurtosis. Figure 14.4 also shows that the largest differences in
higher moments are in the medium-risk portfolios (when comparing the
mean-CVaR and the mean-variance optimization results).

As the portfolio returns increase, note that the higher moment statistics for both optimizations tend to converge. The intuition is that with
increasing expected returns, the focus in both optimizations is on the
expected return, rather than on the "risk" (see also Figure 14.2).

We now compare the two typical institutional portfolios with their
optimal CVaR (5 percent) risk equivalents. By analyzing the risk equivalent CVaR portfolio with a representative insurance portfolio [2.6 percent

F I G U R E   14.4

Higher moment estimates of partially restricted
optimal portfolios

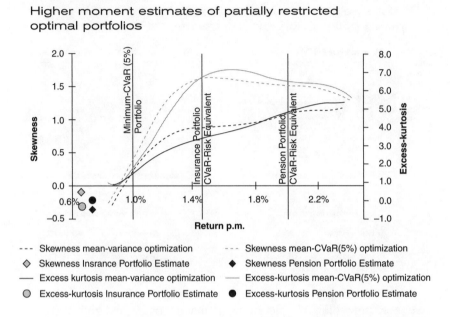

--- Skewness mean-variance optimization   --- Skewness mean-CVaR(5%) optimization
◇ Skewness Insrance Portfolio Estimate   ◆ Skewness Pension Portfolio Estimate
— Excess kurtosis mean-variance optimization   — Excess-kurtosis mean-CVaR(5%) optimization
◯ Excess-kurtosis Insurance Portfolio Estimate ● Excess-kurtosis Pension Portfolio Estimate

CVaR (5 percent)], we find that the return can be doubled to 1.5 percent if we reduce the allocation to U.S. equity from 29 to 6 percent, and the allocation to U.S. bonds from 60 to 36 percent. CepreX U.S. Venture Capital with an allocation of 20 percent and USVC with 10 percent can serve as substitutes for the return driver U.S. equity.

However, while high returns and positive skewness are favorable, USBO and USVC have a higher frequency of extreme returns than U.S. equity. By substituting 20 percent hedge funds for U.S. bonds, we can substantially reduce portfolio risk. Comparing the representative insurance portfolio with its CVaR optimal risk equivalent, we find that both skewness (desirable) and kurtosis are substantially higher for the risk equivalent.

By analyzing the risk equivalent CVaR portfolio with a representative pension portfolio [4.3 percent CVaR(5 percent)], we find that the return can be nearly tripled to 2.0 percent if we substitute 54 percent U.S. equity for 26 percent USBO, 22 percent USVC, and 6 percent REITs. We should also substitute 24 percent hedge funds and 5 percent REITs for the 29 percent U.S. bonds portfolio weight. Again, we find the CVaR optimal risk equivalent exhibits significantly higher skewness and kurtosis than the pension portfolio estimate.

For medium-risk portfolios as measured by CVaR (such as insurance portfolios), we observe the highest diversification. This means the weight restrictions on the portfolio become less important. We also observe the greatest differences in optimal portfolio weights between the mean-variance and the mean-CVaR (5 percent) optimization procedures.

Considering that those are typical institutional portfolios, choosing the correct optimization procedure is even more critical. For CVaR-optimal portfolios, note that the importance of U.S. bonds and REITs decreases as the importance of hedge funds increases in comparison to mean-variance optimal portfolios. Thus, U.S. bonds and REITs each may have up to 15 percent less portfolio weights replaced by hedge funds. Allocation differences for the other assets do not exceed 3 percent each.

Obviously, mean-variance optimization does not capture the favorable downside protection of hedge funds. We also do not observe great changes in the higher moment characteristics of medium-CVaR risk portfolios [see Figure 14.4, portfolios with returns between 1.2 and 1.8 percent and CVaR (5 percent) between 1.6 and 3.5 percent].

By analyzing the portfolios with the highest risk and returns, we find that the asset allocation differences decrease between both optimization procedures. The assets with the highest returns (USBO, USVC, and REITs) exhibit the highest portfolio weights in both optimizations (26 to 30 percent). Hedge funds represent the remaining (12 percent) allocation in the CVaR optimal portfolios for reasons of favorable downside protection. Because mean-variance optimization obviously does not capture those characteristics, U.S. bonds and commodities assume the role of hedge funds. Note that REITs have a higher allocation for the mean-variance optimization such that the 30 percent weight restriction for REITs holds for mean-variance optimal portfolios with average monthly returns greater than 1.7 percent. This is not the case for the CVaR optimization. Here hedge funds basically substitute for REITs, which have a negative skewness and a slightly lower kurtosis than hedge funds.

CONCLUSION

It is important to analyze the return distribution characteristics of alternative assets before considering them as portfolio diversifiers. We find that return estimates vary significantly in the literature, often with mixed results for performance persistence. However, we also find that alternative investments exhibit favorable diversification properties. Consequently, they should be included in a portfolio allocation optimization if the biases are considered and the optimization allows for higher moments.

The results of a CVaR optimization when compared with a mean-variance allocation imply that it is possible to compose a superior mixed-asset portfolio. Because variance as a risk measure does not properly capture the risk–return properties of most alternative investments, investors may over-allocate to assets that do not offer enough downside protection. An example is a typical insurance portfolio. By applying CVaR optimization, we can roughly double the expected return, from 0.7 percent per month to 1.5 percent per month, while maintaining the original risk level of 2.6 percent CVaR (5 percent). Moreover, CVaR optimization implies a nearly 30 percent higher portfolio return than that of the mean-variance optimization, while also maintaining the same risk level.

When considering downside risk, we find significantly different allocations for medium-risk portfolios. For example, expected CVaR is usually 5 to 20 percent higher for medium- to high-risk portfolios, such as insurance or pension portfolios.

We also find that alternative assets are good substitutes for U.S. equity but not for U.S. bonds. For traditional benchmark portfolios (60 percent bonds and 40 percent equity), we find that substituting for U.S. equity with a mix of hedge funds (for downside protection) and private equity (to enhance performance) can significantly improve the risk–return characteristics of the portfolio. For portfolios with higher expected returns, USBO, USVC, and REITs can further increase expected returns while controlling for extreme risks. In this case, hedge fund investments improve the downside protection. Thus, for the riskiest portfolios, traditional assets lose importance.

Ultimately, we find that alternative investments can significantly improve the risk–return characteristics of traditional portfolios. However, U.S. bonds are an especially important portfolio component in low-to medium-risk portfolios.

REFERENCES

Ackermann, C., R. McEnally, and D. Ravenscraft (1999) The Performance of Hedge Funds: Risk, Return, and Incentives. *The Journal of Finance*, Vol. 54, No. 3, pp. 833–874.

Agarwal, V. and N.Y. Naik (2004) Risks and Portfolio Decisions Involving Hedge Funds. *Review of Financial Studies*, Vol. 17, No. 1, pp. 63–98.

Alexiev, J. (2005) The Impact of Higher Moments on Hedge Fund Risk Exposure. *The Journal of Alternative Investments*, Vol. 7, No. 4, pp. 50–65.

Amenc, N., P. Malaise, and M. Vaissié (2005) Edhec Funds of Hedge Funds Reporting Survey—A Return-Based Approach to Funds of Hedge Funds Reporting. Working paper, EDHEC Risk and Asset Management Research Centre, Valbonne, France.

Amin, G.S. and H.M. Kat (2003) Hedge Fund Performance 1990–2000: Do the "Money Machines" Really Add Value? *Journal of Financial & Quantitative Analysis*, Vol. 38, No. 2, pp. 251–274.

Ang, A., M. Rhodes-Kropf, and R. Zhao.(2005) Do Funds-of-Funds Deserve Their Fees-on-Fees? Working paper, NBER, Cambridge, MA.

Anson, M.J.P., H. Ho, and K. Silberstein (2007) Building a Hedge Fund Portfolio with Kurtosis and Skewness. *Journal of Alternative Investments*, Vol. 10, No. 1, pp. 25–34.

Artzner, P., F. Delbaen, J.-M. Eber, and D. Heath (1999) Coherent Measures of Risk. *Mathematical Finance*, Vol. 9, No. 3, pp. 203–228.

Avramov, D., R. Kosowski, N.Y. Naik, and M. Teo (2007) Investing in Hedge Funds When Returns Are Predictable. AFA 2008 New Orleans Meetings Paper, Orleans, France.

Barkham, R. and D. Geltner (1995) Price Discovery in American and British Property Markets. *Real Estate Economics*, Vol. 23, No. 1, pp. 21–44.

Bodie, Z., and V.I. Rosansky (1980) Risk and Returns in Commodity Futures. *Financial Analysts Journal*, Vol. 36, No. 3, pp. 27–39.

Brooks, C. and H.M. Kat (2002) The Statistical Properties of Hedge Fund Index Returns and Their Implications for Investors. *Journal of Alternative Investments*, Vol. 5, No. 2, pp. 22–44.

Brown, S.J., W.N. Goetzmann, and R.G. Ibbotson (1999) Offshore Hedge Funds: Survival and Performance, 1989–95. *Journal of Business*, Vol. 72, No. 1, pp. 91–117.

Capocci, D. and G. Hubner (2004) Analysis of Hedge Fund Performance. *Journal of Empirical Finance*, Vol. 11, No. 1, pp. 55–89.

Chen, H.-C., K.-Y. Ho, C. Lu, and C.-H Wu (2005) Real Estate Investment Trusts—An Asset Allocation Perspective. *The Journal of Portfolio Management*, Special Issue Real Estate, pp. 46–55.

Chen, P., G.T. Baierl, and P.D. Kaplan (2002) Venture Capital and Its Role in Strategic Asset Allocation. *The Journal of Portfolio Management*, Vol. 28, No. 2, pp. 83–89.

Cheng, P. and M.L. Wolverton (2001) MPT and the Downside Risk Framework: A Comment on Two Recent Studies. *Journal of Real Estate Portfolio Management*, Vol. 7, No. 2, pp. 125–131.

Chiang, K.C.H.L. and L. Ming-Long (2007) Spanning Tests on Public and Private Real Estate. *Journal of Real Estate Portfolio Management*, Vol. 13, No. 1, pp. 7–15.

Clayton, J. and G. MacKinnon (2000) What Drives Equity REIT Returns? The Relative Influences of Bond, Stock and Real Estate Factors. Working paper, RERI, Hartford, CT.

Cochrane, J.H. (2005) The Risk and Return of Venture Capital. *Journal of Financial Economics*, Vol. 75, No. 1, pp. 3–52.

Conner, A. (2003) Asset Allocation Effects of Adjusting Alternative Assets for Stale Pricing. *The Journal of Alternative Investments*, Vol. 6, No. 3, pp. 42–52.

Cotter, J. and S. Stevenson (2007) Uncovering Volatility Dynamics in Daily REIT Returns. *Journal of Real Estate Portfolio Management*, Vol. 13, No. 2, pp. 119–128.

Cottier, P. (2000) *Hedge Funds and Managed Futures—Performance, Risks, Strategies and Use in Investment Portfolios*. Bern, Switzerland: Haupt Verlag.

Doyle, E., J. Hill, and I. Jack (2007) Growth in Commodity Investment: Risks and Challenges for Commodity Market Participants. Working paper, FSA Markets Infrastructure Department, London.

Dyment, J. and E. Heavey (2003) Equity Prime Services, Alternative Investment Survey Results Part 2: Inside the Mind of The Hedge Fund Investor. Working paper, Deutsche Bank, London, U.K.

Eling, M. (2006) Autocorrelation, Bias, and Fat Tails—Are Hedge Funds Really Attractive Investments? *Derivatives Use, Trading & Regulation*, Vol. 12, No. 1, pp. 28–47.

Eling, M. (2007) Does Hedge Fund Performance Persist? Overview and New Empirical Evidence. Working paper, University of St. Gallen, St. Gallen, Switzerland.

Embrechts, P., C. Klüppelberg, and T. Mikosch. (2003) *Modelling Extremal Events for Insurance and Finance*. Heidelberg: Springer.

Ennis, R.M. and M.D. Sebastian. (2005) Asset Allocation with Private Equity. *The Journal of Private Equity*, Vol. 8, No. 3, pp. 81–87.

Erb, C.B. and C.R. Harvey. (2006) The Strategic and Tactical Value of Commodity Futures. *Financial Analysts Journal*, Vol. 62, No. 2, pp. 69–97.

Fabozzi, F., R. Fuess, and D. Kaiser (2007) A Primer on Commodity Investing. In F. Fabozzi, R. Füss, and D. Kaiser (eds.), *The Handbook of Commodity Investing*. Hoboken, NJ: John Wiley & Sons.

Fama, E.F. and K.R. French (1987) Commodity Futures Prices: Some Evidence on Forecast Power, Premiums, and the Theory of Storage. *The Journal of Business*, Vol. 90 No. 1, pp. 55–73.

Fung, W. and D.A. Hsieh (2000) Performance Characteristics of Hedge
      Funds and Commodity Funds: Natural vs. Spurious Biases. *Journal
      of Financial & Quantitative Analysis*, Vol. 35, No. 3, pp. 291–308.

Geltner, D.M. (1991) Smoothing in Appraisal-Based Returns. *Journal of
      Real Estate Finance & Economics*, Vol. 4, No. 3, pp. 327–345.

Georgiev, G. (2006) The Benefits of Commodity Investment: 2006
      Update. Working paper, Center for International Securities and
      Derivatives Markets, Amherst, MA.

Getmansky, M., A.W. Lo, and I. Makarov (2004) An Econometric Model
      of Serial Correlation and Illiquidity in Hedge Fund Returns.
      Journal of Financial Economics, Vol. 74, No. 3, pp. 529–609.

Gompers, P.A. and J. Lerner (1997) Risk and Reward in Private Equity
      Investments: The Challenge of Performance Assessment. *The
      Journal of Private Equity*, Vol. 1, No, pp. 5–12.

Gorton, G.B. and G.K. Rouwenhorst (2005) Facts and Fantasies
      about Commodity Futures. Working paper, Yale University,
      New Haven, CT.

Greenwich Associates (2007) New Products and Strategies Shake Up
      "Traditional" Asset Allocation for U.S. Institutions. In Greenwich
      Report, Greenwich, CT.

Herrero, S.G. (2007) Institutional Investors, Global Savings and Asset
      Allocation. Working paper, International Economy and Relations
      Department, Frankfurt.

Hoecht, S., K.H. Ng, J. Wolf, and R. Zagst (2008) Optimal Portfolio
      Allocation with Asian Hedge Funds and Asian REITs.
      International Journal of Service Sciences (forthcoming).

Hoernemann, J.T., D.A. Junkans, and C.M. Zarate (2005) Strategic Asset
      Allocation and Other Determinants of Portfolio Returns. *The
      Journal of Private Wealth Management*, Vol. 8, No. 3, pp. 26–38.

Huang, J.-Z. and Z. Zhong (2006) Time-Variation in Diversification
      Benefits of Commodity, REITs, and TIPS. Working paper, 30th
      Anniversary—Journal of Banking & Finance, Beijing.

Hudson-Wilson, S., F.J. Fabozzi, J.N. Gordon, and S.M. Giliberto (2004) Why Real Estate? *The Journal of Portfolio Management*, Special Real Estate Issue, pp. 12–25.

Idzorek, T.M. (2006) Strategic Asset Allocation and Commodities. Working paper, Ibbotson Associates, Chicago, Illinois.

Jagannathan, R., A. Malakhov, and D. Novikov (2006) Do Hot Hands Persist Among Hedge Fund Managers? An Empirical Evaluation. Working paper, NBER, Cambridge, MA.

Jinliang, L., R.M. Mooradian, and S.X. Yang (2005) Economic Forces, Asset Pricing, and REIT Returns. Working paper, American Real Estate Society, Monterrey, CA.

Kahan, M. and E. Rock (2007) Hedge Funds in Corporate Governance and Corporate Control. *University of Pennsylvania Law Review*, Vol. 155, No. 5, pp. 1021–1093.

Kaplan, S.N. and A. Schoar (2005) Private Equity Performance: Returns, Persistence, and Capital Flows. *The Journal of Finance*, Vol. 60, No. 4, pp. 1791–1823.

Kaplanski, G. and Y. Kroll. (2002) VaR Risk Measures versus Traditional Risk Measures: An Analysis and Survey. *Journal of Risk*, Vol. 4, No. 3, pp. 1–27.

Kat, H.M. (2003) 10 Things Investors Should Know About Hedge Funds. *The Journal of Private Wealth Management*, Vol. 5, No. 4, pp. 72–81.

Kat, H.M. (2007) How to Evaluate A New Diversifier with 10 Simple Questions. *The Journal of Private Wealth Management*, Vol. 9, No. 4, pp. 29–36.

Kat, H.M. and R.C.A. Oomen (2007) What Every Investor Should Know About Commodities, Part II: Multivariate Return Analysis. *Journal of Investment Management*, Vol. 5, No. 3, pp. 1–25.

Krokhmal, P., J. Palmquist, and S. Uryasev (2001) Portfolio Optimization with Conditional Value-at-Risk Objective and Constraints. *Journal of Risk*, Vol. 4, No. 2, pp. 43–68.

Kuhle, J.L.(1987) Portfolio Diversification and Return Benefits—
  Common Stock vs. Real Estate Investment Trusts (REITs). *Journal
  of Real Estate Research*, Vol. 2, No. 2, pp. 1–9.

Lamm, J., R. McFall, and T.E. Ghaleb-Harter (2001) Private Equity as
  an Asset Class: Its Role in Investment Portfolios. *The Journal of
  Private Equity*, Vol. 7, No.1, pp. 68–79.

Le Sourd, V. (2006) Hedge Fund Performance in 2006: A Vintage Year
  for Hedge Funds? Working paper, EDHEC Risk and Asset
  Management Research Centre, Valbonne, France.

Lee, S. and S. Stevenson (2005) The Case for REITs in the Mixed-Asset
  Portfolio in the Short and Long Run. *Journal of Real Estate
  Portfolio Management*, Vol. 11, No. 1, pp. 55–80.

Li, Y. and K. Wang (1995) The Predictability of REIT Returns and
  Market Segmentation. *Journal of Real Estate Research*, Vol. 10,
  No. 4, pp. 471–482.

Liang, B. (2002) Hedge Funds, Fund of Funds, and Commodity Trading
  Advisors. Working paper, Case Western Reserve, Cleveland, OH.

Liang, Y. and W. McIntosh (1998) REIT Style and Performance. *Journal
  of Real Estate Portfolio Management*, Vol. 4, No. 1, pp. 69–78.

Ling, D.C. and A. Naranjo (1999) The Integration of Commercial Real
  Estate Markets and Stock Markets. *Real Estate Economics*, Vol. 27,
  No. 3, pp. 483–515.

Ljung, G.M. and G.E.P. Box (1978) On a Measure of Lack of Fit in
  Time-Series Models. *Biometrika*, Vol. 65, No. 2, pp. 297–297.

Markowitz, H.M. (1952) Portfolio Selection. *The Journal of Finance*,
  Vol. 7, No. 1, pp. 77–91.

Mercer Investment Consulting. (2006) European Institutional Market
  Place Overview 2006. In Asset Allocation Survey and Market
  Profiles. London: Mercer Investment Consulting.

Metrick, A. and A. Yasuda (2007) The Economics of Private Equity
  Funds. Swedish Institute for Financial Research Conference on The
  Economics of the Private Equity, Stockholm.

Moskowitz, T.J. and A. Vissing-Jørgensen (2002) The Returns to
    Entrepreneurial Investment: A Private Equity Premium Puzzle?
    American Economic Review, Vol. 92, No. 4, pp. 745–778.

Mueller, G.R., K.R. Pauley, and W.K. Morrell (1994) Should REITs Be
    Included in a Mixed-Asset-Portfolio? *Real Estate Finance*, Vol. 11,
    No. 1, pp. 23–28.

Mull, S.R., and L.A. Soenen (1997) U.S. REITs as an Asset Class in
    International Investment Portfolios. *Financial Analysts Journal*,
    Vol. 53, No. 2, pp. 55–62.

Myer, F.C. and J.R. Webb (1993) Return Properties of Equity REITs,
    Common Stocks, and Commercial Real Estate: A Comparison.
    Journal of Real Estate Research, Vol. 8, No. 1, pp. 87–106.

Ortobelli, S., S.T. Rachev, S. Stoyanov, F.J. Fabozzi, and A. Biglova
    (2005) The Proper Use of Risk Measures in Portfolio Theory.
    International Journal of Theoretical and Applied Finance, Vol. 8,
    No. 8, pp. 1–27.

Phalippou, L. and O. Gottschalg (2007) Performance of Private Equity
    Funds. Working paper, University of Amsterdam, Netherlands.

Rockafellar, R.T., S. Uryasev, and M. Zabarankin (2006) Master Funds
    in Portfolio Analysis with General Deviation Measures. *Journal of
    Banking and Finance*, Vol. 30, No. 2, pp. 743–778.

Schmidt, D.M. (2004) Private Equity-, Stock- and Mixed-Asset
    Portfolios: A Bootstrap Approach to Determine Performance
    Characteristics, Diversification Benefits and Optimal Portfolio
    Allocations. Working paper, CEPRES Center of Private Equity
    Research, Munich.

Schneeweis, T., V.N. Karavas, and G. Georgiev (2002) Alternative
    Investments in the Institutional Portfolio. Working paper, AIMA,
    London, U.K.

Stevenson, S. (2001) Evaluating the Investment Attributes and
    Performance of Property Companies. *Journal of Property
    Investment & Finance*, Vol. 19, No. 3, pp. 251–266.

Terhaar, K., R. Staub, and B. Singer (2003) Appropriate Policy Allocation for Alternative Investments. *The Journal of Portfolio Management*, Vol. 29, No. 3, pp. 101–110.

Watson Wyatt (2007) 2007 Global Pension Assets Study. Watson Wyatt Worldwide, London.

Winkelmann, K. (2004) Improving Portfolio Efficiency: Risk Budgeting, Implied Confidence Levels, and Changing Allocations. *Journal of Portfolio Management*, Vol. 30, No. 2, pp. 23–38.

Wu, G.Z. and Xiao. (2002) An Analysis of Risk Measures. *Journal of Risk*, Vol. 4, No. 4, pp. 53–75.

Value-at-Risk-Adjusted Performance for Structured Portfolios

Rosa Cocozza

ABSTRACT

The chapter investigates the potential application of value-at-risk metrics to risk-adjusted performance measures in the case of structured portfolios. The main issue is the appraisal of a decision criterion for portfolio choices with reference to either the asset portfolio given a structured bond or the bond structure given an existing coverage asset portfolio. Such indicators are put into an asset and liability management decision-making context, where the relationship between the expected profit and the capital at risk are compared to evaluate the issue of the bond and the expected rate of return of the whole portfolio. An exemplar case provides for practical implementation.

INTRODUCTION

Modern financial markets are characterized by a growing number of structured securities. A *structured security* can be defined as a contract whose payoff can be replicated by a combination of elementary financial instruments and derivatives. As the complexity of the products grows, that is, as the number of implied cash flows increase, so does the number of

349

constituents required to replicate the desired payoff; in other words as the involvement of the product grows, so does the complexity of the replicating portfolio, of the pricing process, and of the managing practice.

As known, constituents of the replicating portfolio will be easier to price, understand, and analyze than original instrument. Everything else being the same, a perfect replicating portfolio must have the same price as the original instrument. Thus adding up the values of the constituent assets, we can get the cost of forming a replicating portfolio. Nevertheless, there is a practical problem that always arises when dealing with financial products—and especially with structured securities—that is the gap between the fair (theoretical) and the real (actual) price.

In a rigorous systematic perspective, the gap should be void, and the price should be fair, in the sense that it should respect the "law of one price." Within this context, the optimal estimate should be the arbitrage-free price as equilibrium value. In a proper business perspective, the actual price of a debt instrument issued by any financial intermediary has to exhibit a value that, on the one hand, can be appraised by subscribers and that, on the other hand, proves adequately profitable to the issuer. Therefore, the cost of forming a replicating portfolio will give the actual price of the original instrument once the market practitioner adds a proper margin. This is the case of any bid–ask differential we can discover on the market for every financial intermediation process; this is also the case of loadings applied to pure premiums, within the insurance context.

The chapter focuses exactly on the inquiry of the adequacy of the profitability of the issue, given a fair valuation of the product. This adequacy has to be appreciated on the basis of both the risk–return trade-off. In a sense, we could remake the question, forcing the attention toward the optimality of the issue, once the pricing is set by usual standard.

This optimality has to be pragmatically evaluated: the risk–return trade-off has to be compared with the return on capital at risk set by top management and/or by shareholders and is, by definition, based on a portfolio approach. At the same time, the main answer is conditional on two other issues:

1. The identification of the factor relevant to the optimality of the issue

2. The measure—or the family of measures—we can use for our
   purposes

If we are able to identify bond or security design variables influencing future outcomes, we can give an answer to the first question. The answer is related not only to the technical features of the bond and to the discretionary parameters but also to the selected investment strategy. As far as the features are concerned, the offer of higher guarantees and/or participation rate should reduce the profitability of the issue. However, the cross section of this information with different investment strategies could give rise to different results if the strategy adopted is opportunely elected. This is the case of a beneficial mismatch between asset and liability, since decision on the (investing) replicating portfolio could make the difference. The selection of a perfect replicating portfolio (a perfect matching strategy) reduces both risk and return, but it does not necessarily turn out to be competitive on the market. Vice versa, the selection of a favorable imperfect matching will increase both risk and return and could give rise to a portfolio whose acceptability has to be carefully evaluated. This takes us directly to the question of the sustainability of the risks arising from a mismatched position. If the increase in the profitability is connected to an increase in the risk of the portfolio, the evaluation has to consider the classical trade-off between risk and reward. In a sense, this is the bridge to our second issue.

The measures—or the family of measures—have to be able to depict coherently the two aspects (Artzner et al., 1999). As a consequence, the main object of our investigation is the distribution of the future net worth of the portfolio on the set of states of nature at the bond maturity, that is to say at the end of the portfolio life cycle. A crucial measurement step is whether the prospective value of the position belongs or does not belong to the subset of acceptable risks, which are positions with acceptable future net worth. The acceptability of the future net worth can be measured by some economic value-added indicator such as the Economic Value Added.

The rest of the chapter is organized as follows. The section The Opportunity Set provides for the logical procedure to follow in establishing a methodological approach to the evaluation of a structured issue.

It defines risk and reward indicators, in a managerial perspective, trying to find a general answer to the issue of the family of measures that can be useful to our scope. The section An Equity-Linked Bond illustrates the technical features of the contract and two possible investment alternatives (a perfect and an imperfect matching portfolio), approaching the question of the profitability of the issue. The section Computation of Results pioneers the applicative section, setting the modeling context and all the computational remarks. The section Findings exhibits the computational results and their significance. The final section Conclusions suggests some future research prospects.

THE OPPORTUNITY SET

Since the object of the analysis is a structured product, the procedure starts with the cash-flow mapping that is the timely decomposition of the complex cash flows into primary flows. By this decomposition we can recognize the elementary flows, and we can analyze also the potential replication portfolio. This step provides us also with a full identification of discretionary parameters defining the risk–return profile of the structured bond. For example, if the bond has to include a minimum guaranteed rate of return and/or the application of a participation rate to the results of the reference asset, the decision on the "size" of these two parameters is a crucial step within the product design. As far as the minimum guaranteed rate is concerned, it has to be lower than the risk-free rate in order to be, at the same time, within the market and sustainable by the issuer. This rate, in fact, is the basic and certain return of an asset potentially offering higher returns: the expected return of such a composite portfolio has to respect the capital market line; otherwise, arbitrage mechanisms will restore the market equilibrium. Similar considerations attain to the participation rate: if the reference asset is exactly the market portfolio, only a participation rate equal to 1 could be compatible with the capital asset pricing model equation.

Nevertheless, the question we want to answer concerns the optimal "size" of such parameters from the point of view of the issuer. At this point, we would like to remark and stress that, in a theoretical perspective, the fair value is that price which is able to conform with the no-arbitrage principle, but that from the practical side an "adequate" margin has to apply. Therefore, the answer we are looking for is relative to a methodology for determining the optimal size of the margins. Recalling the examples, if we want to assess a minimum guaranteed rate, we have to establish the "optimal" distance from the risk-free asset. The appraisal of this optimality can be merely a question of economic equilibrium (spread margin) or of value creation (value margin).

The final decision on the issue has to take into account both the risk–return trade-off and the return on capital at risk set by top management, as a threshold value to set the "acceptability" of the issue and of the backing asset. Within this context, a primary insight can be gained through the analysis of the expected profit and of the linked expected return on equity from the position the intermediary is implementing. These indicators provide the management with an immediate picture of future outcomes and differentials of portfolio alternatives, although they do not weight the information with the risk associated to each strategic choice. As a consequence, the return has to be compared with the risk undertaken: to this aim, value-at-risk (VaR) measures are considered.

In this case, being the VaR is an estimate of the maximum likely loss with a certain confidence level over an identified time horizon, we have to evaluate the probability distribution of the final result with reference to the whole asset and liability portfolio. Therefore, as far as the result is concerned, the focus is on the difference between the initial allocated capital (C_0) and the final value of the entire portfolio ($\mathbf{C}_m$) over a holding period matching the duration m of the bond. As a consequence, the VaR is the threshold value of the loss ($C_0 - \mathbf{C}_m$) that will not be exceeded with probability $1 - c$, that is,

$$\text{Prob}\,[C_0 - \mathbf{C}_m \leq - \text{VaR}_c(m)] = c \qquad (15.1)$$

More specifically, in the risk evaluation of the entire issue, the VaR can be interpreted as the VaR of a portfolio whose initial value is the allocated capital and whose flow dynamic is given by the flows of the initial asset allocation and the subsequent intermediate flows re-allocation. The VaR of the entire value can be interpreted as the VaR of a portfolio exposed to those risk factors that are the changing parameters of the net value itself. It can be measured by modeling the risk factors and by using risk filters to proportionate the effect on the net value. As known, the classical VaR measures suffer from many serious limitations (Artzner et al., 1999), that can be partially overcome by *conditional value at risk* (CVaR), defined as the average of losses exceeding VaR (Dowd and Blake, 2006), that is,

$$\text{CVaR}_c(m) = E[(C_0 - \mathbf{C}_c(m)) | (C_0 - \mathbf{C}_c(m)) > \text{VaR}_c(m)] \quad (15.2)$$

As noted (Hull, 2006), if the VaR estimates the maximum likely loss, the CVaR estimates the average value of losses in the critical area.

In the need of an efficient risk management and the ability to compare different business units risk adjusted performance measures (RAPMs) have become popular in the finance industry. As known, business evolution can be described by means of both the intermediation portfolio (economic value approach) and the income flows (current earning approach). The first approach accounts for the difference between asset and liability at any time of the portfolio cycle, while the second explains the difference between the profit components periodically accrued. In order to compute RAPMs, we used both and concentrated on an average yearly measure, since we are concerned with the global profitability of the issue.

Many acronyms and definitions for RAPMs can be found in the literature. We use the following:

1. The *expected return on equity* (E[RoE]) is defined as the ratio of the expected profit to initial capital, whose annual intensity is set as

$$E[RoE] = \frac{E[\Phi_m]}{C_0 \cdot m} \quad (15.3)$$

2. The *expected coherent risk-adjusted return on capital* (E[CRARoC]) is defined as the ratio of the expected profit to the VaR of the portfolio,[1] whose corresponding average intensity value is given by

$$E[CRARoC] = \frac{E[\Phi_m]}{|\text{CVaR}| \cdot m} \quad (15.4)$$

---

[1] Here we use the term RARoC as a general indicator of return on capital (Matten, 2000). There are lots of variations among institutions, as how they calculate a ratio of economic result to capital. Frequently, almost identical measures assume different names in different context. The choice to use the term RARoC in a broad sense comes from the intent to avoid counterintuitive results arising from the variety of names used in practice as well as in literature.

The last measure can be considered the most useful because it respects the majority of coherence axioms. As far as the value creation is concerned, a general indicator is also selected. A very broad definition of *value added* is given by

$$Value\ Added = \text{Profit} - (TR^*Allocated\ Capital) \qquad (15.5)$$

where TR is a threshold rate setting the acceptability of the future result. The value added should be calibrated to a specific measure of profit, which is the net operating profit and the hurdle rate should be the return on capital at risk set by top management. Here we define the value-added measure (EVA), on an average yearly basis, as

$$EVA = CRARoC - TR \cdot C_0 \qquad (15.6)$$

As can be easily seen, the EVA increases according to the enhancement in the expected profit and the reduction in risk exposure.

AN EQUITY-LINKED BOND

The analysis is applied to a specific equity-linked bond, with the aim of illustrating the potential application, but it can be applied to any structured security, given the opportune refinements. According to the agreement, by paying a predefined amount (U), the buyer will earn—at each predefined time ($t \le m$)—a benefit (B_t) that is calculated at the maximum rate between an annual guaranteed one (g) and a percentage (η) of the annual equivalent total return of the reference asset (s) in the same period. In other words, the benefit it is set by incrementing each year the present value of the fixed payment R_g (the guaranteed payment) by a fraction η (participation rate) of the interest on the investment of the corresponding quota in the reference asset.

Therefore, the buyer will receive at each maturity a fixed amount R_g calculated at the guaranteed rate g, as the installment of an annuity whose present value is the invested amount U, i.e., $R_g = U / \sum_{t=1}^{m} e^{-\delta_g t}$, where δ_g is the force of interest corresponding to the annual guaranteed rate g, and an eventual additional benefit calculated as a percentage (η) of the total

T A B L E   15.1

Buyer flows

Time	0 (issue time)	1	t	m (bond term)
Flow	$-U$	$+B_1$	$+B_t$	$+B_m$

return of the reference asset, conditional on an annual return higher than the guaranteed rate.

At each maturity, the buyer will earn the following cash flow:

$$
\begin{aligned}
B_t &= \frac{R_g}{e^{\delta_g t}} \max\left[e^{\delta_g t}; 1 + \eta\left(\frac{S_t}{s_0} - 1 \right) \right] \\
&= R_g\left[1 + \frac{\eta}{s_0 e^{\delta_g t}} \max\left(0; S_t - s_0\left(1 + \frac{e^{\delta_g t} - 1}{\eta} \right) \right) \right]
\end{aligned}
\tag{15.7}
$$

The cash-flow mapping of the single bond is given by Table 15.1.

Cash-Flow Mapping and Perfect Replicating Portfolio

Since our analysis is aimed at evaluating the profitability of the whole issue, we approach the question on a portfolio basis. The portfolio cash flows are simply obtained by multiplying the individual benefits by the number of issued securities n. By applying a Black and Scholes (1973) valuation methodology to the plain vanilla option portfolios, the value at issue of the single contract can be set as

$$
B_0 = R_g \left\{ \sum_{t=1}^{m} e^{-\delta_{r(0;t)} t} + \eta \sum_{t=1}^{m} \left[\frac{N\left(d_{1(t)}\right)}{e^{\delta_g t}} - \left(1 + \frac{e^{\delta_g t} - 1}{\eta} \right) \frac{N\left(d_{2(t)}\right)}{e^{\left(\delta_{r(0;t)} + \delta_g\right) t}} \right] \right\}
\tag{15.8}
$$

where $N(\cdot)$ is a standard normal distribution with parameters $d_{1(t)}$ and $d_{2(t)}$, defined as

$$d_{1(t)} = \frac{\frac{1}{t}\left(\delta_{r(0;t)} + \frac{\sigma_s^2}{2}\right) - \ln\left(1 + \frac{e^{\delta_g t} - 1}{\eta}\right)}{\sigma_s \sqrt{t}} \qquad d_{2(t)} = d_{1(t)} - \sigma_s \sqrt{t} \qquad (15.9)$$

$\delta_{r(0;t)}$ is the force of interest corresponding to the spot rate $r(0;t)$ for the period $0-t$, and σ_s is the volatility of the reference asset.

Notice that the present value of the investment portfolio (OF_0^P) is equivalent to the sum of the following:

- A portfolio of zero coupon bonds with maturity going from 1 to m whose nominal value is exactly the compulsory t outflow
- A portfolio of plain vanilla call options with varying maturity from 1 to m, increasing strike prices from $s_0 e^{\delta_g}$ to $s_0 e^{\delta_g m}$, and a correspondingly decreasing number of options according to the growing discount factor

Formally,

$$OF_0^P = \sum_{t=1}^{m} \frac{B_t \cdot n}{e^{\delta_{r(0;t)}t}}$$

$$= R_g \cdot n \left\{ \begin{array}{l} \displaystyle\sum_{t=1}^{m} \frac{1}{e^{\delta_{r(0;t)}t}} \\ \displaystyle + \eta \sum_{t=1}^{m} \left[\frac{N(d_{1(t)})}{e^{\delta_g t}} - \left(1 + \frac{e^{\delta_g t} - 1}{\eta}\right) \frac{N(d_{2(t)})}{e^{(\delta_{r(0;t)} + \delta_g)t}} \right] \end{array} \right\} \qquad (15.10)$$

By virtue of the put–call parity property (Black and Scholes, 1973), any equity-linked bond with a minimum guaranteed rate of return is equivalent either to a plan providing a fixed benefit plus a call option or to a plan providing a benefit of the value of the reference portfolio plus a put option. Between the two possible basic strategies, we choose the first one.[2] Hence, the earned sum is considered to be invested into a portfolio made up of bonds and plain vanilla call options, giving rise to the balance sheet structure in Table 15.2.

---

[2] From a theoretical point of view the two strategies are perfectly equivalent. Nevertheless, in a practical perspective, if the reference asset is not directly traded on the market, the put replication can give rise to higher replication cost, for the need to build up on a synthetic. For this reason, we choose the call option strategy. Naturally, whether the reference portfolio is directly traded, the put replication strategy could equally be pursued.

T A B L E   15.2

Perfect matching asset and liability portfolio

Assets	Liabilities
Plain vanilla call options	Equity-linked bonds
Zero coupon bonds	Capital

The related cash flows in Table 15.2 are reported in Table 15.3. Naturally, if we add the writer's capital, the investment outflow will comprise also this quota. If the writer decides to invest the initial capital together with the shareholder capital C_0 in the financial market, he or she will end up with a profit that is:

1. Definitively certain if he/she buys only zero coupon bonds with duration equal to $m;$
2. Almost certain (moderately risky) if he and/or she goes for a rollover bond strategy;
3. Risky if he and/or she selects some other risky assets (stocks, derivatives and so on).

Hence, as long as the selected investing instruments are available—and no dynamic hedging is required—the profit will exhibit the earlier risk ranking. The investment strategy selected, being a perfect replicating portfolio (denoted by superscript P), provides the writer with a final profit (Φ_m^P) substantially conditional on the magnitude of the initial surplus NF_0^P given different levels of the parameters g and η since it can be shown to be equal to

$$
\begin{aligned}
\Phi_m^P &= C_0 \left[\prod_{t=0}^{m-1} e^{\delta_{r(t:1)}} - 1 \right] + NF_0^P \prod_{t=0}^{m-1} e^{\delta_{r(t:1)}} \\
&= C_0 \left[\prod_{t=0}^{m-1} e^{\delta_{r(t:1)}} - 1 \right] + \left[(U \cdot n) - OF_0^P \right] \prod_{t=0}^{m-1} e^{\delta_{r(t:1)}}
\end{aligned}
\tag{15.11}
$$

Consequently, from a security design perspective, relevant variables influencing the outcome are the guaranteed and the participation rate being $\Phi_m^P = f(g, \eta)$ through the value of the initial net flow. Therefore, the acceptability of the outcome can be evaluated with reference to these parameters, in order to asses the most valuable combination of them.

TABLE 15.3

Issue cash flows (perfect matching)

Time	Investment Cash Flows	Bond Cash Flows	Net Flows
0	$-OF_0^p = -\begin{pmatrix} Zero & Coupon & Bonds \\ +Plain & Vanilla & Calls \end{pmatrix}$	$+IF_0 = +U \cdot n$	$NF_0^p = IF_0 - OF_0^p$
1	$IF_1^p = R_g \cdot n\left[1 + \dfrac{\eta}{s_0 e_z^{\delta_x}}\max\left(0;\mathbf{S}_1 - s_0\left(1 + \dfrac{e^{\delta_x} - 1}{\eta}\right)\right)\right]$	$OF_1 = R_g \cdot n\left[1 + \dfrac{\eta}{s_0 e_z^{\delta_x}}\max\left(0;\mathbf{S}_1 - s_0\left(1 + \dfrac{e^{\delta_x} - 1}{\eta}\right)\right)\right]$	0
t	$IF_t^p = R_g \cdot n\left[1 + \dfrac{\eta}{s_0 e_z^{\delta_{z,t}}}\max\left(0;\mathbf{S}_t - s_0\left(1 + \dfrac{e^{\delta_{z,t}} - 1}{\eta}\right)\right)\right]$	$OF_t = R_g \cdot n\left[1 + \dfrac{\eta}{s_0 e_z^{\delta_{z,t}}}\max\left(0;\mathbf{S}_t - s_0\left(1 + \dfrac{e^{\delta_{z,t}} - 1}{\eta}\right)\right)\right]$	0
m	$IF_m^p = R_g \cdot n\left[1 + \dfrac{\eta}{s_0 e_z^{\delta_{z,m}}}\max\left(0;\mathbf{S}_m - s_0\left(1 + \dfrac{e^{\delta_{z,m}} - 1}{\eta}\right)\right)\right]$	$OF_m = R_g \cdot n\left[1 + \dfrac{\eta}{s_0 e_z^{\delta_{z,m}}}\max\left(0;\mathbf{S}_m - s_0\left(1 + \dfrac{e^{\delta_{z,m}} - 1}{\eta}\right)\right)\right]$	0

An Imperfect Replicating Portfolio

As an alternative to the previous investing hypothesis, we consider also a different strategy, which is able to provide the issuer with an higher level of initial surplus and with some *beneficial* mismatching between inflows and outflows, in order to evaluate which levels of profitability different values of parameters g and η offer and to perform a comparative analysis with the perfect matching strategy.

A possibility could be an asset portfolio made up of the zero coupon bonds as in the perfect matching strategy and a portfolio of path-dependent at-the-money up-and-in call options with varying maturity from 1 to m and varying knock-in barriers from $\mathbf{S}_1 > s_0 e^{\delta_g}$ to $\mathbf{S}_m > s_0 e^{\delta_g m}$.

The main difference with the perfect replicating portfolio is the option architecture. In this case, the options come into existence after the barrier is hit. Specifically, being the selected barrier on average higher than the strike, the price of these options is on average lower than the corresponding plain vanilla (Hull, 2006). By applying a Black and Scholes valuation methodology, the present value of the investment portfolio (OF_0^1) is

$$OF_0^1 = R_g \cdot n \left\{ \sum_{t=1}^{m} e^{-\delta_{r(0:t)}t} + \eta \sum_{t=1}^{m} \left[\frac{N\left(d_{1(t)}^{uic}\right)}{e^{\delta_g t}} - \left(1 + \frac{e^{\delta_g t} - 1}{\eta}\right) \frac{N\left(d_{1(t)}^{uic} - \sigma_s \sqrt{t}\right)}{e^{(\delta_{r(0:t)} + \delta_g)t}} \right] \right\} \quad (15.12)$$

where, keeping unaltered the previous semantic, the parameter $d_{1(t)}^{uic}$ is defined as

$$d_{1(t)}^{uic} = -\frac{1}{\sigma_s \sqrt{t}} \ln\left(1 + \frac{e^{\delta_g t} - 1}{\eta}\right) + \zeta_{r(0:t),t} \sigma_s \sqrt{t} \quad \forall \quad \zeta_{r(0:t),t} = \frac{\delta_{r(0:t)} t + \sigma_s^2/2}{\sigma_s^2} \quad (15.13)$$

The intermediation portfolio is depicted by Table 15.4, and the related cash-flow breakdown is given by Table 15.5.

TABLE 15.4

Imperfect matching asset and liability portfolio

Assets	Liabilities
At-the-money up-and-in call options	Equity-linked bonds
Zero coupon bonds	Capital

TABLE 15.5

Issue cash flows (imperfect matching)

Time	Investment Cash Flows	Bond Cash Flows	Net Flows
0	$-OF_0^I = -\begin{pmatrix} Zero \quad Coupon \quad Bonds \\ +Up-and-in-Calls \end{pmatrix}$	$+IF_0 = +U \cdot n$	$NF_0^I = IF_0 - OF_0^I$
1	$IF_1^I = R_g \cdot n \left[1 + \frac{\eta}{s_0 e^{\delta_g}} \max\left[(0; \mathbf{S}_1 - s_0) \middle\| (\mathbf{S}_1 > s_0 e^{\delta_g}) \right] \right]$	$OF_1 = R_g \cdot n \left[1 + \frac{\eta}{s_0 e^{\delta_g}} \max\left(0; \mathbf{S}_1 - s_0 \left(1 + \frac{e^{\delta_g} - 1}{\eta} \right) \right) \right]$	$NF_1^I = IF_1^I - OF_1$
t	$IF_t^I = R_g \cdot n \left[1 + \frac{\eta}{s_0 e^{\delta_g t}} \max\left[(0; \mathbf{S}_t - s_0) \middle\| (\mathbf{S}_t > s_0 e^{\delta_g t}) \right] \right]$	$OF_t = R_g \cdot n \left[1 + \frac{\eta}{s_0 e^{\delta_g t}} \max\left(0; \mathbf{S}_t - s_0 \left(1 + \frac{e^{\delta_g t} - 1}{\eta} \right) \right) \right]$	$NF_t^I = IF_t^I - OF_t$
m	$IF_m^I = R_g \cdot n \left[1 + \frac{\eta}{s_0 e^{\delta_g m}} \max\left[(0; \mathbf{S}_m - s_0) \middle\| (\mathbf{S}_m > s_0 e^{\delta_g m}) \right] \right]$	$OF_m = R_g \cdot n \left[1 + \frac{\eta}{s_0 e^{\delta_g m}} \max\left(0; \mathbf{S}_m - s_0 \left(1 + \frac{e^{\delta_g m} - 1}{\eta} \right) \right) \right]$	$NF_m^I = IF_m^I - OF_m$

The final profit, denoted by superscript I (Φ_m^I), is equal to

$$\Phi_m^I = C_0 \left[\prod_{t=0}^{m-1} e^{\delta_{r(t:1)}} - 1 \right] + \sum_{t=0}^{m} \left[NF_t^1 \prod_{t'=t}^{m-1} e^{\delta_{r(t':1)}} \right] + NF_m^I \qquad (15.14)$$

COMPUTATION OF RESULTS

The portfolio we are studying is exposed to two main risk factors: the dynamic of interest rates and the dynamic of the return of the reference asset. The first dynamic is relevant for all intermediate flows when a rollover strategy is selected in both cases (cf Cash-Flow Mapping and Perfect Replicating Portfolio and An Imperfect Replicating Portfolio in the section An Equity-Linked Bond), while the second one is relevant only for the imperfect replicating portfolio (see Table 15.3 and Table 15.5). Therefore, in the first case the variability of the results is mainly due to the interest rate dynamic and, in a sense, to the investment strategy selected; in the second case, indeed, the volatility of the results is due to the simultaneous variations in the interest rates and in the reference asset. Computation of the final result has been derived by numerical methods, using Monte Carlo simulations for the identified process using 10,000 paths. Since the portfolio is convex, because of the options, we preferred a full valuation (nonparametric) method.

As far as the interest rate is concerned, a single-factor model was selected. The single local source of uncertainty is the spot rate, which is a diffusion process described by a Cox–Ingersoll–Ross (CIR) diffusion process (Cox et al., 1985) by means of the well-known stochastic differential equation:

$$dr_t = \alpha(\mu_r - r_t)dt + \sigma_r \sqrt{r_t} dZ_r(t) \quad \forall \quad \alpha, \mu_r > 0, r_t \geq 0 \qquad (15.15)$$

where $Z_r(t)$ is a standard Brownian motion. As known, this specification assumes a mean-reverting drift, with long-term rate μ_r, speed of adjustment α, and square root diffusion with volatility parameter σ_r.[3]

---

[3] The risk-adjusted parameters of the CIR component of the valuation model were estimated by a two-step procedure developed by Barone and Cesari (1986).

In addition, for the stock market, we assumed a single source of uncertainty, expressed by the stock index S_t; the diffusion process for the stock index is given by the stochastic differential equation

$$dS_t = \mu_s S_t dt + \sigma_s dZ_s(t) \tag{15.16}$$

where $Z_s(t)$ is a standard Brownian motion with the property

$$\text{cov}_t \left[dZ_r(t); dZ_s(t) \right] = kdt \tag{15.17}$$

Thus, we have a geometric Brownian motion, with instantaneous expected return μ_s, and volatility σ_s, which implies a lognormal transition density for S_t as follows:

$$S_t = s_0 e^{\mu_s - \frac{\sigma_s^2}{2} + \sigma_s dZ_s(t)} \tag{15.18}$$

As proposed (De Felice and Moriconi, 2005), the volatility of the stock index and the covariance parameter k can be exogenously specified. With reference to this, we would like to remark that, since the covariance between interest rates and stock prices reveals a slightly negative correlation, we selected a null value of the k parameter. By such adjustment, we consider actually a higher value of the variance of the portfolio and thus we include a sort of "prudential variance (risk) margin" to counterbalance the model risk.

The Procedure

Our goal is the computation of the expected profit at the end of the business together with the connected value at risk in the two hypotheses. To this aim, we applied the formal flow definition from Tables 15.4 and 15.5. The risk sources are the interest rate (modeled on the basis of the CIR process) and the price of the underlying index (modeled on the basis of a lognormal distribution). For each simulation path, the intermediate net flows are reinvested at the corresponding (expected) rates up to the maturity (m) according to the rollover strategy defined in the section An Equity-Linked Bond. Computation provides us with the expected profit $E[\Phi_m]$ at maturity both for the plain vanilla replication $E[\Phi_m^P]$ and the imperfect replication $E[\Phi_m^I]$ as well as CVaR for the whole portfolio at a confidence level of 99%. The two error-term sets for the simulation procedures have been kept constant across different alternatives in order to maximize the comparison results. Since we worked on a portfolio basis, the individual benefit has been multiplied by the number of issued bonds (1,000).

As far as the initial value of the investment portfolio is concerned, the initial outflow connected to the investment process has been set by means of a market consistent pricing procedure as far as both the bonds and the options are concerned. Therefore the corresponding values derive from classical bond valuation and Black and Scholes prices.

All estimates have been based on market data. Interest rates have been calibrated to the Euro Interbank Offered Rate (EURIBOR) data and calibration has been set on 17/04/2008. As far as the index is concerned, we selected the S&P/MIB, measuring the performance of 40 Italian equities and seeking to replicate the broad sector weights of the Italian stock market.[4]

All estimates have been based on the Bloomberg data set and calibration has been set on 17/04/2008. The whole set of input data is reported by Table 15.6.

T A B L E   15.6

Input data set

Symbol	Description	Figures or Reference
U	Nominal value of a single certificate	€2,500.00
n	Number of issued certificates	1,000
C_0	Allocated capital	€200,000.00
m	Maturity	5 years
t	Payment dates	[1, 2, 3, 4, 5]
g	Array of guaranteed rates	[0%; 1%; 2%; 3%; 4%]
η	Array of participation rates	[60%, 70%; 80%; 90%; 100%]
s	Reference asset	S&P/MIB Index (fixing values)
R_g	Minimum guaranteed payment (€)	[500.00; 515.10; 530.40; 545.89; 561.57]
δ_g	Intensity of guaranteed rates	[0%; 0.995%; 1.980%; 2.956%; 3.922%]
s_0	Value at issue of the reference asset	82,905.00
μ_s	Expected return of the reference asset	4.35%
σ_s	Volatility of the reference asset	13.59%
$r(0; t)$	Risk-free spot rate for the horizon $0 - t$	[4.41%; 4.62%; 4.75%; 4.84%; 4.90%]
$\delta_{r(0, t)}$	Interest Rates Intensity $r(0;t)$	[4.31%; 4.52%; 4.64%; 4.73%; 4.79%]
r_0	Starting value of the spot rate	3.91%
μ_r	Long-term mean	4.88%
σ_r	Volatility of the instantaneous rate	5.68%
α	Mean reversion coefficient	0.8
$1 - c$	VaR confidence level	99.00%

[4] The index is derived from the universe of stocks trading on the Italian stock exchange (Borsa Italiana) main equity market. The index has been created to be suitable for futures and options trading, as a benchmark index for exchange traded funds and for tracking large capitalization stocks in the Italian market. It is calculated in real time at 30 seconds (09:05 to 17:31 CET) from the continuous trading phase in the blue chip segment of MTA and MTAX electronic shares market, using the last price of each constituent.

FINDINGS

The Tables 15.7 and 15.8 provide the results of the computational procedure, based on previously defined values and indicators. The value at issue of the entire portfolio allows a primary evaluation of the sustainability of the whole operation. Since the allocated capital is €200,000.00, the combinations that have a net issue value less than the allocated capital (bold figures in Tables 15.7 and 15.8) should be eliminated since they imply that the market maker has to finance with its own resources the obligation assumed towards bondholder. This is clearly incompatible with the intermediary role. As expected, the imperfect replication offers the opportunity to sustain a higher number of combinations with respect to the perfect replication strategy. This implies that an "opportune" imperfect replication strategy provides for higher returns for the bondholders, thanks to a convexity gain (Figures 15.1 and 15.2). Naturally, this simply would imply

T A B L E   15.7

Net present value of the intermediation portfolio
(perfect matching)

Φ_0^P	$G = 0.00$	0.01	0.02	0.03	0.04
$\eta = 0.60$	275,295.23	252,473.32	223,930.06	**189,436.29**	**149,033.19**
0.70	234,193.44	211,952.37	**184,767.67**	**152,389.96**	**114,749.13**
0.80	**193,091.64**	**171,337.95**	**145,225.81**	**114,509.60**	**79,066.42**
0.90	**151,989.85**	**130,661.36**	**105,429.72**	**76,061.88**	**42,411.24**
1.00	**110,888.06**	**89,941.33**	**65,455.28**	**37,212.10**	**5,056.40**

T A B L E   15.8

Net Present Value of the Intermediation Portfolio
(Imperfect Matching)

Φ_0^I	$g = 0.00$	0.01	0.02	0.03	0.04
$\eta = 0.60$	275,295.23	229,042.60	221,975.38	231,478.76	239,907.63
0.70	234,193.44	**191,194.74**	**194,055.39**	216,389.20	237,608.04
0.80	**193,091.64**	**153,346.88**	**166,135.39**	201,299.65	235,308.45
0.90	**151,989.85**	**115,499.03**	**138,215.39**	**186,210.10**	233,008.87
1.0	**110,888.06**	**77,651.17**	**110,295.40**	**171,120.55**	230,709.28

F I G U R E   15.1

Net present value (perfect matching)

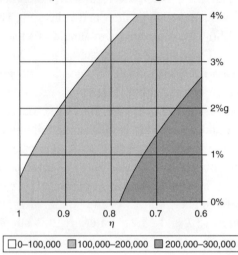

□ 0–100,000   ▨ 100,000–200,000   ▨ 200,000–300,000

F I G U R E   15.2

Net present value (imperfect matching)

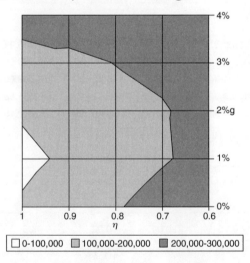

□ 0-100,000   ▨ 100,000-200,000   ▨ 200,000-300,000

that the actual selection of the investment portfolio depends on the risk aversion of the writer. Although this general conclusion is correct, there are many other remarks arising from the risk–return framework.

In addition, the value of the expected profit and of the expected return on equity validates the opportunity to keep up with higher minimum guaranteed rates by means of an imperfect replication strategy. Of course, these results have to be compared on a global basis, that is, avoiding those combinations that are incompatible from the beginning (Tables 15.9 to 15.12).

T A B L E   15.9

Expected profit (perfect matching)

$E[\Phi_m^P]$	$g = 0.00$	0.01	0.02	0.03	0.04
$\eta = 0.60$	155,332.85	125,875.83	89,034.09	44,511.82	−7,637.83
0.70	102,281.38	73,574.08	38,485.87	−3,305.13	−51,889.42
0.80	49,229.90	21,151.68	−12,552.14	−52,198.59	−97,946.30
0.90	−3,821.57	−31,350.97	−63,918.30	−101,824.36	−145,258.39
1.00	−56,873.04	−83,909.68	−115,514.66	−151,969.08	−193,473.53

T A B L E   15.10

Expected profit (imperfect matching)

$E[\Phi_m^I]$	$g = 0.00$	0.01	0.02	0.03	0.04
$\eta = 0.60$	134,790.24	99,438.50	109,529.59	134,586.12	137,271.09
0.70	84,805.80	53,478.57	75,711.89	119,310.47	136,106.69
0.80	34,821.35	7,472.79	41,893.20	103,269.08	133,966.52
0.90	−15,163.09	−38,532.99	8,061.91	85,137.73	131,453.19
1.00	−65,147.54	−84,552.86	−25,884.37	66,797.61	128,675.67

T A B L E   15.11

Expected return on equity (perfect matching)

	$g = 0.00$	0.01	0.02	0.03	0.04
$\eta = 0.60$	15.53%	12.59%	8.90%	4.45%	−0.76%
0.70	10.23%	7.36%	3.85%	−0.33%	−5.19%
0.80	4.92%	2.12%	−1.26%	−5.22%	−9.79%
0.90	−0.38%	−3.14%	−6.39%	−10.18%	−14.53%
1.00	−5.69%	−8.39%	−11.55%	−15.20%	−19.35%

TABLE   15.12

Expected return on equity (imperfect matching)

	$g = 0.00$	0.01	0.02	0.03	0.04
$\eta = 0.60$	16.85%	12.43%	13.69%	16.82%	17.16%
0.70	10.60%	6.68%	9.46%	14.91%	17.01%
0.80	4.35%	0.93%	5.24%	12.91%	16.75%
0.90	−1.90%	−4.82%	1.01%	10.64%	16.43%
1.00	−8.14%	−10.57%	−3.24%	8.35%	16.08%

TABLE   15.13

Conditional value at risk 99% (perfect matching)

	$g = 0.00$	0.01	0.02	0.03	0.04
$\eta = 0.60$	−155,431.88	−125,966.66	−89,114.65	−44,579.96	7,584.22
0.70	−102,365.62	−73,650.33	−38,552.33	3,250.31	51,848.14
0.80	−49,299.36	−21,213.32	12,499.90	52,157.40	97,917.85
0.90	3,766.89	31,303.97	63,880.37	101,797.00	145,243.13
1.00	56,833.15	83,877.33	115,491.11	151,955.70	193,471.71

TABLE   15.14

Conditional value at risk 99% (imperfect matching)

	$G = 0.00$	0.01	0.02	0.03	0.04
$\eta = 0.60$	−134,790.24	−104,581.05	−122,452.71	−156,665.68	−173,292.19
0.70	−84,805.80	−58,553.76	−88,498.82	−140,696.38	−170,495.63
0.80	−34,821.35	−12,526.47	−54,544.94	−124,195.79	−167,699.08
0.90	15,163.09	33,500.82	−20,591.06	−105,845.18	−164,902.52
1.00	65,147.54	79,528.11	13,362.83	−87,494.57	−162,105.96

Clearly, the most profitable solutions are those that exhibit riskier profiles, as can be easily appreciated by Tables 15.13 and 15.14, reporting CVaR values for both portfolios. An efficient picture of the risk−return relationship and of the improvement of the efficient frontier is provided by Figure 15.3.

F I G U R E   15.3

Opportunity set

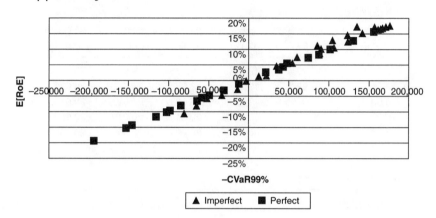

The increase in the risk–return trade-off is backed by the analysis of the evolution of the *coherent risk-adjusted return on capital* (CRARoC) indicators (Tables 15.15 and 15.16 and Figures 15.4 and 15.5), showing the increase in the risk-adjusted performance for the investment in at-the-money knock-in options. The performance rise holds to all the combinations, and indeed, it is more significant for those that are less demanding for the issuer, with a result quite dissimilar from that can be inferred from the profitability analysis.

The EVA analysis is based on Equation (15.6), where a threshold rate was used as the average rate of return on the financial sector in Italian market during last three years. This rate, equal to 6.22 percent, was inferred from the performance of the Italian listed banking companies and was regarded as a proxy of the rate of return required on the investment by shareholders. This rate is a surrogate of the *actual* rate of return because it suffers from many shortcomings, the most important being that it is a gross rate short of any fiscal adjustment. With this respect, we state that an appropriate EVA appraisal should reflect not only the proper *net rate* of return but also a *net profit* measure, the so-called *net operating profit after taxes*. In our analysis we use the gross measure for both the expected profit and the rate of return. As you would expect, in a practical implementation the financial intermediary can adapt all the measures to net values by considering proper fiscal loading and other expenses adjustments.

TABLE   15.15

Coherent risk-adjusted return on capital 99%
(perfect matching)

	g = 0.00	0.01	0.02	0.03	0.04
η = 0.60	19.99%	19.99%	19.98%	19.97%	−20.14%
0.70	19.98%	19.98%	19.97%	−20.34%	−20.02%
0.80	19.97%	19.94%	−20.08%	−20.02%	−20.01%
0.90	−20.29%	−20.03%	−20.01%	−20.01%	−20.00%
1.00	−20.01%	−20.01%	−20.00%	−20.00%	−20.00%

TABLE   15.16

Coherent risk-adjusted return on capital 99% (imperfect
matching)

	g = 0.00	0.01	0.02	0.03	0.04
η = 0.60	100.00%	95.08%	89.45%	85.91%	79.21%
0.70	100.00%	91.33%	85.55%	84.80%	79.83%
0.80	100.00%	59.66%	76.80%	83.15%	79.89%
0.90	−100.00%	−115.02%	39.15%	80.44%	79.72%
1.00	−100.00%	−106.32%	−193.70%	76.34%	79.38%

FIGURE   15.4

Coherent risk-adjusted return on capital perfect matching

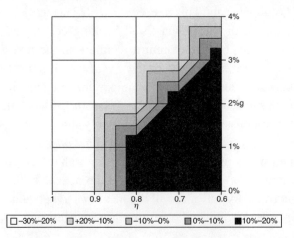

F I G U R E   15.5

Coherent risk-adjusted return on capital imperfect matching

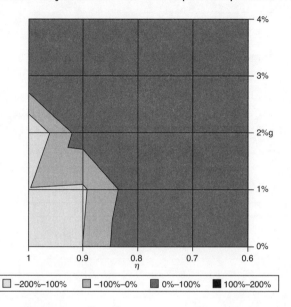

| | | -200%-100% | | | -100%-0% | | | 0%-100% | | | 100%-200% |

The selection of the prospected imperfect replication strategy gives the opportunity to benefit from a convexity gain and therefore to offer to the bondholder a higher guaranteed rate. The sustainability of these two strategies is synthesized by EVA measure showing that both strategies are sustainable and therefore acceptable, but that the imperfect replication creates levels of value far higher that the perfect replication, given different convexities of the two positions (Tables 15.17 and 15.18, Figures 15.4 and 15.5).

T A B L E   15.17

Economic value added (perfect matching)

	$g = 0.00$	0.01	0.02	0.03	0.04
$\eta = 0.60$	27,542.73	27,539.37	27,532.06	27,507.07	−52,714.54
0.70	27,535.29	27,526.81	27,499.25	−53,106.43	−52,463.63
0.80	27,511.86	27,451.99	−52,598.96	−52,463.38	−52,443.40
0.90	−53,012.38	−52,491.85	−52,455.53	−52,442.54	−52,435.99
1.00	−52,459.86	−52,447.21	−52,439.94	−52,435.31	−52,432.16

T A B L E   15.18

Economic value added (imperfect matching)

	g = 0.00	0.01	0.02	0.03	0.04
η = 0.60	187,568.22	177,733.65	166,461.09	159,381.37	145,995.54
0.70	187,568.22	170,233.06	158,670.81	157,168.14	147,228.24
0.80	187,568.22	106,880.14	141,178.07	153,868.66	147,338.35
0.90	−212,431.78	−242,473.90	65,873.21	148,440.40	146,999.61
1.00	−212,431.78	−225,068.20	−399,840.38	140,257.95	146,323.23

F I G U R E   15.6

Economic value added (perfect matching)

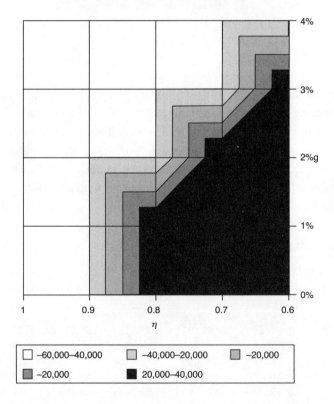

F I G U R E   15.7

Economic value added (imperfect matching)

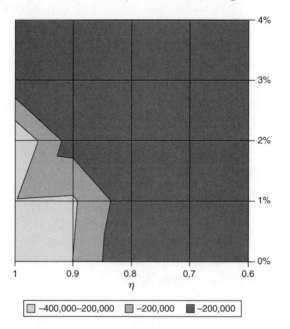

| | −400,000–200,000 | | −200,000 | | −200,000 |

CONCLUSION

The computation of risk-adjusted performance indicators can serve for appreciating the optimality of the issue with reference to both relevant product design variables and investment decisions. Within this respect, we observe that both portfolio and product design decision can be usefully evaluated by the set of indicators we adopted.

The main result is the possibility to optimize the issue by means of the adopted indicators, as reference target in the management of discretionary issue parameter (g and η). The optimization problem, therefore, can be addressed as maximizing the EVA target under the constraint of issue sustainability ($NF_0 \geq 0$) by changing g and η. Of course, the evaluation process can be enriched by including within the optimization problem more investment alternative and eventual capital coefficient where applicable.

As far as limitations are concerned, the development of a simulation procedure is prone to model risk. With this respect, we want to stress that future research prospect should regard the modeling of the financial risk factors with reference not only to the possibility of using multifactor models but also with reference to a complete breakdown of covariance analysis and corresponding simulation techniques. This aspect is particularly important when there are multiple risk factors. This is the case of any multifactor model for the interest rate dynamic and the case of any more complex replicating investment portfolio, as well. As far the specific features of the instruments used, special attention should be devoted to the opportunity to use the entire informative set concerning the volatility surface in order to consider the inner smile effect.

REFERENCES

Artzner, P., F. Delbaen, J.M. Eber, and D. Heath (1999) Coherent Measures of Risk. *Mathematical Finance*, Vol. 9, No. 3, pp. 203–228.

Barone, E. and R. Cesari (1986) Rischio e rendimento dei titoli a tasso fisso e a tasso variabile in un modello stocastico univariato. *Banca d'Italia Temi di discussione*, No. 73, Rome, Italy.

Black, F. and M. Scholes (1973) The Pricing of Options and Corporate Liabilities. *The Journal of Political Economy*, Vol. 8, No. 3, pp. 654–737.

Cox, J., J.E. Ingersoll, and S.A. Ross (1985) A Theory of the Term Structure of Interest Rates. *Econometrica*, Vol. 53, No. 2, pp. 385–408.

De Felice, M. and F. Moriconi (2005) Market Based Tools for Managing the Life Insurance Company. *Astin Bulletin*, Vol. 1, No. 35, pp. 79–111.

Dowd, K. and D. Blake (2006) After VaR: The Theory, Estimation, and Insurance Applications of Quantile-Based Risk Measures. *The Journal of Risk and Insurance*, Vol. 73, No. 2, pp. 193–229.

Hull, J.C. (2006) *Options, Futures, and Other Derivatives*, 6th edition. Upper Saddle River, NJ: Prentice Hall.

Matten, C. (2000) *Managing Bank Capital. Capital Allocation and Performance Measurement*. Chichester, UK: Wiley.

Nefity, S. H. (2004) *Financial Engineering*. Amsterdam: Elsevier.

Wilmott, P. (2007) *Paul Wilmott Introduces Quantitative Finance*, 2nd Ed. Chichester, U.K.: Wiley.

INDEX